_____ *Typhoon in Tokyo*

HARRY EMERSON WILDES

Typhoon in Tokyo

The Occupation and Its Aftermath

OCTAGON BOOKS

A DIVISION OF FARRAR, STRAUS AND GIROUX

New York   1978

Copyright 1954 by Macmillan Publishing Co., Inc.

Reprinted 1978
by special arrangement with Macmillan Publishing Co., Inc.

OCTAGON BOOKS
A DIVISION OF FARRAR, STRAUS & GIROUX, INC.
19 Union Square West
New York, N.Y. 10003

Library of Congress Cataloging in Publication Data

Wildes, Harry Emerson, 1890-
    Typhoon in Tokyo.

    Reprint of the ed. published by Macmillan, New York.
    1. Japan—History—Allied occupation, 1945-1952.   I. Title.
[DS889.15.W54   1978]   952.04   78-16992
ISBN 0-374-98572-3

Manufactured by Braun-Brumfield, Inc.
Ann Arbor, Michigan
Printed in the United States of America

Contents

v

Typhoon in Tokyo

ONE

Occupation Atmosphere

This is the story of the Occupation of Japan, its origins, its personnel, its philosophy, its methods, and its aftermath.

It is the story of 30,000 Occupationnaires who loosed a whirlwind that swept away reaction, wrecked restrictive social barriers, and cleared the way for real, constructive reform. Their 6,000 Instructions, which they called SCAPINS in honor of their chief, Supreme Commander for the Allied Powers, SCAP, and which were written in a special jargon known as Scapinese, comprise a blueprint for healthful revolution. This is the story of how their instructions were obeyed, or were ignored, and of the results that were attained.

This is the story, also, of the greatest civilian overseas commitment ever undertaken by Americans. It is the story of a stupendous but improvised social experiment which used an empire and 74,000,000 people as its laboratory materials, but whose results the Occupation did not care to know.

This volume describes additions to the Occupation program and subtractions from it, by the Japanese. It describes Communist attempts at sabotage, resistance, and counterrevolution.

As no one can tell fully within the limits of one book the whole, far-reaching story of so vast an enterprise, this book concentrates on basic governmental, political, and social matters. It does not dig deep into diplomacy or warfare, nor pretend to settle questions of economics, finance, labor, education, or the arts: these are fields for later cultivation.

Because the basic directives, the initial actions, the patterns of control and of such supervision as Occupationnaires gave, all were phenomena

1

of the first few months, the personalities and accomplishments of General of the Armies Douglas MacArthur and his early staff assistants receive primary attention. This emphasis implies no disparagement of the contributions of his successors, Generals Matthew B. Ridgway, Mark Clark, and John E. Hull, nor of the stream of Occupationnaires who arrived after the Occupation opened. By the time Ridgway replaced MacArthur, on April 11, 1951, the Occupation's work, for good or ill, was virtually complete; the signing in September, 1951, of a peace treaty which came into effect on April 28, 1952, deprived Ridgway, Clark, and Hull of any right to mix in Japanese domestic matters. MacArthur and his men deserve the credit for the good that they accomplished and, equally, the blame for any failures due to their shortcomings.

They faced stupendous tasks. Japan lay prostrate. More than 1,800,-000 of its 74,000,000 population in 1941 had been killed, and unknown millions more were injured, sick, or undernourished. Every family in Japan, officials said, had been seriously and directly affected.

More than 8,754,000 people were homeless. Of 4,447,241 dwelling houses in the cities, 2,259,879 had been bombed or burned; and another 600,000 had been pulled down to open firebreaks that would save the rest. Tokyo, where MacArthur intended to set up his headquarters, was a mass of rubble, having lost 1,066,000 of its 1,650,000 residential houses and apartment buildings.

Other cities had fared badly also. Osaka with 3,000,000 population had lost 57 per cent of its houses; Nagoya with more than a million, the third largest city, was 89 per cent destroyed. Smaller cities had suffered heavily: Hamamatsu retained only 3,740 of its 32,500 houses; Hodachi, 846 of its 16,900; Kofu, 2,901 out of 18,099; and Fukuyama, 1,344 out of 10,154. All these had suffered far more than the better known Hiroshima, which retained 41 per cent of its 61,825 houses, or Nagasaki, 74 per cent of its 54,462 buildings.

Incredible congestion had resulted. In every major city, families were crowded into dugouts and flimsy shacks or, in some cases, were trying to sleep in hallways, on subway platforms, or on sidewalks. Employees slept in their offices; teachers, in their schoolrooms.

A quarter of the national wealth had been destroyed, including a third of manufacturing machinery, one vehicle in every five, a sixth of the waterworks, four-fifths of all vessels, and a fifth of all furniture and household goods.

Such was the situation faced by MacArthur in September, 1945—a nation devastated, hopeless, "flat broke," and leaderless.

The Occupation of Japan did not spring full-blown from MacArthur's head as some of his aides, anxious to glorify their chief, would have had the public believe. Nor was it, when in full operation, wholly, or even in major part, MacArthur's personal plan.

Early in the war, certain State, War, and Navy Department experts, together with specialists from the Office of War Information, the Office of Strategic Services, and other agencies, conferred informally on postwar problems. The sessions, while secret, received wide publicity for their acrimony and their inability to reach decisions. While details were not revealed, many Washingtonians were well aware of violent argument between a China Crowd represented by the leftists and by disciples of *Amerasia* magazine, and a Japan Crowd centering around followers of former Ambassador Joseph Clark Grew. Conversion in February, 1944, of the informal gatherings into an official State, War, and Navy Coordinating Committee (SWNCC) was followed three months later by a Japan Crowd victory when Grew became the State Department's Director of the Office of Far Eastern Affairs.

MacArthur's men, knowing little of the struggles in Washington, were by no means leftists, nor did they read *Amerasia;* but many of them disliked taking advice from Old Japan Hands. MacArthur himself told Russell Brines of the Associated Press that he had but two advisers, George Washington and Abraham Lincoln.

Some influential Occupationnaires took as a handy guide, though one never openly acknowledged, Andrew Roth's *Dilemma in Japan,* written, as Owen Lattimore explained, to represent "the younger school of American experts who are not blinded, as are so many older experts, by myths which even the Japanese do not believe." This volume, which for MacArthur's men had the additional distinction of being hostile to Grew's Japan Crowd in the State Department, called for drastic action.

It urged that the Emperor, if not dethroned, be publicized as a war profiteer and tried for war guilt; that prewar basic economic forces be uprooted; that landlords be dispossessed; that Japan's governmental system and personnel be radically overhauled; that the bureaucracy and the entire Old Gang who had misled Japan be removed from public office, if not jailed; and that everyone who stressed a need for law, order, or stability be distrusted.

The distrust was not alone for such Japanese as the conservative labor leader Bunji Suzuki but applied, specifically and by name, to Joseph Clark Grew, and also to Eugene Dooman, Erle R. Dickover, and Joseph W. Ballantine—all former American Embassy officers, who spoke Japanese and together comprised the State Department's dominant Japan Crowd.

In place of these men, Roth recommended that the Occupation rely upon such determined antimilitarists as Yukio Ozaki, Yukikatsu Takikawa, Daikichiro Tagawa, and Kanju Kato. As all these, except Kato, were either senescent or retired, MacArthur was advised to call upon the "thousands of dangerous thought inmates of political prisons," upon people "interested in a reborn, not a resurgent Japan," and particularly upon the Communist leaders Wataru Kaji and Susumu Okano, better known as Sanzo Nosaka. To point up the pro-Communist nature of the men recommended for leadership, Roth admitted that their policies would be too extreme for America or for Britain; he added that, if the Communists were given free access to press and radio, and if superpatriotic films were banned, reforms would be facilitated.

Above all, Roth noted, the conservative Allies must be extremely careful not to alienate other "major victors," which meant Soviet Russia, and must build international cooperation—which, as it later developed, would have implied a Russian veto on Occupation policies.

Dilemma in Japan strongly appealed to the China Crowd in Washington and to a few middle-brass policy makers in MacArthur's entourage who did not realize that Roth's theories paralleled the Communist line. Particularly impressed by Roth's praise of Kaji and Nosaka as liberal reformers and philosophers, they looked forward to bringing them out of their Chinese exile to assume high roles in Japan's reconstruction; they could not have suspected that both Kaji and Nosaka would turn so violently anti-American that the Occupation would arrest the one and drive the other into hiding for preferring Russian guidance to MacArthur's leadership. Impressed by Ozaki's prewar democratic record, they could not foresee that, grown old and tired and very deaf, he would not be budged from his belief that postwar American democracy was little better than the Emperor Meiji's rule. They could not guess that Kato, hungering for high office, would swing toward rightwing Socialism, or that Takikawa and Tagawa lacked dynamic force. The Roth book, for all its fervor and for all its facile idealism, was flashy and unreliable; it induced false hopes of a Japanese—the Occupation always called it indigenous—leadership that would not be at once available.

Simultaneously the Pentagon, while not rejecting the State Department's Japan Crowd advice, set up special schools to study postwar Occupation problems. Hundreds of picked servicemen, all specialists in various technical fields, attended Civil Affairs Training Schools where they were taught by carefully selected experts. Upon graduation, these officers went to a Civil Affairs Staging Area (CASA) at Monterey, California, to await surrender, when they would be flown immediately to man specific posts to start the Occupation machinery. Each CASA man knew precisely where he was to go, with what friendly Japanese he was to work, and what he was to do.

Meanwhile unpublicized negotiations were under way to bring about surrender. Washington heard hints of this in January, 1945, and President Truman on May 8, 1945, assured Japan that, while unconditional surrender was imperative, enslavement was not envisaged. Senator Homer Capehart of Indiana revealed on July 2, 1945, that only the question of the future status of the Emperor remained to be decided before surrender was announced. As part of these preliminaries, the heads of state of China, Great Britain, and the United States drafted a pronouncement, issued at Potsdam July 26, putting the negotiations on the record and concluding with the threat that rejection of the terms meant inevitable and complete destruction of the Japanese armed forces and utter devastation of the Japanese homeland.

Perhaps the concluding threats deterred Japan from immediate acceptance of conditions to which she had already shown herself receptive; but the delay was costly. The Potsdam Declaration was soon followed by the dropping of atom bombs on Hiroshima and Nagasaki.

In return for her surrender Japan was promised a peaceful and productive life, with sufficient industries for her economy and with access to raw materials and to world trade. The Declaration, however, did not explain how basic industry could pay necessary reparations without also providing a potential source of the war materials that were to be denied to Japan. Nor did it consider such difficulties as preferential tariff walls or international exchange.

Nevertheless the Potsdam Declaration served its purpose and brought surrender. Some Japanese believed it a binding contract; but, on August 11, Secretary of State James F. Byrnes dispelled the illusion, and when, on September 2, 1945, Japan signed an Instrument of Surrender she did so unconditionally. Four days later the United States Joint Chiefs of Staff informed General MacArthur, appointed on August 14 as Supreme Commander for the Allied Powers, that there was no element of contract or of negotiated surrender in the status of Japan, but that every governmental agency, including the Emperor, was at his command.

From this point forward, confusion became inevitable. As General of the Armies, MacArthur was necessarily subject to the Joint Chiefs of Staff and to the President of the United States. As SCAP—a term soon to be applied not only to MacArthur but to the organization which he headed—he was the agent of the Allied Powers, Russia, China, and the British Commonwealth, as well as the United States. In some activities, therefore, he was an officer of the United States Army, in others he was an agent of an international body whose American representative was the Secretary of State. When the War Department, later the Department of Defense, and the State Department saw eye to eye, or when the President assumed control, all was well; when the Departments disagreed, MacArthur drew nice distinctions as to which he should obey.

In most matters, SWNCC sent its communications through the Joint Chiefs of Staff, to whom the President had delegated much authority. Such, for instance, was the case with SWNCC plans for occupation. These were sent to MacArthur for comment, were then approved by President Truman, and, on September 6, were again sent to MacArthur as his official orders.

These official orders known as JCS 10, the United States Initial Post-Surrender Policy for Japan, while published in full in both the American and the Japanese press, were, for some reason, thereafter given a high security classification, the official MacArthur history minimizing reference to it as a source. Japanese politicians understood, however, what types of regulation to expect; they realized, moreover, that MacArthur had little power to modify or soften the requirements. Although well aware that Japan must meet the obligations set forth in JCS 10, and that even protest would be frowned upon, they used their knowledge to appeal, tongue in cheek, against certain of MacArthur's directives. Thus they won public favor by seeming to oppose the Supreme Commander's wishes.

The JCS directive gave MacArthur complete executive authority to carry out its provisions; it also gave him an unexpected freedom of operation. This had not been planned but had grown out of confusion over Russian insistence upon a four-power Control Council, which the United States had refused to approve. Washington proposed, instead, a four-power Far Eastern Advisory Commission to supplement other consultants; but Russia, in its anxiety for absolute control rather than the shadow of control, rejected the proposal. Washington therefore proceeded to operate individually although consulting the British and, less frequently, the Chinese. During the first four months that basic orders were being issued on JCS authority the Russians remained largely out of the picture.

Probably the Russians blundered in not immediately accepting a share in policy determination; they could have played a more important role, even perhaps occupying Hokkaido, and certainly they could have had a voice, if not a veto, on important decisions. They threw away an opportunity to profit by the flounderings that marred the outset of the Occupation.

MacArthur, though his aides later credited him with unerring foresight, had entered Japan with few fixed plans. He knew his general goal as laid down for him by his JCS 10 orders, but his organization was woefully defective.

While still at Manila, he had tentatively chosen Brigadier General William Earl Crist, a Chinese-speaking expert on Far Eastern and Russian affairs, as military governor for Occupied Japan. In preparation for the task which, Washington then assumed, would be carried out in conjunction with the 4,000 CASA graduates, Crist had been sent to Europe to inspect military government operations. While he was absent MacArthur, believing that ample time was available, deactivated the Crist office, in August, 1945.

News of impending surrender caught MacArthur off guard, as far as military government was concerned. As a temporary expedient, he had Lieutenant Colonel Carl Erickson assigned to be acting chief of military government planning. Erickson and three other officers (one of whom came down immediately with appendicitis) and five enlisted men, all crowded within a tiny fourth-floor office in Manila's battered City Hall, were the entire military government force available on August 15, 1945, to administer an empire of 74,000,000 people.

Whether through Crist or through some other officer of higher rank than Erickson, MacArthur planned to operate through *ad hoc* sections within his AFPAC—Armed Forces, Pacific—headquarters; but while such groups were set in motion they had no specific grants of power.

Then the various general-staff sections, the G-Sections, scrambled to annex these special sections and thus take over all nonmilitary and civil-affairs administration.

This would have been his opportunity to call upon the CASA experts; but to do so would have confessed that AFPAC was incapable. Or Mac-Arthur might have copied the suggestions of his army Field Manual for governing a conquered territory; but, perhaps, as Dwight Eisenhower had already followed this advice, MacArthur's pride would not allow him to be second. For two weeks after entering Japan, MacArthur experimented fruitlessly with a wholly decentralized administration only to replace it, on September 10, by military government administered by his 6th and 8th Armies. This, to the Japanese, seemed unreasonable since they had been rebuked for military rule and, as the *Nippon Times* remarked, "If we must have a military government, why not have our own?" And then, when the wide latitude assigned to armies in nonmilitary matters led to confusion of administration and even of policy in differing portions of Japan, MacArthur reverted on October 2 to his Manila plan. He set up a new headquarters as Supreme Commander for the Allied Powers, GHQ-SCAP, with ten staff sections to deal with nonmilitary and civil affairs, in a status parallel, if not equal, to the feuding G-Sections.

Necessarily, GHQ-SCAP fell under military leadership. Headship of the dozen staff sections went to officers whom MacArthur wished to reward for military service, or for whom no other post of commensurate rank was immediately available. Neither ability nor special training was a necessary requisite for appointment to these positions of honor, privilege, and power. Brigadier General Courtney Whitney, leader of Philippine guerrillas, replaced Crist and took over the all-important Government Section with its responsibility for supervising the Emperor, the Diet, the courts, and civil service. Brigadier General Ken R. Dyke, an advertising manager who held no college degree, ruled the schools, religion, the press, and cultural activities. Colonel Raymond C. Kramer, a corporation executive, began the control of Japan's vast economic and scientific structure only to be replaced by Major General William F. Marquat, a former newspaper reporter who, for a year, had been an automotive editor. An assembly-line superintendent without research or writing training received the commission to write the official Mac-Arthur history and to analyze the importance of what the Occupation was about to accomplish. There were also happier selections—for instance, that of Colonel Hubert G. Schenck, Stanford geologist, as chief of Natural Resources Section and Colonel (later Brigadier General) Crawford F. Sams, a neurologist, as head of Public Health and Welfare Section.

Some few CASA graduates filled important slots, but, more often, majors and captains assumed responsible roles. Their staffs, for the most part, consisted of young civilians hastily recruited by Washington procurement officers whom Tokyo called "body-snatchers." Some were specialists in Japanese affairs, and many were expert technicians; but these, unaccustomed to army protocol, floundered in official channels. Often their intimate knowledge of backgrounds, psychologies, and needs led them to conclusions contrary to those desired by their superiors; their careful research methods did not fit the pressing demands for quick action and headline-attracting publicity. Chafing under restrictions imposed upon their freedom of expression, they either resigned or, if they remained, were relegated by their section chiefs to nonoperative posts where they would not interfere unduly. One of the best known authorities on Japan, for instance, was tucked away in a secluded office as a research librarian where his counsel was rarely asked; another, equipped with an impressive title, had virtually nothing to do except keep himself busy in any way he pleased as long as he did not bother his boss; a third, a nationally known labor writer, had nothing to do but was under daily fire for reporting late to do it.

The CASA graduates and the professors were, however, exceptions; the great majority of subordinates were relatively untrained. Some came as transfers from Washington offices reduced in size by the closing of the war, many of the Marquat group were alumni of the wartime economics services; others came for adventure, for curiosity, for study, for service and, frequently, just because the pay was higher than could be obtained at home. In consequence, the quality and efficiency of SCAP employees varied widely. Many of them had come as the result of misleading promises made by the body-snatchers.

Personnel difficulties complicated matters. Occasionally, because army personnel were under call for duty day and night while civilians worked a forty-hour week, with higher pay schedules and overtime allowances, the servicemen were jealous of civilians. Sometimes section chiefs, rightly or wrongly, were criticized for favoring the military; others were accused, as happens everywhere, of inefficiency, drunkenness, idleness, making passes at the girls, and, all too often, discrimination. Civilians chafed under regulations that prevented them from seeking other posts except with the approval of the chief for whom they were working; they fretted under military red tape and petty disciplines. Such internal frictions were, however, of far less consequence than the fact that, taken as a whole, the Occupationnaires were a privileged alien caste living a pampered life amid a conquered people who, whether they deserved to do so or not, were suffering for want of bare necessities: A militarist bureaucracy, comfortably ensconced in never-never land, safeguarded by censorship from realities, lived from day to day in blissful ignorance of how long the paradise would endure.

The bureaucracy was never happy. It suffered from an insidious malaise which especially revealed itself in an intolerance of even the mildest criticism of its policies or of its aims. Even during the war, correspondents had noted an almost morbid suspicion that everyone outside the MacArthur circle was in conspiracy against him. The same fear gripped his Tokyo associates; to protect him against belittlement, they overstated his accomplishments.

They claimed too much too quickly. The Occupation's length became embarrassing. The Public Relations Office, the section chiefs, and MacArthur himself were pushed into a situation where, each month, they added thicker gilding to the refined gold of their previous reports.

They did not dare examine the results of what had been accomplished; to do so might reveal that many widely publicized boasts were based on hope and not on actual proved fact. MacArthur did not stir from Tokyo to see what he had done; his section chiefs were under orders not to leave the capital without special permission. By 1947 Army men in the provinces were pleading with SCAP subordinates to come more often on inspection tours and to accept reports on what was going on; the pleas were passed up to the section chiefs, but apparently went no further.

To question the accuracy of optimistic SCAP statements was counted as disloyalty; devoted section leaders spared MacArthur the pain of reading contradictory details, and subordinates soon learned to delete from their memoranda to the chiefs any unpleasant or disturbing news.

Army officers of every grade, from MacArthur to the juniors ambitious for promotion or for a Legion of Merit ribbon, shared with civilians and bureaucrats the strong conviction that Japanese wartime practices and many of her prewar customs were not only antiquated but dangerous. In many instances this misconception was due to ignorance of past conditions; in others, to devotion to some special formula for reformation; in still others, to hasty and uncritical acceptance of wartime propaganda or to the naïve belief that only Westerners would properly appreciate democracy and freedom.

Characterization of Japanese methods as totalitarian—the usual word among Occupationnaires was "feudalistic"—and of Occidental ways as the sole true path toward social justice facilitated the revolutionary process. Under a gentlemen's agreement each SCAP section operated freely and without undue criticism in its special field, provided it refrained from encroachment on its neighbors. As a matter of form, check sheets were circulated on important matters asking concurrence on policies to be undertaken; but serious disputes upon such matters were rare unless a section chief suspected invasion of his private empire.

One great difficulty lay in the ignorance of most army officers concerning the very nature of their empires. Instructions to MacArthur were, at the outset, loose and broad; his grant of powers to the section chiefs was similarly vague. Each section chief knew that he was expected to build a new and democratic Japan speedily; but few knew what to do. Some, therefore, took quick action that could be interpreted as successful democratization, others claimed success before real action had been taken. All needed wise counsel and close, continued supervision, but few received it.

Suspicion and Uncertainty

God loves Americans, and probably the Oriental gods love Japanese, else the Allied Occupation of Japan could never have succeeded.

The record of the Occupation defied the laws of reason. Students well versed in history, political science, or sociology, glancing at the sketchy initial plans would have predicted that only failure would result; yet, when all was said and done, the Occupation did well. No sane economist, rushing headlong into a series of revolutionary reforms only to reverse himself in full flight, would have expected good results; yet they were, in fact, attained. No well taught soldier, ignorant of the language, customs, traditions, history, or physical conditions of an enemy people, would have ventured, with but a handful of poorly supplied guards, to overturn the foundations of one of the oldest and best established empires of the world; yet this operation, which MacArthur himself called "the greatest gamble in history," was actually attempted.

Not only were the cards stacked against the Allied Occupation but high-placed Allied leaders, deliberately and consistently, threw away the few trumps which they held. Thought had indeed been given to the problem of how to rule conquered Japan, and plans had been drafted by competent experts; but rivalries and jealousies among high officials, together with poor liaison work, sabotaged the execution of the plans.

Much of the disregard of expert advice was intentional, some was due to ignorance, and some, especially among MacArthur's more devoted aides, was traceable to contempt for the opinion of those outside the inner circle of his intimates. But, whatever the reason may have been, the variance was striking between theory and performance.

12

We knew that we must rule a subjugated Empire and so, after studying for eighteen months more than thirty instances of past military occupations, sifting out a dozen different plans and drafting from the best of these an almost foolproof system of administration, we cast all this aside and went in cold and unprepared.

We assumed a joint military occupation shared by British, Chinese, and even Soviet Russian allies, and then denied them any real participation—only the British having even a token share of actual responsibility.

We suspected in February, 1944, that Russians and Chinese would sabotage our efforts, and so we went ahead on the assumption that they would be our loyal friends.

We trained hundreds of expert technicians, drilled them intensively on specific problems of Japanese administration, supplying them with complete information concerning Japanese resources, materials, and equipment, giving them the names of Japanese individuals with whom they were to work, and then sent them off to Manila, Guam, or Saipan, where all this information was wholly valueless.

We scientifically sorted out hundreds of high-ranking college men, sent them to three different graduate schools, first to Charlottesville, then to Harvard, Michigan, or Stanford, and finally to CASA, steeped them so thoroughly in Japanese that we penalized them for talking English and then rejected most of them in favor of persons who could talk no Japanese.

We trained a military government and then threw it away.

We knew that army personnel long fighting in the East would soon return to the United States, and so we gave this temporary and politically untrained personnel long-range assignments on which we knew they could do no more than make a feeble start.

We knew that above all we must be practical, and that we must build carefully upon a firm foundation; yet we set an inverted pyramid of laws, machinery, and obligations upon a theoretical democracy. And when observers criticized us for so doing we called them friends of Communism.

Wartime propaganda rightfully cited the centuries of totalitarianism that had stifled individualism and originality and so, excluding trained personnel from leadership, we expected inexperienced men to bear the heavy responsibility of reconstruction and reform.

Knowing well that Japanese politics had centered about unprincipled leaders, we assumed that colorless and unknown subordinates, stooges, and time servers would at once create idealistic political parties.

Having stressed that centralization had deprived local communities of any vestige of self-government, we entrusted them with the difficult problem of self-administration under bankruptcy conditions.

We frequently and eloquently proclaimed a spiritual revolution that would end the corruption of prewar Japanese administration although we knew that graft, bribery, and intimidation were still unchecked.

We talked of democracy and practiced military autocracy.

We declared the Diet to be the supreme organ of the state, and we insisted that it must be free; yet we consistently dictated its actions and forbade it even to discuss measures unless previously approved by Occupation leaders.

We called the Supreme Court the guardian of freedom but compelled it to rule, against its wish, according to Occupation command.

We knew that Communism was a peril, yet for months allowed it to pose as the favored theory of the Occupation.

We required that schools be free to teach the truth, but we forbade them to teach history or geography lest ultranationalistic propaganda be encouraged.

Yet, despite these contradictions, and despite the fact that much of what was done has since been repealed or modified or even ignored, the Occupation worked successfully. Program after program failed; but its ideals remained.

Japan is back where she started, but with the difference that she is not now, and will not become, ultranationalist or militarist. Reaction exists, as it always exists wherever some few were happier in bygone days; but, with the great majority better off and everyone convinced that it was the army that led Japan to disaster, reaction is but a sentimental relic for a few graybeards. Some Japanese, especially when they think of atom bombs and occupying armies, dislike America, but many more profess warm friendship for American democracy. Japan is loyal to her Emperor but does not worship him, nor has she ever done so; there is no danger that either he or his successors can dominate the government. Japan will not for many years, and perhaps may never, become a Christian country; but neither will she hinder Christianity's consistent progress.

In experimenting with Americanism, Japan found much which, wisely or mistakenly, she deemed unsuitable to her peculiar circumstances; but she did not reject democracy. Failure exactly to mirror American methods would not have been surprising under the most favorable conditions, but Occupationnaires were not the most efficient teachers. Most of the leaders were army officers who, unfamiliar with civilian affairs, resented an assignment which sometimes seemed to them a sidetracking that would not lead to promotion. Many of them had fought the Japanese and had heard well founded tales of Japanese cruelty and deceitfulness, of stabs in the back and of fanatical reaction. For such reasons, some of them had little confidence that Japan could be made a democratic nation.

Those who cooperated wholeheartedly in training Japanese toward democracy sometimes met strange obstacles. Frequently, especially in political affairs, Japan, when ordered to be democratic, had but slight conception of what was actually required. Often, in such cases, Occupationnaires received verbal instructions not to clarify the orders lest Americans be suspected of meddling too much in Japan's internal affairs. Thus the Japanese were forced to guess what was intended and, misunderstanding what they read or heard, seeing only the outward example of Americans in Tokyo, occasionally went ludicrously astray. Military example, especially under Occupation conditions, was no school for pure democracy.

While, in broad and very general outline, Occupation policy aimed at liberalism, democracy, and decentralization, actual practice swung so unpredictably from nagging interference to a scrupulous hands-off administration that Japanese were never certain what they might expect. Thus, although the Occupation professed a major purpose of developing initiative and self-reliance, Japanese fell back upon their traditional habit of relying upon authority for guidance. If the Occupation, or any minor segment thereof, suggested specific action, this was done; if, on the other hand, the Occupation seemed to be issuing recommendations for the record only, or if, as was all too often the case, it showed no real desire to know what action followed its directives, Japanese gave formal and indeed grateful approval and then neglected to do anything.

Ignorance, uncertainty, and the Occupation's occasional lack of interest, coupled with lack of coordination within the various Occupation bureaus, led to uneven acceptance of western ways. Much of what was done was either forced imposition or slavish copying of methods alien to the Japanese background and inconsistent with tradition. However better the innovations may have been, or however necessary for the promotion of democracy and freedom, they were not deeply rooted. As soon as Occupation pressure was removed—even earlier when the Occupation failed to exercise a close and constant supervision—Japan reverted to its ingrained habits and its well worn ruts.

Thus, it is easy to say that Japan became reactionary, and that the Occupation failed; but such a facile argument ignores intangibles. Old laws and governmental practices have, in many cases, been restored, but with the difference that the spirit of enforcement has been altered, the atmosphere is far more free, equality of opportunity has become available. These intangibles cannot be statistically demonstrated; but anyone who knew Japan before the war and since the Occupation knows that they are present, and that they are influential.

Because, among other post-occupation changes, Japan canceled the MacArthur-sponsored police reorganization, reversed decentralization, restored her military system, brought back big business, and stopped splitting up landholdings, many observers felt that the Occupation had failed; others, admitting these developments but sensing a new spirit among the people, discerned salutary reform. Appraisal was almost wholly subjective, depending upon what one wished to discover. Those who went to Japan convinced that the Japanese were sly and treacherous were certain that they pretended democracy only to delude the Occupation; others, thinking of the Japanese as normal peace-loving human beings misled and deceived by propaganda, were confident that true liberalism had been won. Many Occupationnaires believed sincerely that, while the women of Japan were lovely gentle creatures, the men were of an entirely different race.

Nothing even remotely like the Allied Occupation of Japan had ever before occurred in Japan's history. Not only had the Empire never lost a foreign war but, with the doubtful exception of a few of Kublai Khan's attacking Mongols who may have escaped the divine wind, the kamikaze, of the typhoon in 1281, no hostile foreign soldier had ever set foot on Japan.

The revolutionary social, economic, and political reforms, affecting every stratum of society and every individual within the strata, had no precedent. Never before, though Japan had for many centuries eagerly swallowed foreign influence in great quantities, had change been so sudden or so pronounced, and never had it been forced upon her. The greedy gulpings of westernism following the Meiji Restoration of 1868, and of Chinese culture twelve centuries earlier, had extended over years; but, a most important factor, they had been voluntary.

Nor was there precedent for the Americans. With characteristic optimism, many American army officers believed that experience in Cuba, Puerto Rico, and the Philippines had proved their ability to handle occupation problems. Without bothering to study Japanese psychology, history, or backgrounds—they had no time to study, nor were any books available even if time and desire existed—they blithely assumed that anything successful in the United States must necessarily succeed also in Japan. Their mission was to instill democracy, and this, of course, meant imposition of American ideas upon Japan. As far as most Occupation officers were concerned, any other proposal was un-American and Communistic.

Misunderstandings stemmed from uncertainties concerning what the Occupation was to do. Fundamentally, the theory of the Occupation was contained in the Potsdam Declaration. This document offered the stark alternative that Japan must immediately surrender or be devastated, but it bore within itself the seeds of uncertainty. If Japan surrendered she must lose much territory, and some "points" at least of what remained would then be occupied; but where, or how many, these "points" would be and what troops, whether Russians, Chinese, British, or Americans, would garrison the Empire remained undetermined. Japan did not anticipate that "points in Japanese territory" would really mean every square inch of the nation. The proposed length of Occupation was indefinite, the document merely stating that it must last until Japan punished her war criminals, established democratic freedoms, destroyed her war potential, and established "a new order of peace, security and justice." These, certainly, were vague limits, but drafters of the Declaration had considered threatening that occupation must continue until "irresponsible militarism is driven from the world."

If enforced to the letter, Occupation would probably have been eternal, for Utopia always lies far ahead. The best contemporary guess was that it would continue for a year or two, perhaps even three, but, in any case, too short a time to work the miracles required. While the three major powers blustered that no deviation would be made from the Declaration's terms, all thinking people knew that they must be content with something less than perfection.

The misunderstandings invited trouble. In their zeal to comply with Allied demands, the Japanese, even before the Occupation began, introduced reforms in government and administration; but the Allies, considering the changes as insincere and insufficient, refused approval. Shortly after MacArthur's arrival, however, Occupation officials demanded measures which, according to the Japanese, almost exactly paralleled the rejected proposals. Japan therefore, believing that the Occupation was more concerned with taking credit for reform than with the reform itself, complied with little real enthusiasm.

Outside governmental circles, many Japanese, forbidden to criticize openly, whispered that the Allies were hypocritical, that their real purpose was not reform but reduction of the empire to a colony, and that Americans, in particular, purposed to bleed Japan white in order to enslave the people. Confronted with proof that such an evil ambition had been expressly denied at Potsdam, the critics retorted that the variance between the official statement and what seemed to them to be the actual fact merely proved that Allied statements were not trustworthy. Such feelings were widespread, but since, because of censorship, they could not be openly expressed, the Occupation assumed that Japan's smiling cooperation reflected her true sentiments. Later, when the extent of Japanese dissatisfaction became better understood, MacArthur's men explained that Communist propaganda was responsible. Identification of Communism with liberalism, misunderstanding, or dislike of foreign interference induced stricter Occupation rule than was required, so that Japan, misunderstanding the Occupation quite as much as the latter misunderstood Japan, looked on MacArthur's men as irrational and unfair.

Americans, moreover, were impatient. Not knowing how long the Occupation would endure, they rushed to upset the old, established order lest the Allied forces be withdrawn before the work was finished. The absence of the CASA planners was unfortunate, for CASA had blueprints for bettering the social, economic, and political structure, whereas Occupationnaires, as one powerful general jocularly sneered, dreamed up their plans while in flight from Manila to Tokyo. Probably, even had the CASA blueprints been available, they would have been thrown aside as unsuited for making Japan an Anglo-Saxon democracy within a matter of months.

CASA preliminary studies had determined that forceful occupation of Japan would cause revulsion against rather than help Allied aims; and, consequently, only essential areas were marked out for change. Relatively well administered areas of interest—for instance, public health—might, it was assumed, be left for later action, to be democratized after examples had been set by successes elsewhere. Such studies were discarded, if, indeed, the Occupation forces ever saw the drafts. Officers anxious to complete their tasks quickly, and with credit to themselves, attempted to democratize everything completely and all at once.

That Japanese had no real understanding of what they were to do or how they were to do it, that virtually everything in Japanese life and thought opposed such radical upheavals, and that reforms could not live without well planted roots—all this was blithely overlooked. The mere issuance of an order, a directive, was supposed to be sufficient; as one important section chief retorted when told that a projected act was contrary to the folkways of the people, "Make them change their folkways." The orders were that Japan must be remade, which meant that everything must be revamped to American models. If Japan did not comply, or if the result proved inefficient, Occupationnaires charged that the Japanese were reactionaries.

For all this program the Occupationnaire received little if any guidance. Much was said of General MacArthur's understanding of the Japanese psychology and Japanese affairs; yet he gave the Occupation rank and file little direct aid. None of his advice filtered to the personnel, no general conferences benefited by his counsel. Except for a half-dozen top-flight generals, no officer drew upon his wisdom or received instruction from him. He stayed aloof and unapproachable; major generals approached hat in hand through the Chief of Staff, and even they were often put off by a brief memorandum reading, "The Supreme Commander instructs me to say . . ." which neither eased their difficulties nor solved their problems. Actually, MacArthur knew very few of his men and heard of most situations only through brief summaries.

The situation might have been remedied had the top brass been better informed and more accessible, or had they taken more initiative; but all too many modelled themselves on the Supreme Commander's pattern. They dared not bend. Some who tried to do so learned that they had broken etiquette. One high-placed officer who helped a lower-ranking aide was reprimanded for doing work assigned to a subordinate; another was rebuked for exceeding his specific assignment; a third received a written warning against spending time in research; and custom forbade anyone even to talk with a Japanese official not directly concerned with the work immediately in hand. Before the Occupation was one year old, the chief of one of MacArthur's sections denied his men permission to consult attachés of other sections on official business matters.

Except for brilliant and obvious exceptions, top brass knew little of the situation. All were excellent military men; but only a handful enjoyed more than casual knowledge of Japanese civilian affairs, and fewer still were ardent students. Most of them, absorbed in other duties, scorned to study the nonmilitary aspects of Japan, and one or two of them in fact said pointedly that such preoccupation, especially with backgrounds, reflected feudalistic sympathies.

Even had Occupationnaires cared to investigate, research materials were inadequate. Whatever the private resources of the chiefs, official library holdings were extremely slim. Government Section's library contained not a single authoritative modern book, journal, or paper on Japanese political affairs; when Whitney's men worked on Japan's fundamental codes they searched frantically, and for a long time in vain, for a copy of the United States Constitution. Major General Charles A. Willoughby's G-2 commandeered three excellent collections of prewar publications but kept them rigidly off limits to personnel of other sections. Statistics and Reports, the designated SCAP library, owned little else than SCAP-issued documents and, until 1949 at least, forbade use of its shelves even to its own personnel. An SRS rule banned citation of any book issued after 1937; a Japanese book, it was explained, must necessarily reflect militarist philosophy; and foreign books, no matter by whom written, could not have been based on solid, trustworthy sources.

As far as most Occupationnaires were concerned, impenetrable mystery wrapped postwar developments. SCAP's information agencies, intent on reporting plots against the Occupation, failed dismally in supplying data on peacetime progress. Statistics, which SCAP itself distrusted, flowed plentifully, reassurances and promises flooded Occupation offices; but, as trained scholars constantly reminded Whitney, Willoughby, and Dyke, any sound factual reporting was lacking, and virtually nothing came on what Japan was actually thinking.

Nor, apparently, did top brass care to know. Three different staff sections rejected proposals that efficient fact-finding services be established; the need, they said, was small. Except for routine warnings against exposure to disease, troops received little briefing on Japanese conditions; and civilians and dependents heard almost nothing. Except in the very early days when Communist propagandists used the army newspaper to help the Reds, neither the paper nor the army radio carried items dealing with Japanese affairs; Occupation movies ignored even the native newsreels; and, though, from time to time, *kabuki* companies arranged special showings of their drama, only a tiny fraction of army personnel saw it. SCAP officialdom, nourished almost entirely on preconceived ideas colored by wartime indoctrination, lived in a wholly unreal environment.

Occupationnaires arrived with a suspicious and unfriendly attitude. The navy men who led the way into Sagami Bay on August 27, the 150 airmen who landed at Atsugi the next day, and the 8,000 troops of the First Cavalry who followed expected trouble. Seasoned combat soldiers, taught to think of Japanese as cruel and treacherous fanatics, did not trust them.

Japan's peacefulness took everyone by surprise. Days before the first Occupation soldier landed, the Emperor had told Prime Minister Naruhiko Higashikuni to end the censorships, to brighten up the people's daily life, and to cooperate peacefully with the victorious Allies. The Education Ministry had called upon Japan's 20,000,000 students to "dry your tears and please return to gentleness." Home Minister Iwao Yamazaki, carrying out Imperial orders to restore civil liberties, had pleaded for friendly treatment of the invaders. An Occupation officer who did not know of this purged him as dangerous.

The press distinguished itself by its campaign for friendliness. *Yomiuri* assured its readers, on August 20, that, as "the people of all great nations are alike in their good understanding of culture," Japanese need not fear Americans. On the same day Inako Kubokawa, in *Tokyo Shimbun,* pleaded with Japan to try to understand American culture.

Officials helped to calm wild rumors that the invading troops might get out of hand. Prior to surrender the Metropolitan Police Board in Tokyo and the Yokosuka police appealed to every one, particularly women, to maintain prudence and decorum:

People must not worry, must not credit irresponsible gossip, must not show resentment or bear grudges. It was quite possible that some Americans who had been long away from home might be excited at seeing Japanese women; girls therefore should stay at home, but if they could not avoid going outdoors they must be circumspect. "Women will never be sloppily dressed nor bare their breasts in public. If hailed by foreign soldiers with 'hello' or 'hey' or in broken Japanese, the women must pay no attention. They will, wherever possible, avoid walking alone on lonely streets." They must not use heavy make-up, smile or make eyes at the soldiers and must not accept even a cigarette from them.

Press correspondents were amazed at the reception. Some, anxious to dispatch sensational copy, reported the behavior as willfully insulting the Americans by pointedly turning away from foreigners; others, such as the *Nation*'s representative, thought the peacefulness disquieting; it was, the *Nation* said, a proof of insincerity.

The *Nation* was, however, even more concerned with what it termed Japan's characteristic insolence in complaining against outrages committed by the Russians in Manchuria; it praised MacArthur for ignoring the protests.

General William Tardy Clement of the Marines, a Bataan veteran, wholeheartedly complimented Japanese cooperation, saying that it had been flawless. General Robert L. Eichelberger was so pleased that he predicted that, "if the Japanese continue as at present, the Occupation may be washed up within a year," and, in mid-September, MacArthur was so enthusiastic that he suggested cutting down Occupation personnel from 300,000 to 200,000 or fewer.

Others were less pleased. No demonstrations against Americans had occurred except, as Clement said, "an attack by an insane man against a sentry"; and no bitterness was evident. But Americans resented a Yokosuka Liaison Commission protest against the stealing of a wrist watch from a Japanese woman on August 30, the threats on the same day to bayonet a girl, and the stealing of beer at Hodogawa. They objected to publicizing 311 minor incidents against Japanese on August 30, 216 more on August 31, 160 on September 1, 179 on September 2, 85 on September 3, and 33 on September 4. The very fact of the steady drop in numbers indicated that the situation was being brought under strict control and Domei, the official news agency, generously broadcast, "The Occupation has been orderly compared with what Japan has done." It added, perhaps under Occupation pressure, "Reports of alleged misconduct and allegations of rape, looting and robbery have been greatly exaggerated."

These complaints, together with Japanese objections to Soviet advances in North Korea and Saghalien, overshadowed in Occupation minds the very real press efforts toward understanding and friendliness. Almost on the very day that MacArthur praised Japanese cooperation his public relations officer accused the press of sabotaging the Occupation. He told American correspondents of Japanese objections but said little of the friendliness. Lieutenant General Barney M. Giles, commanding the United States Strategic Air Force, demanded that Japan be internationally policed for the next century.

Perhaps MacArthur himself was confused. Edward Musgrove Dealey, president of the Dallas *News,* a newspaperman whose professional competence was far beyond dispute, reported MacArthur as having said that while the Occupation need not last more than six months, "if we are not too ruthless and cruel," he intended "to fix things" so that for the next twenty-five years "the Japanese will have a hard enough time eating." MacArthur's friends immediately denied the statement, but Dealey reiterated its accuracy.

Yet within two weeks the people whom MacArthur was said to intend to hold to a subsistence level had, he reported, begun an evolution which would "restore the dignity of the common man." It was noteworthy that MacArthur in September, 1945, credited the mainspring of the evolution to Japanese admiration of "the free man's way of life in actual action" as evidenced by his GI's, whereas a few months later he was insisting that the change, then classed as revolution, had come about as a result of Occupation directive.

The situation bewildered Occupation personnel. Lacking a clear concept of the situation, none too sure of the nature of the mission, and contemptuous of Japanese psychologies, Occupationnaires operated on the militarist theory that orders alone were sufficient. Since, by definition, MacArthur's directives were invariably wise and disobedience was unthinkable, results could never fail of astonishing success. Major General Willoughby was so certain of this that, before the Occupation had more than opened, he hailed it as "the greatest achievement of its kind since Napoleonic days." The confidence, voiced so seriously in GHQ circles, was a ludicrous parallel to the satire of Gilbert and Sullivan's *Mikado:* When SCAP said, "Let a thing be done," it was as good as done and, if it were as good as done, it was done. And why not say so?

Unhappily, accompanying the bureaucratic and militaristic attitude, the insidious malaise led MacArthur's inner circle to resent what they considered Machiavellian schemings by the President of the United States, the members of the Far Eastern Commission and sometimes of the Joint Chiefs of Staff, as well as by sundry newspapermen, publicists, and jealous politicians, to undermine MacArthur's dignity and power.

To question his wisdom was an act of treason: even though, as Willoughby admitted with a certain pride, MacArthur never read a paper longer than one page, the Supreme Commander understood all things and invariably decided matters with infallible judgment.

Those who doubted, hesitated, or asked the meanings of MacArthur's often turgid prose were suspect. When the Occupation opened, such men were fascist-minded reactionaries who revered the Emperor; later, they were fellow travelers. The malaise struck so severely that one prominent official set secret service agents spying upon a colleague's trusted personnel; he could not, as it was generally believed that he desired to do, unseat his rival's deputy, but he could cause the deportation as dangerous radicals of at least three of his rival's staff.

It was no doubt more serious that the internecine wars among Occupation personnel became known to Japanese who—privately informed by certain SCAP officials that other Americans, identified by name, section, and title, were Red sympathizers—consistently shadowed these individuals and, compiling voluminous dossiers upon their private acts, hoped to use the information for blackmailing purposes.

When the Occupation closed and SCAP control no longer held magazine and book publishers in check, these dossiers became the basis for a number of sensational articles and volumes upon the night life of high-placed Occupationnaires.

Suspicion underlay MacArthur's unfortunate press relationships. Neither he nor his associates had anything to hide, nor were any of the numerous correspondents anything but loyal to their nation; but, all too often, unskilled public relations officers suspected malice, or at least criticism, in the most innocent search for information. Americans who sought other news than the official press releases risked being regarded as Communists; Japanese who failed to print verbose and oft-repeated official statements in their four-page sheets were damned as dangerous reactionaries.

Nor was MacArthur's Public Relations Office wholly above suspicion as a source. Correspondents never forgot that, on the eve of a May Day demonstration in 1946, GHQ released a sensational report that a former reactionary leader had plotted to murder MacArthur. Full details of the conspirator's name, background, plans, and motivation were supplied; but, as no further action followed, newspapermen guessed that the entire incident was a gigantic hoax. MacArthur thought enough of the story to include it in his monthly report.

Distrust was bad enough; inefficiency was unpardonable. No nation, however rich and prosperous, could possibly have fulfilled at once all the varied requisitions by Occupation officers during the first few months following surrender. Certainly a bankrupt people who faced starvation, whose raw materials were scarce, and whose industries were shattered, could not do so. An efficient business organization would, in such circumstances, have created a central planning board, to study needs, survey resources, and allot priorities. This, indeed, the Japanese Government sought to do, within its relatively narrow field of free operation; but the Occupation tied its hands and set up no organization of its own. Each Occupation section remained sovereign, each issued its own commands. Little or no thought was given to relative importance or to over-all effects.

THREE

Rule by Interpreter

To promote efficiency by avoiding duplication of effort, section heads worked out gentlemen's agreements apportioning to themselves specific spheres of influence. Supervision over Japanese affairs was thus facilitated; and, with various ministries and government offices properly allotted to the SCAP section most concerned, the danger of conflicting orders was reduced. Commonly, and unashamedly, an area of interest thus distributed was referred to as a staff section's "private empire."

So jealously were jurisdictions regarded that in many instances contact by outsiders, whatever their rank within the Occupation, was regarded as invasion and, eventually, a general understanding spread that such incursions were tabu. Toward the close of the Occupation the inviolability of private empires had grown so sacred that even MacArthur's historians, in seeking information concerning what had been accomplished, were ordered not to talk to Japanese officials except by express license of the section chief in whose territory they belonged. Even after such permission had been granted—and cases were numerous in which it was refused—no facts thus gathered were to be incorporated in the history unless approved by the section chief concerned.

The tabu was typical of a certain provincialism rife in Occupation circles. Uncharitable observers held that this was due to the lack of proficiency among the section heads and a consequent unwillingness to invite comparison by others; but this, of course, was an exaggeration. More probably it sprang from grievous experience in trying to extract information from the Japanese; for, what with inexact statistics, fallible

26

memories of Japanese officialdom, and the seeming impossibility of obtaining comparable data, each section had been obliged not only to set its own standards but also to select those facts which seemed most flattering. Rival investigators were certain to create confusion by discovering, and possibly publishing, contradictory detail. Brigadier General Sams expressed the philosophy bluntly but accurately when he said, "No statistics on public health are acceptable unless they come from my office."

It was less understandable that, as far as possible, each staff section insulated itself against undue contact with its colleagues. With the exception of Civil Information and Education and Natural Resources Sections and, to less degree, Economic and Scientific Section, staff sections cloaked their activities in mystery. Some sections carried the isolation policy to such extremes that workers at adjacent desks were often ignorant of what their neighbors were doing. Occasionally the rival interests of Occupation leaders led to thinly veiled hostility; at such times a section leader might require a visitor from another empire to produce a letter, in the nature of a passport, from his section head, with no assurance that even this would bring about admission. Such distrust was particularly rife between civilian staff sections and sections dealing with matters of military security.

Protection against competition or invasion, while designed for efficiency, promoted less desirable results. Laziness, incompetence, and indifference could not be checked. During the first three years each section contributed, for inclusion in MacArthur's Summation of Non-Military Activities, a monthly report in which its chief included whatever seemed to add luster to his record; but, in the absence of unbiased reporting and without adequate checking, the Summation advertised claims rather than accomplishments. Summation editors, forbidden to seek independent data or to do more than challenge obvious statistical errors, forbidden strictly also to interpolate explanatory comment, background, or comparative material, especially any pertaining to the Austrian or German Occupations, were allowed only to correct punctuation and paragraphing.

Under such a system, no failures, no shortcomings, and no policy changes were reported, the Summation being merely a journal of triumphs. The situation led the shrewd W. Macmahon Ball, British Commonwealth member of the Allied Council for Japan, to state with some acidity that the real fault of the Occupation was not that it accomplished so little but that it claimed so much.

Perhaps the various Supreme Commanders may for their private information have insisted upon complete and honest reporting from their section chiefs—this, it would seem, would have been indispensable; but, if so, little information was sought from mere subordinates. Field workers—for instance in military government teams—compiled exhaustive monthly reports which, as far as GHQ-SCAP was concerned, moldered in corps headquarters at Sendai or Kyoto, arriving at Tokyo, if at all, in closely edited and abbreviated form, and after months' delay. Presumably workers reported to branch chiefs, who reported to division heads, who passed on pertinent details to section chiefs; but each stage involved condensation, and, the higher the ladder was mounted, the less familiar was the officer in charge with actual conditions.

Economic and Scientific Section, CIE, and Government Section failed most notably in such respects since none possessed machinery adequate to check developments within their respective fields. ESS, indeed, produced monthly statistical reports upon economic developments, but without much confidence in the accuracy of the reporting. Ken Dyke and his successor, Donald Ross Nugent, formerly a teacher in a provincial school, shrugged off such matters by pointing out that no one really could know how effective educational changes were until twenty years after they were instituted. Whitney claimed repeatedly that Japan had grown democratic, his subordinates carefully keeping from him any data that might disprove the claim.

In Whitney's case the need for adequate reporting was particularly serious since his assignment was elastic. JCS directives called merely for encouragement for founding and supporting democratic political parties; but, as this by interpretation, and certainly by necessity, might be stretched indefinitely, he undertook also to supervise such parties as existed. The lack of clear directive for this extension may explain his predilection for indirect advice rather than concrete written orders.

For such encouragement and guidance, Whitney had available two nationally known political economists, each thoroughly experienced in Japanese affairs, Professors Harold S. Quigley of Minnesota and Kenneth W. Colegrove of Northwestern. Quigley, to be sure, was stationed in another section where his talents were not fully employed, but Colegrove was Whitney's own adviser. Separately, or as a team, these experts would have been admirable mentors for a democratic movement.

Whitney, however, preferring military to civilian aid, assigned responsibility for this vital task to an inexperienced major. MacArthur then dispensed with the service of an excellent Political Adviser from the State Department.

The major's task was complicated by a policy akin to a conspiracy of silence. Perhaps because the mission was less clear in the supervision of political parties than in the administration of the purge, the reform of government administration, or extension of the electorate, Government Section studiously refrained from overt interference in Japan's political affairs. By JCS directive Japan was to be democratized; but the major was under no compulsion to explain just what was thus required. To earnest Japanese who asked for guidance he replied that Japan itself must implement the order. To party politicians who inquired how best to convert boss-government into democratic rule he answered that a careful study of Western party management might offer a good clue; but he himself avoided specific answers, nor were publications available to clarify the matter. The selfsame politicians who had been active in prewar politics were thus expected to plan and manage their own reform. The major considered himself duty-bound to make no explanation.

This neutralism faithfully echoed Government Section policy. The obsession of aloofness lay so deep that in every political crisis Whitney categorically commanded subordinates to refrain from talking with, or even meeting, any Japanese official or political leader lest some stray word be construed as an attempt to influence the situation. Similar prohibitions forbade Government Section personnel from conferring with purgees even though such individuals might be the only possible source of valuable data upon political affairs.

Even in normal times, much if not all Government Section information concerning political trends came from the public press—which other MacArthur aides dismissed as an uninformed and wholly unreliable source—or from such Japanese as voluntarily appeared to report on current developments. A few Government Section attachés essayed independent investigation; but this, while at first tolerated, was later frowned upon and then almost entirely ceased. Thus Government Section, and through it MacArthur, unwittingly repeated special pleading by a biased, sometimes subsidized, and always closely controlled press.

Because Government Section did not ascertain the impact of its

activity, Japanese took advantage of its ignorance. Early in the Occupation, the New Japan Political Party, although founded and controlled by racketeers, convinced a naïve Whitney attaché that it was
a warm defender of democracy and, as such, received enthusiastic welcome as an idealistic reform group. This allowed the gangster chiefs
to delude donors of campaign funds into believing that MacArthur was
the party's patron. The founder and the chief propagandist of the
Cooperative Party, professing one of the more reactionary political
creeds, invited Whitney's chief political expert to a feast and then
displayed pictures of the dinner party to prove that Government Section endorsed its aims. Another small party printed letterheads listing
a Government Section member as its "adviser," while yet a fourth,
inducing two of Whitney's men to sit upon the platform at its inaugural
ceremonies, implied that it was the Occupation's preferred party. Yoshio
Shiga, the Communist editor, who was a frequent visitor in Whitney's
offices, went so far as to assert in public speeches that MacArthur's
aides were Communists, and that the Occupation demanded support for
Communist candidates. Government Section's isolation from first-hand
knowledge of political activity, and its underlings' practice of suppress-
ing published information that might embarrass or annoy their chiefs,
kept all such matters from MacArthur's, and even from Whitney's, ears.
Top brass did not know that Sanzo Nosaka, the Communist leader, was
boasting that the political expert had called him "the most astute and
learned statesman in Japan," and that he was further regarded only as
"a harmless and much misunderstood theorist who had no ties to
Moscow."

Each major party delegated an English-speaking member as a liaison
officer to propagandize within the ill informed Occupation. Such visitors
arrived daily to relay as "confidential information" the news appearing
in the vernacular papers, which most of MacArthur's men were unable
to read. Government Section's willingness to accept such data was unpardonable since it received daily an admirable digest of the Japanese
press; but many of the personnel were too busy, and some were too
uninterested, to read this thoroughly.

Tadao Wikawa, who represented his fascist Cooperative Party as
democratic followers of the Dutch and Danish cooperative movement,
and Yusuke Tsurumi, long-time propagandist who delighted to describe himself as the "brains of the Progressive Party," were masters
of the method; they press-agented their parties of old-line political

bosses as democratic youth groups. When Tsurumi was eliminated by the purge his place was filled by his disciple, Ken Inukai, another smooth talker who subsequently became Yoshida's Justice Minister.

Others exploited the lack of liaison not only between various staff sections but also within the sections, using this as a means of setting one group against another. A few, particularly among Socialists and Liberals, discovering that some of the higher brass were willing, and occasionally anxious, to undercut their own subordinates, flattered the upper echelons.

In this the Socialists were especially successful. The slim, elegant, and politically astute Shizue Kato, formerly the Baroness Ishimoto of birth-control fame, played upon the hunger for exciting revelations. Her frank disclosure of "plots" by rival factions of her own party against the Occupation made her such a favorite that after February, 1947, the Occupation was generally regarded as favoring Socialist left-wing policies.

Government Section, aware of this accusation, retorted that it supported Socialist politics because the voters had shown their preference for such leaders, and that the Diet had selected Tetsu Katayama as prime minister; but, long before the election, Mrs. Kato's close Government Section connections had inspired rumors that MacArthur hoped for Socialist success.

While Shigeru Yoshida's Liberals were usually dominant their propagandists were less successful on the lower levels. The choice of a back-slapping liaison officer who modeled his behavior upon the pattern of college movies repelled many of the Occupationnaires; the brashness of one of Yoshida's special protégés incurred the ire of Whitney's staff. The Liberals also, like other conservative parties and like the right-wing Socialists, were deliberately sabotaged by leftist interpreters who reported that the party was composed of bosses, gangsters, and venal reactionaries.

Yoshida himself, however, more than compensated for the shortcomings of his underlings. As Prime Minister he had access to MacArthur; and, even when out of power, he assured his intimates that MacArthur continued to rely upon him. More than one rival was removed from public life because of a Yoshida hint that MacArthur thought the person purgeable.

Such high-level but wholly unofficial liaison gave Japan advantage. Graduates of the American army and navy language-training schools, while well equipped for ordinary conversation, rarely possessed the expert knowledge needed to conduct technical discussion. The few Japan-born Americans available, particularly of the officer class, were monopolized by high-ranking Occupationnaires, so that the bulk of translation work was entrusted to American-born Japanese, Nisei, from Hawaii or California. These young high-school graduates proved both willing and competent for ordinary assignments, such as interrogations or readings for the Allied Translator and Interpreter Service; but for specialized interviews they sometimes were inadequate. As enlisted personnel, or more rarely as lieutenants, they dared not admit ignorance in either language on any topic assigned to them. They hesitated to ask their superiors to stop talking so that they might translate or to explain a complicated phrase; hence they passed on in Japanese, in greatly modified form, only as much of the torrent of words as they remembered. Similar shortening and editing of the reply resulted in both sides having but a hazy general idea of what was under discussion. Eavesdroppers at home in both languages therefore suspected at times that in some technical discussions Japanese, Americans, and Nisei alike were so bewildered that none really knew what the others were saying. In at least one instance, relating to interrogations concerning Japanese war plans and strategy, an American lieutenant resourcefully created from his own imagination an elaborate report, complete with names, dates, and alleged documentary source, to support the theories favored by his commanding officer.

School-trained interpreters used the Tokyo dialect; Nisei, mostly descended from ancestors who used the Okayama or Okinawa patois, often floundered in talking with Japanese from other provinces. High-placed Japanese complained that Nisei, innocently or by design, insulted them by speaking low-caste language without proper honorifics. Occupation officers, unaware of dialect difference or considering honorifics undemocratic, ignored the complaints or dismissed them as due to jealousy or hate. To avoid such complications one section chief, who considered himself far better equipped scientifically than any Japanese he was likely to encounter, ordered his staff, regardless of their proficiency in Japanese, to use English only. Thus he was certain that instructions were given in exactly the form that he desired while problems of accurate interpretation were purely a Japanese concern.

Documentary translation lessened difficulties somewhat by eliminating localisms and by avoiding the stress of speed and strain; but other problems rose. Even in scientific matters Japanese often prefer indirection, allusion, and perhaps vagueness while Occidentals favor specific, direct, and accurate reasoning; to translate Japanese documents into English often therefore requires not only knowledge of both languages but also appreciation of the overtones and implications that might be involved. Occupationnaires, accordingly, used such documents as sparingly as possible.

Personal interviews, however, were heavily relied upon. Occupation officials desirous of understanding background or current conditions summoned Japanese to appear to answer questions. Such summonses, especially in the early Occupation years when Japanese leaders were being jailed or purged, would in any case have thrown politicians and businessmen into states of fear; but when delivered by a police agent, as was usually the case, the summons was often terrifying. Many Japanese arrived at Occupation headquarters in such trepidation that they could not coherently present their cause. Interpreters who failed to understand the psychological situation, or who, for ideological reasons, were hostile, held such men at their mercy; for interpreter reports, whether honest or distorted, were the basis for judgment, opinion, and action.

Japanese who sought interviews but could not speak English often brought their own interpreters—a custom also followed by those who knew English but desired time to express their thoughts more accurately, especially when replying to questions that might embarrass them. Michinari Sugawara, for example, a political manipulator, thus talked for hours before admitting that he was a University of London graduate. When taxed with his knowledge of English and asked why he had concealed it, he replied, simply and with perfect truth, "You didn't ask me."

A few self-possessed Japanese used Occupation interpreters to good advantage. When asked for opinions they were not accustomed to expressing or cross-examined too severely, they fell back, Oriental-fashion, upon cloudy imagery or answered in such abstruse language, couched in ultrapolite Chinese style, that interpreters were beguiled into long side colloquies which might in time produce a proper answer, but which more often made the inquisitor so impatient that he either abandoned or forgot his question. Men like Tetsu Katayama and Sanzo Nosaka thoroughly enjoyed tantalizing the amateurs and entangling the Nisei as did former Finance Minister Tanzan Ishibashi until, on one occasion, he absent-mindedly wandered into headquarters carrying an English-language magazine.

Perhaps the most famous translation incident concerned the Constitution. Soon after arrival in Japan, MacArthur held a consultation with former Prime Minister Prince Fumimaro Konoye. In discussing Occupation requirements, Konoye asked if MacArthur had any suggestions concerning changes in the "make-up of the Government," meaning the relations of the military and naval Cabinet ministers to the civilian officials. The interpreter, however, translated "make-up" by its English equivalent "constitution," which MacArthur understood as a proper noun. Although heretofore little attention had been given to the thought that a new Constitution should replace the Meiji Constitution of 1889, MacArthur replied that Constitutional changes would indeed be necessary.

Konoye still further misunderstood the Supreme Commander to mean that he, Konoye, was to draft a new fundamental law and also to form and lead a new political party pledged to democracy. None of this was in MacArthur's mind; but Konoye left the conference with the impression that he had been thus commissioned. Upon returning to meet Mac-Arthur on October 4, he reported that the Emperor had approved the plan to write a revised Constitution. Konoye completed the task, but his draft was rejected as insufficiently democratic.

A post-Occupation Japanese myth developed that the rejection caused Konoye such loss of face that he committed suicide. The truth was that he took poison rather than face arrest and trial as a war criminal; and this was well understood while the Occupation continued.

Shigeru Ozu, former chief groom of the Imperial stables, told of an interpreter misunderstanding that saved Hirohito's face. Following a boast that an American would ride the Emperor's famous white horse, Lieutenant Dick Ryan visited the Imperial stock farm, where he saw an Arab stallion, Hatsushimo, or First Frost, which, he was told, had a pedigree extending back to Napoleon's Shagyias. Ryan asked if this were the Emperor's horse and was assured that it was, indeed, Imperial property. Ryan therefore paid 1,000 yen, then the equivalent of $66, and announced that he had fulfilled the boast. Later he took the animal to the United States where it was widely exhibited although, as Ozu revealed, Hatsushimo was only a stud horse which Hirohito had never mounted.

Government through interpreter developed in many cases into government through mistresses. From the beginning, Japanese relied upon women as weapons to win the Occupation; and, at one time, they seriously proposed to enroll all housemaids and waitresses as spies. Almost upon arrival, high-ranking officers were offered feminine companionship, and many enthusiastically accepted. Ladies who had lived abroad, especially those with embassy experience in English-speaking countries, were particularly favored; and if, in addition, they bore titles the lure was irresistible. Japan reckoned rightly that an official who preached equality of rank would be delighted with a countess as a friend.

Variations on the theme were numerous. An heir to the prewar Black Dragon Society, the man who boasted that it was he that had made Shigeru Yoshida Prime Minister, planted his son to spy in the home of a commanding general; but this was unusual since women were preferred. A clever politician, learning that flirtation was afoot between a leading Whitney adviser and a bright young lady in his office, offered his mansion for whatever private use they might require; another gave a summer home at the seashore, next door to an Imperial villa, for similar purposes. Wataru Narahashi, chief secretary for Prime Minister Baron Kijuro Shidehara's Cabinet, planned to capture Whitney's entire Government Section. At frequent parties in the palatial mansion of the Rubber King, Narahashi entertained lavishly, detailing pretty girls of noble families to dance with the Americans while Cabinet members sat glumly waiting for American canned rations. Nothing was untoward, in fact two women attachés were also entertained; but friendships were encouraged, and Occupation officers were offered every opportunity to invite the girls to more intimate surroundings.

Thus, when Narahashi wished to suggest informally that Government Section might take certain action, when he wished informal or advance information on Occupation activities, his channels were prepared. The scheme worked well, both in Government Section where a handsome lady of title was extremely effective and in Legal Section where a vivacious widow formerly of London played her part with skill. Narahashi was pleased to find that Whitney's deputy chief, Colonel Charles L. Kades, spoke French fluently, for while few top Government Section men were apt at Japanese, Narahashi could speak French. It did not save him from the purge but Narahashi thought that it postponed the evil day.

Similar amenities were offered to other sections, with attention concentrated on Marquat's Economic and Scientific Section through which big business was controlled, and by which contracts were approved. In these instances, since the bait was dangled by industrialists rather than by diplomats and statesmen, the approach was sometimes cruder. Akira Ando, powerful transportation magnate with fleets of taxis, private motorcars, and trucks, who aimed at monopolizing both stevedoring and construction work, showered gifts on Occupation leaders. At his elaborate Dai-An, Great Ando, night club, frequented both by gangsters and by the more frivolous top nobility, he gave costly geisha parties for Americans in a position to award contracts. He placed his eighteen bordellos at their disposal. Ando, however, offered bribes too openly, and when he boasted that a powerful American general was his chief protector he was arrested for possessing black-market goods. He went to jail for six months and paid a fine of 50,000 yen, equivalent to $3,300, but upon his release in September, 1947, received a contract for crating and transporting machinery and tools for reparation payments. His guest book, which reportedly contained the names of the hundreds of Occupation officers whom he had befriended, was confiscated and disappeared from sight.

Ando was unique only in that he was punished; hundreds of others, ranging from the high personage who prepared a suit of medieval gold armor as a gift for MacArthur to little fellows who bought favor by "presentoes," marked the progress of the Occupation. During the first year of the Occupation it was almost impossible to find an American who had not been approached with some sort of "deal."

That these offers often were accepted is evidenced by the fact that, until the turning of yen into dollars was declared illegal, the armed forces remitted to America each month a sum approximating $8,000,000 more than their total pay. Colonel Harold R. Ruth, the fiscal officer, charged that the excess was the profit from black-marketing. Later, plans grew more grandiose, as when a certain prince arranged to import shiploads of cigarettes so that he and his American colleagues might make enough money on the black market to buy a controlling stock interest in the Japanese steel industry; the plan failed only at the last moment, after having been approved by lower Occupation echelons.

Dispatches to both the *New York Herald Tribune* and the *New York Times* during 1947 that certain American officials were misusing their positions to grow rich illegally, followed by the conduct by important personnel of private business with the very men whom they had previously supervised, confirmed Japanese suspicions that the Occupation was not above illegal methods. Rumors spread rapidly that key officials had been bought, and when the great Showa Denko scandal revealed billions of yen in corruption, not only Japanese but jealous Americans in other staff sections whispered that huge graft had been collected.

These were rumors not proved, although Japanese ladies hitherto connected closely with the central figures insisted that the rumors were entirely accurate. There were, however, other proved incidents. Provost marshal's men and some MP's went to jail for black-marketing. Colonel Edward J. Murray, accused of misappropriating diamonds entrusted to him at the Bank of Japan, was jailed for attempting to smuggle gems into California. The disappearance of gold and diamonds worth more than $2,000,000 after two American majors took them into custody led in August, 1952, to an investigation by the Diet. Other charges of theft were lodged against minor officers and men, and while unimportant both in numbers accused as compared to the thousands of Occupationnaires and in value as contrasted to Japan's own swindles and robberies, they undermined confidence in the integrity of the Occupation. Japanese were unaware that many military and civilian officers were being quietly shipped home on similar suspicion.

The unhappy, and no doubt unfair, result was a firm conviction among Japanese, to whom such practices were not surprising, that Americans could be bought, whether by women or by bribes. Thus the innocent also were suspect as venal. Nor was this attitude confined to Japanese; many Americans also suspected that their fellows who defended or explained Japan were influenced by their lady friends or had been "reached" by Japanese associates. This, added to the always lurking willingness to regard the nonconformist as a bad security risk, went far toward poisoning the Occupation atmosphere.

FOUR

Revolution from Above

As propaganda the Potsdam Declaration was admirable; as a specific guide to peacetime action it was inadequate. Perhaps, indeed, its assumption that Japan had latent democratic tendencies requiring only revival and strengthening was mistaken, if not actually harmful. Acting upon this document, however, President Truman—on the advice of his Joint Chiefs of Staff and apparently without consulting other Occupation powers—ordered MacArthur to help Japan create any peacefully inclined and responsible democratic government which it might desire. At the same time he forbade MacArthur to impose upon Japan any form of government which Japan did not wholeheartedly approve.

These instructions, which in effect prevented the overthrow of the Emperor system, insisted upon democracy and, by implication, liberalism; but failure to define the qualifying clauses left wide latitude for interpretation. To many Japanese and to some Occupationnaires as well the injunction that MacArthur must veto reactionary or totalitarian rule carried hints that Japan might swing as far leftward as she pleased provided Occupation interests were not imperiled; they looked upon the orders as an open invitation for a New Dealism, or a Welfare State, which they misunderstood as Communism.

MacArthur's friendly gesture of inviting Russian generals to dinner as soon as they arrived in Japan made Japanese fear he was a Communist. His obedience to orders in requiring abolition of the secret police, unbridled criticism of the Emperor, release of radicals from political imprisonment, and freedom for Communist propaganda, together with his flat injunction against criticism of any Allied power, including Soviet Russia, intensified the false fears. Irrespective of the justice or the need for such requirements, these matters had for years been taken in Japan as ultra-Marxian proposals supported by no conservative and by few, if any, liberals. To amazed and frightened Japanese, MacArthur's actions seemed to be identical with the Moscow line. Soviet sympathizers fanned their fears by assuring Japanese that MacArthur and his chief aides were really Russia's friends, and that he would be pleased if they, too, joined the Reds. Worried conservative Socialists hastened to Government Section to inquire if MacArthur had demanded that they form a united front with Communism. Employees of the three major Tokyo newspapers, whose influence was paramount throughout Japan, blustered to their editors and owners that MacArthur wanted the press to prove its democracy by coloring its news in Moscow's interest; when the executives and owners balked, the employees themselves assumed control. Russian-inspired labor leaders marched into employers' offices to demand employee control of industry as a proof of industrial democracy. Yoshio Shiga boasted in public speeches that his release from jail was proof that Russia ran the Occupation.

Some Occupation officers, a few of them in key positions, welcomed these actions as evidence of a healthy democracy; and one or two were believed by ultraconservative Japanese to have encouraged radicalism. Others, caught wholly unaware by the Red propaganda, if indeed in their general ignorance of the language and conditions they even knew about it, were slow in counterpropaganda. As Occupation censorship forbade speeches or publication that might conceivably annoy the Russians or any other Ally, the misconceptions went uncontradicted, a fact which, to worried Japanese, seemed to indicate that Shiga and his friends were echoing Occupation wishes.

Quite probably Lieutenant General Kuzma Derevyanko, the Soviet representative in Tokyo, realized the misuse of MacArthur's legitimate demands for justice and freedom; and he may, in fact, have directed it. If so his participation was unofficial. Perhaps by his advice Russia, modifying its stand, agreed at Moscow in December, 1945, to join a new directorate, a Far Eastern Commission (FEC) originally of eleven members and later of thirteen, to formulate policy and, if it desired, to cancel MacArthur directives. At least three of the four major parties —China, Britain, the United States, and Russia—were to have power

to reject or approve fundamental changes in the Japanese Constitution
or governmental system. This FEC was to meet at Washington; a less
important body, the Allied Council for Japan (ACJ) with a delegate
from each of the four major Allies, was to meet fortnightly in Tokyo.

No doubt the Russians hoped to use these agencies for propaganda,
if not for direct intervention in administration; but MacArthur, both
by temperament and by design, was armed against the possibility. Because of the security classification already given to JCS 10, his assistants
were giving the impression that policy directives had been drafted by
the Supreme Commander personally.

A reissue of that document, as JCS 18, on November 8, allowed them
to cite JCS 18 instead of JCS 10 for actions taken in September and October. They let readers infer that the Joint Chiefs had ratified rather
than initiated his policies. By declining to explain why certain steps
had been taken MacArthur, operating independently, completed his
actions before recommendation or advice could be received. They
might, thereafter, be canceled or modified, but only at the risk of discrediting the entire Occupation.

Russia's belated effort to intervene merely tightened American control. Essentially the Occupation was an international activity under FEC
control and ACJ supervision; but because it was administered by Mac-
Arthur as an American army officer, and because the greatest number
of his civilian assistants were American, the international color faded
rapidly. MacArthur tacitly, and his assistants more or less insistently
and vocally, ignored the FEC, sneered at the ACJ, and took their cues
directly from the American Joint Chiefs of Staff, usually without publicly acknowledging that they were doing so.

Policy directives, sent by FEC through the Joint Chiefs of Staff,
were orders for MacArthur; but the Allied Council for Japan, being
merely consultative and advisory, had less standing. Supposedly Mac-
Arthur was to call all matters of substance to ACJ attention in advance, but only if the exigencies of the situation should permit; and
he was the judge of those exigencies. Not only were such consultations
rare, but MacArthur, as holder of a decisive vote, could overrule the
other members.

At its first meeting, April 3, 1946, MacArthur put the ACJ in what
he considered its proper place by reminding it of its function as adviser; he failed to mention that if any member disagreed with him on
matters affecting the regime, on fundamental constitutional changes,

or on alterations in the government as a whole, such matters must await decision by the FEC. The reason was obvious; MacArthur had no intention of changing the control regime or of regarding anything he might desire to do as a fundamental amendment. Thereafter he not only permitted his aides to ignore or even to insult the ACJ, but himself pointedly neglected even to mention it in any of his own reports.

MacArthur could not ignore the Far Eastern Commission; but, as far as possible, he by-passed it, gave it no credit for assistance, and omitted any mention of it as a source for constructive information or advice. Only after the FEC had pleaded with him for four years was he persuaded to send it a liaison officer—a man of but a colonel's rank. Through General Whitney he urged his staff to draft a new constitution for Japan by working day and night. His purpose may have been to finish it and, if possible, to have it accepted before the FEC could send him orders on its contents. So jealous were Occupation leaders of possible FEC interference that a civilian received a lecture and a virtual reprimand for having even talked to Nelson T. Johnson, the FEC secretary-general. MacArthur, the civilian was informed, owed nothing to the FEC.

The new Constitution, thus drafted in a hurry, was an afterthought.

Upon arrival in Japan, MacArthur apparently had little if any idea of replacing the 1889 Constitution by an American-dictated draft. Nor did his JCS orders empower him to do so; for, although they gave him permission to require changes in governmental machinery, they did so only in the event that the Emperor or other Japanese authority failed to carry out the surrender terms in satisfactory fashion. He could, to be sure, "permit and favor" any modifications of feudal or authoritarian aspects of the government; but these, it was intimated, were to be initiated by the Japanese.

Under the Potsdam Declaration Japanese citizens must be guaranteed civil liberties, respect for fundamental human rights, and the removal of obstacles to the revival and strengthening of democratic tendencies; but, as these rights had been accorded at least in principle by the Meiji Constitution, no major change was contemplated. These civil liberties had not, in fact, been extended to the people, but the restrictions had been imposed by legislation which could be repealed by Diet enactment or by issuing ordinances. Both Japanese and Occidental lawyers construed the Meiji Constitution as a highly elastic document amenable either to authoritarian or to democratic interpretation.

The point had long been argued. Since the Meiji Constitution was, by definition, a basic law graciously granted by the condescension of an Emperor who retained all sovereignty and all rights of legislation, execution, and judicature, and since it premised respect for the Imperial ancestors, especially the sun-goddess, Amaterasu Omikami, few responsible scholars dared examine the degree to which the Emperor might directly interfere in governmental matters. But since for a thousand years or more personal intervention had been non-existent, with ministers acting in the Imperial name, debate was possible as to their competency and efficiency.

Conservatives, led by such professors of constitutional law as Shinkichi Uyesugi of Tokyo Imperial University, held that the Emperor, although he had granted a Constitution, remained unbound by it. Liberals, such as Tatsukichi Minobe, also a Tokyo Imperial University professor of law, challenged this traditional view by saying that the Emperor had surrendered a portion of his power and, ceasing to be absolute, had become a partner in the government, an organ of the state in which sovereignty now rested. Both sides were heard attentively, with Minobe probably attracting a larger following until, during the 1930 decade, reactionaries attacked him in the Diet, and then shot him, although not fatally, for lese majesty.

It was, however, clear that reform, even along the lines of the Potsdam Declaration, was possible either by a loose construction of the Meiji Constitution or by surrounding the Emperor with more liberal advisers. More than a week prior to MacArthur's arrival, Prime Minister Higashikuni announced his intention to guarantee civil liberties, especially free speech, and to call a new election so that the voice of "fair public opinion" might be represented in the Diet. Later, both he and the Emperor promised to convert Japan into an empire modeled on British constitutionalism.

Probably the idea of a completely new Constitution came to Japan through an overseas broadcast by the Office of War Information. This message, delivered in the name of Admiral Harry E. Yarnell, commemorated Bill of Rights Day in the United States and suggested that Japan might incorporate such principles into her fundamental law. Soon afterwards, Prince Konoye, reporting both to the Emperor and to MacArthur, received what he understood to be a mandate to draft proposals.

Although, in conformity with his orders, MacArthur did not initiate

Constitutional reform—leaving it, as the Joint Chiefs of Staff had directed, to the Japanese—he set the tone for it by insisting upon democratic innovations. As early as September 15 he fulfilled his instructions to require press freedom and, on October 4, he demanded the other JCS 10 requirements for civil liberties. These, he told Konoye, included woman suffrage and broader education privileges. The formal press statement issued on this meeting, did not mention a Constitution.

The demands, together with the necessity for dismissing various police officials as well as the current Home Minister, Iwao Yamazaki, caused the replacement of the Higashikuni Cabinet by that of Baron Shidehara, an antimilitarist diplomat. Konoye then passed on to Shidehara the hint that MacArthur wanted a new Constitution.

Shidehara, like most Japanese, saw no essential need for a new Constitution, believing that a reinterpretation of the Meiji charter would be sufficient, but he seized the opportunity to make Japan, if not an Oriental Switzerland, at least a nonmilitarist nation. At his suggestion a clause was drafted forbidding any military force, renouncing war, and denying Japan even the right of belligerency. This won enthusiastic approval from MacArthur but not from Konoye.

Once Japan had decided by Konoye's misconception upon Constitutional revision, numerous groups prepared drafts. Konoye and Soichi Sasaki, professor of constitutional law at Kyoto Imperial University, headed a committee appointed on October 11 by the Emperor. State Minister Joji Matsumoto and Tatsukichi Minobe led a rival committee named the same day by the Cabinet. Each major political party and various private individuals, among them Yukio Ozaki, drew up outlines.

Since all were subject to the Potsdam Declaration, the JCS directives, and SWNCC instructions, all drafts were basically similar. Necessarily, each included equal suffrage, a Diet with full powers, a government fully responsible to the people, and an executive who must resign upon losing the Diet's confidence. Elective governors and democratic local assemblies, in prefectures, cities, towns, and villages, were also required.

All plans envisaged the retention of the Emperor as a symbol, only the Communists suggesting his dethronement; and most of the suggestions revived the prewar plans of reducing the power of the House of Peers and of the Privy Council. A favorite proposal was the introduction of some sort of functional, or vocational, representation into the upper house.

Whitney's advisers, regarding this proposal as fascist, and disappointed because Japan continued to regard the Emperor as ruling by divine descent, rejected all the drafts. Some of the more radical officers favored a plan proposed by Tsunego Baba, editor of *Yomiuri* newspaper, and Tatsuo Morito, a Socialist theoretician, for an elective president, the initiative and referendum, social insurance, a compulsory eight-hour working day, and proportional representation; but, as this received no support outside Socialist ranks, it was dropped.

By the end of January, 1946, MacArthur became convinced that Japanese if left entirely to themselves, even with the help of his directives, would not produce a satisfactory document. He and Whitney, conscious of their roles as men of destiny, prepared to write a basic law for Japanese acceptance. This, however, required haste since the Foreign Ministers had decided at Moscow in December that any fundamental change must be approved by a Far Eastern Commission. As this Commission was soon to meet, any Occupation-sponsored plan must be prepared at once.

Whitney therefore turned his Government Section into what he termed a "constituent assembly" and, on February 4, assigned each of his staff, "as a Thomas Jefferson," to specific duties in drafting a Constitution for Japan. Secrecy was imposed, lest the Far Eastern Commission hear of the project, and the staff was ordered to work day and night, if necessary, to finish the job within a week. Nothing was said about anticipating the FEC, but the staff was urged, as a patriotic symbolism, to have the Constitution accepted by Japan on Washington's Birthday.

MacArthur gave but little guidance, confining himself to four basic points: that the Emperor was to remain as a symbol of the state, his throne descending to his heirs; that government must be responsible to the people; that all should be equal; and—the Shidehara idea—that war should be outlawed, with Japan having no armed forces. Colonel Charles L. Kades and his assistants expanded these brief notes into full-fledged constitutional provisions.

Other Government Section personnel, some of whom studied the Soviet Constitution, suggested additional provisions. Some were ruled out at once as ultraradical; others were seriously considered, including the right of the Diet to overrule the Supreme Court, a clause protecting the Constitution by forbidding amendments for ten years, the prohibition of political activity by religious groups, and a detailed specification of social guarantees. A proposal to make the Bill of Rights inviolate, so that it could not be repealed or weakened, was stricken out by MacArthur himself, according to Whitney.

The draft, completed February 10, was laid before Yoshida and his constitutional draft adviser, Joji Matsumoto. Acceptance, Whitney said, was not compulsory; but if Japan refused it MacArthur would himself lay it before the people. Yoshida delayed, explaining privately that he did so because Matsumoto, a big businessman, a lawyer, and a bureaucrat, was a Socialist who preferred a more circuitous "jeep way over bumpy roads" to this American airway approach. The Cabinet split, Yoshida and Matsumoto opposing the Whitney draft and Prime Minister Shidehara favoring a compromise. The Emperor, however, intervened directly and advised the most far-reaching reform, even if it involved the loss of his prerogatives. Eventually, by adding Narahashi and another pro-revisionist to the Cabinet, a majority was procured.

Matters now took a strange and somewhat tortuous course, designed to hide the fact that this draft Constitution was an American production, and that it had been forced upon Japan. On March 5 the Emperor issued a Rescript expressing his earnest wish that the Meiji Constitution be revised by popular consent upon a basis of respect for fundamental human rights. Presumably this was the initiation of the drafting process, since the Whitney assistance had been kept strictly secret; but the next afternoon Yoshida produced the complete draft, announcing that it had been prepared "after an extensive study of contemporary foreign constitutions." MacArthur at once endorsed the document as "a new and enlightened Constitution" which, he said, was "throughout responsive to the most advanced concept of human relations." He admitted that it had been drafted after frequent conferences between the Government and the Occupation, but he did not say that it had been written by Americans.

Whitney, in fact, laid a tight embargo upon any revelation that Government Section had participated, and when, four months later, news leaked to the American press he set up a commission of inquiry so that he might discover and discipline the informant. Whitney's fiction was that the new Constitution was wholly a Japanese product, both in inspiration and in execution. Few Japanese were deceived, but a close censorship prevented any but the most guarded references from appearing in print. Yoshida, cooperating in this respect, solemnly denied before the Diet that the draft had been forced upon Japan.

This satisfied the strict letter of FEC requirements. Anticipated by Whitney's speed-up constituent assembly, the FEC insisted that it be thereafter kept informed of what was going on, that it be permitted to pass on the final draft to see that it was consistent to the Potsdam Declaration, and that Japan be assured full freedom to choose between the Whitney draft and any other draft that might be offered. It was, however, unlikely, after both MacArthur and the Emperor had approved a draft Constitution, that any Japanese legislative assembly would prefer another document.

FEC also required a full discussion of provisions and ample time for study so that the Constitution might represent the free will of the Japanese electorate and of their representatives. It also required that the new fundamental law be adopted in legal conformity with existing legislation.

These were easily assured. A general election for the Diet followed a month after the publication of the draft, and many candidates campaigned upon the Constitution as a platform plank. When therefore the new session convened in June, all members were familiar with the proposed provisions and with the reactions of their constituents. Yoshida introduced the draft on June 20 and, after long discussion in subcommittees, a special seventy-two-man Special Constitutional Committee, and the House of Representatives itself, the bill was passed August 24 by a vote of 422 to 8, most of the negative ballots being those of Communists. A similar procedure in the House of Peers resulted in its passage by 298 to 2. The Privy Council approved October 29, and finally, on November 3, the Emperor sanctioned and promulgated the Constitution, to be effective May 3, 1947.

These successive steps fulfilled every requirement of the Meiji Constitution relative to amendment, the new law, sometimes called the Showa Constitution, being, in effect, an amendment of the old. By thus observing all legal formalities the legislation was protected against attack on the ground of illegality. It was further protected by the Emperor's careful observance of custom in reporting the important step to his ancestors by special rites before three shrines.

During the six-months interval between the promulgation and the coming into effect of the Constitution, the Diet revised such laws as were out of harmony with the new concept of the Emperor as a politically powerless symbol and with the transfer of sovereignty to the people of the empire. These revisions concerned Imperial Household regulations, national administration, the function of the Cabinet and of the Diet as the chief organ of the state, finance, judiciary, and local government.

Not until the publication in 1949 of Government Section's report did Whitney permit Japan to learn officially what it had long known unofficially: that Americans had written the Constitution. Meanwhile those members of Government Section who had participated had received from the Emperor commemorative medals and special gifts as his appreciation for work they were forbidden to admit that they had done.

No admission was ever made that Occupation officials also inspired, if they did not wholly write, legislation needed to place the Constitutional requirements in effect. This process, like that of preparing the Constitution, was kept under cover; every effort was made to conceal the extent of Occupation activity. The usual practice was to send the Japanese government a directive, SCAPIN, requiring action. The Cabinet thereupon, usually through the Minister directly concerned or through the Chief Cabinet Secretary, consulted an appropriate SCAP section for advice. This advice, while invariably given in the form of guidance or as a suggestion and usually offered verbally rather than in writing, carried the force of an order but could not legally be cited as such.

Having learned what specific legislation the Occupation's staff section desired, the Japanese then proceeded to draft the necessary law. This was done by the ministry concerned and was later checked by the Cabinet Bureau of Legislation (or after February, 1948, with the Attorney General's Office), which corrected phraseology, examined constitutional questions, and couched the measure in proper form. When the revised bill was returned to the ministry which had drafted it a further conference was held with Occupation officials, who, if they approved, cleared it for introduction into the Diet.

Government Section received copies of all proposed legislation and polled other SCAP divisions for possible objection. In the event that no objection was registered the Diet received permission, again verbally, to pass upon the bill. No legislation not endorsed by MacArthur's lieutenants had any opportunity to pass.

In the event that Occupation-endorsed legislation was defeated or delayed in the Diet, the desired goal could be, and on several occasions was, attained by requiring the Cabinet to issue a special order, called a Potsdam Ordinance, which had the force of law. This method overrode the Diet and, because of that fact, was violently opposed by Japanese who believed in the Constitution's statement that the Diet was the sole legislative agency. The by-passing was, however, defended on the ground that democratic results were essential, and that if the Diet did not create such results emergency devices were justified.

On other occasions the Occupation, finding that the Constitution inconvenienced its operations, calmly if not cynically overrode its provisions. Not only was the Diet by-passed, often when Occupationnaires were loudly proclaiming its preeminence, but judges, even of the Supreme Court, while not required to rule in any specific fashion, received strong intimations—carrying a force equivalent to command—that certain decisions would be welcome. Occupation security forces, enjoying extraterritorial privileges over foreign nationals, sometimes extended their right over Japanese. Insistence upon warrants in the case of search and seizure, of habeas corpus, and upon limitation on the length of detention without trial applied to Japanese police but not to the Americans. Similarly, while Japan was required by Occupation directive and by its new Constitution to abolish secret police and censorship, the Occupation, for security purposes, retained such methods.

No doubt, military exigencies, particularly the threat of sedition and subversion if not of invasion, fully justified the policies, just as the maintenance of Occupation discipline may have justified the retention of caste systems forbidden to the Japanese; but the unhappy effect was to convince many Japanese that the Occupation was not only inconsistent but hypocritical.

As Occupation policy, like that of the United States, shifted into a stiffer anti-Russian attitude, the constitutional antiwar clause, much praised in 1947 by MacArthur himself, became a source of much embarrassment. Serious Communist-inspired riots and fear of general strikes convinced the Occupation, even those members who had been most insistent upon weakening the police strength, that greater protection was required; in July, 1950, therefore, MacArthur directed the establishment of a special security organization for national internal defense.

To all intents this new force of 75,000 men under centralized direction constituted the nucleus of an army; yet, as the Constitution specifically forbade military force, MacArthur maintained the fiction that the body thus created was merely a police force—a National Police Reserve—to supplement ineffectual local forces. Apologists pointed out that, as the NPR had no tanks or aircraft, no artillery, no engineers or chemical warfare equipment, no communications or transport organization, no armored cars, no military police, and no court-martial system it could not be an army. This, however, was disingenuous, for plans were in contemplation for all these matters, beginning with machine guns, mortars, and light tanks and progressing to ordnance and aviation; and in the meanwhile the NPR was being clothed, disciplined, and treated as an embryonic military body. MacArthur himself, upon being relieved as Supreme Commander, boasted proudly that the NPR had, under his direction, become the nucleus of an excellent ground force.

This implied admission that the Constitution was being circumvented caught Japan off guard. Some publicists hastened to deny the MacArthur statement; others, to insist that the prohibition against military force applied only to aggression overseas; still others, to argue that police action required military weapons and military methods. Yoshida's dominant political party, fearing loss of face by admitting that the Constitution had been by-passed, privately favored rearmament but dared not admit it openly; but the Democrats (now the Progressives), being in opposition, came out as early as March, 1951, in favor of a 200,000-man army for Japan. One newspaper, *Jiji Shimpo,* courageously insisted that the antiwar clause was "a miscalculation which should be repealed." *Tokyo Shimbun* published an editorial saying, "The problem is not whether Japan should rearm but when and how it should do so."

Two years later, Vice President Richard Nixon, who probably had never heard of the *Jiji Shimpo* editorial, frankly admitted to a Tokyo audience that the "no war" clause had been a mistake.

Although public opinion polls showed a gradually increasing support for rearmament, the Liberals continued to dodge the issue. While some, like Secretary-General Eisaku Sato, supposedly echoing Prime Minister Yoshida's opinion, stressed a need for autonomy, independence, and stronger self-defense measures, they coupled their statements with remarks that real rearmament was premature, and that nothing should be done until the United Nations officially invited Japan to rearm. Chief Cabinet Secretary Katsuo Okazaki, later Foreign Minister, went so far as to deny in September, 1951, that rearmament was even under consideration, or that Constitutional revision was being planned. When, however, the Socialists attempted to block change by appealing to the Supreme Court to declare the NPR unconstitutional as violating the antiwar clause, the Supreme Court rejected the plea as "unprecedented," "abstract," and "theoretical"; the Socialists, said the Court, must wait until they could prove they had been injured in their rights.

Meanwhile the politicians prepared the way for Constitutional amendment by drafting provisions for effecting changes in the fundamental law. A forty-six-article bill was introduced into the Diet calling for passage of Constitutional amendments by a two-thirds majority of each house, following which a public referendum must be approved by a majority of those voting. If rearmament was thereafter found impracticable by indirect means, the process would be invoked to change the Constitution.

FIVE

The Purifying Purge

Too many Occupation leaders shared the naïve assumptions that all Japanese in high position had been selfish, brutal, and malignant, but subordinates were usually good men and true; that big business executives and the superpatriots who had so often tried to murder them worked harmoniously for common interests; and that all Japanese agreed with Occupation views about responsibility for Japanese misdeeds.

Some Occupation leaders, moreover, were deluded into thinking that top leadership could be stripped away without harm; that postwar officials, regardless of previous bureaucratic or political background, would judge war guilt without prejudice, rancor, or partisanship; and that, despite age-old Japanese customs, younger subordinates could and would do the work of their superiors with equal efficiency.

Under such misconceptions the great purge program, designed to remove socially cancerous elements from Japanese public life, was undertaken by administrators not too sure of what they were expected to accomplish and none too certain whom they must remove.

The Potsdam Declaration required the elimination "for all time" of men who had misled or deceived Japan. This broad and vague category required more precise definition. President Truman and the Joint Chiefs of Staff, therefore, softening the Declaration by omitting the phrase "for all time," ordered MacArthur to arrest top military and naval officers, chief ultranationalists and militarists and other advocates of aggression. He was to bar from all posts of "public or substantial private responsibility" or from supervisory or educational posts all career

51

military or naval officers, all active militarists or militant nationalists, and all influential members of ultranationalistic, terrorist, or secret patriotic societies.

Considerable leeway was thus afforded for interpretation, both in the definition of what was militarist or ultranationalist, and in what was meant by leadership or influence. The uncertainty was increased by a further requirement that MacArthur remove from important economic positions any individuals who "do not direct Japanese economic effort solely toward peaceful ends."

Undoubtedly the first two requirements were punitive, if not vengeful; but MacArthur used the third to explain that the entire purge program was purely a preventive measure. His application of the purge varied from the strict letter of his orders. While promptly arresting many leading servicemen, he not only spared others who seemed to be of equal guilt but placed them on the Occupation pay roll and gave them special privilege.

These men, who certainly should have been purged if the JCS orders were to be obeyed, included two lieutenant generals of the Army General Staff, Torashiro Kawabe, military attaché in Germany during the Hitler regime and later head of the surrender mission to Manila, and Seizo Arisue, the Army's intelligence chief. Neither of these spoke English; but they communicated in German with Willoughby, who had been born in Germany, and whose name was originally von Tscheppe und Weidenbach. A third Army man protected by MacArthur was Colonel Takushiro Hattori, Tojo's military secretary and chief of operations for the General Staff. The Japanese Navy was represented by Admiral Kamesaburo Nakamura, the Navy representative who met MacArthur upon arrival, and Captain Toshikazu Omae, who was regarded as the Navy's master strategist. Clarke H. Kawakami, attached to this group as American editor, reported that Japanese servicemen working with Arisue, Kawabe, and the rest were ordered to accord to them their former military titles in all daily contacts, but less fortunate Japanese, including princes, were pulled down to ordinary levels. In addition to the purgeable officers receiving special privilege, Dr. Mitsutaro Araki, former exchange professor to Nazi Germany and his artist wife were also raised above their fellow countrymen though both had been particularly close to German diplomatic circles during the war.

Presumably the fifteen high-ranking officers, most of whom were General Staff members, were working on a Japanese history of the war, though Willoughby later denied that any such history had been in progress but Occupationnaires who knew the men assumed that they were coordinating Japanese and American intelligence concerning Soviet activities. Derevyanko, in fact, charged that Vice Admiral Minoru Maeda, formerly a Navy intelligence chief, and Lieutenant General Shuichi Miyazaki, Army chief of operations, were so employed, though not in the Arisue-Kawabe group; but George Atcheson, then Mac-Arthur's deputy on the Allied Council for Japan, replied that they, too, were merely researching war history.

If MacArthur, for whatever reason, did not purge all high career military and naval personnel who fell directly under the JCS directive, he did obey the order to break up the secret Japanese police. On October 10 he required the expulsion of Home Minister Iwao Yamazaki, a high police official since 1940, all other higher police personnel, and all the 1,176 so-called protection and surveillance officers. This was accomplished within ten days, affecting 4,960 Home Ministry officials.

Elsewhere, the purge was slow in getting under way. Occupation leaders did not know whom to name as civilian ultranationalists. Save for the arrest of war criminals, the only important action prior to 1946 was the ousting on October 11, 1945, of eleven Rikkyo University officials and professors for the "inexcusable and unjustifiable subversion" of this former mission school to ultranationalist purposes. The action followed reports that vandals had slashed the marble altars with swords and had pulled down stone crosses, but within three years the purged officers were quietly reinstated, and records of the affair had vanished from the files.

Not knowing whom to purge, the Occupation asked the Japanese Government to supply lists of leaders in economics, press, publication, radio, dramatics, and ultranationalism; a directive, on October 7, required the Government to name every member of each of the 1,250 political organizations. This practice led to unexpected prolongation of the purge program, more names being discovered from time to time of men whom the Government had forgotten to mention.

Wrangling within the Occupation delayed full application of the purge. Some leaders, such as Max Bishop, the Political Adviser, and General Willoughby, argued that the JCS directive called only for elimination of the more active and influential militarists, and that even this should be undertaken gradually, so as to minimize the dislocation of normal Japanese political and economic life. Others, notably Courtney Whitney, insisted on a broad interpretation that would bar at once virtually every leader of almost every activity. By December, Whitney had become victorious, and MacArthur agreed to a far-reaching and immediate expulsion of thousands of prewar leaders to be chosen purely on a basis of their officeholding, regardless of any word or deed they might have spoken or performed.

Thus, from the beginning, the purge program was planned as a mechanistic process, ignoring any circumstances that might be extenuating, failing to balance evil against any possible good that had been done. Certainly Whitney was no Communist, nor had he sympathy with Communist procedure; but the purge pattern that developed oddly paralleled the methods used in Iron Curtain countries, for one false step, one minor deviation, in the past canceled out a lifetime of liberalism. The method opened the way to the worst excesses of back-stabbing and delation, for an anonymous accusation of guilt, offered without proof, was sometimes accepted as sufficient evidence. Japanese angrily asserted that leftist agents within the Occupation not only inspired such charges but distorted the defenses; and while these were partisan exaggerations the fact remains that opportunity was afforded for malpractice. Some Occupation underlings pointed out the possibility of abuse but were ignored.

A resultant directive, issued January 4, 1946, barred all persons specified in the JCS instructions sent to MacArthur four months earlier but added other categories not definitely stated in those instructions. These covered people who, between July 7, 1937, the date of the Marco Polo Bridge incident near Peking that precipitated the China Incident, and September 2, 1945, were: (1) holders of important posts in financial or development companies exploiting overseas areas; (2) holders of important office in occupied territory; (3) influential members of the Imperial Rule Assistance Association (IRAA), Imperial Rule Assistance Political Society (IRAPS) or the Political Association of Great Japan.

A final broad provision, Category G, brought under the purge an indefinite number of people who had denounced or seized antimilitarists, instigated or perpetuated violence, or played "an active and predominant governmental part" in the Japanese program of aggression. This was sufficiently dangerous because of its vagueness but was made even more so by the inclusion as purgees of those who "contributed" to such undesirable actions, or whose speeches, writings, or actions might be judged as militant, ultranationalist, or aggressive.

Any person who had held an office in the banned categories, irrespective of acts performed while in office, or who had been approved by Prime Minister Hideki Tojo as a Diet candidate in the 1942 election was barred from public post of responsibility or of policy making in the New Japan. In practice he also was barred from responsible posts in industry, finance, commerce, publishing, or agriculture, for while he might be legally acceptable it was difficult for him to obtain clearance for any position which interlocked with other industry or which helped mold public opinion.

The potentialities of the program, especially of the all-inclusive Category G, were at once apparent. For most of the groups the holding of the office was objective evidence; and, although in some cases the position had been purely honorary, its occupancy was conclusive proof of guilt. Category G, like the use of the words "influential," "active," and "important," opened up a wide range of subjective evidence whose validity varied with the official who administered the purge. No one could clearly define "instigated" or "contributed," nor could any authority offer a definite gauge to measure whether any given speech or article was, or was not, of militant or aggressive nature. Decisions, therefore, were neither objective nor unbiased.

While the announced purpose of ridding Japan of evil leaders who had misled and deceived the people was laudable, Occupationnaires, from the beginning, implied that a further purpose was to clear away top leadership so that new men might appear. This, of course, assumed that lower echelons in Japanese affairs had necessarily been democratically minded, and that inexperienced men would work as efficiently and with as great influence as those whom they replaced.

These fallacies were minor flaws; a more serious outcome was loss of faith in American integrity. MacArthur and his men preached justice; yet their purge convicted men on the unsupported word of anonymous informers, denied purgees a fair trial, requiring a victim to prove his innocence, violated the individual human rights which MacArthur had insisted that Japan recognize, and, by a later extension, punished a man's relatives, to the third degree, for acts which they themselves had not committed. The purge was certainly necessary; but careless and mechanical administration and deliberate misrepresentation of its nature were inexcusable.

For Occupationnaires were less than honest. Although purge regulations were drafted in compliance with a JCS directive, and although Whitney's staff gave direct guidance, the Occupation long maintained the fiction that the purge was wholly a Japanese action. In the sense that few directives had been issued, this fiction was perhaps defensible, although misleading; but every Japanese knew that his government was but a puppet. Upon announcement that a purge would be required, Prime Minister Kijuro Shidehara had attempted to resign—only to be informed that if he did so he might thereafter be acceptable to the Emperor or to the Diet for high office but never again to Douglas MacArthur. Tatsuo Iwabuchi, an active purge administrator for the Japanese Government, told, after the Occupation ended, how Japanese had hoped to identify and to punish their own war criminals but had angered General Whitney by singling out only 3,000 offenders. According to Iwabuchi, Whitney complained that 300,000 Nazis had been purged under an identical program in Germany, and that Japan must match, if not exceed, that total. The report, as far as General Whitney was concerned, may have been exaggerated or even untrue; but many Occupationnaire division and branch chiefs felt that to list a large number of purgees would testify to their zeal in cleansing Japan of reactionaries and to their alertness and efficiency.

Pressure to expel from public life a total that would compare favorably with the German purge led not only to the widest possible latitude in application of the method but also, in some cases, to toleration of known inequities. Not only were reactionaries barred from posts of power and prestige but also men who, although nothing had been proved against them, might conceivably have been guilty of offenses not yet discovered. One Government Section official, in admitting this possibility, excused it by citing the analogy of a surgeon who, while cutting away cancerous tissue, knowingly and purposely also removed healthy muscle to prevent recurrence of malignancy.

Despite its denials, the Occupation pulled the strings of purge administration, specifically telling the Government whom to expel from office, sometimes by written command, more often by verbal suggestion, and, when it wished to widen the purge, not only forced the protesting Yoshida to break his promises but vigorously denied that changes had been made.

From the announcement of the purge, Japanese had feared its impact. That it would affect vast numbers was apparent, there being 109,-991 career officers alone, plus 38,590 ex-servicemen's association leaders, 35,099 IRAA members, and 31,075 other ultranationalists. Indefiniteness of the categories and uncertainty of how they were to be applied made it impossible to guess how many more would be included or what else might befall those purged. Many, therefore, who knew themselves to be involved, voluntarily resigned in order to avoid possible further penalty. Half of Shidehara's Cabinet quit, virtually every governor resigned, and scores of bureaucrats, Diet members, and other top officials followed their example. So, too, did thousands of teachers, policemen, and minor employees. The number quitting was never known but was conservatively estimated as about 100,000.

Compliance by the Japanese Government, on February 27, 1946, with demands that it establish legal machinery for questioning and screening officials threw all responsibility for removing the guilty and for approving the eligible upon the Japanese.

When taken in conjunction with all factors, the purge stripped leadership from the professionals. The Progressives, then the majority party, lost 247 of their 274 Diet members and all but one central executive committeeman; the Liberals, 20 of their 50 representatives; and the Socialists, 10 of their 17, together with 3 party founders. Only the Communists were unaffected. Amateurs replaced those purged, but the new leaders were not necessarily more honest, more democratic, or more altruistic than those whom they replaced.

A powerful Occupation faction, including some leftists, demanded equally drastic action in the economic field. On January 4, 1946, Whitney's office required Japan to bar from public life "upon its own initiative" all former high officials, except technicians, of twenty overseas development companies and twenty-seven other expansionist organizations. Two months later, 127 corporations were added to the list. Many men thus to be affected, not knowing what consequences might follow a purge order against them or, perhaps, eager to cooperate with Allied desires, resigned rather than be expelled from office.

Their voluntary withdrawal and the requirement that Japanese and not Occupationnaires do the actual purging, permitted Whitney to say with perfect truth that his Government Section had not interfered with industrial or economic progress since only 296 business executives, other than notorious militarists, were purged by his command during the first half of 1946. He did not add that the displaced leaders, purged or voluntarily retired, included virtually the entire managerial and administrative staffs of all the largest organizations.

Meanwhile candidates for the Diet election of April, 1946, were doubly screened, the obviously undesirable being forbidden to run and the dossiers of the successful being reexamined. This second scrutiny, by a committee containing several members whom Japanese considered leftist, eliminated eight Diet members, all of them executive committeemen of the conservative parties. Among them was Ichiro Hatoyama, founder of the postwar Liberals, who expected to become prime minister.

Hatoyama, who had received the largest plurality of any candidate, was the prime Communist target. A genial, fun-loving bon vivant, a dilettante of music and the arts, he had in prewar times favored liberalism, equality, and parliamentarianism; but he had also showed a notable Red phobia. Together with Yukio Ozaki and Hitoshi Ashida, later a prime minister, he had appealed to General Kazushige Ugaki to halt the advance of militarism; and he had opposed the Tripartite Alliance with Hitler's Germany and Mussolini's Italy. For this he had earned Hideki Tojo's hatred, and so he had spent the war years in political exile.

His parliamentary record and the fact that his Liberal Party, founded November 9, 1945, professed reformist principles of responsible democratic government, civil liberties, equal rights for women, antimilitarism, and laissez-faire economy caused Government Section at first to look upon him favorably. Leftists, however, retorted that all these protestations were mere window dressing, required by the Potsdam Declaration and by the surrender terms. Supported by at least one foreign envoy, they pointed to Hatoyama's advocacy of the Emperor system (though always with the proviso that the monarch, like the British sovereign, reign but not govern), derided him as "feudalistic," and insisted that he be barred from public life.

Throughout the 1945–1946 winter, the Occupation argued over Hatoyama. Realists, especially those familiar with prewar Japan, contended that, while his liberalism was outdated, his hatred of militarism and his very real devotion to parliamentarianism could, under wise Occupation guidance, lead to good government. Leftists, ardent for quick and drastic change, considered him as a symbol of past evils, including militarism, big-business domination, and ultranationalism.

Had Hatoyama acted as wisely as Toyohiko Kagawa, around whom similar debates were swirling, he might, like Kagawa, have emerged safely.

But Hatoyama was unwise. Following Japanese custom, he gave elaborate dinners to Americans, often with expensive presents, which opened him to suspicion of attempted bribery. He argued for civil rights but made it clear that this did not extend to Communists. He talked too volubly, first in customary Japanese circumlocutions which led to accusations of double-talk and then, trying to speak frankly in a language he only partially understood, fell into verbal traps laid for him by guileful interviewers. The Japanese press, then largely leftist, misrepresented him, and foreigners who read the colorful and provocative statements attributed to him ignored his liberalism but scented insincerity, anti-Americanism, and hunger for revenge.

Occupation officials who had talked with him were not deceived; both Counterintelligence Corps and Civil Intelligence Section reported that his record was clear. Mark Gayn of the Chicago *Sun* and John La Cerda of the Philadelphia *Evening Bulletin* reported that the high brass was so friendly to him that they were forbidden to investigate the charges brought against him.

Leftist sympathizers, however, kept on Hatoyama's trail. Two sources, one a lower Occupation officer, the other Kentaro Yamabe, a Communist just freed from four years' imprisonment, reported that he had once published a book, *Sekai no Kao* (Face of the World), praising totalitarianism and proposing that Japan strip China of six northern provinces.

La Cerda, checking the questionnaire which Hatoyama, like other Diet candidates, had been required to file, found no mention of this publication; Gayn turned up passages in praise of Hitler and Mussolini. Four days before the April, 1946, election, they invited Hatoyama to a dinner after which they produced the book and asked for explanations.

Hatoyama, who had never faced a battery of such expert newspapermen, brushed the book aside as a diary of a private trip taken to refresh his knowledge of world conditions. In a savage five-hour cross-examination the reporters forced him to admit that the trip was really a mask to cover a secret mission as Prime Minister Fumimaro Konoye's confidential agent. When he explained that failure to mention the book in his questionnaire was due to the fact that he had not himself prepared the report and had not seen it, the newspapermen showed him his signature and accused him of lying. The charge was strengthened after Hatoyama first denied membership in the Imperial Rule Assistance

Association and the Imperial Rule Assistance Political Society, then said that he had been enrolled without his knowledge, and finally declared that he had resigned after a period which he variously described as from three days to six weeks.

Following publication of reports of this grilling—an ordeal which Occupation chiefs sedulously avoided—Whitney changed suddenly to implacable opposition. The change was only partially attributable to Hatoyama's shiftiness but resulted also from Hatoyama's failure to cooperate with Government Section. After a long succession of unnecessary interviews with Whitney underlings, Hatoyama, wearied by the constant summonses to Dai Ichi Building, snappishly answered yet another call by retorting, "If they want me, they know where to find me." A Government Section major, construing this as an insult, reported to Whitney that Hatoyama was undemocratic.

Whitney waited until after election and then demanded that the Japanese reexamine Hatoyama's record. As every high official was a Hatoyama protégé, a reply came back that this was unnecessary since everything, including *Sekai no Kao,* had been investigated and found innocuous. Whitney reiterated his demand, which the Government correctly interpreted as an order for his purge.

Yoshida, who thought he knew MacArthur's mind, advised Hatoyama to step aside temporarily in Shidehara's favor. This, said Yoshida, would satisfy Whitney and would save Hatoyama from the purge.

Quite possibly Hatoyama might have been named Prime Minister had he been pliant. As the Liberals had not won a clear majority, some form of coalition government was necessary. The Socialists, then in Government Section favor, were prepared to work with him if he would name their men as Welfare Minister and to all the economic posts; this arrangement, it was reported, would be acceptable to Whitney's office. Hatoyama, however, thinking the price too high, held off for better terms; instead, he received a stinging letter on May 3, 1946, signed by MacArthur, barring him from any governmental post.

The assigned causes for this action included the *Sekai no Kao* passages but, for corroboration of Hatoyama's undesirability, went back to prewar days. Hatoyama had been Chief Cabinet Secretary from 1927 to 1929 for Prime Minister Giichi Tanaka, supposedly the author of the Tanaka Memorial, Japan's *Mein Kampf;* and although the memorial, even if authentic, had been drafted prior to his appointment the purge order accused him of complicity. As further proof of antidemocratic activity, the letter alleged that Hatoyama had violated academic freedom as Education Minister in 1932.

The charge concerned the dismissal of Andrew Roth's friend, Yuki-tatsu Takikawa, professor of political science at Kyoto Imperial University Law School, who, in teaching that crime was the product of social maladjustment and in urging the emancipation of women, had been unjustly accused of radicalism and immorality. Hatoyama had been called upon to fire him from his professorship, but had demurred; although he eventually signed the order, he did so only under instructions from the Cabinet.

The incident, while notorious at the time, had been relatively insignificant in comparison to the 6,903 arrests for Communism, many of them teachers, which had taken place in 1931 prior to Hatoyama's assumption of the Education Ministry. It was, thereafter, less than accurate to charge, as did MacArthur, that the affair "gave momentum to the spiritual mobilization of Japan which, under the aegis of the military and economic cliques, led the nation eventually into war." The attack upon Takikawa may have been unjust, but it was neither begun nor notably furthered by Hatoyama. The military and economic cliques leading the nation toward war would have continued to do so had Takikawa never lived. Reliance upon the case to purge Hatoyama suggested that the case against him was weak.

With Hatoyama out of the way and the purge of national politicians effective, Whitney, Marquat, and Nugent pressed the purge. Over the protests of the Diplomatic, Civil Communications, and the four G-Sections, they put through an order, June 5, 1946, requiring Japan to screen all corporations doing a gross annual business of more than $60,000; all banks, insurance companies, and cooperatives with assets exceeding $3,000,000; all chambers of commerce and manufacturers' associations and any similar companies "associated with the economic life of Japan." To relieve the Occupation from responsibility, the Government was required to produce and publish by August 20 a comprehensive plan for purging undesirables.

None of these corporations, unless engaged in overseas exploitation, had been included in the directives sent to MacArthur by the Joint Chiefs of Staff.

Added to this was a requirement that purge procedures be applied also to local officials, down to the smallest village—an extension that did not seem required either by the Potsdam Declaration or by JCS directives. A further provision declared all mayors and headmen, or their deputies, whose incumbency antedated September 2, 1945 ineligible for reelection during the next four years. This action, applying to everyone irrespective of any possible guilt or innocence, was said to be required because, as Home Office appointees, they must necessarily be bureaucrats.

Prime Minister Yoshida violently protested. Admitting that some form of purge was required, he objected to the methods used. To purge a man merely because of a remote, superficial, or even undesired connection with a militarist organization, he said, was not only uncalled for but unreasonable; to punish the little fellows who acted under duress with no chance to voice their opposition was, he said, unjust. It was unthinkable, he said, to class village IRAA chiefs as "influential members." To apply the extended purge requirements—which Whitney refused to admit was an extension—would, he declared, involve the very faith and integrity of the Japanese Government.

MacArthur received the Yoshida protest on the evening of October 31; he rejected it the very next day. Yoshida made a further protest against Whitney's demand that relatives to the third degree of purgees be forbidden for ten years to succeed them; it was, he said, a prohibition not even applied to murderers. This protest, also, was rejected.

Since nothing more could be done the Government, "of its own free will," extended the purge to village officials, thus requiring screening of 232,863 candidates for elective office, and to 246 additional major business enterprises.

Local screening committees, working with a central committee headed by seventy-three-year-old Tatsukichi Minobe, examined 745,000 questionnaires.

Not all these were militarists or totalitarians. The purge was applied to all persons who made serious errors in filling out their questionnaires, who forgot pertinent detail, or who misrepresented facts. Punishments were also given to purgees who talked, even on innocent matters, to officeholders, who revisited their former offices, and were even held as a threat over those who wished to exercise a citizen's privilege of sitting in the Diet gallery. The avowed purpose was to prevent intimidation of the innocent and to avoid indirect control by the purgees; but this laudable desire did not explain why Government Section personnel were forbidden to talk with men who had been purged.

That restrictions upon normal social relationships of men who had not been convicted of crime violated constitutional guarantees was considered unimportant. One man was penalized for submitting an article to a magazine which he had founded, and of which he still owned nearly all the stock; another, for editing a manuscript; a third, for making a public speech on economic theory; and yet a fourth, for asking his former colleagues to a party. Fusanosuke Kuhara, an eighty-year-old copper magnate with a totalitarian political record, faced an eight-months' jail sentence for giving 500,000 yen to his son-in-law. The excuses were, no doubt, ingenuous, but the strictness of enforcement went so far as to defeat its own purpose. Japanese law enforcers had little enthusiasm for pressing charges, and even Occupation officers kept straight faces and tight lips when Tokyo judges acquitted an ex-mayor of purge violations which Occupationnaires had witnessed.

Purge enforcements slowed notably in journalistic, education, and economic fields. Nugent refused to press charges against publishers who during wartime had printed anti-Allied articles; he was unhappy when Whitney wanted Tanzan Ishibashi purged for having published, prior to Pearl Harbor, some thirty articles forced upon him by the military.

Increasingly, moreover, as anti-Yoshida politicians uncannily fell under the purge, charges spread that purge administration was becoming partisan. The fiction that the purge was Japanese-sponsored also stirred resentment, and a Government Section spokesman's boast, "No Japanese purge has ever been reversed by the Supreme Commander," set off gales of laughter.

No one can ever know how many persons were affected by the purge. Records and reports were incomplete and badly kept; many were destroyed in a fire which Government Section called "mysterious." Whitney's official report showed a total, as of June, 1948, of 8,781 purgees out of 717,415 questionnaires examined; but an additional 193,-180 non-officeholders, most of whom were career military men, must also be included. Thousands more resigned in fear of being purged.

Undoubtedly more men were purged than either the Potsdam Declaration or the JCS directives had envisioned. In January, 1948, Under Secretary of the Army Kenneth C. Royall, wryly commenting that MacArthur had purged too enthusiastically, warned that further purges would endanger Japan's economic recovery.

Although Royall probably did not realize it, such a suggestion was a red rag to the Occupation. Over and over again Whitney and his deputy, Colonel Charles L. Kades, had denied any such danger. Even before any result of the as yet incomplete economic purge could possibly be gauged Whitney had written on January 31, 1947, for MacArthur's signature, an angry blast refuting predictions that the purge would damage the economy. Kades, some months later, followed this by declaring, "It is nothing short of absurd to claim that industrial efficiency and production have been seriously disturbed because a couple of thousand odd persons have been removed." Kades added that the very few persons dislodged from private industry were "not only free but are encouraged to engage in any other business of their choice."

This was not the generally accepted view. Colonel Frederick Pope, whom MacArthur invited to survey the chemical industry, reported that it had been hurt because the top men—most of whom, he said, were honest, hard-working and qualified—had been removed. He also said that the officer who had purged them was a mere lad ignorant of his subject.

By 1949 it became evident not only that the purge was unpopular, but that a reverse tendency was imminent. Yoshida promised reexamination of those disqualified merely because of the offices they had held; and, while he was promptly checked by Whitney and his purge official, Lieutenant Colonel Jack Napier, 5,706 educators and publishers were reinstated. Kades termed the talk of possible "depurge" a whistling in the graveyard by such "extreme rightists" as Hatoyama and insisted that this extreme right was a greater danger than Communism to Japan; but by this time Allied military leaders were looking longingly on purged servicemen as a bulwark against Red dangers. Yoshida was therefore permitted to set up a Purge Appeals Committee to reinstate for "gross injustice done or for error committed."

The purge, thereafter, hit Communists who had been previously exempt. Dr. Walter Crosby Eells, of Civil Information and Education Section, toured universities to recommend the dismissal of Red professors—the same procedure, incidentally, as that for which Hatoyama had been purged. Marquat's Labor Division stood idly by while 10,608 workers were fired for Communist activity. Although Napier denied the charge, Japanese insisted that he had issued verbal orders to dismiss Reds and fellow travelers from private, as well as public, industry.

Meanwhile purgees were reinstated. In October, 1950, with Napier's approval, 10,090 purgees were cleared out of 32,089 cases reviewed. In the following month 3,072 young service officers, all those who had entered military or naval academies after Pearl Harbor, were restored, many of them joining the embryonic army called the National Police Reserve. In January, 1951, the Occupation permitted the release of 21,195 labor bosses. After May 1, 1951, when General Matthew Ridgway approved the release of all but convicted war criminals, the purge drew to its close, Hatoyama being restored in July. The last step came in 1952, just prior to the signing of the Peace Treaty, when top service officers and Tojo's Cabinet members were restored to full rights.

None of the feared aftermaths occurred. Purgees were not a bitter, vengeful gang, nor did they at once return to their prewar posts. They showed themselves to be, as every rational person had anticipated, a group of sincere, patriotic citizens.

SIX

Who Ruled Japan?

Quite possibly the greatest postwar revelation for the Japanese was the discovery, in 1946, that Emperor Hirohito, the embodiment of Nipponism, the central symbol of the Empire, owned suits of Western clothing by the score, a dozen military or naval uniforms, and numerous pairs of Occidental shoes, but not one Japanese kimono and not a single pair of geta. That he ate bacon and eggs and toast for breakfast, with black Formosan tea, instead of standard Japanese bean soup and fish was shocking, too; but his clothing and his foreign bathroom appointments seemed to mean that he was somehow not truly Japanese.

Such an accusation would be wholly false; but it would be no stranger than the misconceptions under which MacArthur and his top lieutenants embarked upon their treatment of the Emperor. Americans who knew a little Japanese confused the term Tenno Sei, which means Imperial System, with Tenno Seiji, which means Imperial Rule, and they assumed that because Hirohito was the Emperor he therefore was top dog. They thought that he was worshiped, which he certainly was not, that he was himself responsible for both the war and the decision to surrender; they thought of him as being the wealthiest individual in the world with full power over every stick of property, as well as over every person, in the Empire; and, because a clumsy newspaperman a quarter of a century ago believed that he had tried to steal a young man's girl, they thought of him as a lecher, even perhaps, like his father, Emperor Taisho, mentally abnormal. One reporter, who should have known much better, had him chasing palace maids about the gardens while his wife, Nagako, screamed out curses.

The stories were more picturesque than true. So also was the rumor that Hirohito and his brother Chichibu were bitter enemies because Hirohito was legitimate whereas Chichibu was falsely said to have been sired by a certain minister of the Imperial Household. For this untrue reason, and because certain reactionaries had plotted in 1936 to make Chichibu the regent, he was, the rumors stated, in disgrace. The fact was that Chichibu was ill, suffering from the tuberculosis which killed him in 1953, but the slanders were readily believed by those anxious to hear the "real dirt on the Imperial Family."

Perhaps MacArthur's men, disappointed by inability to dethrone the Emperor, went further than was necessary in taking away his prestige. Mistakenly crediting him with more real power than he actually possessed, believing that anyone who, in the least degree, disturbed the Imperial tranquillity must immediately commit suicide, they thought him a tyrant of the Hitler-Mussolini breed.

Most of their beliefs were true in basic theory only. MacArthur himself realized, after having been for some time in Japan, that the Japanese Emperor, like the British King, reigned but did not govern, and that, as the Supreme Commander sometimes told his callers, "The Emperor is to Japan what the Stars and Stripes are to the United States." But these realistic appraisals were, for some odd reason, not made available to Occupation rank and file, MacArthur's interviewers being cautioned not to quote him directly on the matter. Occupation administrators, intent on rooting out feudalism in a hurry, overnight if possible, continued on false assumptions to eradicate a situation that did not, in fact, exist. While MacArthur and Whitney knew better, the division chiefs under them continued, as far as Hirohito's power was concerned, to fire howitzers at shadows.

Not for a thousand years had any Emperor ruled Japan. By custom and tradition, Emperors confined themselves to spiritual duties, performing highly conventionalized rites designed to win the favor of the gods while secular officers performed the necessary public duties. Most powerful among these deputies were the army chiefs, the shoguns, who headed the military dictatorship. The shoguns, like the Emperors, attained the office by heredity, and they, too, were often figureheads for whom, also, hereditary advisers did the actual work.

These under officers who, for want of better names, were called regents, prime ministers, or councilors, knowing only what their underlings, the civil servants, told them of national affairs, thus converted

Japan into a vast bureaucracy capped by an Emperor and a shogun who, for the most part, were but dimly aware of actual affairs.

Few if any Emperors mounted the throne with any idea that they would govern. Most of them were immature at their accession. Of seventy Emperors since A.D. 823, thirty-eight ascended when less than fifteen years of age; and ten of them were babies. Hirohito at twenty-six was the oldest mentally normal man crowned since 1770. In 1868 the shogunate was abolished; but, of the thirty-nine men who had held the office, more than half were minors.

That this was a deliberate policy was evident because, in ninety-three instances out of one hundred and twenty-three, eldest sons were deliberately passed over in choosing a new Emperor so that a minor might be selected, this discrimination happening in all but six of the last twenty-one new rulers. Prior to Hirohito the last succession of an eldest son was in 1747. Similarly, fewer than one-third of the shoguns were eldest sons, the last such choice having occurred in 1760.

Lest the nominal rulers develop, as they matured, a taste for power, regents and prime ministers induced or forced them to abdicate. Of eighty-nine Emperors after A.D. 700, fifty-six retired from office: twenty-one during their twenties; nine more in their teens; and two before the age of five years. More than half the shoguns, also, abdicated although, as a rule, at a slightly greater age.

Japanese, accustomed in all phases of political and social life to such distinction between real and nominal power, accepted this figurehead system as desirable. The Throne, but not the Emperor, became a symbol for all desirable traits of character, the source of virtue, of power, of justice, mercy, and protection. The Emperor, as mortal, might be youthful, weak, incompetent, vicious, intemperate, or, like Hirohito's father, mentally incompetent; but the Throne retained its power and its glory. Dissociation of the Throne from the individual who sat upon it precluded any thought of revolution that might overturn the monarchy. While some rulers might be expelled or ignominiously treated, the Throne was venerated and esteemed.

When therefore Japanese statesmen credited the Imperial virtue as inspiration for their performance they spoke of the Throne; when they laid all accomplishments at his feet they credited the symbol not the man. Thus the Emperor Meiji, who ruled from 1868 to 1912, attained exceedingly high rank among world rulers; yet, as Etsujiro Uyehara dared to point out even in Meiji's lifetime, there was no record that he ever took an independent action. Statesmen such as Hirobumi Ito invariably ascribed good policies and achievements to Meiji's suggestion, advice, and guidance; but much of this was sheer politeness. Hirohito, Meiji's grandson, followed this course.

Americans who themselves distinguished perfectly between the Presidency of the United States and the individual who held the office, revering the one while sometimes venturing to criticize the other, failed utterly to understand the Japanese distinction. Knowing Japan to be totalitarian, they supposed its Emperor to be dictator. Reference to the Italian situation and, as a democratic antithesis, to the British government, would have readily dispelled misunderstanding; but wartime propaganda, working on the general ignorance of Japanese affairs, simplified the matter by pinning all blame on a name which every foreigner remembered.

Thus Hirohito, the shy and rather pathetic little fellow who wanted nothing more than to study his marine biology, became a sinister international menace while his advisers, save Tojo, the new shogun, remained virtually unknown.

Some Imperial advisers were individuals, such as the Lord Keeper of the Privy Seal who countersigned all laws, the Imperial Household Minister who managed the estates, or the Grand Chamberlain who directed court etiquette. These men, his daily associates and, as far as was possible, his personal friends, were customarily experienced and conservative by temperament, most of them favorable to the nineteenth century evolutionary constitutionalism that in Japan passed for liberalism. Their preference for parliamentarianism rather than for totalitarianism caused some of them to be marked for murder during the reactionary movement of the 1930 decade; but, later, the militarists planted their own agents in the court.

Advice came also from such groups as the Privy Council and a special council of princes. When, after the downfall of the Tokugawa Shogunate in 1868, the seventeen-year-old Emperor Meiji gained nominal control, though in an extremely restricted sense, three powerful court nobles and five revolutionary leaders guided his actions, the group developing into a body called the Genro, or Elder Statesmen. The clique won such importance that, until 1912, it monopolized the Prime Ministry and, until the death of its last member, Prince Kimmochi Saionji, in 1940, exercised a veto over the choice of subsequent Prime Ministers. While at least two of the Genro had been professional soldiers, and while one of them, Prince Aritomo Yamagata, was notably conservative, the Genro, especially in the later years, furthered parliamentary government.

After 1924, when Saionji had become the sole survivor among the Genro, he proposed the creation of a new body, the Jushin, or Senior Statesmen, to be composed of the Lord Keeper of the Privy Seal, the head of the Privy Council and all former Prime Ministers. The Diet, however, objected that such a group, perpetuating the veto power of the Genro, might interfere with the unrestricted growth of parliamentarianism. Militarists stood firm against creating any organ that would stand in their way by recommending, like Saionji, moderates and politicians instead of servicemen. Slowly rising labor and proletarian groups protested that the Jushin would be too bureaucratic and too conservative, an argument in which, strangely enough, Fusanosuke Kuhara, representing big business, concurred. The Jushin, therefore, failed to function officially but nevertheless met informally to advise the Emperor.

The Privy Council, a most important body created by Ito as the final constitutional consultant for the Emperor, exercised tremendous power. This, too, a body of indefinite number whose members were named for life by the Emperor, not only advised the Emperor but also, by informal prior consultation with the Cabinet, virtually vetoed the introduction into the Diet of measures which it disapproved. No one could join the Privy Council until he was forty years of age; but, in actual practice, the average was well over seventy, so that this group still further influenced the Emperor toward old-line liberalism. From its creation in 1888 until its dissolution in 1945, no law was promulgated and no treaty ratified without the prior consent of the Privy Council.

Thus, although Hirohito like his predecessors was theoretically an absolute monarch, he acted only as his advisers recommended. At least until the complete capture of Japan by the military in 1940, they were Victorian liberal and parliamentarian in their principles, and Hirohito, as far as he was allowed to have any choice whatever, was an antimilitarist and antitotalitarian. When, however, the army seized control by usurpation, murder, and manipulation of the popular vote, appointing new advisers to the monarch, Hirohito necessarily did as he was told. For a thousand years or more, no Japanese Emperor had dared take any other action. Had Communists, instead of military reactionaries, won control, Hirohito would have done as they demanded just as, under the Occupation, he dutifully signed every document required of him by the Allied Occupation or its puppet Governments.

Prior to surrender, Allied military and diplomatic officers had thought seriously concerning the role which the Emperor should play during the projected occupation. A strong contingent, headed by John Carter Vincent, Far Eastern expert for the State Department, Thomas A. Bisson, editor and economist serving with the Strategic Survey Board, and Andrew Roth of Naval Intelligence, vigorously argued that to punish Hirohito as a war criminal would convince Japanese of the enormity of Japan's offenses. These men, although more familiar with Chinese than with Japanese affairs, carried great weight because of their access to periodicals. Their thesis had strong support in Australia, Canada, China, the Philippines, Russia and, less notably, Great Britain.

Similar views were held among MacArthur's men. Less tolerant and more doctrinaire than the Washingtonians, they simplified the Japanese problem as a vast conspiracy of fanatical assassins, greedy monopolists, feudal landlords, and superstitious Shintoists for whom the Emperor was a sacred focus. To certain MacArthur advisers the reform of Japan was relatively simple: all that was required was to jail the hotheads, strip monopolists and landlords of property, break up the union of church and state, and kick out the Emperor.

True, there might be difficulty in getting rid of Hirohito. A highly regarded colonel who fancied himself as an expert in psychologic warfare had assured MacArthur that Japanese would defend their Emperor to the death; but he proposed to turn this devotion to American advantage by painting Hirohito's picture upon every Allied tank and by having each American soldier carry a button with his image. This, he suggested, would safeguard Allied forces against attack. But the same colonel insisted that it would be safe to execute Hirohito as a war criminal.

Opposing these extremists were such men as former Ambassador Joseph C. Grew, Eugene H. Dooman, Joseph W. Ballantine, and other State Department experts who had served in Japan and knew its history. Accepting the view that the Emperor mirrored the attitudes of incumbent leaders, they insisted that under an occupation he would become a useful tool, and that the people would obey his orders. This opinion was endorsed by authorities upon Japan, particularly such university professors as Claude A. Buss of Stanford, who was working with the Office of War Information, and John F. Embree of Chicago, a State Department consultant.

By the summer of 1945, Washington had grown fairly well convinced that retention of the Emperor system was probable, if not desirable, unless the Japanese themselves demanded a change; but the future of Hirohito himself remained in doubt. In America, as in Japan, a belief was growing that it would be politic for Hirohito to abdicate to clear the way for a new ruler not smirched by war responsibility; but no conclusions had been reached upon the matter.

Such was the situation when on August 15, 1945, Japan formally announced her willingness to surrender. MacArthur's group, not knowing what turn might develop, found itself in difficulties. A Japanese mission was to arrive at Manila on August 19 to learn the details of surrender ceremonies, but MacArthur, uncertain of Washington's policy, dared not insist upon the tough policy his advisers desired.

Major General Charles A. Willoughby, his intelligence officer, moreover, had conjured a new, daring plan. This was to enlist the Japanese delegates as partners in an anti-Communist movement. He therefore provided them with every comfort, including a turkey dinner that, as one delegate said, "frightened our wartime stomachs," and won their cooperation as secret intelligence agents for the Occupation. The vice chiefs of the Army and Navy General Staffs were thereafter paid American assistants. As for the Emperor, he was to be surrounded by liberal advisers to become a symbol for speedy and efficient regeneration of Japan.

Whoever may have drafted the decision, whether MacArthur or his Washington superiors, the Occupation thus reached essentially the same conclusions and followed the same general patterns as had the feudalistic Tokugawa shoguns. As realists steeped in military thought Occupationnaires, like Iyeyasu Tokugawa in 1603, reduced the Emperor to an innocuous symbol. Like Iyeyasu they forbade the Emperor to meddle in political affairs, drastically reduced his staff of servants, slashed his budget, and left him with no responsibilities save the performance of meaningless rites, the composition of poetry, and the contemplation of nature. Like Iyeyasu also, they cloaked their action under the most formal courtesy while refraining carefully from showing even the slightest sign of personal friendliness or even of human understanding.

No doubt the parallel was unintentional, since few Occupation leaders had read deeply into Japanese history; but it was apparent to Japan. So close, indeed, was the parallel that certain Japanese suggested that it be carried to somewhat the conclusion that had occurred under Emperor Komei during the last days of the Shogunate when a young Imperial princess was betrothed against her will to the Tokugawa Shogun. Why not, it was suggested, merge the two lines by betrothing yet another princess to the young son of General MacArthur? But this proposal, if ever made officially, won no support from either side.

Perhaps as a return for secret collaboration, whose real purpose was to unite intelligence forces against possible Russian plots, the Occupation entered Japan in a mood more friendly to the Emperor, and to the Japanese, than anyone had anticipated. The unexpected friendliness was also traceable to Washington activities. Japan's acceptance of the Potsdam Declaration as a basis for surrender had been accompanied by a proviso that no demands prejudicial to the Imperial prerogatives be imposed. It is true that Secretary James F. Byrnes, in replying on August 11, had insisted upon unconditional surrender, and upon obedience by the Emperor to any order given him by the Supreme Commander; but he had evaded all mention of the prerogatives, and this, in Japan's view, conceded the condition. Japanese drew a fine distinction between the unconditional surrender of the Japanese armed forces, to which they agreed, and the surrender of Imperial sovereignty, to which they never consented. The distinction might be meaningless in practical administration, but it was very real to Japanese.

It soon became apparent that, to Japanese, the Imperial prerogative embraced far more than Anglo-Saxons considered as a sovereign's special privilege. Hirobumi Ito, in his official commentary on the Constitution granted in 1889 by the Emperor Meiji, had clearly set down four general principles: inviolability and the right to be reverenced; freedom from derogatory comment; recognition of the Emperor as sole source of legislative power with the Diet as a consultative body only; and absolute supremacy over all other authority. In addition, he claimed for the sovereign all powers omitted from the Constitution or not clearly stated therein so that, as he put it, "The Emperor is the state."

If this interpretation were to be accepted, Japan could never without her consent establish the new order of peace, security, and justice envisaged in the Potsdam Declaration. Such changes must therefore be accomplished by the Japanese through their own government and officials. By this reasoning, the Emperor seemed safe; to depose him would unquestionably violate his special prerogative.

The problem, which in Allied capitals centered about the question of the legality or the desirability of dethroning the Emperor, appeared in Japan as a question of abdication. By ancient custom those in high position, whether actually or theoretically controlling, showed their concern for errors committed by their underlings, for catastrophes which should have been avoided, or for mistakes in judgment by resigning their positions. On lower planes, a police official felt it incumbent to resign, if not to kill himself, for having carelessly led an Imperial procession astray, and school principals resigned for mispronouncing words of an Imperial Rescript. For like reason, the Emperor worried whether he should abdicate to show his deep sense of responsibility for the calamities that had overwhelmed the nation. He therefore, on August 29, told Marquis Koichi Kido, Lord Keeper of the Privy Seal, that if it should be necessary to avoid a national crisis he would retire in favor of Crown Prince Akihito, permitting his own younger brother, Prince Chichibu, to act as Regent.

As the statement was not made generally public, no widespread discussion followed; but the Court and high political circles argued vehemently. Traditionalists, die-hards, and totalitarians approved, particularly those who in the past had planned armed rebellion for this very purpose. Their spokesman, Prince Naruhiko Higashikuni, the Emperor's cousin and since August 17 the Prime Minister, enthusiastically approved; he urged Hirohito to sign the surrender documents and then, showing his remorse for Japan's downfall, to abdicate. This, as it happened, was precisely the plan recommended by the Soviet authorities, who wished to abolish the entire Imperial system and set up a people's democracy, so that, while each group of participants would have violently repudiated any thought of cooperation with the other, the strange spectacle occurred of Communists and ultranationalist reactionaries working for exactly the same purpose.

But while the superpatriots and the admirers of the beautiful customs of Old Japan acclaimed the idea, ardent parliamentarians, men like Ichiro Hatoyama, Yukio Ozaki, and Takao Saito, scented danger. Recalling the assassination plots of 1932 and 1936 aimed directly for a Chichibu regency, they suspected the motives of those who wanted Hirohito to resign.

Others, notably bureaucrats like former Shidehara and his close friend, former Ambassador to Britain Shigeru Yoshida, also protested earnestly. Westerners, they pleaded, would not understand the Japanese concept of resignation to assume responsibility. To resign at such a time would to them imply Hirohito's opposition to surrender; it would undoubtedly make peace conditions harder. At home, moreover, it would encourage hotheads to rebel and, by imperiling the peacefulness of the Occupation, would prolong its length.

Hirohito, still convinced that he must abdicate but unwilling to sabotage the Occupation, rejected the Higashikuni proposal for immediate action but desired to ask MacArthur what time would be most appropriate. Protocol, however, delayed their meeting. Both men were understandably curious about each other, but neither wished to take the initiative. The Emperor, realizing that he was subject to MacArthur's orders, hesitated to suggest a conference and expected to be summoned to the presence. Whitney and others suggested to MacArthur that Hirohito be called in, but the Supreme Commander, not yet knowing how he was supposed to treat the Emperor through whom he was to administer Japan, turned down the idea. "Let him," he said in effect, "come to me." To take other action, MacArthur believed, would put him in the position of a suppliant; but, if Hirohito called upon the American commander-in-chief, Japan would know that even her Emperor must yield to Allied wishes.

The situation, therefore, was a stalemate; but it redounded to the best interest of both Japan and the United States. Japan had time to think, to draft a program intended to combine outer compliance with inward spiritual resistance to Allied demands. This program, as it happened, was not long pursued after Japan realized that the Occupation Army entered without vindictiveness and with no thought of making martyrs of the people. The delay, moreover, allowed the Emperor to share, at least in part, the credit for political and social changes leading toward democracy, thereby removing both from Japanese and from Americans a measure of the wartime hostile feelings. The Americans, in turn, profiting from the wise JCS counsel of working through established governmental agencies, found that radical reforms, thus countenanced by the Emperor, met little or no resistance. Yet the general situation remained only in abeyance; the basic problem had not yet been solved.

Throughout September, the Emperor was ready to quit, and Mac-

Arthur was prepared to accept the abdication. His orders bound him merely to use Hirohito, not to support him; had Japan installed a puppet, a republic, or a people's democracy, MacArthur had no authority to interfere unless Occupation safety was imperiled.

Thus, for eighteen days following surrender, while the situation thus hung fire, the Russians had their opportunity. Had Lieutenant General Kuzma N. Derevyanko, their Tokyo observer, used his revolutionary techniques cleverly, the Communists might then have dethroned the Emperor and set up a regime more pleasing to themselves. Luckily, whether because there was a lack of sound Japanese Communist leadership, or because Moscow sulked at having been denied equality upon a control commission, or merely because Derevyanko failed adequately to report the situation, Russia contented herself with inspiring noisy mass meetings under MacArthur's office windows. The precious opportunity passed with no real gain to Russia, but with the Occupation alerted to a possible assault which neither Russia nor the Japanese Communists were ready to launch.

Hirohito, however, increasingly perturbed about the demonstrations, ventured then to ask an interview. To his delight, MacArthur readily accepted. On September 20, therefore, the Emperor dressed punctiliously and was driven to the American Embassy to find MacArthur in open-throated shirt, without medals, decorations, or campaign ribbons. This took the Emperor aback and so shocked the Japanese that censors tried to forbid newspapers from publishing the picture; but they laid it to ignorance of etiquette rather than studied insult.

The interview was secret, but reports leaked through interpreters that both principals were ill at ease. MacArthur let Hirohito set the tone. The Emperor began by thanking the Americans for occupying Japan so peaceably and MacArthur politely replied that this was wholly due to Hirohito's cooperation. A quarter-hour of casual verbal fencing followed, with MacArthur avoiding any verbal lead, and then the Emperor timorously suggested that it would be interesting to know what future historians would say about responsibility for the war. Although MacArthur then had on his desk an order to start trying war criminals as soon as possible, he made no reply, and so the Emperor, true to the Japanese custom of bringing up the most important problems only at the very end, sounded him out on the all-important abdication issue. MacArthur again dodged the issue, and Hirohito withdrew, after thirty-eight minutes in which he had learned absolutely nothing.

MacArthur promptly teletyped Washington a full report, not omitting the war-guilt reference and the hint of abdication. While he was waiting a reply, Hirohito, five days after visiting the Embassy, again broke precedent, by receiving two American newspapermen, Hugh Baillie, president of the United Press, and Frank Kluckhohn of the *New York Times*. Through these two correspondents he sent to America carefully worded statements implying that Japan was about to become a constitutional monarchy of the British type.

The press reported the three interviews without comment but the Home Ministry suppressed the issues. Occupationnaires thought the action due to pictures showing MacArthur towering over Hirohito and to Kluckhohn's saying that the Emperor had accused Tojo of misusing the Imperial seal; Japanese explained that it was to conceal MacArthur's bad manners in dress. The Occupation ordered the news and picture published.

Washington, in considering what instructions to give MacArthur, balanced the Emperor's releases with increasingly strident demands that Hirohito be forced to abdicate and then be tried as a war criminal. Again deciding that it was less dangerous to use Hirohito as a tool than to risk setting him up as a martyr around whom reactionaries might rally, the Joint Chiefs of Staff, on October 6, forwarded top-secret directives renewing the order to start war-crimes trials as soon as possible but not to take action against the Emperor.

MacArthur confided to his intimates that he did not know if Hirohito would abdicate but he was sure that he would not be tried as a war criminal. Referring to Hirohito as a sincere liberal, he said, "I came here ready to treat him sternly, but that has not been necessary."

It is, of course, unlikely that MacArthur's orders leaked to the Japanese, but it is a noteworthy coincidence that within two days of their receipt, Shidehara was denying that Hirohito would be forced to abdicate. A few days later Imperial Household Minister Sotaro Ishiwata officially announced that the Emperor had no intention of resigning, and Konoye, who had seen both Hirohito and MacArthur, repeated the assurance.

SEVEN

That Sacred Emperor

To all intents the issue was decided, yet new complications rose. Whitney, in expanding his Government Section to take over control of local, provincial, and national administration, received an admirable staff of high-caliber men, several of them lawyers and, unlike the personnel of other sections, many of them well versed in Japanese affairs. Had these men been permitted to function without interference, Whitney's section would have stood foremost in the Occupation set-up; but, instead, their hands were sometimes tied. Whitney distrusted people who had known Japan before the war; he called them Old Japan Hands and, not in the least jokingly, charged that they still rose at dawn to bow in the direction of the Imperial Palace. Although himself a conservative, he was certain that every phase of Japan's prewar government was "feudalistic," and that only by a violent and thorough-going change, in directions which his critics called pinkish, could reform be achieved. His phobia against centralization was particularly strong; he wanted every governmental activity broken into independent local units. This, moreover, must be done by Japanese initiative; thus he insisted that his section issue as few directives as possible and, instead, inspire Japanese to shoulder all responsibility. Government Section, accordingly, developed the most skilled needlers, nudgers, prodders, and innuendo mongers of the Occupation. With all this, Whitney, a choleric and extremely sensitive individual, was suspicious that everyone was plotting to undermine MacArthur and himself; once harboring such feeling, he seemingly never thereafter forgot, forgave, or tried to understand.

78

The Imperial Family early gained his enmity as the focal point of feudalism. Although, following MacArthur's lead, he later referred to Hirohito as a great liberal "adept at understanding the broad principles of democratic government," he did so only after dealing crippling blows that cut the myopic little Emperor down to nothingness. The powers of government that Hirohito had never dreamed of exercising were stripped away, and Prime Minister Tetsu Katayama was verbally blasted even for telling Hirohito that he had resigned. The protection of lese majesty laws was removed so that Hirohito, whose only means of fighting back were also lost, was open to unbridled and unfair insult; the attempt to prosecute a Communist who called the Crown Prince illegitimate was scathingly condemned as an effort to restore feudalistic ideas.

Whitney stood quietly by when attempts were made to discredit Hirohito, as an illegal ruler. In November, 1945, an imposing envelope, heavily sealed with the Imperial chrysanthemum crest, arrived for "Marshal MacArthur, Heavenly-Sent Messenger to Japan." Within were documents asserting that Hirohito was a usurper, and that the throne rightfully belonged to Hiromichi Kumazawa, a storekeeper of Nagoya, as the nineteenth direct descendant of the Emperor Go-Kameyama, or Kameyama II, who had been deposed in 1331.

MacArthur, committed to the view that Hirohito was a sincere liberal, had neither power nor desire to pull the throne from under him; at the same time he did not wish to defend him. He had no authority to depose the Emperor unless some grievous offense had been committed against Occupation interests; but neither was he obliged to support him if other forces threatened to unseat him. He therefore looked the other way when news of the Kumazawa papers leaked to a little ring of correspondents.

These men, who apparently were not thoroughly familiar with the history of Japan, scented a sensation. Not knowing that the story had been widely printed in Japanese histories, and that it was readily available in English, they reported as hot news that, six hundred and fourteen years before, the Ashikaga shoguns, supporting one group of Imperial Princes against the ruling branch, had expelled Go-Kameyama and forced him into exile. They did not, however, report that many years later Go-Kameyama had returned and, by compromise between the rivals, officially installed his very distant kinsman as rightful ruler of Japan. Nor did they know that the Nagoya claimant for whom they claimed the throne was not a blood descendant but an adopted member of the Kumazawa family. In a series of excited articles, in which the official Occupation newspaper, *Stars and Stripes*, joined, they demanded Hirohito's abdication.

Their efforts failed when research showed that Japanese historians had already thoroughly investigated, and dismissed, the same claims; but the publicity resulted in similar claims by at least seven other pretenders, all of whom, like Kumazawa, based their cases upon the theory that eldest sons should necessarily succeed to the throne. Kumazawa himself grew cool when his own eldest son returned from captivity in Siberia as a professed Communist and said that he wished only to be "the first democratic Japanese president." In February, 1951, the Tokyo District Court declared all claims baseless.

Misconception concerning the nature of the aristocracy also entered. When the war ended, Japan had 14 princes of the Imperial blood, 19 other princes, 49 marquises, 112 counts, 390 viscounts, and 434 barons, exclusive of Korean peers no longer included in the Japanese nobility. The 1,018 peers had such special privileges as a guarantee against bankruptcy proceedings, immunity from certain other legal processes and membership, or representation, in the House of Peers, but no exclusive political power. Socially they ranked high; but the general public was so far from thinking them superior that the common description was that they had "boiled sweet-potato faces."

Their origins were various, but most of them were fairly recent titles. None of the Imperial princely families, for example, except those of the Emperor's three brothers, antedated the Meiji Restoration. The one hundred and twenty-one emperors prior to Meiji had, to be sure, fathered numerous children, one succession of eleven Emperors having produced a total of two hundred and ninety-eight children; but court regulations provided that descendants who did not themselves mount the Throne must gradually lose status until, in the third generation, they became "commoners." The three long reigns, totaling one hundred and ten years, preceding Meiji left only one Imperial prince, Motohiko Kanin, surviving; and he, an adopted son, had held the dignity for but a year.

Upon Meiji's gaining nominal power, a plentiful supply of heirs became desirable. Unaware that the sickly boy would, in due course, with the assistance of a wife and five concubines, produce fifteen children, four Kanin brothers were commanded to form princely families, a genealogical chart being contrived to show their descent from a ruler who had died five hundred years before. Later four other Kanins were ennobled, two of them for marrying Meiji's illegitimate daughters.

The princes of the blood were men of dignity and wealth, holders of high position in religion or the armed services; but few were more than figureheads. There was no danger of their establishing an entrenched aristocracy, and eight of the fourteen, including the Emperor's brothers, Takamatsu and Chichibu, were childless.

More than half the other nobles held titles that had originated since 1884. In that year Ito had converted the old Tokugawa feudal nobility of court retainers, daimyos, and priests into a modern system, grading them according to their wealth: three Tokugawa princes, three great daimyos, and twelve families of the court nobility became princes; the other major nobles were made marquises, while minor figures became counts if their yearly revenues exceeded the equivalent of 500,000 bushels of rice, viscounts if more than 50,000, and barons if below 50,-000.

Such was the aristocracy which Whitney wished to abolish. Few Japanese, not even the aristocracy itself, defended the system. A few, like Prince Konoye, of the old court nobility, volunteered to resign their titles to show their sense of responsibility for Japan's misfortunes, but Hirohito disapproved the resignation as unnecessary; he also disapproved Higashikuni's suggestion in November, 1945, that every noble except the Emperor's three brothers, become a commoner.

While Hirohito disapproved, Whitney welcomed the suggestion; it became his chief demand upon the nobility. Most Japanese were willing to accept a proposal that titles die with the current holders, but Whitney insisted upon immediate abolition of all titles and upon the inclusion in the new Constitution of clauses forbidding not only any title of nobility but also the continuance of any honor or decoration beyond the lifetime of the recipient.

At Christmas, 1946, therefore, fifty-one members of princely families lost their special rank and became commoners, only the Crown Prince and the three Imperial brothers retaining titles. The favored individuals who had hitherto been free of ordinary cares, and who, indeed, had never known the liberty of ordinary citizens, registered at city offices, received ration cards and, like others, stood in line for personal and household necessities.

Those divested of their rank and titles received financial settlements nominally ranging from 100,000,000 to 800,000,000 yen; but a 90 per cent capital levy was imposed, and certain other taxes had to be paid, so that the gross totals were illusory, and the heads of eleven families, as career military officers, received no settlements whatever. As few, if any, of the recipients had previous business experience, much of the settlement money vanished, either through the schemes of sharpers or by unwise investments.

Some former princes, such as Prince Asaka who rented his mansion as the Foreign Minister's official residence, or Prince Kitashirakawa, landlord for the Speaker, received steady incomes; others experimented variously as proprietors of hardware, noodle or drug stores, as chicken raisers or swine breeders or farmers. One princess gave dancing lessons; another sold cosmetics in a department store. Prince Kuni sold his mansion to the International College of the Sacred Heart and invested the proceeds in the flourishing Marigold Dance Hall. Prince Higashikuni led, perhaps, the most adventurous career, being in turn a restaurant proprietor, a speculator, a notions storekeeper, and finally, a priest. Since after long meditation he could not decide whether his priesthood should be Christian or Buddhist he compromised by establishing a new sect having what he thought the best elements of both.

Only the Emperor's immediate family retained titles—including the Dowager Empress Sadako (now called Teimei), the Empress Nagako, Crown Prince Akihito and Prince Yoshi, the Princesses Kazuko and Takako, his brothers, Chichibu, Takamatsu, and Mikasa, and the two sons of Mikasa. Reviving the Tokugawa period legislation, only Akihito and Yoshi would transmit imperial titles to their descendants, the princesses ceasing to have family membership upon marriage and the brothers and nephews losing imperial status at Hirohito's death.

Financial support came entirely from the Diet, the Imperial family losing all right to buy, sell, or transfer property as long as the Occupation lasted without consent of the Supreme Commander; thereafter, all property was to be transferred to the state although hereditary estates might be retained for use, but not in fee simple, provided appropriate taxes were paid.

On this score, also, misconceptions colored Occupation thinking. As emperors, it was believed, were costly luxuries, Hirohito, one of the world's richest rulers, must necessarily be expensive; his expenditures must, therefore, be reduced.

The fact, however, was that Hirohito's court had so steadily retrenched since his accession that his Imperial Household Ministry, which, with all its far-flung interests, had accounted for 0.3 per cent of national expenditures in 1926, required only one-tenth of that ratio in 1945. Indeed, the Occupation, in seeking to restrict the Emperor, began by granting the Ministry a larger ratio than it had enjoyed, allowing it 0.04 per cent of the national expenditures in 1947, instead of the 0.03 per cent it had previously collected. When, despite pruned Imperial Household activities and a reduction in staff to 902 officials (only 17 of whom were above GS 11 rank and only one above GS 13), the allowance rose to 0.18 per cent in 1950, the cost to each Japanese was 1.39 yen per year instead of the 1.08 the Imperial system had cost him in 1947, or the 0.27 yen it had cost in 1945.

The great wealth of the Emperor, moreover, proved to be more potential than immediately realizable, more than three-quarters being in forest; revenue from these and from securities or other assets brought the Imperial Household approximately 15,000,000 yen annually, to which was added a fixed appropriation of 4,500,000 yen from the budget. When the properties were taken over by the state little financial relief resulted, the annual budget appropriations for Imperial care exceeding yearly the increased revenue from all government property thus received. On paper, however, the democratic movement scored a notable victory since the wealth of the Imperial Household was sharply reduced by legal confiscation.

The fortune thus sequestered was estimated in October, 1945, as 1,500,000,000 yen (then worth $100,000,000); the 90 per cent capital levy tax, local taxes, and other charges cut it down to 25,600,000 yen (about $71,000) in February, 1951.

There was, however, no danger that Hirohito would sink into the financial difficulties that had beset some of his remote ancestors, one of whom was said to have been so hard up that he could not afford to bury his Imperial father for a month after death. As an economy move 75 per cent of the Palace employees were dismissed; but much necessary work was done by volunteer "sweeping parties" organized and paid for by villages which sent squads of laborers to care for the 1,600-acre Palace grounds. More than 25,000 persons a year came to Tokyo, some of them booked a year ahead, to carry out what was considered to be as much a national obligation as the climbing of Mount Fuji or a visit to the Ise Shrines.

The custom indicated that the campaign to deflate the Emperor's popularity had won but slight success. In January, 1946, a public opinion poll showed that 90.1 per cent favored Hirohito, and that all but four of the eighty-nine political parties registered in Japan supported him; a similar poll in 1951 gave him 90.3 per cent support, with only the Communists opposing him. Twice yearly, on New Year's Day and on April 30, his birthday, several hundred thousand people thronged the Imperial Palace Plaza to sign his visitors' guest books, regardless of the weather. The crush was so great on New Year's Day 1954 that 16 persons were trampled to death and 30 were injured when 380,000 people, half of those who visited the Palace, suddenly rushed forward to enter the grounds. The Police Chief resigned because he had failed to foresee and prevent the tragedy.

Communist opposition persisted. On a visit to Kyoto in 1951 about five hundred university students surrounded his motorcar and heckled him, singing the Communist "Song of Peace" while they demanded that he reject rearmament proposals; but this was an unusual occurrence. So also was the refusal of the eccentric leftist, Jiichiro Matsumoto, vice president of the House of Councilors, to attend an Imperial reception because he would not "walk like a crab" and did not wish to make "worshipful obeisance." Others of Matsumoto's Socialist Party, however, attended, although Education Minister Tatsuo Morito wore a hunter's cap and Labor Minister Mitsutsuke Yonekubo shocked sedate palace attendants by appearing in a soldier's brown boots.

Following surrender, the Imperial advisers, probably with some covert advice from within Occupation circles, planned Imperial inspection tours to various regions of Japan. Russians promptly protested that this was a capitalistic plot to fasten Emperor rule upon Japanese struggling to be democratic, and even the Canadians and Australians objected; but Whitney told MacArthur that the net result would be beneficial. When, he said, the people saw for themselves that their Emperor was not a martial and imposing figure but rather a weak-chinned, round-shouldered, nervous fellow with a bad tic at the corner of the mouth and a high-pitched speaking voice they would no longer pay homage to him. MacArthur consented, and within the two years following surrender Hirohito made more personal appearances in more parts of Japan than during his entire preceding quarter-century as Prince Regent or Emperor.

Hirohito cut a poor figure on these tours at first. Clumsy, shabbily dressed, and ill at ease in conversation, he fell far short of expectations, as Whitney had anticipated. His subjects dutifully cheered and then went off to gossip about "Mr. Is that so?"—mocking Hirohito's nervous "Ah, so desu ka?" response to explanations of farm processes, factory procedure, or social conditions. The gossip, however, was friendly in tone, only the Communists attempting to discredit him.

But the tours, while they made Hirohito better known, caused bitter comment. Town authorities complained that Hirohito's ninety-man entourage was too large and its personnel was far too haughty. They did not like providing the food and other necessities required. Nor did taxpayers, as a rule, approve the costs that were involved. New roads and bridges were constructed so that the Emperor might see his country at its best; schools and factories were burnished; streets were swept. Toyama, it was said, spent 5,300,000 yen for such a visit; Nagano, Osaka, Okayama, and Niigata spent millions also. A Communist party-line magazine well described the situation by declaring: "The Emperor is a broom; everywhere he goes he sweeps the country clean." But the magazine accompanied its statement by a cartoon picturing the Emperor as a broom; and this audacity led to an indictment for lese majesty from which Whitney had to rescue it.

Instead of losing stature by the tours, Hirohito actually won so much prestige that a public opinion poll in August, 1948, reported him the most popular man in Japan.

He easily weathered also the blow that many in the Occupation thought would utterly demolish him. Foreign misconception of the Japanese devotion to the nation, with the Emperor as its symbol and the throne as the center of loyalty, had distorted the complex situation into the simple but misleading idea that to Japan the Emperor was divine. When the constitutional scholar Niichiro Matsunami wrote, "Japan is an absolute, a tennocratic, state," Westerners, knowing that *tenno* was the Japanese word for "emperor," leaped to the conclusion that Japan was yet another ancient Oriental land that deified its ruler. Etsujiro Uyehara, in whose experience no Emperor was godlike, wrote, "Divine right is the fundamental principle of Japanese polity," meaning only that Japan was favored of the gods and that exercise of power must be tempered by worshipful awe of the divinities. When Nobushige Hozumi, a famous interpreter of law, said, "Worship of the Imperial ancestors is the foundation of our Constitution," he had no thought of deifying the living Emperor.

To Japanese the Emperor was a moral focal point. The new Constitution accurately and with historical correctness described him as a symbol of the state. His personality was unimportant—he might be dissolute, drunken, or diseased—but his office remained the embodiment of virtue. He was not, and never had been, a god; men who so described him either misunderstood Japan's philosophy or used the propagandist's license.

For these reasons, the Occupation's deep concern to have the Emperor renounce all claims to divinity meant little to the Japanese. When General Ken Dyke's Civil Information and Education Section proposed to the Shidehara Cabinet that he do this, the Prime Minister and his Education Minister Tamon Maeda had much difficulty in explaining what was wanted. Shidehara, however, drafted a declaration in English, secured Dyke's approval and then presented it to Hirohito. He read the statement on New Year's Day, 1946, as a message to the people, telling them it was an error to regard him as a divinity, that Japanese were in no wise superior to other peoples, and that relations between Emperor and subjects rested on firmer bases than belief in myths. Since it was an Imperial pronouncement the Japanese press highly praised it, as did MacArthur; but the press had but little idea what the talk was about. Japanese never had thought of the Emperor as divine, and the declaration of equality seemed to them to be merely a polite compliment—the relationship was obvious. While people overseas looked upon the renunciation as evidence that Japan had truly become liberal and democratic, as indeed MacArthur told them, the Japanese saw far deeper importance in Hirohito's pointed reiteration of his grandfather Meiji's Charter Oath of 1868 when he had promised popular participation in government. Of this, however, neither MacArthur nor the Western press made mention.

As the Occupation closed, Hirohito's conservatism reasserted itself. Conforming to ancient custom, he visited the Grand Shrine of Ise and the tombs of his ancestors—particularly that of the Emperor Jimmu, who had founded Japan in 660 b.c.—and reported that Japan again was free. Although the Occupation had specifically objected to mounting Imperial photographs in the schools lest they lead to veneration, if not adoration, Hirohito in July, 1952, revived the practice of sending portraits to schools requesting them. To replace Imperial household regulations abolished by the Occupation, Hirohito set up commissions to study ceremonies useful in post-Occupation years. The talk of abdication that had flourished during 1945, and that Higashikuni and his aristocratic clique had revived in 1947 and 1948, died down completely when on Constitution Day, May 3, he announced his intention of ruling, promising to render himself worthy by "constant self-exhortation and mature deliberation in the light of recent history and the trend of public opinion." No one any longer suggested, as President Shigeru Nambara of Tokyo University had done in December, 1945, and as several observers had done following a visit by Bishop Fulton J. Sheen in June, 1948, that the Emperor might become a Christian.

Family relations revealed him at his most conservative. Not until November, 1953, did the Emperor and the Empress attend the theater together; and this was the first time in thirty-one years that Hirohito saw kabuki. Whitney and the Civil Information and Education Section, both under Dyke and under his successor, Nugent, had insisted on equality of the sexes, particularly the right of young men and women to choose their own mates without family dictation; but Hirohito reverted to former practice. When two daughters, Atsuko and Kazuko, were marriageable, he allowed his mother, the Dowager Empress Teimei, to pick their husbands; when all was settled and the young men had been notified, the girls were told. When Crown Prince Akihito came of age in 1951, Hirohito asked the court officials to comb the list of eligible princesses among the eleven former princely families; they narrowed the choice to eleven-year-old Princess Kitashirakawa as favorite, with three other slightly older girls as possibilities.

Hirohito's brother Mikasa, sometimes called the Red Prince, objected that this was feudalistic and was a violation of the Constitutional provision guaranteeing the inviolability of fundamental human rights, but he was overruled. Nothing would be done immediately, Mikasa was told, because the court was in mourning for Teimei's recent death; but at the proper occasion Akihito would be instructed which girl to marry, and he would do so, or waive his right to the Throne.

On Akihito's twentieth birthday, in December, 1953, Director-General Michihara Tajima, of the Imperial Household Agency, implied that the Crown Prince would announce his engagement, by November, 1954, to a girl "of suitable social standing" who would then be given two years' training in etiquette before her marriage.

Mikasa, youngest and least conformist of the Imperial brothers, was well accustomed to rebuffs. A student of both Marx and Christianity— he studied German and Hebrew, but not Greek, in order to compare the two in the original—he was not favored in court circles because he opposed rearming and because he sometimes echoed Soviet slogans. He incurred disfavor in 1947 when he refused to attend the official ceremony of proclamation of the Constitution because his wife was not invited although the Constitution promised equal rights to women. Not only had he repudiated Shintoism as a personal belief, but he revealed that few of his relatives really had faith; for this he was again rebuked. A prince who rode the streetcars to classes in Western history at Tokyo University, he angered his fellow princes by saying that it was unethical to use money from the national treasury to speculate in private business. Hirohito himself lost patience when Mikasa refused to comment favorably upon the Emperor's new book, *Opisthobranchia of Sagami Bay,* beautifully bound and sold for 3,000 yen in an edition limited to 3,000 copies, because he did not know what it was all about. Similarly when the Emperor sent seven poems to *Kaizo* magazine and refused a fee of 10,000 yen for them, taking instead five copies of the magazine, Mikasa suggested that the five copies were a truer approximation of the actual worth.

The return of conservatism did not, however, presage a return to prewar mysticism or obscuranticism. Those who saw Hirohito in the flesh wearing a battered hat, old shoes, and an askew cravat no longer believed the myth of an individual so dainty that he must use golden chopsticks to assist him at the toilet. The legend of a shadowy figure dressed in white silk and sleeping on a pillow patterned with cherry blossoms and stuffed with chrysanthemum leaves dried in the shade, eating pheasant boiled in sake and diamond-shaped rice cakes baked by a woman wearing white silk gloves passed, together with the legend that he bathed in three tubs, each with its own soap and towel. The Emperor, like most other middle-aged gentlemen of wealth and distinction, was conservative; but Japan knew that he was human.

Conservative influences following Japan's resumption of independence favored a new concealment of the Emperor behind the prewar Chrysanthemum Curtain. A new court etiquette based upon ancient precedent supplanted the simpler, more democratic codes imposed under the Occupation. Such instances as the funeral of the Dowager Empress Teimei, Akihito's coming of age, and his recognition as Crown Prince showed preference for old customs. Although Education Minister Teiyu Amano declared in November, 1951, "The Emperor is the moral center of the nation, and from him emanate all faith and love," it soon became obvious that, as Mikasa declared, "the Imperial Family is a prisoner."

In January, 1953, the relegation came clearly into focus. Hirohito, suddenly aware that his brother Chichibu was dying, planned a midnight motor drive to visit him; but court chamberlains denied permission, and Chichibu died before the Emperor could make a daylight trip. Again, when funeral ceremonies were held, the court officials prevented Hirohito's attendance at the rites—it would, they said, not only involve the high costs of a state funeral but break precedent.

The publicity resulting from disclosure of this interference, while not releasing the Emperor from court control, indicated a freedom of criticism that would have been impossible before surrender. Two other innovations, post-mortem examination and cremation of the body, departed from ironbound custom; but it also became known that Hirohito had been unable to permit a surgical operation that might have bettered Chichibu's condition while alive.

While the magic of the Imperial name and presence had grown thin in the Occupation period, signs were multiplying that efforts would be made to restore the prewar attitudes. Prominent among the plans was a bill drafted by Yoshida to restore the prewar system of decorations, honors and court rank which Whitney had ordered abandoned.

EIGHT

Battling the Bureaucrats

The Occupation intended not only to modernize public service and to make it more efficient but also to transform government personnel from petty tyrants into servants of the people.

The need was obvious. For decades, officials of every grade had been a privileged caste dedicated to their Emperor but with no obligations to private citizens. Their code called for obedience and deference to superiors; but toward subordinates they were pompous, haughty, and tyrannical. Flattery, obsequiousness, and subservience received reward in rank and honor, but merit, while desirable, was secondary. Even the wholly incapable were certain of promotion if they played the game according to accepted rules; but nonconformists or men devoid of personal loyalty could never mount the ladder.

Within this tightly knit circle favoritism and nepotism had created a still narrower clique, high among whom were graduates of the Tokyo First Higher School who had studied administrative law and technique at Tokyo or Kyoto Imperial University. Courses had been specially designed to teach precedent and method; trimmed precisely to meet the needs of civil service, they produced a standard type of public servant. Graduates of such schools readily passed civil service examinations, particularly as their professors often set the questions and graded the papers. Loyal alumni fired by a special esprit de corps aided one another to advance. Some high officials were merely figureheads, and some were incompetent; but the great majority were adequate though wedded to red tape and formalism.

Virtually all levels of the population resented the routine and the

90

traditionalism thus promoted. On few other matters was public opinion so unanimous. Much public outcry rose, of course, from unhappy personal experience, from identification of unpleasant duty—for instance, paying taxes—with the personality of the assessor or collector; yet, with all allowance for distortion, bias, or personality, there still remained good reason for public criticism. Parliamentarians protested the civil servant's basic distrust of democracy; publicists hated old-fashioned ways and lack of imagination in the conduct of official duties; businessmen condemned stodgy and reactionary commercial regulations while militarists sometimes went so far as to brand civilian government officials as traitors who blocked the efficiency of Japan's armed forces. When hotheads conspired in the 1930 decade to murder those whom they regarded as enemies to the nation, government personages stood high among their prospective victims.

Opposition centered not so much upon the rank and file as upon an élite corps of fewer than 2,000 *chokunin,* or Imperial appointees: the so-called bureaucrats who manned top administrative posts. Of these, 737 in 1941 staffed cabinet bureaus or commissions; another 1,092 managed such enterprises as the national railways, posts, telecommunications, the monopoly bureau, or official financial organs.

Subordinate were a second rank of 22,423 *sonin* in 1941, who held commissions approved by the Emperor, and a third grade of 182,592 *hannin* named by the department chiefs. Of these, 14,299 sonin and 61,480 hannin worked in Cabinet bureaus. Membership in these three groups had risen from 134,537 in 1931 to 206,844 in 1941, and increased during the war to 328,592 in 1945. The increase was chiefly in the hannin class, the number of chokunin falling from 1,829 in 1941 to 1,788 in 1945.

The élite corps, and particularly the 700 top chokunin within the ministries, wielded tremendous influence. As career administrators and executives they advised cabinet ministers, and virtually directed diplomacy and justice, managed home affairs, including the police, education and local administration, and guided economic policy in all its varied branches. Even the Emperor followed the recommendations of the Imperial Household bureaucrats. But while the influence was powerful it was irresponsible, beyond control by the electorate or by the Diet.

The Occupation determined not only to reform the civil service, break up cliques, and loosen the hold of favored schools upon appointment to high position, but also to pare the pay rolls and to transfer power to elected officers.

Striking success was claimed in certain of the aims. National Public Service Acts in 1947 and 1948 guaranteed tenure, assured adequate pay, required modern job classification, and provided retirement pensions. Written examinations testified to the technical competence of every civil employee below the rank of Cabinet Minister, and promotion was to be by merit alone.

Accomplishment in such fields was comparatively simple, especially as Japan already possessed laws nominally covering such matters; but elsewhere difficulties were encountered. The chokunin, whose numbers had been dropping, and who had never in any previous year exceeded 1,906, suddenly increased under Occupation rule to 3,744 in 1948. Sonin more than doubled, from 26,481 in 1945 to 57,299 in 1948. Hannin, who had totaled 300,323 in 1945, jumped to 545,983 in 1948. An Occupation pledged to reduce the civil service pay roll actually increased the top officials by 84 per cent within three years.

Traditional classifications were thereafter abolished in favor of fifteen civil service categories. It was impossible to compare new ratings with old rankings; but 3,375 officers in the new GS 13, 14 and 15 brackets performed by and large the tasks previously assigned to 3,744 chokunin, indicating that little saving had been effected. Despite decentralization moves transferring many national operations to local jurisdiction, the total of national employees, exclusive of armed service personnel, which had been considered dangerously high at 517,859 in 1931, hit 1,567,638 in fiscal 1949. Later cuts reduced the total to 1,423,840 in 1952.

Savings may have been illusory. Posts under the Cabinet, where bureaucracy had been most firmly entrenched, actually increased from 392,845 in 1946 to 503,100 after the 1951 readjustments. Whatever personnel economies may have been effected in national administration, moreover, were more than offset by a startling increase in local government. Town, city, and prefecture employees had numbered 394,773 in 1931, many of them serving without pay, but prefecture employees numbered 380,357 in 1951 against 13,096 in 1931; and city employees, 375,217 against 41,390. In addition 544,594 town and village employees, in 1951, brought the total of government employees to 1,300,168, virtually all of whom were paid.

Not only had the Occupation failed to prune officialdom, but it had failed to weaken the prewar civil service clique. Occupationnaires, by transferring to the bureaucrats many powers formerly wielded by industrial and commercial councils and control associations—some of them operated under a semblance of a guild system—actually intensified bureaucratic strength.

Even had bureaucrats received no access of power they would have profited by the purging of their rivals, the militarists, the politicians, and big businessmen. No one intended such exemption, but civil servants, by the nature of their work, eluded purges. Had the Occupation wished to exclude them from public life—a decision never publicly announced—it would have been difficult to find a reason since bureaucrats for the most part had been administrators, not makers of policy decisions. The experienced civil servants, however, had fortified themselves against even remote contingencies by burning all records that might have incriminated them, and then exchanging positions—some going to remote localities where their previous activities were not well known. Preserving there an attitude of cautious watchfulness, attracting no unfavorable attention, they lived and worked in unobtrusive fashion.

Thus the civil servants, and particularly the top bureaucrats, weathered the purge and, following traditional courses, gained prestige and power. Perhaps to their own surprise the members of this élite group, which had been trained to consider Western thought as leading only to disruptive individualism, became leading agents in the introduction and dissemination of democracy.

The development followed a carefully worked-out plan, invented and executed by a band of former Foreign Office attachés. This cohesive group, speaking English perfectly and well versed by residence abroad in Western preferences, volunteered as liaison officers between the Occupation and the Japanese Government. Thus they were in excellent strategic position to present Japan's needs in the best possible light and also, through their savoir-faire and diplomatic skill, to win friends in high position. Few were actually on the list, drafted by State Department officers, of possible friends of the United States; but some—for instance, Shidehara and Yoshida—had suffered militarist persecution, thus attesting to their democratic tendencies. Others, especially former students in American or British universities, knew well what slogans would please the foreigners. MacArthur's aides, charmed and perhaps indeed flattered to be courted by internationally known personalities, trusted them to institute reforms. With certain obvious exceptions, no more unlikely circle could have been selected.

In trusting the élite group to reform itself the Occupation overrode clear warnings. As early as November, 1945, Lieutenant Milton J. Esman, an officer with experience in personnel management, had pointed out the grave deficiencies of Japan's administrative system. When Whitney nevertheless ordered the government to rid itself of feudal traits, Esman reported on January 20, 1946, "The present bureaucracy is neither willing nor competent to reform Japan nor to manage a modern democratic society." His conclusions were reenforced by Dr. John M. Maki, who made systematic surveys of the entire administrative structure and of the personalities involved.

Government Section, however, pigeonholed the Esman-Maki reports and put its confidence in Shidehara and Yoshida. These veterans of the Foreign Ministry bureaucracy proposed a revision of the civil service system, including improvements in the salary and promotion methods, and, despite lagging by the bureaucratic Board of Legislation, succeeded in obtaining a draft of suggested amendments.

Their plan pleased no one. The press scoffed at its mildness; politicians protested that it could not be properly enforced; bureaucrats complained that they, the special agents of the Emperor, were suffering discrimination. Whitney himself was unenthusiastic: the draft, he said, was "only a satisfactory beginning toward simplification and democratization."

Even the minor civil service workers, the rank and file without clique connections, found little merit in the bill designed for their protection; it seemed to threaten that perhaps 30 per cent of civil service workers would be dismissed.

Nor did Government Section's draft of a new Constitution suggest serious reform; it went no further than to instruct the Diet to legislate on civil service matters while allowing the bureaucrats in Cabinet offices to administer such laws as it might pass.

Few believed that Yoshida and Shidehara, veteran bureaucrats, had any real desire to weaken the bureaucratic system; almost no one thought that their Liberal Party, largely composed of bureaucratic leaders, intended radical innovations. Yet even their mild proposals split the Cabinet, some ministers battling the reforms as dangerous to established custom and vigorously criticizing the decision, whether taken under Government Section pressure or for the sake of votes in an imminent election, to put the changes into effect by Imperial Ordinance.

Tanzan Ishibashi's Finance Ministry, a stronghold of old-line bureaucracy, sought delay by suggesting a special American advisory commission on civil service affairs. MacArthur then appointed Blaine Hoover, president of the Civil Service Assembly of the United States and Canada, to survey the situation.

Hoover arrived in November, 1946, during a period of intense political turmoil. Difficult living conditions, for which inept administration was unfairly held responsible, had caused unrest. Nascent labor organizations, engaging in political activity, were demonstrating constantly. Hoover was appalled to find civil service workers waving red flags in noisy public demonstrations just below his office windows.

Frightened into thinking that labor generally, and civil service workers in particular, were going Communist, Hoover announced that no public servants should be permitted to join unions, to bargain collectively, to strike, or, contrary to a Far Eastern Commission directive, to enter politics.

The announcement was unfortunate. Labor leaders, who had been counted as allies in the war against bureaucracy, called Hoover fascist. The rank and file of civil servants, whom Hoover was trying to protect, regarded him as stripping them of their last defenses against bureaucratic tyranny. The general public, already seriously confused about the meaning of democracy and rights of labor, misconstrued Hoover's recommendations as violations of human dignity and of the fundamental rights guaranteed by Japan's new Constitution.

Even within the Occupation, Hoover's suggestions were opposed. Certain labor experts, already under fire for allegedly leftist tendencies, privately egged on Japanese protests. Others, not in the least radical, worried lest the proposals violate Truman's instructions to encourage unionism. Government Section itself was somewhat displeased lest the Hoover plan centralize rather than decentralize administrative controls.

None of the furore directly concerned the top bureaucratic clique, but apparently the public reacted in its favor. The ensuing general elections of 1947 indicated that popular opposition to bureaucracy, assumed for decades to be strong, was almost negligible. Voters in thirty-two of the forty-three prefectures reelected sitting governors, every one of whom was bureaucratically supported, or chose candidates with bureaucratic backgrounds. Diet members also reflected bureaucratic influence; upon election, they showed no independence but took their orders from their bureaucratic bosses. Socialists as well as Liberals followed the trend.

Nevertheless, under constant Occupation prodding, civil service reform went forward; and, on October 21, 1947, the Diet passed an act creating a National Personnel Authority (NPA) of three members—to be named by the Prime Minister and confirmed by the Diet—to set standards, adjudicate complaints, and coordinate personnel operations in all government departments. The ban on striking was omitted.

Hoover's associates, however, were not pleased. Although MacArthur himself hailed the new law as one that "tempered the inordinate bureaucratic power by requiring all public officials to justify the trust of public responsibility and answer for their acts directly to the people"—without explaining how tempering had been achieved or how the bureaucrats were answerable—Government Section wanted stricter regulation.

To convince the public of the need for action, a double campaign opened, attacking top bureaucrats as well as warning against unionization and striking by the rank and file. Colonel Kades, Whitney's right-hand man, linked the bureaucrats with an illegal underground which, he charged, was stronger than the actual government. Commander Guy J. Swope, liaison officer for Diet affairs, accused the bureaucrats of conspiring to restore Imperial autocracy. Colonel Frank E. Hayes, the legal expert, charged them with undermining the authority of the courts. Although Tetsu Katayama, the Socialist prime minister, promptly denied the existence of an underground and disclaimed any intention of restoring the Emperor, the barrage served its purpose. Hoover, and Whitney himself, insisted that protection be afforded; they also demanded the passage of the strike ban.

MacArthur therefore, on July 22, 1948, ordered the new prime Minister, Hitoshi Ashida, to enforce the entire Hoover program.

Protests again arose. Katayama predicted that labor gains would be imperiled. Unions demonstrated angrily. Within the Occupation, James S. Killen and Paul Stanchfield, heading the Labor Division, took the unprecedented step of demanding the reasons for actions which, they said, were treacherous to democracy. Army discipline would not permit a direct answer to so irregular a demand; but when Whitney implied that collective bargaining infringed upon the Diet's sole legislative rights, and Hoover reported a Communist plot for a civil service strike, Killen and Stanchfield resigned. Government Section willingly took over their work as far as public officials were concerned.

Neither Ashida nor his Labor Minister, Kanju Kato, had any such easy recourse. The former frankly admitted that he was a puppet and could not help himself; and Kato, former Roth favorite and a veteran union leader, excused himself by reporting that Hoover had commanded him to stay in office and carry out orders. Consequently, as the Diet was not in session, a Cabinet order, July 31, put the Whitney-Hoover program into effect.

The order permitted civil servants, except police, firemen, and the coast guard, to form unions for welfare and social purposes but not for collective bargaining. Strikes by public officials were outlawed. Less controversial provisions gave the NPA stronger power to enforce the merit system, to set pay rates in accordance with duty and responsibility, to require in-service training, and to revise pension and retirement plans.

Before the Diet met in December to ratify the order, the Ashida Cabinet resigned, only partly because of public opposition to its stand on civil service, and Yoshida again became prime minister. Since he had already sharply condemned labor leaders as malcontents, and inferentially as enemies to the state, he welcomed the opportunity to restrict their activity. He was happy also, as prime minister, to be in a position to name the NPA and to control civil service reform.

In submitting the Cabinet order for Diet approval, Yoshida added a provision calling for a 5,330 yen monthly wage base. Ashida's Democrats, no longer obligated to support the measure, asked 5,809 yen, and Katayama's Socialists 6,307, a deadlock ensuing. Although Dr. Justin Williams, Swope's successor, assured lawmakers that they were free to act as they saw fit, both Whitney and Marquat, Killen's former chief, told Yoshida to accept the Socialist proposal—perhaps in order to soften labor resentment against the accompanying restrictions. Passage on December 10, 1948, of amendments to the National Public Service Act enacted the full Hoover program into law.

Labor's gratitude for the 68 per cent rise in wages was somewhat lessened by the simultaneous increase in working time from thirty-six to forty-eight hours weekly, which, it was said incorrectly but vigorously, actually reduced the hourly wage. This argument proved ineffective; but the rise in living costs was real, and in 1949 the workers received year-end bonuses costing the government 5,380,000,000 yen, their base pay being raised to 7,981 yen in January, 1951.

The wage increases were, however, so graded that the greatest benefits went to the élite corps: the GS 13 bracket receiving 18,300 yen monthly; GS 14, 21,500 yen; and the GS 15, 28,000 yen.

Both to hold down costs in spite of higher wage bases and to pare the pay rolls, Hoover called for a ceiling of 871,000 higher-grade em-

ployees, and this was theoretically embodied in a Personnel Strength
Act of May 31, 1949; but the law proved ineffective. Only a few employees were actually dismissed, and they alleged that their separation
had been due to politics. Yoshiji Nishiyama of the Economic Investigation Board insisted, for example, that his staff had been cut by 70 per
cent in reprisal for its disclosure of black marketing operations, embezzlements, and connivance in evasions. Within forty-eight hours,
Nishiyama, who had uncovered hoarded goods worth more than 24,000,-
000,000 yen, was himself dismissed.

Personnel improvement, undertaken simultaneously with the unsuccessful efforts to hold down expense, also met sly, and on the whole
effective, sabotage.

Despite Hoover's consistent emphasis upon promotion by merit and
the passage of laws requiring it, three years elapsed before he could
apply it to the top bureaucracy. While Japan had since 1885 required
civil service examinations for initial appointment to the civil service,
promotion had been based upon seniority, nepotism, and the favor
of school cliques. Chokunin and their successors in the highest posts,
including vice ministers, had been exempt from any tests.

Hoover's insistence that these men be examined caused unprecedented
furore. So strong was the opposition that Chief Cabinet Secretary
Kaneschichi Masuda called upon the NPA to waive the examinations;
when it replied that it could not override Hoover's command, Masuda
appealed to Government Section to countermand the order, Chairman
Kiyoshi Asai of NPA joining in the request. Whitney replied that only
the incompetent, unfit, and unqualified need worry about the test,
whereupon Prime Minister Yoshida took the matter directly to Mac-
Arthur.

So certain were the bureaucrats that these protests would be effective
that, as late as a week before the scheduled examination date only 125
of the almost 3,000 incumbents bothered to register; but when Mac-
Arthur rejected the appeals all took the test, together with some
5,000 outsiders anxious for appointment to the high positions. A total
of 8,076 applicants took the two-part ninety-question examination held
at eleven centers on January 15, 1950.

Whether by the skill of the school clique or by the connivance of the
NPA—which, to the intense indignation of the bureaucracy was itself
exempted from the test—the questions favored the incumbents. Special
administrative practices and the peculiar knowledge imparted at the

Tokyo and Kyoto University law schools provided keys to proper answers. Only 4,859 candidates won passing marks on technical problems, and only 2,900—virtually all of whom were incumbents—passed the administrative questions. No candidate scored more than 86; the average paper was graded 48. While Hoover had anticipated, and perhaps hoped, that approximately one-third of the incumbent bureaucrats would be disqualified, all but a few emerged successfully. Not all Japanese were convinced that the examinations had been fair.

Hopes that the examination system would open top civil service ranks to women were also dashed. Only nineteen passed the technical tests, and only twenty-five the administrative sections; one woman alone placed among the leading two hundred candidates.

No civil service examination was thereafter held for top positions in the bureaucracy.

Hoover's death in September, 1950, ended effort to revolutionize the civil service structure, but Yoshida doggedly continued his attempt to reduce swollen personnel. Well aware that the 871,000 ceiling level for higher-grade employees had long been ignored, and that new bureaus and agencies were increasing pay rolls dangerously despite supposed decentralization, Yoshida called repeatedly for 30 per cent cuts.

Welfare Minister Ryugo Hashimoto undertook in 1951 to drop 173,000 persons from the pay roll; but bureaucratic opposition, reenforced by labor union and Socialist objections, induced the Cabinet to pare this cut to 123,000. The proposal then went to the Diet, which first reduced the cuts to 88,000 and then, after flagrant lobbying by thirty-one Agriculture-Forestry Ministry executives, to 60,127. This figure, however, indicated no actual dismissals since annual resignations and retirements, together with the fact that many positions in the table of organization had not been filled, more than equaled that amount.

Yoshida, who despite his loyalty to his former bureaucratic associates sincerely favored personnel reduction, reacted angrily against this cut of less than 10 per cent when he had asked for three times as much. He demanded the dismissal of the thirty-one lobbyists, and they were fired within a month. Hashimoto resigned, ostensibly because of failure to win sufficient appropriations for wounded veterans' pensions, and Yoshida in January, 1952, ordered State Minister Tokutaro Kimura, head of the Administrative Management Board, to bring about the required 30 per cent cut in personnel.

But again, despite Yoshida's mastery of a Liberal Party that was committed by its platform to reform the bureaucratic system, and that held a 284-vote majority in the House of Representatives, action lagged. Bureaucratic influence within the ministries caused Cabinet delays; an increasing membership of ex-bureaucrats in the Diet strengthened parliamentary opposition.

By this time, with the peace treaty removing Occupation pressure toward civil service reform, idealism had become secondary; but personnel cuts remained a major issue. After the highly publicized improvements, and despite the wide decentralization programs, the central corps of chokunin, sonin, and hannin had risen from 328,592 in 1945 to 607,026 in 1948 and their replacements were now exceeding the 681,000 level set in 1949. Unquestionably government offices were overstaffed; and, in addition, new bureaus, sections, and divisions were being established. The ministries were not so much at fault, there having been but two new ministries set up since 1932; but almost a thousand new subordinate agencies had been created.

Yoshida desired to streamline the structure, but he could not count upon support. Public opinion, while remaining highly vocal in opposition to bureaucracy, proved to be singularly tolerant at the polls. The 1953 Diet elections, for example, sent 103 bureaucrats to seats in the House of Representatives, and others entered the House of Councilors. Only a small group of civil service workers were themselves interested in administrative changes; the great majority, long living insecurely because of Yoshida's constant plea for 30 per cent cuts in personnel, wanted little more than to be left alone.

Thus, although an Administrative Reform Committee, drafting a Japanese version of Herbert Hoover's Reorganization Plan of the United States, recommended reductions of 187,000 from the national pay roll and 196,000 more from local government employment, virtually nothing was accomplished. Chairman Ichiro Honda of the Administrative Supervision Agency, who was supposed to sponsor a Diet bill to this effect, confessed in February, 1953 that he had little stomach for the plan; the Diet itself adjourned in April without taking action. Early in 1954 the agency began to cut personnel, but only by 10 per cent, and even this over a three-year period. The press, noting the general reluctance to discharge personnel, doubted if the full 81,668 employees scheduled for dismissal would actually be fired.

Relegation of the once powerful NPA to impotence was readily accomplished, and that agency, whose chairman once had aspired to rank immediately below the Chief Justice and the Speaker of the House, became subordinate to the Prime Minister.

Nor was much more to be hoped in further reform. The inner clique remained intact, supported, after 1953, by a Yoshida Cabinet itself chiefly drawn from Tokyo Imperial Law School graduates and therefore bound by training, loyalty, and interest. Little vestige remained of the Occupation effort to transfer power from appointed to elected hands nor of the decentralization movement. Yoshida himself, while stubbornly insisting that the government service was overmanned, devoted his efforts to bringing under central authority teachers, policemen, and perhaps large segments of other local officials, and thus forbidding unionization and strike privileges to them. In 1953 he secured a law forbidding strike privileges to transportation, coal-mining, and electric power workers. In 1954, he sponsored a law forbidding teachers to support or oppose any candidate for office, to solicit funds, to parade or demonstrate for or support any political cause or to write for, edit or display any writings on political affairs.

NINE

Political Machinery

Japanese party government may be a hothouse plant, a forced and artificial growth incapable of survival without continued careful nurture.

Appearances are deceptive, for while Japan apparently possesses a well developed party system with full party responsibility and with established loyalties and traditions, the parties in reality bear but slight resemblance to those existing in the West. Little evidence appears that the general public has grasped the nature of party government, or that the parties fully understand the duties and obligations involved in such a system.

Like other Oriental institutions, the outer surface of Japanese politics does not reflect the inner motivating spirit; there is no surer way to misunderstand the political situation than to assume, as Occupationnaires assumed, that the names, platform planks, slogans, pronouncements, or methods used bear any necessary relationship to the same used in the West. While Japanese politicians outwardly resemble their foreign counterparts, even in appearance, they think and act in strangely different ways.

Political parties date from the Aikokukoto, or Patriotic Party, in 1874, but contemporary parties are all postwar creations, even the Communists having made a fresh start. During most of the period since the surrender Japan followed a three-party system. The Jiyuto (Liberals), formerly termed Minjuto (Democratic-Liberals), usually held a plurality of seats in the Lower House; but a second conservative party, Kaishinto (Progressive Reformist), standing only slightly to the left, posed a constant threat; it had previously been called Shimpoto (Progressive), Minshuto (Democratic), or Kokumin Minshuto (People's Democratic). The chief rival, the Shakaito (Socialist, but formerly referred to by the mistranslation of Social Democratic Party), held the prime ministry briefly during 1947. Minor parties are legion and vary widely both in strength and in policy.

Virtually all parties are similarly organized, each having a president (Shigeru Yoshida for the Liberals, Mamoru Shigemitsu for the Reformists, and Jotaro Kawakami for the Socialists), a powerful secretary-general, a central executive committee, and various other standing groups. These leaders and committee chairmen constitute a tightly organized clique removed, for the most part, from control by their subordinates and recognizing virtually no obligations to the voters who support the party candidates. While national conventions, and occasionally local conferences are held, the membership is never selected by the rank and file but consists almost entirely of headquarters officials, Diet members, and the more influential local chieftains, who are either self-selected or appointed by the Tokyo officers.

Party government works primarily through the House of Representatives, relatively little attention being paid to local offices. Parties, therefore, exert strength only in so far as they have power in the lower house; and party politics, while voicing occasional platitudes concerning local government, pays slight attention to it.

Carrying out prewar traditions of the House of Peers, the House of Councilors has special parties of its own. Of these the largest has been the Ryokufukai, Green Wind Society, so called because it was formed in May when fruitful breezes rejuvenated the fields—and, by implication, politics. A conservative party, it usually, though by no means invariably, sides with the Liberals; the possibility of its independent action has seriously worried Prime Minister Yoshida's adherents since 1947.

Except possibly the Communist, no Japanese party has historic roots or basic principles. Theoretically, the Liberals descend from Count Taisuke Itagaki's Liberal Party of 1882 by way of the prewar Seiyukai while Reformists stem from Count Shigenobu Okuma's Reformists through the prewar Minseito; but these chains of descent involve considerable distortion of the historic record. Other claims, that the Liberals are Mitsui followers and the Reformists Mitsubishi men, or that Liberals are landlords and farmers whereas the Reformers are small business men, cannot be historically defended. Only the Communists and the laborite Socialists can be accurately classified as having any specific color.

Nor are platforms helpful as a guide. These, like platforms elsewhere, echo generalities and platitudes against which no one takes offense; but the double talk of platforms in Japan consists of pious exhortation. No American party would write an agricultural plank promising merely to "respect the farmer"; yet upon that issue the Liberals swept the rural districts in 1946. The vagueness is a Japanese tradition; in 1918 Takashi Hara frankly confessed that he had no program but that his platform was a blank page to be filled in as circumstances might require, and in 1952 Tadao Oasa declared his intention of forming a Japan Reconstruction Party but would decide later what the party would support.

Personality, not principle, rules a party; the leader, not the issue, is the focus. The party label is relatively unimportant; voters rally about a politician who, through power, prestige, money, or those vague attributes which collectively the Japanese describe as character, possesses mass appeal.

Loyalty to leaders rather than to a party name results in groups similar to private clubs in that membership is by invitation and approval rather than resulting from support by ballot. Thus party primaries, which the Occupation strove to foster, gained no support, Japan having no comprehension of a democratically organized and managed party whose voters had a right to choose the candidates. Iron discipline becomes possible when the leader can expel a follower who has deviated from the rigid party line. Easy shifts are facilitated, even between parties which theoretically are diametrically opposed. Yukio Ozaki, veteran liberal, wandered in and out of parties, or set up his own. Japanese saw nothing incongruous when Baron Kijuro Shidehara, Prime Minister of a Liberal Cabinet, deserted to head the rival Progressives or when he returned to become supreme adviser of the party he had left. So fluid are party memberships that in one postwar Diet session more than half the representatives shifted their allegiance, three of them five times each before running for reelection, successfully, on a sixth party ticket.

Even before the war signs were manifest that these easy transitions were diminishing, and that a faint form of party responsibility was coming into existence. This tendency continued after surrender, as was made evident by factional struggles within each of the major parties. As the party in power with patronage to share, the Liberals long resisted the tendency to break asunder; but two Socialist parties and two Democratic parties (the latter sharing the same small office building) warred vigorously upon their brethren of the same name.

Thwarted ambitions and jealousies, the latter a particularly chronic evil among Socialists and labor parties, motivated many of these shifts. A bitter personal feud between two strong leaders resulted in the founding of two postwar conservative groups, rather than one; the hatred of a powerful clique against a man who, it was alleged, had been an ingrate a dozen years before continued the separation. A judicious distribution of Cabinet posts won back the dissidents, but the parallel conservative parties remained because of the convenience of exchanging members. On at least five different occasions large blocs of Democratic or Reformist Diet members moved en masse into Liberal ranks.

Party instability is evidenced by change of heart, the present Reformist Party, for example, having since its 1945 birth as the Progressive Party, shifted from conservatism to "streamlined capitalism" to "modified socialism"; it made deals for coalition with the reactionary Liberals, the fascist-like Cooperatives and both the left- and the right-wing Socialists.

Minor parties followed similar courses. In their almost complete ignorance of prewar political history, Occupation officials were astonished to hear that Japan had some 1,250 registered political parties in 1946, each of which, it was naïvely assumed, had a specific political philosophy. All but a very few, however, were either local units of a major group, or unimportant bands of irresponsibles. Not realizing that Japanese form a club, ornamented by a resounding title, at the drop of a hat, the Occupation assumed that the surprising total indicated Japan's eager assumption of democratic principles, that each group was a legitimate organization deserving a full public confidence, and that party government was completely understood. MacArthur's advisers were pleased when twenty-five small parties won thirty-five seats in the first Diet under the new Constitution; they could not understand why immediately after election twenty-seven of these members accepted offers from larger parties while the remaining 8 formed an Independent Party which itself later merged and vanished. The pattern, carried over from the prewar era, was repeated in each succeeding general election.

Campaigning by personal appeal rather than by party label led to the election of an unusual number of "independent" candidates; but the independent in Japan is far less likely to be a Yukio Ozaki than to be an opportunist. To be nonpartisan implies no independence of spirit nor freedom from boss control; usually it means that the candidate, or his controlling backer, is waiting for persuasion. After each of Japan's twenty-six general elections, among the ten to a hundred independents chosen for the Diet (the number was 79 in 1946), all but half a dozen shopped around for the best major party offer for their votes. In prefectural and local elections where national issues are not strong the independent is an even more common phenomenon. At the 1951 local elections 152 of the 192 successful mayors reported themselves as unattached, as did 50 of the 66 whose candidacies were uncontested.

Japanese themselves recognized the dangers inherent in their system. Councilor Kinichi Saionji, whose father by adoption was Japan's last influential elder statesman, bewailed that purely personal factors and absence of established ideals render successful party politics impossible. Tsunego Baba, veteran liberal and editor of one of Tokyo's most powerful newspapers, feared that the interests of Japanese were sacrificed upon the altar of personal prestige. The influential English-language *Nippon Times* reported that kaleidoscopic political maneuvers dictated by expediency, regardless of popular will, endangered democratic government.

"No combination is so bizarre as to be altogether beyond consideration," a *Nippon Times* editorial declared. "Changes are so fluid and so rapid that none but a relatively few initiates can keep up with the complicated moves. The general public does not know what it is all about."

This cynical and irresponsible behavior, with the corollary that the general public must be kept politically immature, wrecked confidence in parliamentary government during the 1930 decade and facilitated totalitarianism. Wartime propagandists abroad mistakenly ascribed the fall of party prestige to army intrigue, and this of course was surely evident despite rigid prohibitions dating back to 1878; but party politics, and with it democracy in Japan, were doomed by inner weaknesses. Despite pious postwar protestations, no Japanese party ever received firm grass-roots support. Except at election time voters have sedulously been ignored, and in the few instances where workers or farmers have been organized their interests have all too often been betrayed by those whom they elected.

A basic cause lies in the fundamentally undemocratic character of Japanese political parties. No party allows the individual voter even the faintest voice in the determination of its policies, the choice of its officers, or the selection of its candidates. Primaries are non-existent, nor do conventions nominate the candidates. Bylaws usually provide that local branches may suggest both policies and candidates, and these, if satisfactory, may be accepted; but central headquarters retains the right to dictate policy, to impose candidates for both national and local office (*rakusan,* or "parachute" candidates), and to exact forced contribution—all this under penalty of expulsion if the interference is resented. No party member in the Diet and no party executive may deviate from the party line set down for him; those refusing lose their party privileges. Every political party in Japan since surrender has thus expelled numerous supporters; the Democrats in 1949 split into nearly equal factions, each of which solemnly expelled the other.

Yoshida as head of the Liberals, in the same year, clearly expressed the general philosophy of all party heads when he condemned intra-party criticism of his action. "It is impertinent," he said, "for party members to question what the party president does."

Yoshida's assumption of a party presidential dictatorship revived the prewar idea of personal political rule. In other postwar parties, the presidents held merely the shadow of power, the real administrators remaining hidden; but Yoshida rebelled against restriction. Although by preelection agreement the Liberal Party reserved party management to a small old-guard clique of professionals, Yoshida insisted not only on naming the Cabinet but also on approving or vetoing mergers. His refusal to join leftist Socialists—that "mermaid party with a fishy smell"—gave no offense; but his welcoming, in 1948, of bureaucrats who had consistently opposed political control and of men ungrateful to their old-guard sponsors caused violent resentment. His open support, in 1949, of Ken Inukai, whom the old guard detested, and his preference for Shidehara as Speaker, added to his continued interference with party management, widened the breach; but the old guard had no other candidate with whom to replace him.

The field from which a party president may be drawn is limited. Most often he is an elderly man—preferably of high prestige in diplomacy, like Yoshida, Shidehara, Shigemitsu, or Ashida. He is not necessarily a politician. Prior to heading the Liberals Yoshida had never been elected to the Diet nor had his friendly Progressive Party rivals, Shidehara, or Shigemitsu. Though the late Marquis Tsuneo Matsudaira, former ambassador and Court official, disliked political prominence, every major party except the Communists invited him to become its president. Admiral Kichisaburo Nomura and President Naotake Sato of the House of Councilors, both former ambassadors, also declined such postwar invitations.

Such men are sought as screens behind whom the real manipulators may operate as the old guard planned to work behind Yoshida. Although conditions changed rapidly, each party has shown the same phenomenon: Inukai calling the turn for Shidehara; Mitsu Kono and Jotaro Kawakami, for Katayama; Sanahiko Yamamoto, for the Cooperatives; and, more openly, Sanzo Nosaka and Kyuichi Tokuda, for the Communists.

During the Occupation few postwar party presidents were politically adroit. The expert campaigners and political manipulators were, for the most part, subject to purge, Ichiro Hatoyama, founder and first president of the Liberals, being the great exemplar. Wataru Narahashi, long considered second only to Hatoyama as a party manager, built or reorganized half a dozen postwar groups, including Liberals, Progressives, and Democrats, but never sought a party post higher than the secretaryship. So, too, Ichiro Kono, Tsuruhei Matsuno, and others whom the Japanese call "Gods of Elections" stayed modestly in the background.

These constituted the respectable front for the political scene; through them funnelled the essential campaign funds. Generally speaking, the postwar party president is not necessarily a money raiser although Yoshida's support from his wealthy son-in-law, Tagakichi Aso, assures his independence from the old guard. More usually the financial backer works through the manipulator. Thus Seijiro Ishibashi, Japan's rubber king, supplied funds to the Liberals through Hatoyama, whose son married Ishibashi's daughter, and, through Narahashi, to certain of Hatoyama's rivals. Major contractors, especially in railway and construction work, contributed millions to managers of all the parties without discrimination, and one of the most important, Usaburo Chizaki, who sought harbor contracts, even included the Communists.

To keep the party as respectable as possible, the more tainted contributions—those from gamblers, vice lords, racketeers, bribers, and fixers—flow more indirectly to the party treasury. Only infrequently, therefore, are party presidents smirched by corruption charges, though both former Prime Minister Hitoshi Ashida and his financial agent, Michinari Sugawara, were detained on charges of complicity in the Showa Denko scandal.

Collection of campaign contributions by others than the party president or the party managers weakens the grip of the figurehead president upon party machinery and facilitates both interparty shifts and supposedly independent action. Each leader in party management may withdraw, taking with him his financial following, as did Ashida and, in 1952, Hatoyama, in seceding from the Liberals, and Shidehara and later Inukai when deserting the Democrats and Progressives. The influential leader need not rely upon local support but, secure in his supply of funds, may wholly disregard his constituency after election.

Necessarily the query rises, Why, if local groups are impotent, individuals are repressed, and independence is easy, should party membership be thought desirable? The answer does not lie in patronage; for patronage—at least in the American sense—is not distributed through local branches, nor even, usually, through the Diet members. Rather, the explanation is peculiarly Japanese, turning about the concept of gratitude and duties owed to the feudal lord. The boss can do no wrong, and his subjects are his personal property. A further, but oddly enough no stronger, reason is that public office is a source of income and prestige, that election is expensive, costing far more than the rather limited amounts set legally, and that, as money contributions pour into central headquarters, reelection is usually impossible unless by Tokyo assistance. If the candidate is not one of the few fortunates possessing his own "sphere of influence," he needs money from the central headquarters.

Thus the "independent" or minor party candidate appears in somewhat different light. He may be, and often is, an actual free-lance supported and financed by local bosses entrenched so strongly that they fear no rivals; as a Diet member he is free to pick and choose the party offering the highest bid. When a party is in national discredit, he may be a silent unacknowledged sympathizer prepared to show his proper colors after election. At one election, when Progressives feared they could not win in Hokkaido, every party candidate campaigned and won as an independent. Instances have also been common when major parties have made deals, the favored candidates running unattached to conceal the agreement.

Little can be done to reduce the number of independent candidates for whom such deals have been arranged; but usually the camouflaged candidate can disguise himself but once. For this reason, the 114 successful independent and small-party men in the 1947 elections fell off to 24 members for five small parties and 12 independents and in 1952 to 4 splinter-party men and 19 independents. The general situation, however, remains far from satisfactory.

To cure obvious evils whose cause and probable implications he did not comprehend, a wholly incompetent Occupationnaire embarked upon a dangerous experiment.

Not realizing that despotic political parties could not possibly create democracy, and not bothering to consult political experts who were readily available, a Government Section attaché told Japanese that party loyalty was more important than capable candidates. To choose independents, he said, imperiled democracy. Rejecting the argument that straight-party voting had proved dangerous, he demanded that Japanese vote party labels, irrespective of candidates. A split ticket, he said, was a crime against good citizenship. He went so far as to propose that ballots be prepared containing only party names and emblems, so that after election each party president might select for office the number of candidates proportionate to the party votes cast. Although critics of his plan were incorrectly assured that this was a command decision verbally received from General Whitney, they persisted in their opposition and defeated the proposal.

Soon afterwards, a successor, equally unqualified by education or experience, drafted another scheme designed to eliminate independents and small parties from campaigning. His proposal forbade parties to amalgamate or to dissolve, except by majority vote of all members—the term was undefined—and banned party shifts or expulsions within three months after election or between the resignation of a Prime Minister and the choosing of a successor. No party was to appear upon the ballot unless it had at least one Diet member or had cast, at the preceding general election, at least 1 per cent of the total vote for the

House of Representatives. Parties were excluded from contesting for seats in the House of Councilors unless they had received 6 per cent of the vote in a local, or 10 per cent in a national, election.

The Japanese press, usually silent when the Occupation proposed legislation of which it disapproved, burst out in chorus, *Yomiuri* thundering that the proposal would forever continue bossism and *Jiji Shimpo* declaring that the plan was "Fascist, absurd and betraying an ignorance of psychology." Shizue Kato, whose relations with Government Section had always been extremely cordial, said publicly that the Occupation officer whom she held responsible knew nothing of political science but, "tired of having always been a policeman, wished to be remembered by some constructive piece of legislation."

The answer to the unanimous press opposition was a House of Representatives subcommittee amendment to the bill, denying recognition to parties that held fewer than twenty seats unless they had cast 2 per cent of the vote at the last preceding election for Representatives or, in the case of Councilors, 12 per cent in the local and 16 per cent in the national constituency. In all probability these requirements were raised to impossible heights in order to assure the bill's defeat, for, under its provisions, only the Liberal, Democratic, and Socialist parties could have campaigned for locally elected Councilors, and only the Socialists could have run candidates on the national ticket. If this was indeed the purpose the maneuver proved successful, for the bill died.

Consideration of these extraordinary measures during 1947 when an Occupation, supposedly dedicated to democracy and free enterprise, sought to freeze in power the corrupt feudal bosses and to prevent Japan from competition in the political field concentrated attention upon the need for reform. While, as *Jiji Shimpo* said, politicians could not be purified until the intellectual and moral levels of society were raised, and while Occupation fiat could not raise these, a start was possible if party regulations were revised. Half-hearted movements among the Liberals and the Progressives had already produced a partial change under which Diet party members would select members of the executive committees, and insurgent movements in all parties had somewhat liberalized machinery; but much remained to be accomplished.

Yet progress had been made. The parties were not democratic, but the boss system was no longer headed by unified big business; and so it was easier to shatter. Control by profit-seeking contractors existed, but on a lesser scale; and its vulnerability was shown in 1948, when the engineering and contracting syndicate behind the Socialists was dragged into the open and pried loose. Underworld influence continued on the lower levels, but racketeers vanished from Diet membership. Laborers and peasants did not yet enjoy their proportion of political management, but they, like women, were increasingly conscious of their rights. Although democracy had not arrived the ground swell was running strongly.

Withdrawal of the Occupation removed the need for much hypocrisy. Parties no longer mouthed alien slogans to win MacArthur's favor. Yusuke Tsurumi no longer pretended that his platform was a "blend of Gandhi, Sun Yat-sen, and the New Deal"; nor did Inukai proclaim that he was working for a Welfare State.

Optimistically, the Occupation boasted that political rejuvenation was an important indication of Japan's spiritual revolution; but evils necessarily resulted from its failure to impose political integrity, or even common honesty, upon politicians unprepared for democratic ways. Thus, Japan seemed to retrogress—but only from a lofty peak which existed only in the Occupation's own imagining; for, having claimed rejuvenation, Occupation officers dared not report its non-existence but, on the other hand, felt an impulsion to show still higher ascents.

The true level of Japanese political maturity is low—far below that which the Occupation claimed, but higher than before the war. Issues are still between persons and not policies; but at least they may be fought out honestly. Japan blended its new democracy with ancient custom, but by a healthy evolution rather than the unions of discordant elements which the Occupation tried to bring about.

TEN

Puppet Diet

The Diet fought a losing battle.

Holding all the high cards under the 1947 Constitution whereby it became the highest organ of the state, the sole source of legislative power, with all Government agencies under its command, the Diet threw away its assets. The Prime Minister, whom it elected from its membership, and the Cabinet, half of whom must also be Diet members, were subject to its orders; but in actual fact they dominated the legislative branch. Increasingly, power gravitated to the Prime Minister, or reverted to the bureaucracy, a process seldom slowed down by Diet opposition.

Certainly the postwar Diet started with everything in its favor. MacArthur's men, following directives from President Truman and the Chiefs of Staff, not only insisted that the Diet be supreme but ruthlessly purged from public life all those who hesitated in making laws to that effect. Nor were laws alone relied upon; Cabinet members came down from their high seats to places on the floor of the chamber as visual symbols of their loss of status, while the Speaker of the House, like the Chief Justice, received precedence not only in court rank but in access to MacArthur.

But, accompanying this increased prestige were indications that the Occupation itself was not impressed by the Diet's newly granted dignity. Notwithstanding the acclaim of the Diet as sole legislative agency, Government Section made it clear that every Diet step must follow Occupation orders. By constitutional provisions the Diet had full rights to pass upon the eligibility of its members and to discipline itself; but

113

in practice it could do nothing without Government Section approval. No bill or resolution could be introduced, much less debated or enacted, until it had been cleared by Whitney's office. A Diet member never dare initiate or improvise; he must guard his tongue in speeches, and he must heed advice upon his vote.

No doubt such strict controls were needed for security as well as for efficient advancement of free government; and had this iron discipline been openly admitted it could have been condoned. Seldom, if ever, had the Diet in the past been free to act as it desired; but Occupation-naires mistakenly attempted to conceal their guidance. High Occupation officers in public statements, press releases, and inspired comment praised the freedom granted to Japan, while simultaneously they issued orders that could not be ignored.

Occupation apologists could, and often did, deny that such orders were given to the Diet; and, strictly speaking, none were issued. The entire list of more than 6,000 SCAPINS—instructions from the Supreme Commander for the Allied Powers—contains not one command to the Diet. No written orders were dispatched. Little can be shown to indicate that certain action was required or other proposals flatly disallowed; but, daily, politicians of all ranks and from all parties, including the Prime Minister and his Cabinet Ministers, came humbly to the sixth floor of MacArthur's headquarters in the Dai Ichi Building to ask Whitney or his underlings for guidance. A politician wishing to shift his party membership, to join or shun a common front with Communism, to hold commemorative exercises in honor of war dead, even to move his lodgings, humbly craved permission. Perhaps the caution was unnecessary, as Government Section personnel sometimes pointed out; but so fixed was the belief that every move was dictated by Occupation wishes that few but the Communists dared disregard precautions.

As in the prewar days when Diet members were dominated by bureaucratic bosses, so, under the Occupation, legislators learned to read between the lines. Government Section, as well as other Occupation offices, carefully refrained from giving clear and definite instructions; but politicians gleaned from hints, a smile, or a frown an understanding of what would be approved and what would be rejected. A casual flippancy from one high-placed colonel concerning a politician of whom he had never heard and of whose policies he knew nothing caused a party rift that wrecked a Cabinet.

Of course, the system was abused. Liaison officers coming from the Diet to consult GHQ officials returned with verbal "orders" never intended, and often never even spoken, by any SCAP official. Thus marplots disarmed the opposition, permitting bills to pass that otherwise might have been delayed, and strengthening their hold upon both their party and the Diet itself. Sometimes interpreters, aware that only one or two section chiefs and few members of their staff could speak formal Japanese, distorted matters for their own peculiar ends. Naïve Occupationnaires, warned that such skullduggery was rife, disregarded the warnings as vicious rumors spread by malcontents.

Under such conditions the legislative body had no real freedom. Occupation wishes, transmitted through soft suggestions of Commander Swope and Dr. Williams, Whitney's legislative officers, were far more potent than even the orders of prewar bureaucrats and military men, who had at least permitted opposition voices to be heard, even if they later expelled the recalcitrant from Diet membership. No one, except the Communists, dared publicly criticize an Allied "request" or "suggestion".

Perhaps, indeed, the system really saved the Diet's face. If the laws passed under Occupation pressure were acceptable, the Diet took the credit; if they were bad, politicians shifted blame to Occupation orders. It also served MacArthur's purpose by permitting the myth that Japanese, filled with democratic spirit, initiated changes, and that the Occupation held reins loosely or not at all. Thus, if reforms succeeded, GHQ-SCAP reaped a reputation for wise guidance, especially in America; if by any mishap they failed, no blame fell upon MacArthur's men.

The method, apparently sometimes endorsed by MacArthur himself, was no monopoly of Government Section. Professor John Phillips of Yamagata University noted, for example, that while SCAP's Civil Information and Education Section had implied in May, 1948, that it held essentially major responsibility for educational reform, its chief, Colonel Nugent, had written to him in December, 1951, explicitly disclaiming the implication. Nugent insisted that CIE had made no attempt at any time to impose or enforce patterns or techniques but had merely recommended, without directing, action. The disclaimer would have startled Japanese educators, few of whom had ever dared disregard a CIE suggestion.

Diet members, having no stomach for political suicide, heeded anyone who seemed to speak for GHQ. Diet initiative was low, if not non-

existent; but, in all fairness, it must be recognized that this was nothing
new. Seldom in the Diet's sixty-two-year history had members taken
an aggressive or determined stand, or challenged precedent; such exceptions as Ozaki and Saito were rare. Similarly, postwar editorials in such
great newspapers as *Mainichi, Yomiuri,* and *Asahi* complaining that
the Diet was intellectually bankrupt echoed prewar accusations.

Ironically, since few Occupation executives were well versed in Japanese political history many Diet members who had stood firm against
the militarists became anathema to the Occupation. Ignorant or forgetful that leading prewar politicians had fought for parliamentarianism
against totalitarianism, unaware that virtually every Diet since 1890
had battled against clan government and bureaucracy, Occupation officers ruthlessly purged Diet members who had survived. A touchstone
was the vote against Takao Saito in 1940 when he had challenged the
army's China policy. Diet members who, for whatever reason, voted
to expel him fell automatically under the purge, which of course eliminated the diehard militarists; but members who voted to retain him in
the Diet, whether because they were pacifists or because they were more
militarist than Tojo, were praised. A second criterion was endorsement
by Tojo in the 1942 campaign. No Diet member who failed both tests
remained in public life. Thus, few experienced prewar Diet members
who had held important party or official posts were eligible for early
postwar Diets.

The purges further weakened Diet power since, during the greater
part of the Occupation period, only untried men or second-raters were
left available for office. The situation may be readily visualized in a
parallel: Had a victorious Japan imposed surrender terms upon the
United States, could a powerful Congress have been composed of pro-
Japanese, pacifists, and neophytes?

Justin Williams, who was perhaps closer to the Diet than any other
American, believed that even the most seasoned legislators were at the
mercy of the all-powerful political organizations. Although he realized
the Japanese passion for group action, for individual anonymity, and
for collective responsibility, he battled manfully for recognition of the
dignity of the individual Diet member. Yet, at the very moment that
he strove as chief of one Government Section division to break the
party shackles, a colleague of equal stature clamored for tighter party
discipline. While Williams urged the Japanese to elect able men regardless of their party his neighbor pleaded that they vote a party label

regardless of the candidate. Wise leadership would have prevented or resolved the conflict that so bewildered Japanese voters; but the leadership was not forthcoming.

Lack of leadership or of adequate explanation prevented certain innovations from winning headway. Americans desired to substitute for the formal interpellations customary in the Diet the more spontaneous rough-and-tumble of floor debates; they thought that chaotic heckling should give way to politer cross-talk; they urged Diet members to adopt a "free discussion" system whereby a legislator might raise such questions as he thought important. These policies were suggested to the Diet leaders and were accepted at least in theory, because desired by Occupation leaders; but when the Occupation contented itself with this the innovations failed to flower. Few Japanese had any real idea of what was wanted; nor were they told in any great detail.

Plans to popularize the American committee system also lagged. This had greater possibility of success since it seemed to be in close conformity to Japanese preferences and, if successful, would help promote the myth of unanimous decision. Committees were accordingly set up, as before the war, and chairmen were dignified not only in prestige but by such tangible benefits as official motorcars and free gasoline; but little was accomplished. Committees became miniature Diets, with the same formal interpellation system and with even greater pressure by bureaucrats and politicians upon committee members than upon the Diet members as a whole. Even the Western-minded *Nippon Times* denounced the committee innovation; it asserted that consideration of controversial matters in small groups facilitated bribery and, by relieving the greater number of Diet members of responsibility for decisions, induced carelessness and recklessness in legislation.

Still less success followed efforts to promote independent action. Under prewar Diet rules speaking time had been allotted, patronage had been awarded, and perquisites had been doled out not to members personally but to the parties to which they belonged; moreover, parties with fewer than twenty-five adherents were largely excluded from such advantages. Although Williams deplored the practice he faced such strong opposition, not only among traditionally minded Japanese but within his own Government Section, that he could accomplish no lasting reform. "The individual member," he concluded, "stands for nothing; the party is all-powerful." For such reasons no Japanese Diet member became well known unless he was a party official, a Cabinet minister, or a member of such long standing that he could not be ignored. The independent member enjoyed respect and deference but comparatively little power.

Not only was the would-be independent thus virtually gagged unless he accepted the party shackles which Williams tried in vain to break, but, unless he was as outstanding as Ozaki, he faced difficulties in re-election. The peculiar election laws, proposed by Japanese but unthinkingly endorsed by one of Whitney's amateurs, favored party spokesmen, bosses, bureaucrats, and their obedient stooges but handicapped the independent. Forbidden to use freely press, radio, or television, limited in the length and frequency of campaign speeches, denied editorial or cartoon support, restricted in the use of posters or automobiles, forbidden even to ask a next-door neighbor for his vote, the individual could not make himself widely known to the electorate. Even if a strong ground swell existed for him, he gained little advantage since newspapers were forbidden either to conduct public opinion polls on preferences for candidates or to publish the results of those taken by others.

Obedient party members, while subject to precisely the same restrictive regulations in campaigning, profited by boss or party support. The use of the party label, denied to aspirants not formally endorsed by party leaders, was of course a valuable aid; but the receipt of party funds was even greater. In the 1952 Diet election, for example, the Liberal Party had 229,000,000 yen to spend—an average of more than 500,000 yen for each contested seat, which was much more than the individual candidate was himself legally allowed; other parties, with smaller campaign funds, ran fewer candidates but lavished huge amounts upon their favored members. As a large part of the great sums was given by corporations—Japan's biggest iron and steel company contributing 13,000,000 yen to the four major parties—the successful candidates were expected to be properly appreciative.

Former Agriculture Minister Rikizo Hirano told a Diet committee in February, 1954, that corruption struck deeper. The Hozen Keizai Kai, a bankrupt loan company with political support in the three major parties, had, he said, given 24,000,000 yen to five Diet members, including two other former Cabinet ministers, and to the Liberal Party. Hirano, whose past record had not been immaculate, admitted receipt of 3,000,000 yen, a motor car and what he described as an office building.

The confession inspired other charges. Rumors had long been current that nine large steamship companies had distributed lavish bribes in order to obtain operation subsidies; in addition, three high company officials had been indicted for embezzling 150,000,000 yen. Yasuhiro Nakasone, one of the Young Turks of the Progressive Party, then charged two Cabinet ministers, neither of them noted for financial rectitude, with having accepted bribes of 1,000,000 yen each. Nakasone had previously attained some notoriety for a boast—wholly without foundation—that it was he who had induced Vice President Nixon to call the no war clause an American mistake but on this occasion he seemed to have some basis for his charge. A Liberal Party executive returned 2,500,000 yen sent to him "by mistake" but was none the less indicted for alleged corruption.

Nowhere was the weakness of the Diet member more apparent than in his inability to push legislation through the Diet. Swope and Williams tried to teach the Western custom of dropping bills into the hopper for consideration on their merits; but even yet no Japanese law is commonly referred to by its sponsor's name, as are American enactments. Private members might introduce bills, and were no longer humiliated by seeing them remain at the foot of the calendar until all Cabinet bills were disposed of; but results were negative. In the first five Diets following surrender only two such laws, beyond ten bills necessary to put the Constitution into effect, were enacted, and one of these was to regulate horse racing; but two hundred and twenty-four Cabinet laws were passed. This, too, reflected prewar custom since, in the 50th Diet in 1925, said to have been the most democratic prewar assembly, the Cabinet passed fifty-one of its fifty-five proposals whereas, of forty-two private bills, all but four were beaten. In 1952 Yoshida ordered his Liberal Party to cut down on private bills. "They impair the dignity of the Diet, undermine the people's confidence in parliamentary government, and lead to fascism."

Subdued and regimented Diet members, while theoretically masters of the Cabinets whom they elected, remained mere members of a debating society free only to choose their leader. Propagandists alleged that the subordination grew out of Ito's plot to give Japan the façade but not the reality of democratic government, or out of the theories of the Tokyo Imperial University clique headed by Shinkichi Uyesugi to keep the Emperor as dictator. It resulted rather from Japan's legislative immaturity and a social and political system that suppressed individualism. Tatsukichi Minobe's teaching that the Emperor is but an organ of the state with the Diet as his independent legislative partner, while approved by the Occupation, was too advanced for Japanese. The new Constitution disarmed the Emperor; but the Cabinet, and especially the Prime Minister, reigned in his stead.

Condemnation of all private bills as pork-barrel legislation designed only to build up personal popularity reflected the tendency to consider the individual member not as a representative of his constituency but as a cog in the political machine to serve the interests of the Prime Minister and his administration.

Minor triumphs, to be sure, were achieved. Cabinet members no longer sat in lofty splendor above the level of the legislators; their bills no longer took precedence, nor might the Cabinet withdraw a bill once offered to the Diet. Unless a minister was recognized from the chair he had no right to speak; but if called upon by either house he must appear and account for his actions. These were advances in democracy over prewar methods, but they were secondary. It was more significant that the Cabinet controlled the Diet, that all important bills were Cabinet-directed—according to the *Mainichi* private bills are chiefly graft and gambling licenses—that the Diet waited lethargically until the Cabinet decided upon action, and that the Cabinet too frequently usurped legislative rights.

Unhappily, this usurpation was done by the example and, probably, by the inspiration of the Occupation itself. Early in the Occupation, in order to assure prompt compliance with requirements of the surrender terms and of Occupation orders, the device called "Potsdam Ordinance" was developed—an Imperial or a Cabinet decree issued in time of emergency and having the force of law. How many such decrees were promulgated is impossible to ascertain, since the Potsdam Ordinances were but units in hundreds of other regulations; but at least seventy-eight in a two-year period dealt with matters of political and social interest.

When, therefore, a Diet balked at passing legislation desired or favored by the Occupation, or by the Cabinet, a Potsdam Ordinance appeared. Farmers, for example, demurred at surrendering to the Government more rice than had been set by quota; they termed the demand for more "unfair discrimination" and alleged that they were penalized to help the city dweller. Two Diets failed to pass the bill, nor could Dr. Williams' strongest efforts change the vote. Accordingly, in December, 1949, a complaisant Cabinet, even though a Diet was in session, put the law into effect, at the very time, it happened, when the Agriculture Minister was promising that a Potsdam Ordinance would not be issued. Similarly, in 1950 the Cabinet by-passed the Diet to put through an ordinance reorganizing the electric power industry.

ELEVEN

Highest Organ

Disregard of the highest organ of the state may have been unavoidable; but after all the enthusiastic propaganda praising the Diet it seemed to be yet another demonstration that Japanese democracy was superficial, and that even the professed liberals of the Occupation scorned parliamentary methods. The Cabinet heard protests that it had insulted the Diet, that it had preached hypocritically of legislative supremacy by cynically adopting prewar totalitarian methods, and that Potsdam Ordinances negated democracy itself. Yoshida was accused of reverting to his bureaucratic past.

The charges were not only unfortunate but, as applied to the Cabinet, uncalled for. Irrespective of Yoshida's individual preferences and those of his Cabinet, the fact remains that Douglas MacArthur had forced the unpopular actions. It was bad enough that the Occupation thus undercut its own high principles; but it was unpardonable that it obliged its puppets to shoulder the responsibility. Yoshida did not feel free to tell all the truth about the situation. Not until the furore over the electric power ordinance had died down did International Trade and Industry Minister Shigemi Yokoo or Chief Cabinet Secretary Katsuo Okazaki dare admit that MacArthur not only had ordered its issuance but had drafted its contents. They did not, however, venture even then to publish the contents of the MacArthur command.

Japanese disinclination to wrangle publicly compromised four other clashes in which the Diet, after vigorously protesting Cabinet pronouncements, did, of its own accord, precisely what the Cabinet had said must be accomplished. In 1946 the Speaker, Senzo Higai, objected to a Cabinet announcement that it would revise the rule of parliamentary procedure; the matter, he insisted, was the Diet's own affair. Accordingly, the House of Representatives proceeded to consider the revision and put forth the Cabinet's proposal, retaining forty-eight of the rules adopted in 1889, modifying forty-one other rules, accepting four prewar Diet regulations, and copying two more from the Meiji Constitution. Most of the remaining thirty-seven paragraphs were those recommended by Government Section.

Twice during 1947 chief Cabinet secretaries, Joji Hayashi and Suyehiro Nishio, a Liberal and a Socialist, informed the Diet that the Cabinet would tell it when and how long to meet. On each occasion the Speaker protested; but Takashi Yamazaki was overruled in January, and while Komakichi Matsuoka thundered resoundingly, "The Diet receives no direction on such matters," he did as he was ordered. It may be wholly coincidental that Yoshida thereafter disciplined the two Liberal Party Speakers, Higai and Yamazaki, severely, giving other reasons.

An argument in November, 1948, caused by Yoshida's boast that he would dissolve the Diet, involved Occupation authorities. Yoshida was not in power at the moment, but everybody knew his accession was imminent. The tottering Socialist-Democratic coalition, weakened by graft accusations that involved the Prime Minister, retorted that only the Diet could dissolve itself—a statement ratified by Government Section. Yoshida, however, went to General Headquarters and returned with assurances that "the highest quarters" had given permission. Accordingly, the Diet was dissolved; but, to save everybody's face, authorization for the dissolution was given both by Yoshida and by the coalition.

The Cabinet thus carried its point on four occasions, although never in a clear-cut victory; but the Diet failed in counteroffensives. Yoshida's failure to attend Diet sessions, once because he had a cold, again because he had "liaison business" with an American, but more often because he thought the session was insufficiently important to warrant his attention, roused storms of protest from an Opposition which accused him of "ignoring the importance of the Diet." Impeachment was threatened, but no action was ever taken. In 1949, also, a hothead Liberal, Eikichi Kambayashima, in an excess of national pride demanded the impeachment of Finance Minister Hayato Ikeda for sponsoring Joseph M. Dodge's demand as financial adviser to SCAP for a balanced budget.

Yoshida retorted by insisting that Kambayashima be expelled from the party. Cooler heads prevailed, and Kambayashima thereafter received neither party nor Diet preferment. The Dodge plan was adopted.

Not only did the Diet fail to hold the leadership bestowed upon it by the Constitution, but the House of Representatives lost prestige. According to the Constitution the numerically larger House of Representatives—466 members as compared to the 250-member House of Councilors—is the ruling body. Any bill passed by the Representatives but defeated by the Councilors or pigeonholed for sixty days becomes a law if the Representatives repasses it by a two-thirds vote. Budgets and treaties become law when passed once by the Representatives, irrespective of action in the Councilors. In conference committees and in all other joint activities the Representatives always have a majority; and the Speaker presides over joint sessions and is the Diet's spokesman on all formal occasions. The President of the House of Councilors (successor to the House of Peers), formerly an extremely high state officer, now ranks below the Prime Minister, the Speaker, and the Chief Justice.

Subordination of the Councilors, though they serve six years as against the Representatives' maximum of four years and though they hold office irrespective of a dissolution that unseats the Representatives, rose from anxiety to prevent the reappearance of a privileged upper house. The House of Peers had never been popular, and revision of it had been planned even prior to the war, with vocational representation instead of hereditary membership of the nobility. Following surrender, the resignation or forcible removal of 178 members out of 415 afforded opportunity to carry through reforms.

Conservative Japanese, including a special committee in the House of Peers itself, proposed the vocational representation plan, specifying lawyers, doctors, scholars, scientists, educators, and literary men as worthy of membership. State Minister Tokujiro Kanamori and Home Minister Seiichi Omura, briefed by Government Section, dismissed the idea as totalitarian and insisted that both Representatives and Councilors be selected by the same voters, citizens over twenty years of age, with all the Representatives chosen by districts and half the Councilors chosen at large and the other half by prefectures. The Kanamori-Omura proposal was adopted, but the idea of vocational representation did not die; as late as 1952 a committee on constitutional reform revived the recommendation.

The truth is that most Japanese wholly failed to understand the function of the House of Councilors; they see no need for two houses each chosen by the same electors, particularly as Representatives were understood to be national, and not local, officers. In spite of the lack of privilege accorded by the Constitution, they looked upon the Councilors as of higher status.

The official Election Management Commission apparently shared this misconception. In May, 1950, it issued thousands of explanatory posters reading, "The Upper House restrains the Lower House when the latter becomes an arena of political struggle or when the majority party in it becomes oppressive." Only the *Jiji Shimpo* newspaper appeared to be shocked by the implications that the Councilors were a restraining force, that the House of Representatives should be anything else than "an arena of political struggle," or that majority rule was somehow undesirable.

Much of the higher regard for the Councilors sprang, no doubt, from misbehavior in the House of Representatives. This, too, was a prewar heritage which new-found responsibility failed to cure. On at least a dozen occasions after surrender large-scale brawls—some of them involving a score of members and one, in March, 1947, lasting eleven days— turned the House of Representatives into a free-for-all. A five-day roughhouse in November, 1947, set off by acrimonious charges of bribery and marked by drunken misbehavior, caused the usually conservative *Nippon Times* to head an editorial "Diet or Zoo," and inspired the veteran Ozaki to demand resignations of those responsible for disorder. When the resignations were not offered, he sadly wondered whether self-immolation was required of him to bring Diet members to their senses. Belatedly the Discipline Committee suspended two members for thirty days and another for fifteen days.

Save for a seriocomic interlude in December, 1948, when the drunken Finance Minister, Senroku Izumiyama, bit a woman Diet member on the cheek and loudly assured her, "I love you more than the supplemental budget," the Diet remained peaceful; but in April, 1949, Williams found it necessary to remind the members that they must maintain the Diet's dignity. Within a month, however, the most spectacular riot in the Diet's history occurred, induced by a Socialist charge that the Cabinet had, of its own volition, amended a pending measure. Speaker Kijuro Shidehara and Deputy Prime Minister Joji Hayashi offered assurances that this would not again occur; but meanwhile a Liberal Party member, Toramatsu Konishi, had seized a Communist by the necktie, and the Communist had retaliated by striking him upon the head. Konishi, insulted, summoned twenty gangsters to "restore the honor of their boss" by assaulting Communist members. "Had this happened outside the House," Konishi declared, "every one of these thirty-five Communists would die." The matter was ended when the Communist permitted Konishi to strike him twice upon the head. None of these incidents harmed any of the participants, all being reelected except the Communist, and he had been purged.

Actions such as these called forth another *Nippon Times* editorial denouncing the "national disgrace." Gang fights and street brawls, the paper said, were not the actions of responsible men in their right minds. "It's no wonder that public confidence in the Diet has remained at a low ebb." Yet five days after the Konishi outbreak, sixteen Councilors fought to pull the vice president off the rostrum. The effect upon the general public was profound, since there had never been a disturbance during the fifty-six years' existence of the House of Peers.

At the expiration of the 6th postwar Diet in December, 1949, Yoshida took the members to task for mud-slinging, vituperation, and violence. "Pandemonium reigns in both houses," he said. "It is a shameful spectacle that shows we have not mastered the rudiments of parliamentary government." He repeated his strictures against the Diet in 1952, accusing it of undermining popular confidence in democratic government.

Instead of inducing reform, the rebukes led to angry complaints that Yoshida had insulted the Diet. Unbridled heckling and rowdyism continued. Despite constant editorial warnings, every Diet session was marred by such turbulence that tram conductors quelled drunken outbursts by reminding passengers, "This is a streetcar, not the Diet."

Little shame was shown by Diet members. A parliamentary vice minister assaulted an opposition member because "I wanted to prove I was not drunk." A deputy secretary-general of the majority party, objecting to shrill heckling by a woman Opposition member, turned angrily and shouted, "Shut up, you streetwalker." But these affairs occurred during the unprecedented heat wave of August, 1953, and the House disciplinary committee graciously decided to overlook the incidents.

Far from feeling ashamed of rowdyism, at least one Diet member, caught by newsreel cameras in the act of storming the Speaker's rostrum, distributed hundreds of free movie tickets to his constituents that they might witness and, he assumed, admire his exploits.

The Diet could assume a lofty attitude when it desired to do so.

Yoshida, whose quick temper frequently flared into angry outbursts, lost his head in the heat of interpellations in March, 1953, and muttered that his tormenter was *bakayaro,* which may be politely translated as "damn' fool." Both the Opposition and disgruntled Hatoyama Liberals seized upon this "slip of the tongue" to censure him for seriously insulting the Diet's dignity and passed a no-confidence motion against him. Yoshida immediately dissolved the Diet and called for new elections. In the *"bakayaro* campaign" which followed, Yoshida's party was returned with a sharply reduced majority.

Militant minorities have seldom won such spectacular success as in the unprecedented discipline motion against Yoshida or the no-confidence vote. They therefore usually resorted to filibusters, seven of them within the first five years under the new Constitution, and perfected a new technique in 1953 of so surrounding presiding officers, especially committee chairmen, that the latter could not adjourn sessions or even leave the chair to visit washrooms. This method, copied from precedents established by Communist repatriates returning from Siberia, replaced earlier practices of walking out of proceedings.

Violence and filibustering were bad enough, shaking what *Mainichi* in August, 1953, called "the by-no-means stable foundation of democratic parliamentary politics in this country"; corruption was much worse. While this, too, was in the Japanese tradition, the era following surrender, supposedly one of spiritual regeneration, broke all records for bribery and malpractice. Within fifteen months after the new Constitution became effective, fifteen Diet members had been arrested; and only one of them was acquitted. Nor were these the sole offenders; the Procurator's Office, in an official statement, regretted that amnesties and stays of prosecution had prevented trying thirty-nine others.

Similar wholesale prosecutions, especially for election frauds, were threatened in the closing days of 1952. The House of Representatives in a precedent-making move, suddenly announced over the protest of the House of Councilors that the Diet would be prolonged an additional ninety-nine days. As no pressing legislation was under consideration the press virtually unanimously declared that the only purpose of extension was to extend the Diet members' period of immunity from arrest until the statute of limitations would prevent offenders—including, it was said, Foreign Minister Katsuo Okazaki—from being brought to trial. The charge seemed to be borne out by the singular reluctance of opposition parties to oppose an otherwise purposeless Diet prolongation.

The series of disorders, incompetences, corruptions, and political maneuvers, according to Yomiuri, brought the prestige of the national Diet to the brink of ruin—a statement which other papers echoed.

The postwar period produced the most far-reaching bribery case in Japanese history, with corruption by the Showa Denko engineering and chemical interests of at least a score of Diet members, among them leading political figures and Cabinet Ministers that periled even former Prime Minister Hitoshi Ashida. During the course of this and other revelations, political *kuromaku,* vote-peddlers, lobbyists, and fixers, freely implicated scores of Diet members as having taken bribes. Few violators were punished, even though admitting their guilt; and one man, former Deputy Prime Minister Suyehiro Nishio, was acquitted because he had received cash "in his private capacity and not as a political leader."

Even when the Diet maintained order it seemed to be unable to function efficiently. Failure to agree upon agenda, indecision of party leaders, and slothfulness of arrival caused sessions to open late, and two-hour delays occurred twenty-two times in the 1st National Diet, twenty times in the 2nd Diet, twenty-one times in the 3rd Diet, and seventeen times in the 4th.

While Japanese laid far more stress than Americans upon regularity of attendance, absenteeism was chronic. When Yoshida laid the draft Constitution before the House of Representatives only 96 of the 466 members were present, with 110 spectators (including 46 schoolgirls) in the galleries. A year later Speaker Yamazaki warned 137 absentees that they must attend; but 239 stayed away the next day. Only 35 of the 466 members attended every session; and 56 members missed every meeting of what *Mainichi* called the Truant Diet. In April, 1948, General Whitney wrote a letter virtually commanding Diet members to appear in the House; but, even then, the best attended session had 184 absentees. In spite of telegrams summoning delinquents to attend, 221 members were not on hand to hear Yoshida's policy speech in December, 1948.

Among the Councilors a similar situation prevailed. Less than half the membership attended the opening sessions in 1949, and after fifty-eight days four members had not yet appeared. One Councilor answered every roll call, but only twenty attended even one-third of the sessions.

Spectator interest also lagged, average daily attendance in the galleries falling from 596 in 1946 to 567 in 1947 and 480 in 1948. The decline was camouflaged by a practice of clearing the galleries every fifteen minutes so that guests who tarried were counted twice or oftener; thus daily attendance records showed an average of 1,500 in 1950 and 2,672 in 1951.

A partial explanation for the lack of interest may be the deadening effect of the set-speech policy, spectators finding Diet proceedings dull unless unhappily enlivened by rowdyism or heckling; but some of it is traceable to Diet disregard of public participation in its affairs. Williams and other Occupation officials urged the public to assist the Diet by submitting petitions, appeals, and memorials for consideration. In the first fifteen Diets following surrender, 20,059 petitions were received by the House of Representatives; but more than 25 per cent were thrown into the scrap basket and, while 14,830 were referred to the Cabinet—not to the House of Representatives—very few were ever considered. Of 9,386 appeals filed in the Lower House, only 133 received committee attention. By March, 1953, the Diet's Recording Office admitted that it did not even bother to acknowledge receipt of such communications.

Tamotsu Murayama, a veteran press political analyst, reported that visitors object to what he termed the Diet's "feudalistic policy." No ordinary visitor, he pointed out, entered the ornate main entrance. All Japanese were "frisked" for weapons; but, even so, guards stood on watch, facing the guests and backs to members, to prevent untoward incidents. This practice was a carry-over from the turbulent 1925 session when an irate ultranationalist flung a live snake into the middle of the crowded chamber. Murayama, moreover, deprecated the custom of addressing every Diet member, irrespective of age or ability, as *sensei*— the respectful salutation supposedly reserved only for the learned.

Diet managers showed faulty planning. Custom calls for lengths of sessions to be set in advance: regular sessions, which must begin within the first ten days of December, usually are announced for 150 meetings; and special sessions, of which there have been sixteen since surrender, are estimated at whatever length seems necessary. Of twenty-four Diets convened since surrender, however, thirteen required more than the allotted time, the 5th Diet in 1949 and the 13th in 1952 each requiring five extensions. Three Diets, the 1st, 2nd, and the 13th, broke records for length of sitting. Of the eleven Diets held within the estimated limits, four were dissolved; three more were short convocations called for one specific purpose; and four could not be lengthened because another Diet was to meet next day.

Inefficiency was not due to lack of facilities. A special library, housed in the Crown Prince's former palace at Akasaka and stocked with books from the South Manchuria Railway collection, was available and was to be moved, under the able direction of Dr. Tokujiro Kanamori, to a new five-story ferro-concrete building on the site of the old German Embassy at Miyakezaka, adjacent to the Diet. Incorporation in it of the Ueno Municipal Library and the large Morrison Library of Oriental books, and purchase of other books, it was announced, would raise the collection to 10,000,000 volumes, making it the largest library in the East. As the Education Ministry had only recently announced that all the libraries in Japan then held only 9,600,000 books, few people took the announcement seriously. In 1954 the Diet Library owned only 1,000,000 books.

The Diet Building, an imposing white structure completed in 1936 at a cost of 26,500,000 yen, contains offices for Diet officials, for Cabinet ministers, for each of the standing committees, and for each party with more than twenty-five members. Much pride was voiced in the Diet Building as Tokyo's chief tourist attraction, replacing the Meiji and Yasukuni Shrines and the Sengakuji Temple, shrine of the legendary forty-seven Ronin, in popularity.

Quarters for individual members, particularly office space, have been restricted, but a special Office Building was erected near the Diet. To accommodate out-of-town members who could not easily find living space the Diet purchased the mansion of the former Prince Kitashirakawa. This relieved the strain on one Representative who had been living with nine regular members of his household, and two or three guests nightly, in a three-room house; of another whose family of four shared space equivalent to a room ten feet by eight; and of a third who lived in the party headquarters.

While salaries, as everywhere, were never as large as desired, the minimum for Diet members was placed at the highest rate paid to any Government official. Until the Prime Minister's pay was increased, in 1947, Tetsu Katayama, who then held the office, preferred his salary as Diet member to that as Prime Minister because as Diet member he received allowances for clerk hire, telephoning, hotel bills and transportation. The salary schedule was raised six times between May, 1947, and December, 1952, when it reached 78,000 yen a month. Diet members also enjoyed the franking privilege and free passes on the government railways; the Speaker, Vice Speaker, and all Cabinet ministers had free official residences.

Diet members themselves seemed to be quite content with their conditions. A twenty-four-man inspection committee, sent to America at the suggestion of Justin Williams, returned in 1950 with only minor recommendations. The innovations it recommended included forbidding the introduction of private bills unless sponsored by the Cabinet, by committees of the Diet, or by political parties, and opening committee meetings, as well as plenary sessions, to questions from the floor.

An earlier proposal to keep the Speaker nonpartisan failed. In 1946 after Speaker Higai asked his fellow Liberal, Prime Minister Yoshida, to change a Diet subcommittee's recommendation, Government Section spurred an agitation to take the speakership out of politics. Although a motion of no-confidence in Higai failed, 229 to 179, etiquette required Higai to resign. His successor, Takashi Yamazaki, a Government Section protégé, then announced that he would follow the British tradition by resigning his party membership, although he resumed it during the next campaign. Subsequent speakers, including three Liberals, rejected Yamazaki's precedent, one of them, Bamboku Ono, vigorously using the Speaker's prerogatives as a weapon in the 1953 campaign.

A precedent, however, had been established that the plurality party, regardless of ability to control the House, shall hold the Speakership with the second-ranking party winning the Vice Speakership.

While Japanese consistently and almost unanimously condemned the Diet for shortcomings, Occupationnaires usually professed pleasure over its progress toward democratic ways. Because the former considered immediate situations while the Occupation discerned long-range trends, MacArthur in 1948 praised the Diet for its "full implementation of the basic concepts of the democratic Constitution" at the very time that such newspapers as *Mainichi* were rebuking it for "setting a record for inefficiency." This was the Diet which, according to the *Nippon Times,* passed no good law except the Daylight Saving Act.

Few Japanese believe that postwar Diets compare favorably with probably imaginary high prewar standards. Lack of interest became apparent in the 1953 election, when only 1,042 candidates contested for 466 seats, an average of only 2.2 candidates per seat at a time when Japan had five major parties in addition to the Communists and a half-dozen splinter groups.

TWELVE

Yoshida, the Paradox

Japan forswore totalitarianism but did not uproot one-man rule, the Diet merely rubber-stamping the Prime Minister's decisions. Its weaknesses were apparent; but, since the Diet chose the Premier and could dismiss him, a façade of democracy veiled the continuing autocracy. Steadily power gravitated into Prime Minister Yoshida's hands until bureaucracy, civil service and budget affairs, economic control, foreign policy and treaty making, central police and army administration, relation with local communities, and special commission activities, all funneled through his office. The Prime Minister not only by-passed the Diet, in the rare instances when it proved to be recalcitrant, by himself issuing ordinances with the force of law; he sometimes overruled the Supreme Court by compelling rehearings of cases once decided.

Personnel increases reflected his power annexation, his staff more than tripling from 53,545 in 1946 to 164,498 in 1951, while he was clamoring for personnel reduction elsewhere. No other ministry as much as doubled its staff during the period, and several vitally important departments, including finance, welfare, labor, and construction, actually lost personnel.

An Occupation which preached democracy tolerated the growing autocratic trend. Military men who expected instant compliance with commands disliked a slow parliamentary process which opened opportunity for criticism, but thoroughly approved a system whereby they might order one responsible individual to produce immediate results.

Yoshida precisely fitted Occupation patterns. An old-fashioned mid-Victorian bureaucrat with a record of opposition to Japanese militarism, his psychology was virtually identical with that of many Occupation leaders. As Premier or Foreign Minister in all but thirteen months during the entire period after surrender he cooperated faithfully, and in the main successfully, with overlords whom he disliked and who cordially detested him.

Neither side concealed its feelings. When compelled to sponsor a measure which he thought socialistic, Yoshida obeyed; but, while doing so, he flaunted the white rose of a medieval rebel clan. Time and again he openly defied Occupation orders against consorting with purgees. Candidly and with unexampled courage, he told MacArthur that Occupation policies on police, civil service, and land reforms, purging, and budget matters were foolish. Occupation officers, in turn, damned Yoshida as a bullheaded, testy autocrat. They admitted, however, that he was no hypocrite, some of them admiring his unconcealed contempt for the Diets by whom he was elected to high office.

The stubby, portly Yoshida would have admitted cheerfully that few persons, Westerners or Japanese, liked him personally. A realist and a cynic, he understood thoroughly that he was a political accident, named as Prime Minister because no seasoned leader was available, and twice retained by minority vote only because the Opposition failed to agree upon a suitable replacement. He realized the intended insult when many Diet members, even in his own party, absented themselves or cast blank ballots in the vote for Prime Minister, and he made no effort to hide his low opinion of those who voted for him.

As Diet chief and president of the dominant Liberal Party, Yoshida found the cards stacked against him. Legislative and political personnel were second-rate, the upper strata of trained men having been skimmed off by the purge and the new administrators having no freedom of action. Yoshida, wholly inexperienced in political give and take, with neither aptitude in free discussion nor desire for it, with no ability to persuade and only the sketchiest knowledge of parliamentary practice, headed a Diet to which he had never previously been elected and led a political party of which he had never been a member, and which was not wholly loyal.

As Prime Minister he faced even more grievous problems. Japan was beaten, bankrupt, and disheartened; her industries were in ruins, her people faced famine, and leftist sentiment, seemingly under Occupation sponsorship, was rising dangerously.

No immediate recovery was feasible, yet Yoshida was buried under blame when Japan's future did not at once become bright and cheer-ful. Required to comply with Occupation demands, of which many were vaguely stated and some were distasteful to him, Yoshida assumed the thankless and politically dangerous task of introducing and enforc-ing unpopular requirements whose real sponsorship he was forbidden to divulge.

Thus, for five occupation years or more, Yoshida suffered constant attack and violent vilification by his political opponents, many of whom were fully conscious of the unfairness of their attacks. The cry "Down with Yoshida," voiced by Communists, was echoed stridently by Socialists, right-wing Progressives, and dissident Liberals.

Yoshida, while implacable in denouncing his enemies, offered surpris-ingly slight defense against their personal attacks. "I take things easy," he said. "Things will take their predestined courses." When Chikao Honda, president of the powerful *Mainichi* newspapers, advised him to cultivate political reporters, to hold more press conferences, and to talk more frequently to the people, he refused. To do so, he said, would be cheapening; to issue formal statements but once or twice a year would enhance his dignity.

Except in the heat of election campaigns, Yoshida was far from cultivating the press, or, as he would say, toadying to it; he would raise his walking stick to break the camera of a news photographer or would dowse a reporter with a glass of water.

Yoshida's actions, like his character, have been paradoxical. A tradi-tionalist, he steered Japan through political and social revolution. A cherisher of custom, he sponsored legislation that struck at the heart of social practices. A stickler for etiquette who fired a high-ranking subordinate for leaving a party before he himself was ready to go, and who, in Tokyo's tropic summers, insisted that Cabinet Ministers wear wool coats and sit at strict attention, he horrified tidy housewives by striding in dirty wooden clogs over the clean mats of his polling place. A practicing politician, he scorned the voter. To Japanese his white *tabi*, native socks, were symbols of reforms he sponsored; but when loyal followers sent him new pairs Yoshida flouted both elemen-tary politics and ordinary politeness by not even acknowledging them. Such people, he would have said, were unimportant folk not worth his while. An advocate of parliamentary government, who liked to be called "Japan's Churchill," he scorned legislative procedure, dictated the votes of his party members, and forbade them to introduce bills without his consent. A promoter of education and culture, he advised the Crown Prince to be an "English gentleman," with skill in riding, hunting, and fishing. It was, he said, not necessary for such a man to read too much. "Reading," he told the Prince, "is the beginning of worry."

Yoshida, who led Japan in democratic paths, was essentially an aristocrat and did not like the commoners. All Japanese who can afford to do so live secluded behind a wall, a hedge, or bamboo fences; but Yoshida went deeper into isolation. In Tokyo he occupied the French Renaissance style mansion of Prince Asaka, within extensive landscaped grounds; and although in theory it was the Foreign Minister's official residence he would not relinquish it. He much preferred, however, a seashore house at Oiso, forty miles from Tokyo, or a Hakone mountain retreat belonging to his friend Count Aisuke Kabayama. Both were more constricted than the Asaka palace and, by Western standards, would have seemed overcrowded; but he liked the neighbors better. The Mitsui and Sumitomo millionaires were close at hand, as was Fusanosuke Kuhara, the copper magnate, Marquis Muneaki Date whose ancestor sent the first Japanese envoy to the Vatican and Marquis Naomitsu Nabeshima who married an Imperial princess.

He held, moreover, one standard for himself and another for his people. As a prerequisite for economic recovery, he warned, Japan must live a Spartan life, economizing and rigidly eliminating every luxury lest essential foreign exchange be drained away; yet for himself he reserved choice foods and liquors, heavy Churchillian cigars, imported woolens, and one of the very few Rolls-Royces in the nation. He urged hard work for everyone yet prided himself on his laziness and procrastination. Insisting upon loyalty and justice, he antagonized even his closest friends by breaking firm promises. A bitter hater of secret political deals, he plotted and counterplotted to remain in power.

Yoshida was born September 22, 1878, in the year of the tiger, which means that he was destined to be determined and implacable. He came from Kochi on the island of Shikoku, a region famous as the home of the reformist Tosa clan and of people who demanded the right to do as they pleased. Shigeru was the fifth son of Dr. Tsuna Takeuchi, a laissez-faire economist and Diet member; but, as fifth sons have little chance to prosper, he was adopted as the heir of Kenzo Yoshida. After graduation from Tokyo Imperial University, whose Red Gate is the entrance to state preferment, he went into diplomacy. Marriage to

Yukie, eldest daughter of Count Nobuaki Makino, a trusted member of the inner Imperial circle, no doubt facilitated this career. Within seven years after passing through the Red Gate he had been sent to Tientsin, Mukden, and London and was secretary to the Governor General of Korea. He went to Washington in 1916, back to China in 1918; and in 1919 he was part of the Japanese peace delegation at Versailles. After further service in China and Sweden he became Vice Minister of Foreign Affairs for the Giichi Tanaka Cabinet and, when this fell, became ambassador to Italy and to England. In 1936, just after the army mutiny, Prime Minister Koki Hirota asked him to become Foreign Minister; but the army, disliking Count Makino, refused to accept his son-in-law for so important a position. This, as it happened, was fortunate because Yoshida took no part in the ultranationalist movements that followed, and retired two years later when he reached sixty—the age when, as Orientals believe, a man's life span is complete and he is reborn. Thus he escaped involvement in any activity which might have made him subject to the postwar purge. Although service in Giichi Tanaka's Cabinet was given as a reason for barring Ichiro Hatoyama from postwar public service, it was not applied to Yoshida.

Another Shigeru Yoshida, seven years younger, who had been Welfare Minister in the Yonai Cabinet during 1940, was not so lucky; he was purged as a war criminal. The two men, though bearing the same name, were not related.

Makino's son-in-law became a martyr for democracy. In 1945, when Japan's military star was setting, he asked Prince Konoye to make peace. For this he was arrested and jailed, but only briefly; emerging soon he became Foreign Minister in September, 1945, in the first postwar Cabinet under Prince Naruhiko Higashikuni. Yoshida insisted that he was Foreign Minister in fact, if not in title, continuously thereafter. Even during the thirteen months when he was nominally out of office, he says, he was MacArthur's agent to relay orders to the government. The boast may or may not have been true, but it was important that his Liberal Party members believed it to be true.

Whatever Yoshida may have known concerning the wishes of the Occupation, he knew comparatively little of Japan. Like MacArthur, Yoshida kept aloof from the people, talking to few and listening to fewer. His information, like MacArthur's, filtered through an ever narrowing circle of informants who told him only the things they wanted him to know. At first he drew upon old-time bureaucratic associates and upon fellow diplomats like Shidehara, nominally a political rival but in reality a close and trusted friend. He listened to his father-in-law Count Makino (who was adviser also to the Emperor)—and to his neighbor Seihin Ikeda, manager of the great Mitsui business interests. Yet another trusted confidant, with far more practical political experience, was Kazuo Kojima, a powerful behind-the-scenes figure both in the prewar Seiyukai and in the Liberal Party.

Yoshida, himself inept in public relations, gained a somewhat unwarranted popularity as the protégé of these important elder statesmen. Makino, the son of Toshimichi Okubo, one of the great leaders of the Meiji Restoration, lent special luster to Yoshida's reputation, and Kojima, a stickler for Confucian concepts of justice, required him to play fair and act honorably, thus making him seem to be a rare and thoroughly desirable statesman with but little thirst for power.

Yoshida began his political career by leaning heavily upon the statesmanship of Ichiro Hatoyama, long the idol of postwar Liberals. Hatoyama fully expected to be Prime Minister (Whitney's political advisers for a time encouraged him in that ambition) with Yoshida as Foreign Minister.

But in May, 1946, upon the very eve of accession to the premiership, Hatoyama was purged by MacArthur and, when four other Liberals refused to be considered in his stead, offered the top post to Yoshida.

After nine months' experience of the Occupation it was only too clear that a Prime Minister could merely be a puppet, and Yoshida had no desire to take the job. Content as Foreign Minister, though overseas relations were virtually non-existent, and advised by Kojima to curb his ambition for greater power, he demurred. In deference to Hatoyama's wishes, however, he talked to Shidehara, the retiring Prime Minister, who stressed a puppet's troubles; to Chuji Machida, leader of the Opposition conservatives; to Kojima, who had refused the appointment for himself; to Ikeda; and finally to Count Makino. All these had been purged; therefore Yoshida broke Occupation rules when he talked to them on governmental matters. All advised him to reject the offer, and so, in characteristically perverse reaction, he accepted it.

Yoshida agreed to become actual Prime Minister and nominal Liberal Party president, with full power over diplomatic and administrative matters but none over party patronage or management. He solemnly promised as Hatoyama's stopgap, "a son-in-law under an apprenticeship," to retire as soon as Hatoyama was depurged.

No one really wanted Yoshida as Prime Minister or as party president; but his political career opened in a friendly atmosphere. Occupationnaires, especially those susceptible to the magic of big names, acclaimed him as one who knew his way around the West, who required no interpreter to relay his beautiful English, and whose manners could be impeccable when he condescended to turn on his charm. Japanese reformers hailed him as a sincere, if moderate, liberal; and antimilitarists recalled his dislike of Tojo's policies. Politicians, knowing through Kojima the circumstances of his choice, expected a figurehead who would follow Occupation orders, but who was pledged not to invade their private party province. Hatoyama trusted him to keep his promise.

Yet, almost from the beginning, Yoshida swerved from the expected course. Not only did he clash with the Occupation by refusing to play the yes man, but he attacked MacArthur's judgment and, when overruled, yielded ungracefully. His liberalism was Gladstonian, unadaptable to postwar Japanese conditions, and his desires for reform were but a feeble smolder. For months, openly at first and then clandestinely, he conferred with Hatoyama weekly. Then, growing self-reliant, and using Occupation pressure as excuse, he drifted from his mentor. Kojima, disappointed at what he called "this breach of honor," expressed displeasure at Yoshida's violation of the Confucian code of justice.

Politicians, moreover, were amazed that Yoshida, whose antiradical phobia led him to brand even some Liberals as leftists, set up a brain trust from a "professor group" of enrolled Socialists. His insistence upon naming one of them, Hiroo Wada, as Agriculture Minister stirred a storm in the Liberal Party. Such old-line economists as Finance Minister Ishibashi, editor of the influential *Oriental Economist,* protested that Wada had been a radical, jailed in 1941 for criticizing the Emperor; but Yoshida made the appointment.

"Yoshida," said Japanese wits, "dislikes Communism but not its pink **fringe.**"

Actually, Yoshida looked upon the Socialists as little better than the Reds. He called upon the Socialist professors for opinions, at least in the first year or so of his premiership, because they clarified for him the meaning of the vague economic policies required by Occupation edict, and he tolerated Wada because certain leftist-minded Occupation officers ordered his appointment as Minister of Agriculture. But while he asked for professor-group advice he seldom followed it.

Once having drained the professors of their information and having satisfied MacArthur's men that agricultural and economic reforms were under serious consideration, Yoshida discarded his professors as he had discarded Hatoyama.

He could not discard his critics as readily as he had cast off his advisers. Hatoyama supporters within the Liberal Party, constituting the old guard, resented his treatment of their leader. Never anxious for Yoshida as party president, they plotted to replace him but had no first-class candidate to offer except the purged Hatoyama.

Yoshida's insensitivity to the feelings of others was accompanied by a notably thin skin where his own feelings were concerned. Forgetful of Kojima's injunctions, he reacted angrily. As Japanese director of the purge, executing Occupation suggestions, he was well aware of its value as a political weapon. Whenever, in early 1946, rival leaders set up efficient organizations to challenge the Liberals, the purge cracked down so opportunely that opponents doubted that the action was sheer coincidence. MacArthur himself had used the purge to rid himself of Hatoyama. When, therefore, men like Ishibashi criticized the Prime Minister, or when the old guard moved to hamper Yoshida's activity, the purge was soon invoked. Both Yoshida and Occupation leaders stoutly denied, however, that this was done for political considerations.

Perhaps for additional self-protection against suspected plots, perhaps because of that appetite for power against which Kojima had warned, Yoshida steadily encroached in areas believed tabu to him. Although he had solemnly pledged himself not to interfere in party management, he insisted upon naming party managers, upon writing platforms, and upon dictating policy. When the old guard demurred, he eliminated or sidetracked the objectors into relative obscurity. Whitney's special protégé, former Speaker Yamazaki, unwittingly trapped in a political plot, was dropped from the party hierarchy despite his frantic protestations of innocence and his hurried resignation from the Diet.

To replace the old guard, Yoshida turned to his prewar bureaucratic associates. Many of them, to be sure, had been purged from public life and thus were unavailable; but others, especially those who had retired from service prior to 1937, had not been included in the purge and could be recalled to service. Steadily these older men were recruited both for party office and for high administrative posts. The bureaucratization of the governments ran counter to expressed Occupation aims but violated no law or regulation.

Return of prewar officials attested to Yoshida's loyalty to the bureaucratic clique, but often it produced new headaches. Such men had seniority privileges, and some rebelled against One-Man Yoshida's assumption of complete authority. Others, wedded to prewar ways, refused to follow Occupation methods. A few used public office to recoup their fortunes. Many found postwar government office under Yoshida far less attractive than they had anticipated.

Personnel shufflings in Yoshida's five Cabinets not only reflected his growing preference for bureaucrats, including some who had served in Hideki Tojo's Cabinet, but also testified to his inability to work harmoniously with his associates. Cabinet changes had always marked government administration in Japan, but Yoshida's 143 ministerial appointments far surpassed the previous high records of 82 changes under Ito and 75 under Konoye.

Most Cabinet tenures were short. Yoshida alone served in all five of his Cabinets, and no one else survived as long as five years. Most appointees, unable to endure his dictatorial ways or his constant meddling with their departments, resigned or were dismissed within two or three years, and the majority of these either joined Yoshida's opponents or retired from politics entirely; few continued to defend him.

Similar dissatisfaction characterized Liberal Party management. The all-important secretary-generalship passed into four different hands within the 1951–1953 period alone, one man twice tendering his resignation before being allowed to quit. The Political Affairs Research Committee, which supposedly decided party policy, also was headed by four chairmen within the same three-year period, while the party's Executive Board had three different chiefs, one of whom thrice submitted his resignation before it was accepted.

Of all the men who revived the prewar Liberal Party after surrender, but two remained in 1953 as high party officers; and both of these, Masazumi Ando and Tsuruhei Matsuno, had been politically inactive during the greater portion of the postwar period, because of the purge. All others who had helped Hatoyama form the Liberals were either driven from its ranks and in active rebellion against the man they had raised from political obscurity to high office or, if still in the party, were silent and ineffective members of the rank and file.

THIRTEEN

How to Play Politics

The passing of potential rivals left Yoshida in complete control. Unhappily, the withdrawal or removal of the living coincided with the deaths of Makino, Shidehara, Ikeda and Kojima, the seniors who were among the very few that Yoshida respected.

Wise advice from senior statesmen no longer curbed his autocratic tendencies, no longer restrained his innate contempt for less important people, his scorn for public opinion, his short temper, his arrogance, or his intolerance. More and more relying upon intuition and gratifying his whims, Yoshida grew self-contained. He lived within a very narrow circle of cronies.

Most of these were amateurs in politics and were cordially disliked by the men to whom they issued orders in the name of Yoshida. One of the more important was Jiro Shirasu, fifty-year-old Cambridge graduate and son-in-law of Aisuke Kabayama, prewar professional friend of American and British diplomats. Shirasu, with little of his father-in-law's sweetness and charm, alienated both Occupation personnel and old-guard Liberals; the former recoiled from his backslapping manners, and the latter resented his boast that he could be named Cabinet minister whenever he desired.

Whitney lost his temper when Shirasu burst in upon him unannounced. Marquat complained that his statements sometimes varied widely from the facts. Both agreed with Willoughby that Shirasu purposely set one Occupation section against the other. When later, Shirasu, after failing to be appointed ambassador to the United States, retired

140

to head the Tohoku Electric Power Company, few foreigners or old-guard politicians were unhappy.

A second important Yoshida crony was Tagakichi Aso, a wealthy Kyushu coal operator who married Yoshida's third daughter, Kazuko. Aso himself was a successful Liberal politician in a heavily Socialist constituency; but the old guard, which worshiped seniority, considered him as an upstart.

Kazuko Aso, a charming and resourceful lady, supplied the graces which her father often scorned. Her tactfulness salved wounds inflicted by his brusqueness and smoothed relationships which he had disturbed. Her activity was so successful that the radical magazine *Shinso*, forgetful of the new equality conferred upon women, burst out indignantly, "She has the shameless effrontery, woman though she is, to interfere in the affairs of government and of the Liberal Party."

Kazuko was more than tactful; her father relied upon her for sound appraisals of personality and character. To win her confidence was almost a certain road to his favor; to incur her disapproval was to sink into the ranks of the forgotten.

Her influence even affected Yoshida's personal relationships. After the death of his wife he was attracted by Kiyoko Sakamoto, whom he called Korin-chan; but Kazuko's strong opposition led him to postpone his plan of secret marriage.

Yoshida read character less shrewdly than did his daughter. Unwilling to trust the judgment of friends and too impatient to study the records for himself, he failed to give due weight to conflicting factors and sometimes capriciously chose as helpers men who were nothing more than smooth talkers. Against protests at honoring men who, rightly or wrongly, were regarded as undesirable, Yoshida's anger flared. He was unable to accept frank criticism and, resenting even mild demurs as disloyalty, stubbornly refused to yield.

Certain *causes célèbres* tested Yoshida's devotion to the ancient codes. A samurai kept his word, which, once given, could never be recalled. Prior to the 1949 election, which he did not expect to win, Yoshida promised Inukai, leader of the Progressives, that, regardless of the election's outcome, he and Inukai would be included in a Cabinet that, to some degree at least, would be a coalition government. When the Liberals swept to overwhelming victory, the promise proved to be not only unnecessary but inconvenient since Hatoyama's old guard violently disliked Inukai; but Yoshida, having given his word, could not retract.

The old guard protested, and some threatened to secede from the Liberals if the Inukai appointment was made; but Yoshida persisted.

Since a promise was sacred, devious means were justified for its fulfillment. When old-guard Liberals, holding a majority in the Diet, would not countenance a coalition government, Yoshida proposed Inukai's admission into Liberal Party membership. Hatoyama's friends objected so successfully that a delay ensued, whereupon Yoshida, to soothe Inukai's disappointment, suggested (according to Shinnosuke Abe, a well informed source) that he take a trip abroad with all costs paid by Yoshida's financial backers. Meanwhile an understanding spread, although it was not solemnized into a promise, that Inukai might enter the party on the condition that he receive no important party or Cabinet office. Soon after entry Inukai, on October 29, 1952, became the Justice Minister and, to commemorate the event, changed his given name from Ken to Takeru, which means expert or matured but which may also mean raging.

From ancient times, Japanese leaders, *oyabun,* have protected their loyal followers. When a drunken brawl brought about a Cabinet vacancy Yoshida named a hitherto unknown figure, Hayato Ikeda, as Finance Minister. Thereafter two other Cabinet Ministers resigned, alleging inability to work with Ikeda, and, in November, 1952, the Diet voted no confidence in him.

Although Liberal Party members advised jettisoning Ikeda to ease the internal party strains, Yoshida, because of oyabun obligations, refused. Under the Constitution, he was compelled to find another Finance Minister; but he stood by Ikeda by forcing his appointment as chairman of the Liberal Party Political Research Committee. Within five months Ikeda quarreled again, and a third Cabinet member resigned. Soon thereafter Yoshida made him his personal envoy to Washington and London.

An oyabun's obligations were no stronger than the obligations of his follower, the *kobun,* to render loyal service. Yoshida, who cherished feudal etiquette, was outraged, therefore, when one whom he trusted and whom he had raised to perhaps unwarranted eminence showed ingratitude. This was the political comet Kozen Hirokawa, who in June, 1950, flashed out of obscurity to become Yoshida's Agriculture Minister.

Hirokawa's checkered career had afforded but little preparation for the troubled Ministry of Agriculture, whose difficulties proved too great for eight different men within a three-year period. Trained as a Buddhist priest, he had also been a postman, a primary-school teacher, a sake and soy sauce dealer, a firewood vender, and a confectioner; but he was always, and above all else, a local politician. Although he had once been a Socialist he had later followed Bamboku Ono, of the old guard, who built him into a power in Liberal Party politics.

His gratitude was limited. Realizing quickly that the old guard was weaker than Yoshida, he turned his back on Ono and, gathering twenty or thirty Diet followers, became Yoshida's most vocal and insistent defender. Blasting the old guard, he refused in August, 1952, to support Ono, a Hatoyama man, for the Speakership.

Politically the atmosphere was stormy. Hatoyama, depurged in 1951 and almost immediately stricken by paralysis, had sufficiently recovered to demand that Yoshida keep his promise to step aside. Although Kojima, who was then alive, advised the Prime Minister to observe propriety and etiquette by doing so, Yoshida remained in office. He professed to believe that Hatoyama was too ill to lead.

Hatoyama thereupon blasted Yoshida as ungrateful, inefficient, and undemocratic. He pleaded "a revolution of brotherly love whereby the people might reform themselves," and charged that Yoshida was too sly and deceitful to be trusted.

Behind these personal differences were other oppositions, typified by the opposing views of former Finance Ministers Ikeda and Ishibashi. Neither man, perhaps, was as completely frank as might have been desired. The former, backed by Yoshida, talked of sound finance and of the need for stabilizing public livelihood, although actually prices had risen approximately 50 per cent within a year and living conditions had deteriorated. Ishibashi, a Hatoyama man, favored subsidies to industry and mild inflation through bond issues but knew that Japan had little credit, and that only American largess and huge war orders were keeping the economy afloat.

Ishibashi and Hatoyama openly favored rearmament and speedy replacement of American troops by a revived Japanese army; Yoshida and Ikeda, declaring that Japan could not have both guns and butter, professed abhorrence of rearmament but steadily built up a so-called police or security force that was an army in everything but name.

With tempers rising high, and flying accusations of deceit, ingratitude, and what Hatoyama called Yoshida's "Rasputism," the Liberal Party seemed ready to fall apart. On August 28, 1952, Yoshida surprised his opponents by unexpectedly demanding and securing the Diet's dissolution after Ono had served but three days in the Speakership. This was a daring step which many thought would unseat Yoshida as Prime Minister even if the Liberals were not actually defeated.

Most observers expected that the new elections to be held in October, 1952, meant the restoration to Diet membership of Hatoyama and other old-guard leaders experienced in prewar politics. Yoshida had no hold over them, and their parliamentary skill added to the strong anti-Yoshida feelings already existing would, it was anticipated, cause his ruin.

Hirokawa, the shrewd opportunist, shared these expectations; but, like Yoshida, he thought that Hatoyama was too ill to be Prime Minister. With Yoshida about to be replaced and Hatoyama incapacitated, he saw opportunity for himself. He gambled everything upon a Yoshida victory. Should the old guard win, either Hatoyama or one of his kobun, perhaps Ishibashi, would become Prime Minister. Accordingly, Hirokawa campaigned vigorously for Yoshida, larding his speeches with denunciations of the Hatoyama clique.

The gamble paid off. Of the 35,294,000 votes cast the Liberals received 16,983,000, or 48 per cent, as against 44 per cent in the 1949 election. True, the Socialist vote, left and right, rose even more, with 21.3 per cent as against 13.5 in 1949, and Progressive strength, while dropping from 19.1 per cent in 1949 to 18.2 in 1952, showed a gain of 600,000 votes. The sixty-six-vote Liberal majority fell off to a paper-thin seven-vote margin.

Yoshida's majority, moreover, was only theoretical. Hatoyama's defection would imperil him at any time. With one hundred and thirty-nine prewar politicians sent to the Diet after having been depurged, competition for leadership intensified. Hatoyama's personal supporters numbered only forty, but all were skilled parliamentary tacticians.

Gizo Tomabechi, a Progressive leader defeated in the election, caused some embarrassment by filing a suit against Yoshida on the ground that the dissolution in August, 1952, had been illegal. In October, 1953, the Tokyo District Court upheld his contention that, because fewer than half the Cabinet members had signed a petition for an Imperial rescript of dissolution, the Cabinet's advice and consent had not been given, and so Yoshida's action had violated the Diet's constitutional rights. The judge, therefore, awarded Tomabechi, and presumably all other Diet members, 285,000 yen in salary as a Diet member until the January,

1953, election. The Government appealed the case to the Supreme Court.

To defend himself against loss of power, Yoshida called in a skilled publicist for the first time in his career. This was Taketora Ogata, former high executive of the *Asahi* newspapers, and member of the last two wartime Cabinets. Ogata had also been Chief Cabinet Secretary for the Higashikuni postwar Cabinet, but until 1951 had been purged from public life.

Ogata's newspaper experience had been on a journal whose once high ideals of press freedom had been corrupted by totalitarianism. His formula for Yoshida's defense was to create an official central news agency which, by censorship or by filtering all information that reached either the Japanese people or the world at large, would build an impression favorable to Yoshida.

Hirokawa, observing these developments, judged the situation favorable. With public opinion crystallizing against Ogata's proposed press controls, he reasoned that neither Yoshida nor Hatoyama would insist selfishly upon preferment, and they might compromise on Kozen Hirokawa. Both men feared radical upswings, and though the Communists had waned from 2,980,000 popular votes in 1949 to 890,000 in 1952, losing every one of their twenty-two Diet seats, the presence of fifty-four leftist Socialists, representing 3,461,000 voters, imperiled the seven-vote Liberal majority.

Hatoyama, indeed, reacted as Hirokawa anticipated but less sharply than he wished. Approaching Yoshida, Hatoyama offered peace. The terms were harsh, but Yoshida, again as Hirokawa guessed, accepted. The deal gave Yoshida his coveted Prime Ministership; but he was forced to promise to rule more democratically, to give responsible party posts to Hatoyama's followers, and to repudiate "inner politics," as practiced by the "cronies" Aso, Shirasu, Ikeda, and Hirokawa. In October, 1952, Yoshida was reelected, receiving 247 of the 453 votes cast. Ono was reelected Speaker by almost the same vote. Yoshida then made Ogata his Chief Cabinet Secretary and Deputy Prime Minister.

Aso and Shirasu, profitably ensconced as presidents of important business concerns, offered little objection, and Ikeda was not dropped; but Hirokawa, who lost his Agriculture portfolio, felt seriously abused. Not even a belated reinstatement, in December, was enough to soothe his feelings. Moved partly by his pique and even more by the idea that Shigeru Yoshida was losing power, he plotted with Yoshida's opponents.

Assuming that Hatoyama would win eventually, he leagued with Bukichi Miki, one of Hatoyama's political manipulators, with Yoshizaku Miura, a behind-the-scenes wirepuller, and with Yoshio Kodama, who had amassed a fortune in military contracts. These men favored Hatoyama, but Hirokawa planned to swing them to his own interest.

To questioners of his sincerity, Hirokawa answered that he was promoting unity among conservatives. The need was apparent, especially among Liberals, and several prewar politicians, professing the same purpose, had set up a "neutral" faction to arrange internal peace. This group, reflecting the confusion within the party, was itself conglomerate. Some, like Speaker Bamboku Ono, Tsuruhei Matsuno, and former Deputy Prime Minister Joji Hayashi, regarded Hatoyama as oyabun. Others, especially former Railway Minister Yonezo Maeda, were old-time Hatoyama enemies, while still others including former Construction Minister Shuji Matsutani, had been Yoshida protégés. Hirokawa, anticipating little real success from a badly divided neutral group, saw himself as the one man upon whom everyone would unite.

Yet, with the possibility that the Liberals, thus split into Hatoyama, Yoshida, and neutral groups, would cut their own political throats, Hirokawa further strengthened his position. Knowing that Hitoshi Ashida was dissatisfied with his place in the Progressive Party councils, Hirokawa crossed party lines and sought a deal. Hirokawa and Ashida, in much the same sort of arrangement as Yoshida had made with Inukai, agreed upon under-cover collaboration; but each desired the Prime Ministership, and so the stability of the deal was far from firm.

Superficially the plans were airtight; yet Hirokawa failed. Rumors of his numerous arrangements undermined confidence in his integrity, and when the time came in late 1952 and early 1953 for choosing party officers few recommended him. Hirokawa, eagerly campaigning for the secretary-generalship, saw himself passed over by Yoshida, who nominated Eisaku Sato, and by the neutrals; even Miki, who professed to favor him, was only too willing to sacrifice him for the sake of party harmony. Ashida, seeing Hirokawa's weakness, hastily broke off negotiations for collaboration.

Of these machinations Yoshida knew little and suspected less until January, 1953, when Hirokawa openly opposed his choice for secretary-general. Even then Yoshida was loath to credit the disloyalty; but when Hirokawa ducked a roll call in March, 1953, when the Diet disciplined Yoshida, the Prime Minister immediately fired him from the Cabinet.

Hirokawa, with fifteen followers, bolted the Liberal Party. His small band, after a brief existence as the Doshi Kai, or Brotherhood Club, joined Hatoyama's group. The defection of these men, while not in itself important, cut the slim Liberal majority and left Yoshida vulnerable to a no-confidence motion. On March 14, 1953, he unexpectedly dissolved the Diet again and called for a new election.

This second dissolution, even more startling than the August action, caught his opponents off guard. Hatoyama even questioned its constitutionality: the movement, he said, was convincing proof of Yoshida's "unmitigated dictatorial ways, high-handed administration, and contempt for the Diet"; it was also an invitation for "the rise of Fascism and the spread of Communism."

Hatoyama's anger was explainable. The Liberals, as the Government party, had a prestige advantage over his men; Yoshida needed smaller campaign funds than opponents whose treasuries had been drained so recently. In the open break that followed between Yoshida's Liberals and a hastily created Hatoyama Japan Liberal Party, the former held most of the high cards.

Yoshida had lost Hirokawa, now firmly in the Hatoyama camp; but this time he had aid from several Hatoyama henchmen who, while loyal in their thoughts to Hatoyama, foresaw his defeat looming. Ono, cherishing his Speakership, and refusing to work with Hirokawa, stayed neutral. Tsuruhei Matsuno, perhaps the most skilled vote estimator and manipulator in Japan, allied by marriage to the wealthy Mitsui interests, and Masazumi Ando, a power among Buddhist youth, deserted to Yoshida.

Liberal dissension cost only 420,000 votes, the total dropping to 16,-520,000 votes in a poll of 34,602,000, or 47.7 per cent as against 48 per cent in October, 1952, but the combined Socialist vote shot up to 9,186,-000, or 26.5 per cent as against 21.3 in 1952. The Progressives virtually stood still, dropping to a 17.9 percentage as against 18.2 in the earlier election. Once more the Communists fell down, registering only 1.9 per cent as against 2.5 in 1952.

Yoshida's strategy, usually credited to Ogata, Matsuno, and Ando, with help from Yonezo Maeda, a depurgee, succeeded, but at heavy cost. Yoshida's Liberal faction won 199 seats, a loss of six, while Hatoyama lost 5, retaining only 35 seats. Hirokawa was among the unsuccessful candidates. Thus the combined Liberal Party, assuming a non-existent perfect harmony, held a single-vote majority.

Although it was unlikely that 76 Progressives would work against him in unison with 72 leftist and 66 rightist Socialists, much less 12 Independents, 5 Labor-Farmers, and a Communist, Yoshida could take no chances. His reelection as Prime Minister in May, 1953, showed clearly that his position was precarious since only 204 votes favored him, with 116 opposing, while 146 Diet members abstained. It was the second time he had been elected by a minority vote.

Nor could the Liberals command majorities in other tests. Though Ono was tossed overboard in retribution for neutrality, the Liberals lost the Speakership to a Progressive, 252 to 206, and the Vice Speakership to a leftist Socialist, 223 to 220. They could not carry the House of Councilors, where Matsuno received but 95 votes against the Opposition's 135, 20 Councilors abstaining.

Yoshida called upon his new-found political magicians to rescue him from peril. Collecting a slush fund estimated at 100,000,000 yen (about $275,000), his agents gunned for Progressive Party converts, offering as much as 3,000,000 yen per vote. Few openly accepted, though rumor reported that one geisha party netted ten Diet members who would cooperate when needed.

Whatever its accuracy, the report coincided with Yoshida's known practices. In at least five previous crises when recalcitrant Liberals threatened his leadership Yoshida had offered inducements ranging, it was said, from relaxation of the purge to Cabinet preferment and recruited enough Progressives to swing the balance in his favor. One defeated sports-minded rival dubbed the Progressive Party the Liberal farm club. Later, in November, 1953, Hatoyama and most of his following returned to the Liberal Party, thus strengthening Yoshida's position. The return was almost unconditional, Hatoyama gaining only a promise that Japan would rearm, a decision already made in order to assure continued American aid.

Some great men profit by experience, but Yoshida saw no need to mend his ways. Arrogating to himself full credit for casting off Occupation shackles and restoring full sovereignty to Japan, for directing an exceptional postwar recovery and raising the standard of living, he cherished his gruff and solitary manners.

Even within his own party, publicists generally reported general dissatisfaction with his policies and personality; yet Yoshida, for whom no one cheered, had become Prime Minister more often than anyone else in Japanese parliamentary history. The democratically chosen

Diet writhed under his contempt but elected him to longer service than even the eminent Prince Ito had served. No Prime Minister had sustained more prolonged or more vicious criticism, yet, after six years of concentrated attack, the electorate twice within seven months had given his party the mandate to govern.

Perhaps voters did so because no other leader was available; but it is more likely that, for all Yoshida's stubbornness and tyranny, they admired his blunt honesty and rocky independence.

The voters proved, also, that they were capable of good judgment in spurning such opportunists as Hirokawa and Ono—each of whom was suspected in 1954 of having been implicated in major corruption scandals. These men vanished from important political activity. In their stead Ogata rose steadily and with him a hitherto retiring figure, former Commerce and Industry Minister Nobusuke Kishi (brother of Eisaku Sato) who, it was expected, would compete with Ogata for the Prime Ministry whenever Yoshida might vacate the post. Probably Yoshida would prefer Ogata but Kishi, like Hirokawa before him, cultivated friends in other parties, too. He was particularly friendly with Mamoru Shigemitsu.

FOURTEEN

Grass-Roots Reform

After State Minister Kiyohide Okano, banker and lawyer, had wrestled with Japanese local government problems for a year, he went to Great Britain to study local administration. The trip was necessary; few people in Japan possessed sufficient understanding of the matter.

No one, least of all the Occupation, was pleased with postwar local government. National administrators confessed themselves bewildered; mayors and headmen were confused; the local entities were bankrupt. The electorate, which had watched with growing disappointment the fading of bright promises, was frankly cynical.

Even prior to the war, local government had not worked well. French administrative methods had been applied to backward and old-fashioned rural areas whose people, despite the legal abrogation of feudal fiefs in 1878, continued to obey their hereditary local lords. While centralization had grown stronger it had killed off whatever democratic tendencies may have been inherent in cooperative neighborhood associations, communal public works, and elective local officers.

Misreading Japanese history, Occupationnaires fallaciously compared prefectures to American states, assumed that tiny villages had been governed democratically, almost along New England town-meeting lines, and that Japanese not only were eager for American concepts of home rule but thoroughly understood them. Misled by the idea that various reactionary movements of the Meiji Restoration period, intended to restore power to local lords, had really been steps toward democracy, they urged Japan to follow policies that had been planned for the revival of feudalism. Similar misunderstandings had, of course, under-

150

lain the Potsdam Declaration's promise "to revive and strengthen democratic tendencies."

A first step was to cancel a 1943 order consolidating the forty-six prefectures into nine regional groups. In recommending this move Major Cecil G. Tilton, chief of Local Government Division of Government Section, argued that home rule for the prefectures, for the 253 cities and the 10,419 towns and villages, would revive grass-roots democracy, break down totalitarianism, encourage independence, stir pride in local activity, and, by accustoming citizens to participation in local affairs, would encourage more efficient administration. He believed that the more citizens knew about their police, fire, health, welfare, education, labor, and fiscal affairs, the more wisely they would vote and the more jealously they would insist upon efficiency and honesty.

Tilton's plan directly contradicted the existing system whereby the Home Ministry dictated local affairs through the governor of the prefecture, or ken, appointed by the Emperor on its own nomination. This officer, a national rather than a local official, and usually not a native of the province he controlled, managed ken property, collected ken income, kept the records, compiled the budget, and drafted bills for assembly consideration. He supervised elections and decided any contests arising therefrom.

Minor chief executives—the mayors, appointed by the Home Minister on nomination by city assemblies, and town headmen, elected by local assemblies—held similar powers within their communities.

Tilton's proposal that governors be elected shocked the Home Ministry; his further suggestion that governors yield to the wishes of their assemblies, even to resigning after a vote of no confidence, met flat rejection. While Home Minister Etsujiro Uyehara agreed to a limited type of popular election, an Imperial Council overruled him April 12, 1946, offering to have governors selected by prefecture electoral colleges subject to ratification by the Home Ministry. Tilton then suggested a primary election to weed out candidates; but this, too, was refused.

Tilton also proposed higher status for assemblies. Previously these had been deliberative bodies of strictly limited power, meeting but once a year and then only for a thirty-day session. Members were permitted to vote on bills drafted by the governors, but not to introduce bills or increase budget items. They did not choose their own officials, could not override a veto, and were subject to dissolution by the governors. Usually they worked in secret because the governor, or any three members, could require closed sessions. Tilton demanded full powers for assemblies, especially freedom from the fear of dissolution. The Home Ministry conceded most of his requirements but insisted on retaining the right of dissolution if 10,000 voters petitioned for such action. No prefecture had fewer than 400,000 electors, so that the reservation was tantamount to a proposal that the Ministry close down the assembly whenever it desired to do so.

Over strong opposition by two American political science professors who were advising him, Tilton agreed to allow the governor and any ten assemblymen to hold secret executive meetings when the assembly was not in session.

Usually, when Occupation officers and Japanese leaders disagreed, the former issued directives compelling the Japanese to comply; but Tilton preferred persuasion to coercion. He and his men therefore spent nearly a year visiting every prefecture and every city to stress the need for home rule, free election, and the desirability of the initiative, referendum, and recall.

This cultivation of democracy at the grass roots resulted, September 27, 1946, in the passage of four laws revolutionizing local government. On April 17, 1947, a Local Autonomy Law granted to assemblies full power to legislate, to investigate, and to control elections. It also gave them the right to lease or enfranchise public utilities, but no franchise might be given for more than ten years unless approved by public referendum.

The political scientists were again overruled when, despite their advice that legislative bodies be kept small, high memberships were allowed. Each town council had a minimum of 12 members, even when, as in the case of Ashinoyu in Hakone, there were but 25 households; communities under 50,000 population elected 31 assemblymen, and Tokyo had 120. By the 1947 local elections, Japanese voters were asked to choose 2,617 ken assemblymen and 190,496 city, town, and village assemblymen, together with 10,419 headmen.

For propaganda purposes, much was said about the popularity of these elections, particularly of the trooping to the polls of 81.2 per cent of eligible electors; but, in point of fact, elections for local assemblymen were relatively unimportant. Only 249,074 candidates contested for the 190,496 places, an average of but 1.3 candidates for each post to be filled. In the 1951 elections, with 170,279 seats at stake, 224,965 candidates appeared, an average only slightly higher than in 1947. The same lack of interest appeared in elections of headmen, only 20,593 persons contesting for the 10,419 seats in 1947 and 13,296 for the 6,726 vacancies in 1951.

Not only was the advice of political scientists ignored by thus increasing the number of local legislators by more than 35,000 above the 1938 level, but expenses soared. While local government expenditures rose ninefold between 1946 and 1948, the costs of the assemblies rose 28.5 times. Much of this was due to the Occupation's insistence that each of the 190,000 lawmakers must be paid, the theory being that unpaid service would, as in the past, lead to corruption.

While pay did not assure a higher type of public servant nor prevent an increase in bribery, it did create a new vested interest, that of the professional office seeker, who, as in Tokyo in 1951, clamored for such special privileges as separation allowances upon retiring from office and pensions for life.

As the political scientists had warned, the swollen legislative bodies became unwieldy, direction drifting into the hands of bosses who operated secretly. In large assemblies, especially those using the committee system, the contribution of individuals could not be readily identified, so that some members shirked responsibility and others sold their votes. The same evils that had afflicted the old-fashioned city councils of the United States prior to the modernization of local government reappeared in postwar Japan.

Local Government Division sold well its panacea of local initiative. Each of the twenty-three Tokyo wards claimed that, because it had an elected ward chief and an elected assembly, it, too, was an independent entity. As such, it demanded management of its own affairs, principally the award of contracts for street repairs, sewerage, and waste disposal. These had once been locally managed, but the experiment had failed. In 1951, however, when ward officials learned that approximately 3,000,000 yen yearly could be made by selling garbage to swine raisers, and that about 78,000,000 yen more could be made in fertilizer sales through the establishment of incinerators, they called for decentralization of the services. They sought also the right to name all personnel, thus building up their own political machines, and demanded that each ward separately administer its schools, parks, bathhouses, health centers, and other activities. At one time the Tokyo ward chiefs seriously believed that each ward should maintain an independent police and fire service.

Before the Occupation closed, it had become evident that decentralization had been forced upon local entities long before they were prepared for it. The plan was excellent, but it presupposed an Anglo-Saxon understanding of democratic practices and an interest in local government which the average citizen did not have. This had been anticipated, but it had been mistakenly assumed that understanding and interest would develop rapidly in time of need; and, this, regrettably, had not occurred. (The parallel may certainly be carried too far, but conditions in Japan's local units were not too dissimilar to those in American cities during the period when great blocks of newly naturalized voters were enfranchised.) Since ballots were blank, voters being obliged to write in the names of their candidates, well known candidates enjoyed a great advantage. These usually were incumbents, bureaucrats, and professional politicians rather than independents or reformers. Thus the conservatives, elected by the people's free vote, gained status, and the boss system became riveted upon the local entity—seemingly, through the will of the Occupation which had required the changes.

Far from working hand in hand toward common democratic goals, national and local governments clashed sharply. They differed on areas of jurisdiction. By the intention of the innovators, Tokyo would surrender much of its concern with local matters; actually, the central government not only retained its local offices but established more of them. From the inauguration of the Local Autonomy Law, governors formally complained of Tokyo's encroachments. National and local authorities differed on questions of relationship, the national government insisting that since it sent subsidies to finance operations it should supervise administration. They differed also, in cases of duplication, whether local offices had equal status with national or were subordinate. They differed whether Tokyo interference was merely a survival of past conditions which would disappear in due course, or would continue indefinitely.

None of this enhanced the average citizen's confidence in local government, for, in virtually every case, the more experienced and better financed central agency overshadowed the newcomer. Citizens, observing the greater efficiency of the well established bureaucrat, looked with scorn upon officials who could not do as well.

Unwittingly the Occupation sabotaged decentralization. Supposedly Occupation General Headquarters in Tokyo issued directions, but operational activities were directed until 1950 by the 8th Army, whose liaison with GHQ was far less than adequate. Policy was laid down in Tokyo, but each local area, down to the smallest village, found itself theoretically free to apply the policy as it desired. Since this permitted a highly undesirable variation, especially in the more remote communities, GHQ itself restricted local freedom; residents, noting the dependence of their villages upon the governor or the Tokyo authorities, grew skeptical about the degree of local independence.

The gravest difficulties sprang from the assumption of expensive activity without the financial resources necessary to maintain them. As the bulk of taxes continued to flow to Tokyo, local communities were obliged to find new revenues or to surrender their privileges in return for central government subvention.

Transfer of schools, roads, buildings, and other facilities to local control pleased local pride. At first few worried seriously over the costs that would be incurred. Without thinking much about the matter most local politicians assumed that Tokyo would continue the old practice of paying at least half the costs of many activities. Politicians and contractors anticipated patronage and profit.

Local budgets therefore leaped. Assemblies anxious to demonstrate their modernism voted extensive improvements. While total local government expenditures were multiplied by 90 between 1940 and fiscal 1948, payments for social and labor facilities were multiplied by 290, reaching more than 22,000,000,000 yen. On the other hand, health and sanitation expenses, which Occupationnaires had hoped to see increased, were multiplied only by 70 over the 1940–1948 period.

Taxation alone could not, and was not planned to, cover the vastly increased postwar expenditures. National contributions, in one form or another, had accounted for 88,000,000,000 of the 294,000,000,000 yen local expenditures in fiscal 1948; and, while this percentage was expected to decline, sizable grants were anticipated. The hope, however, collapsed when a special American tax mission, headed by Dr. Carl S. Shoup of Columbia University, recommended a drastic cut in national grants. If, he said in effect, local home rule is to continue, local entities must pay their own expenses; no local government can be strong unless it has its independent income. No national authority, he warned, would continue to appropriate money over whose expenditure it had no control; nor was it logical that decreased centralization should be accompanied by increased flow of bounty from the national treasury. In short, if local areas wanted better services they must raise the taxes to pay for them.

This did not mean that all subsidies would be stopped, but it did mean drastic reduction. It meant, moreover, that much of the money would come as loans to be repaid with interest rather than as outright gifts. The sums granted would be graded according to need, with better terms accorded to poorer neighborhoods; but richer areas would not, as heretofore, receive special aid.

The difference may be illustrated by the school appropriations. Under the educational reform laws of 1947–1948, the national treasury was to pay half the costs of education during the compulsory school years and 40 per cent of costs in the post-compulsory years. This was cut sharply. Of the total school bill of 156,000,000,000 yen paid by local units in 1951–1952, the central government contributed but 4 per cent. Prefectures paid 52 per cent; smaller entities, 30 per cent; and the remaining 14 per cent came from outside sources, particularly contributions from parent-teachers associations. Such contributions had supposedly been outlawed as contrary to the principle of free public education; but without them the schools could not have continued.

Prefectures, cities, towns, and villages, therefore, sought new tax sources. Cities, as a rule, found amusement and recreational activities lucrative, the Diet allowing a tax of 100 per cent to be levied upon admission fees; but rural areas did not have this resource. Most prefectures increased income taxes and taxes upon real property, Miyagi prefecture doubling its land tax and raising its tax upon houses from 150 to 250 per cent. Special taxes of many sorts were imposed, including head taxes, taxes upon automobiles, sewing machines, radios, gardens, and advertising. Not all these could be collected, at least 60 per cent being delinquent in some areas in 1951. Because of this, and the desire to win votes in the 1951 elections for the House of Councilors, the Liberal Party sponsored a tax reduction bill halving the levies on admission fees, food and drink, sports and lodging. The estimated loss in revenue was estimated at 6,000,000,000 yen.

Although tax yields rose from 191,000,000,000 yen in 1950–1951 to 208,000,000,000 in 1951–1952, the local areas would have been bankrupt had they been left to their own resources, as was planned. Even with prefectural aids and with various subsidies, loans, and equalization grants from Tokyo, the financial situation was desperate. In March,

1953, 767 local entities were officially reported as having deficits total-ing 10,000,000,000 yen. In March, 1952, the Local Finance Committee, surveying the situation, had reported that the five largest cities faced a deficit of 6,000,000,000 yen; 180 other cities were 5,500,000,000 yen short; and 9,128 towns and villages, 8,000,000,000. A supplementary report in July, 1952, revealed that only two municipalities out of twenty-six investigated were solvent.

The situation seriously undermined official morale. Within the first two years of local independence, no fewer than 2,179 of the 10,628 mayors and headmen resigned their posts because of conflicts with the assembly or with their constituents, and so tense were feelings in many cases that new candidates could not be found for the positions. With the reduction of national aid and the increasing financial strin-gency, more resignations occurred. By 1952, voters were resorting to the recall to show their anger at increased taxes, there being ninety-two recalls in Fukui prefecture alone and thirty-four in Kanagawa prefec-ture. Only 60 per cent of incumbent chief executives had been reelected.

The lack of confidence in personnel was accompanied by a more seri-ous tendency. Increasingly, the larger cities sought national aid through the operation of special legislation which, while bringing additional subsidies, cost them much of their prized local freedom. Cities eligible for national help received funds for construction work and for improve-ments, provided they placed themselves under the guidance of national committees on which they themselves had only partial representation. Thus, during 1950 Hiroshima received 180,000,000 yen, and Nagasaki 90,000,000, as "international cultural cities." This gave them special prestige and assisted in reconstruction work; but it also obliged the mayors to report twice yearly to the Construction Minister and to accept his direction.

Under the new Constitution no such special cities could be created unless approved by a referendum of the electorate; but this was no deterrent. Beppu, Atami, and Ito voted overwhelmingly in June, 1950, to become "International Hot Springs Tourist Cities"—the last named by a five-to-one vote. Sasebo by thirty-five to one, Yokosuka by eleven to one, Kure by twenty-seven to one, and Maizuru by a smaller majority decided to become "Naval Port Conversion Cities." Yokohama and Kobe surrendered much of their freedom as "International Port Cities," as did Kyoto, Matsue, and Nara as "International Cultural and Sight-Seeing Cities."

The Kobe program, to cost 42,000,000,000 yen and to spread over a five-year period, included extensive interurban railways, enlarged port facilities, and thirty-four first-class roads (30 to 50 meters wide) as well as eighty-nine second-class roads. A suburb, Ashiya, therefore, to attract foreign residents sought and received classification as an "Ideal Residence City," gaining a national subsidy for a yacht harbor, golf course, zoo, botanical garden, and recreation zone, together with an international hotel.

By a special Diet act, overwhelmingly approved by the citizens, Tokyo became a special city, receiving 4,500,000,000 yen as part of a 400,000,000,000-yen project for a new metropolis with scientifically planned transportation, commerce, water, sewage, and public utilities, parks, roads, and public buildings. The entire city was to be fireproof, if the plans were carried out as envisioned, and it was to become a city of "sun and fun." In return, Tokyo placed itself under a nine-member Capital Construction Committee appointed by the Prime Minister, on which the Tokyo representation consisted of its mayor and one member of the municipal assembly.

The special city movement, thus rapidly moving forward, was a reversion to a prewar plan which also included, when first suggested about 1921, the independence of the five largest cities, Tokyo, Yokohama, Kyoto, Kobe, and Nagasaki, from the prefectures in which they are located. The movement was then opposed by the rural population which, except in Tokyo and Kyoto, outvoted the city dwellers. Only Tokyo, the capital of the empire, won freedom, annexing five cities, three counties, eighty-four towns, a large amount of outlying farm land, and a number of islands miles distant from the center of the city.

By 1950, thoughtful Japanese were admitting that local autonomy, while theoretically desirable, was probably too costly a luxury. Some of the 10,200 towns and villages, ineligible for special city classification, merged with their neighbors, first in police and school administration but later in all fields, so that by 1954 only 9,659 remained. Tanzan Ishibashi urged that Occupation innovations be canceled, and that Japan revive the wartime plan to substitute regional districts for independent prefectures. It was in connection with this movement that Okano went abroad to study how, if American theories were discarded, or postponed, the British democratic local government system might be applied to Japanese conditions. By 1954 a Town Amalgamation Promotion **Law** had been passed, requiring the merging of neighboring villages so as to reduce the total number to a third.

Pending his report, the central government moved tentatively to re-capture those areas which resisted surrender of their local freedoms. The first sign of this appeared in May, 1950, when the Diet, in considering a bill for local government finance, strongly criticized an Occupation proposal as unworkable. Three times the Chief Cabinet Secretary, Kaneshichi Masuda, asked GHQ to modify the terms; and when the requests were refused the Diet took the almost unprecedented step of rejecting an Occupation requirement. To everyone's astonishment, MacArthur professed to believe that this was nothing more than a pre-election maneuver and, after elections were over, again called upon the Diet to pass the bill. Face-saving changes were made, and the bill passed; but the Diet was on record as having opposed continued local self-government.

Emboldened by this, the national administration then ventured further attack upon local interests. Hitherto, local officials had been uncontrolled, although at Whitney's insistence the rights to unionize and strike had been denied to civil service employees since October, 1947. In anticipation of assembly elections in April, 1951, the Liberal Party executive proposed that local employees be similarly restricted. The ostensible reason was to unify procedure; practically, the Liberals, aware that 1,350,000 local civil servants and 400,000 teachers had joined unions favorable to the Socialists, were taking out insurance. If this was the real motive the plan succeeded, because in the prefectural elections the Socialist vote dropped by 25 per cent while in the vote for Councilors the vote for Socialists fell from 30 per cent of the total to 15 per cent. Pursuing its assault in 1952, the central government, through the Liberal Party, suggested first that all Tokyo ward heads be appointed by the governor; when this stirred too great antagonism it modified the plan to have the ward assemblies choose the ward chiefs. The purpose, in either case, was to reduce wards from small, independent entities to the status of administrative units.

This measure, introduced by Okano as one of the fruits of his study tour abroad, carried with it a proposal that ward chiefs so chosen should be subject to approval of the Tokyo governor, reviving on a small scale the prewar plan whereby mayors had been chosen. Coupled with it was a provision for reducing by at least 10 per cent the number of prefecture, city, and town assemblymen. There was every indication that further, and more serious, attacks would be made upon a local autonomy system which most Japanese felt was an unsuccessful experiment.

FIFTEEN

Spiritual Revolution

Almost overnight, MacArthur told the Japanese people on September 2, 1946, they had experienced a spiritual revolution. It was, he added in a metaphor that was not above reproach, no thin veneer but a convulsion unparalleled in world history.

The information probably astounded his audience. They knew well that the first year of the Occupation had been marked by black-marketing, corruption, graft, and fraud, that crime rates were soaring, that gangsters dominated their communities, that vice was rampant, and that elections (for all MacArthur's high praise for the efficiency with which democracy had been implanted) had gone to the highest bidders. It was much easier for MacArthur, high above the battle, to discern a spiritual revolution than for the people among whom he said it was occurring.

But again on March 19, 1947, when MacArthur granted the only press conference of his proconsulship he made the assertion, this time to foreign correspondents. They, too, saw little evidence of the phenomenon. By using their excellent newspaper techniques they had found, and reported, the theft of military goods and civilian supplies worth billions of yen. They had heard rumors that one Setsuzo Hinohara, president of the Showa Denko (Showa Electrical Industry Company), had won his position by pretending that Marquat's Anti-Trust and Cartels Division had ordered his election, and that he was spending millions in bribes. They knew also that greedy contractors had corrupted large numbers of government officials, that political machines were being paid by seekers of special privilege, that business interests were evading taxes and controls, that large sections of the press were filled with

160

filth and were using blackmail, and that all these evils had been emphatically denounced by the Occupation itself. It was therefore difficult for them, as well as for the Japanese, to believe that MacArthur really knew the facts. The more charitable assumed that the Supreme Commander was talking merely to uphold morale.

The unhappy circumstances were not unusual. Never had Japan's public life been free of major stain—malfeasance and corruption had always been regarded as a prerogative of the official caste; but never had the evils struck so deep nor carried such serious consequences.

For this, the postwar chaos, the uncertainties of livelihood, and the breakdown of morale certainly shared responsibility. The presence of the American combat soldier, with that fine sense of self-respect, self-confidence, and self-control, that spiritual quality to which MacArthur paid tribute, could not, in so short a time, cure evils that had been so long ingrained. Nor could the passage of half a hundred laws, forced through the Diet under Occupation pressure, correct conditions that had endured for centuries.

At the very moment that MacArthur was telling the press that a spiritual revolution had occurred, Japanese publicists were loudly bewailing the degeneration of the times. Government Section had but recently forwarded a complaint that "the young people of today are becoming more and more stained with social evils because of the examples set them by their elders." Yukio Ozaki, the ninety-year-old sage, was charging that all politicians were corrupt, that voters lacked political training, and that newly enfranchised women had failed lamentably in their civic responsibilities. MacArthur was also aware, through Government Section reports, that campaign financial reports were untrue, inaccurate, and incomplete, that candidates had failed to account for money received, and that party leaders had failed to report moneys spent. The top legal expense for any candidate was 30,000 yen; yet seasoned observers were declaring that success in election cost upwards of 2,000,000 yen.

MacArthur insisted that democracy had struck roots deep within Japan; yet those who had probed deeply into actual conditions felt far less confidence. The cities, they knew, were gang-ridden and corrupt; the countryside also failed to reflect spiritual reformation. Not only was electoral dishonesty condoned—few people suffering severe punishment for bribery or fraud—but villagers resented publication of corruption. As late as 1952, seven years after the beginning of the

Occupation, the entire village of Ueno in Shizuoka prefecture, near Tokyo, boycotted the family of a high-school sophomore who wrote a civics paper describing ballot-box frauds.

The boycott, which lasted into 1954, took the form of reviving an ancient form of ostracism—*mura-hachibu*—which excluded criminals from social contacts with the community in any relationship except those required by funerals and fires: no employer would hire any member of the family; the farm cooperatives refused seeds and tools; no one would visit the house nor speak to any person associating with the ostracized. From the standpoint of the Ueno populace the revelation of election corruption was unimportant in comparison to the "disgrace" said to have been brought upon the village by publication of the facts. "Even if the fact existed," the high-school authorities said, "it is against etiquette for anyone to expose it."

For such reasons the confessed bribery of at least forty Diet members in 1946, admitted both by the bribers and by the receivers, was wholly hushed up, no one being penalized. The receipt of millions of yen as bribes when coal nationalization was under discussion, misappropriations of 1,500,000,000 yen of salt monopoly revenues, the series of incredible scandal cases revealed by Diet investigation committees, wholesale election frauds, illegal campaign contributions, and political party corruptions, all stirred interest but led to little action. Hundreds of indictments were threatened; but few were laid, and fewer still resulted in jail sentences. Not since the great Teikoku Rayon scandal of 1934 had so many Diet members been indicted as during the first years of the Occupation. The spiritual reformation was by no means evident in political circles nor in popular resentment against official malfeasance.

Corrupt politics produced corrupt administration, Procurator-General Tosuke Sato reporting 69,239 instances of malfeasance, bribery, or theft during six years of the Occupation's spiritual reform. National Rural Policemen arrested 6,877 "bureaucrats" during 1950 and an even larger number during 1951, and Finance Minister Hayato Ikeda, in demanding a clean-up, alleged that more than a thousand tax officials annually had been caught embezzling; but convictions on such charges were few and, when found, brought light punishments.

Theoretically embezzlements were impossible. Elaborate inspection machinery supposedly safeguarded the expenditure of public funds: a Board of Audit examined national payments; the Cabinet had an Administrative Supervisory Board to inspect accounts; an Economic

Investigation Board passed on business transactions between the government and private enterprise; each house of the Diet had an Accounts Settlement Committee to check budget payments and, in addition, the Lower House had a special Administration Inspection Committee. Inspection committees also existed within each ministry, each prefectural government, and each local agency.

This very multiplicity of safeguards, complex and overlapping, afforded loopholes for illegalities. Few inspecting bodies had exclusive jurisdiction, and final authority was uncertain; therefore each was inclined to pass the buck when difficult or delicate problems arose. None cared to assume responsibility for questioning or delaying necessary reconstruction work or activities in which the Occupation had expressed an interest.

Occupationnaires, concerned primarily with security, paid little heed to purely Japanese activities, and thus the peculations mounted to extraordinary heights. In comparison with a prewar yearly average of 100 major embezzlements, fraudulent conversions, and forgeries in governmental affairs, the Board of Audit reported 175 in fiscal 1948, 750 in fiscal 1949, 1,113 in 1950, and 1,198 in 1951. These important offenses increased not only in number but in amount involved: 660,-000,000 yen in 1949, 3,500,000,000 in 1950, and 3,000,000,000 in 1951. Ikeda broke precedent in 1951, by warning fellow Cabinet members to watch their accounts more carefully, but with so little result that Yoshida took his administrators to task in 1953, for what he termed "laxity in official discipline."

Close Yoshida associates, however, were not exempt from suspicion. Former Finance Minister Tokutaro Kitamura charged in the Diet that Yoshida associates had illegally refunded 2,000,000,000 yen to coalmine operators by reducing an interest rate set by the Occupation on Reconstruction Finance Bank loans, while Hideo Kurita, a Progressive Party leader, demanded that the Diet probe the grant of a billion yen and special franchise rights to a power company headed by one of Yoshida's favorite advisers. The favor, said Kurita, was extended in return for a 650,000-yen donation to the Liberal Party's campaign funds.

An odd feature of the spiritual reform lay in the fact that the few culprits who were caught and placed on trial pleaded guilty but gave extenuating circumstances. The head of the Mineral and Industrial Products Trade Company, an official agency from which 300,000,000 yen had been embezzled, contended that the money was profit that had resulted from his efficiency, and therefore he should not be penalized. Numbers of high-placed politicians, including former Cabinet ministers, excused themselves for money gifts from contractors on the ground that they had received them "in their private capacities" and not because of their official positions. The Economic Investigation Board, in reporting on the shortage of 8,000,000,000 yen in eight government corporations, expressed a similar philosophy in declining to publish details of the defalcations "because it might produce a bad moral effect."

Perhaps the most spectacular instance of postwar corruption was disclosed in the three-and-one-half-year trial of half a hundred leading political and industrial figures indicted in the great Showa Denko Electrical Industry Company case. This scandal, arising out of negotiations for a 2,000,000,000-yen Reconstruction Finance Bank loan and the distribution of the funds thus borrowed, revealed a widespread pattern of gifts from companies seeking loans or contracts, purchase of political support by donations to all major parties, solicitation of bribery and kickbacks on orders to purchase goods. Methods by which high-placed officials took money indirectly, thus avoiding direct contact, went into public record; the names of principals and intermediaries received nation-wide publicity, together with the precise amounts paid by the donors, drawn off as commissions by the middlemen, and received by the beneficiaries. Disclosure of these details caused the downfall of the Ashida Cabinet in 1948. This, it might be noted, was the Cabinet which had come to power immediately after MacArthur's jubilation over "spiritual reform."

The sensational trial resulted in the conviction for bribery of former Deputy Prime Minister Suyehiro Nishio; former Finance Minister Takeo Kurusu; President Setsuzo Hinohara of Showa Denko; and five other prominent personages. Ashida was acquitted on the ground that he was innocent of bribery in spite of being suspected of receiving 2,000,000 yen, because he held no official responsibility and exercised no jurisdiction over the funds from which the bribe was alleged to have been taken.

Jail sentences were imposed upon the convicted; but most were softened by stays of execution which, in effect, released them on probation.

Although *Asahi, Mainichi, Yomiuri,* and the minor press thundered incessantly at what *Asahi* termed "the bottomless pit of public corruption," the electorate showed little real resentment. Twenty-eight other Diet members, including at least one high-placed Cabinet Minister, were triumphantly reelected in 1953 while awaiting trial for frauds in the 1952 election.

Public tolerance of official malfeasance, although largely an ancient heritage, may also have reflected Occupation attitudes. None of the Supreme Commanders had been ignorant of the situation. MacArthur, in particular, received ample information, not only through the English-language press but also in daily digests supplied both by Willoughby's Allied Translation and Interpreter Service and by Whitney's special reports. To have recognized reality, however, would have risked embarrassing consequences. Occupationnaires, committed to the myth that Japan managed its own internal affairs, could not interfere openly without destroying the fiction that they had themselves created; nor could they nudge and needle corrupt public officials into sending themselves to jail. To publicize the evils, moreover, would have been to confess that the Occupation had been negligent or inefficient, and that its spokesmen had been hasty in proclaiming a spiritual regeneration. The Occupation therefore did little to correct the situation, and the Japanese did less.

In consequence, the evils steadily increased, the closing months of the Occupation being marred by a dozen major scandals. Peculations, frauds, and briberies reported by police and justice officials as totaling millions, or in some cases billions, of yen marked the administration of postal, railway, telephone, food, tax, and education offices. Few officials were punished, many of those who confessed to embezzlements being let off scot-free.

After the Japanese Government recovered actual, as well as theoretical, control of its internal affairs, more stable conditions reappeared. Corruption diminished, although still rampant in government offices dealing with railways, power, and international trade. The cause, however, was not enlightened public morality but rather lessened opportunity, now that funds were reduced and supervisory responsibility was centered in some specific authority. In February 1954 the Diet again heard charges of corruption involving high officials of each of the three major parties, by an investment company whose methods exactly paralleled those of Showa Denko. Simultaneously other graft charges were pending in army, railway, shipping, tax, and welfare cases.

Almost irretrievable damage, however, had already been done. Japan, while fed high-sounding platitudes and buttered with praise for her non-existent spiritual regeneration, had learned that crime in high places incurred but little penalty. More than ever cynical, she doubted the integrity not only of her own officials but of those imposed upon her from abroad. Wholly unfounded rumors spread that leading Occupation officials had been bribed, and that Occupationnaires, as well as Japanese officials, had pocketed huge sums of public money.

Shattering of the administrative structure into tiny autonomous pieces and wrecking of the supervisory structure increased opportunity for grafters. The corruption spread rapidly from Tokyo into prefectures, cities, and villages. While necessarily upon a more limited scale in any given entity, the evil became exceedingly serious, not only because of the numbers of offices involved but because discovery of guilt, difficult enough in Tokyo, was almost impossible when it came to small offenders in the local areas. Nor was the money cost so grievous as the loss of public confidence in the integrity of leaders, small as well as large. In all too many instances, possession of public office was no longer as in the past a mark of distinction and dignity, but cause for public suspicion, especially if they played mahjong, to which, it was said, all officials except Yoshida were addicted, for winnings at this game often covered bribery. Tokyo had 1,282 mahjong parlors in 1954.

During the first three years of the Occupation, Niigata prefecture arrested 360 officials; Nagano, 90; Hokkaido, 78; Miyagi, 48; and Osaka, 42. In 1951 Procurator-General Sato, while not breaking his figures down by prefecture, reported 1,303 metropolitan and prefectural offenders and 1,577 city officials as guilty of corrupt practices. Among the offenders had been governors of Miyagi and Saitama, the mayor of Tottori, the mayor and the entire membership of councils of a smaller city of northern Japan, the mayor of Shibuya, and the vice mayor of Aomori. That public sentiment did not run too harshly against such men was shown in August, 1952, when a former governor implicated in a bribery and misappropriation case was vindicated by election as governor of another prefecture.

During 1949 and 1950 many local communities, desperate for funds, connived with gamblers to tolerate dishonesty. Professional bicycle racing, introduced into Kyushu in November, 1948, spread rapidly throughout Japan, the local authorities agreeing to license racing in return for a portion of the money wagered. At least 150 tracks opened, and at most of them well substantiated charges of fixed races, bribery, and other evil practices followed. Angered patrons started riots, and in some cases set fire to wooden structures. By the summer of 1950 scandals were so numerous that bicycle racing was officially forbidden; but political interests prevailed upon the Yoshida government to reinstate it. After November, 1950, the Ministry of International Trade and Industry assumed supervision of the tracks, and the worst evils subsided. The possibility of revenue, however, induced the Diet in June, 1951, to legalize dog racing on condition that the national treasury receive 25 per cent of profits.

Licenses for bicycle and dog racing were concessions to the passion for gambling that swept over Occupied Japan. While convictions for gambling fell sharply in 1949 and 1950 after an almost uninterrupted rise since 1902, the decline apparently was due to lack of enforcement because pinball gambling, in addition to legalized lotteries, bicycle, horse, and dog racing, and "flower-cards," suddenly increased. From the 7,152 establishments (or *pachinko*) with 169,384 machines reported by the Local Finance Commission in October, 1951, the pinball industry rose to 22,500 establishments with 995,000 machines in 1954. The galleries in Tokyo increased from 845 to 4,700.

The growth paralleled a feverish increase in amusement seeking. A Local Finance Committee survey in July, 1952, revealed that taxes paid during 1951 on amusements outside the home totaled 35,000,000,-000 yen, or slightly less than $100,000,000, which—at a tax rate ranging from 40 to 100 per cent—indicated a total payment of almost double that sum; and during the second half of 1951 there was attendance of at least 167,870,000 at movies, 6,780,000 at bicycle races, 3,780,000 at horse races, 2,790,000 at dance halls, and 3,070,000 at amusement parks, while there were 2,120,000 players of mahjong.

Tokyo alone had 1,060 high-grade restaurants, 7,742 taprooms, 3,752 teashops, 1,996 cafés, 2,524 inns, and 328 movie and other theaters. Its monthly bill for pleasure outside the home was at least 3,000,000,-000 yen. Much of this was spent upon legalized vice, there being thirteen red-light districts with a total of 670 licensed houses of prostitution in September, 1948. These, however, were insufficient, and steps were taken with the connivance of officials to open three more districts before the residents of the areas were aware of the purpose of the new houses being erected. At Ikegami new brothels were about to be opened where fifteen schools were concentrated within a mile radius; but public protests forced cancellation of the licenses. At Uji, also in Tokyo, another licensed quarter was stopped by public protest, only to be reopened quietly a few months later. In addition to these licensed houses, at least 5,000 clandestines operated in Tokyo during 1950, being divided into two groups, the White Bird Society which patrolled central Tokyo and the White Chrysanthemums who centered in the populous Shinjuku and Shibuya districts. A regiment of 912 White Birds served the Ueno railway station, and 754 others the Asakusa amusement park. Arrests of 9,425 streetwalkers, *pan-pan* girls, during 1950 failed to limit their activities.

Although these prostitutes catered primarily to Japanese, some pan-pan girls and those who called themselves "onlies" specialized in GI's and other foreigners. In 1952 the Welfare Ministry counted 70,000 such girls who, the Economic Stabilization Board added, illegally brought into Japanese economy about $200,000,000 yearly in foreign exchange. A *Jiji Shimpo* columnist, no doubt intending to be humorous, suggested that they be decorated for their promotion of international good will.

GI's, however, were not the only offenders. In August, 1952, the Education Ministry, after surveying eighty-two junior high schools in the Tokyo district, reported that at least 30 per cent of the girl students had been "subjected to indecent influences" by movies and other undesirable conditions.

It is impossible to interpret Japanese delinquency statistics accurately because offenders under twenty-five years of age are classed as juveniles, and because such offenses as "meetings of lovers," "strolling about holiday resorts," "pretending to be students," and "actions that are not good" are lumped without discrimination into the same statistics as more grievous crime; but detention of approximately 4,000 monthly in Tokyo during 1950 indicated a 30 per cent rise over the 1949 statistics and a doubling since 1948. Prior to the war there had also been a rise, of 14 per cent in 1936–1940 and 43 per cent in 1940–1944; but the postwar figures showed a 48 per cent increase in 1948 over 1944. If only the criminal code arrests are considered, the juvenile offenders, who in this category included only those under twenty years of age, rose from 33,048 in 1940 to 111,790 in 1946. In the first six months of 1953, the National Rural Police reported that 62,413 youths were arrested and 157,012 were placed under surveillance.

Gambling, prostitution, and narcotics traffic necessarily implied laxity in police control. In March, 1951, the *Yomiuri* newspaper exposed widespread collusion between the police of Yodobashi station and racket leaders of the Shinjuku red-light district. *Yomiuri* specifically named the chairman of the ward assembly, the president of the hotel men's association and the most important restaurant keeper as leaders of a corruption ring—all three being prominent members of three different police assistance societies—but could not bring procurators to consider indicting them. Eiichi Tanaka, chief of the Metropolitan Police Board, while admitting underworld activities in Tokyo's amusement resorts, promised only to investigate the charges which *Yomiuri* had already carefully documented. No further action seems to have been taken, and no punishments announced.

Similar indifference greeted protests later in 1951 against the licensing by the Construction Ministry of a new and luxurious Turkish bath establishment where male patrons were attended overnight in private rooms by attractive young masseuses. Little, if any, official public action was taken against government officials who spent huge sums as expenses in pleasure resorts while supposedly on official business. An epidemic of strip-tease dancing in approximately 150 Tokyo cafés and cabarets and in the half-dozen Tokyo burlesque theaters roused no strong public resentment.

Nor were Japanese particularly concerned with the cruelty to animals revealed in an Osaka proposal in 1952 to legalize dog fighting— a move stopped only by applying a new interpretation to an act against committing misdemeanors—or in the carting around Japan, for exhibition, of a harmless brown bear in a cage too small for it to stand upright and too narrow for it to lie comfortably. These evils were checked chiefly as the result of strong protests by an American, Mrs. Lindesay Parrott, after Japanese officials had waved the matters aside as unimportant.

The child slavery evil continued to curse Japan, without a sign of a spiritual revolution. Responsible officials of three Cabinet ministries— Welfare, Labor, and Education—and a special Diet investigation committee, policemen, and social workers agreed that sale of young people into forced labor, a traditional practice in impoverished rural Japan, was not only continuing but increasing. In 1949 the Welfare Ministry uncovered 3,136 such cases in northeastern Japan, and between January, 1949, and the end of the Occupation in 1952 it reported 5,959 instances of sale of young girls by their parents for sums as low as 3,000-yen advance with royalties to follow from their services in Tokyo brothels. The bad rice crop of 1953 intensified the evil, the Welfare

Ministry reporting that 1,489 children had been sold (89 per cent of them 17-year-old girls). In addition, the Procurator's Office charged, 29,007 Japanese were "sold into jobs."

Such abuses had been supposedly illegal since 1881, and the laws prohibiting these sales were strengthened under the Occupation; but, despite repeated assurances that the statutes would be enforced, few persons arrested for exploiting children suffered seriously. During 1949, for example, twenty-seven cases were tried; but only three persons went to jail for as much as a year, nor was anyone fined as much as $50. Following a drive in 1950 against the evil, 101 individuals were brought into court and 66 defendants received jail sentences—none for more than a year; but 50 of the 66 were paroled during good behavior. Of the twelve fines imposed, the largest was a nominal $50.

Japanese, in fact—even such an official as Kiyoshi Kikuchi of the Crime Prevention Society—defended child slavery by drawing a specious comparison to the bound servants of colonial America. Selling a girl into slavery, they said, helped the child. Her health improved because she ate more and better food; her housing was more satisfactory, and a physician was especially assigned to guard against and cure illnesses. Socially, moreover, she was better off; her rural village had few facilities to offer, but the Tokyo contacts opened wide horizons. The reasoning was particularly stressed when factory labor was discussed, but the benefits were usually more apparent than real.

SIXTEEN

Underground Empire

MacArthur's staff sections, refusing to believe facts long in their possession, may have helped racketeers control Japan. Because of sectional jealousies and unwillingness to publish data contradicting the Supreme Commander, they kept feudalism alive.

Lack of clear jurisdiction played a part. Under the gentlemen's agreement, section chiefs kept well within the limits of the "empires" assigned them in October, 1945. Each chief was anxious to make a showing that would pin another star upon his shoulder. Each was willing to annex responsibility not elsewhere allotted, but none would venture into the gray shadows that lay as a no man's land between the empires.

Gangster activity was such an area. It involved police and economic interests, government and social welfare, taxation and labor, mines and transportation, covering the fields of at least a dozen Occupation staff sections. And since it was no man's monopoly no staff section chief wished to burn his fingers on it.

Occupationnaires knew little of this tangled racketeer domain, and Japanese refrained from telling much about it; but when Allied intelligence agents warned of danger the Occupation closed its ears and shut its eyes.

Eventually it took action, but belatedly and under almost unsurmountable difficulties. Gangsterism and racketeering were evils to be stopped at almost any cost; but the curative methods employed by Americans who did not know the problem were almost useless.

To explain modern Japanese gangsterism is to court misunderstanding; yet basically, as in the medieval European feudalism to which it is

171

so loosely comparable, a balance of service and protection prevailed. The ethical conception, however, varied widely. In Japan, unlike the West, leaders acknowledged no obligations and no duties; nor did followers talk of rights and privileges. This, to Westerners, seemed like surrender of will, perhaps imposed by force; but no such violence or bargaining or voluntary agreement had occurred. Harmony was paramount, a harmony of subordination willingly offered by men unconscious of making any sacrifice; far from feeling robbed or cheated of his rights, each member felt comfortable in his status.

This, to be sure, oversimplifies a complex situation highly charged with emotion; but the Occupation wholly failed to understand even the elementary principles of Japanese gangster groups. Considering the groups solely as criminal conspiracies organized for graft or vice or crime, the Occupation firmly believed that all that was necessary was to jail the leaders, unconcerned by the fact that this meant striking at the very heart of Japanese reaction, not only in crime but also in political and social relationships. Recognizing clearly that the gangs were hostile to the democratic spirit, the Occupation deluded itself into thinking that a mere order to dissolve a gang would be sufficient.

As in the instance of the purge, stress upon leaders and on formal organization ignored reality. Jailing the leaders would not wipe out loyalties; dissolution of criminal conspiracies would not prevent their reestablishment. Undoubtedly the Occupation was well within its rights in seeking to uproot the gang; but its hasty identification of those gangs with the illegal mobs of prohibition times in the United States once more showed its unfamiliarity with Japanese conditions. In the laudable campaign to wipe out racketeering the Occupation unwittingly took on a war against a foundation of Japan's social system.

This was the idea of fixed status—an idea which for centuries had been so carefully fostered that each Japanese knew his proper station and all that this involved in etiquette—precisely as every American service officer expected not only to receive the rights proper to his rank but also to act with proper decorum toward his fellows. Deference to leaders, unwillingness openly to criticize a senior, modesty in thrusting one's self forward, hesitancy in expressing an original opinion—these were virtues admired both in an army camp and in Japanese society. Yet American officers who would have shrunk from violations of their own code demanded that Japanese ignore their fundamental principles.

For the leader-follower system, the *oyabun-kobun kankei*, was inherent not only in the gangs but also in politics, in management of industry, in education, and in virtually every other type of social relationships. The Occupation, while properly appraising it as hostile to democracy, erred in considering the system as nothing but a variation of the gang. Thus, in warring upon the gangs and secret societies, a relatively minor manifestation, a perversion of the oyabun-kobun system, the Occupation met surprising opposition: while Japanese rarely would defend or excuse the gangs, they did resist attacks upon social relationships entrenched in centuries-old tradition.

For centuries Japanese had been familiar with secret societies whose members pledged loyalty to their leaders, and whose leaders protected their men. Fantastic tales of outlaws bound together by tasting each other's blood studded Japanese romances; dramas of the legendary Chuji Kunisada, knight of chivalry, were favorites upon the stage. Every Japanese child knew the stories well; but Occupationnaires either had never heard of them or credited the explanation that Kunisada was the Japanese equivalent of Robin Hood.

The gang leader, oyabun, had little similarity to the underworld character of the American prohibition era. He had few, if any, of the characteristics of the Hollywood master criminal. Seldom did he fit the stereotype of the suave and soft-spoken but deadly gentleman, well tailored and polished but ruthless. He had no deep-laid plots, nor was he the cold and scientific Brain of the detective stories. The oyabun was the boss, the executive who because he had a little capital, the know-how, political connections, energy, or some other special qualification assumed leadership in time of stress. Around such a man gathered the friendless and the unfortunate, the uprooted and those in need; in return for food, clothing, shelter, and protection they owed him labor and unquestioning obedience.

The oyabun system rose readily when communities were wrecked by war. Japan knew that the oyabun groups of Tokugawa days persisted, especially in country districts where the leader was the big landlord and in the slums of cities where the leader was the padrone who gave day labor or the political boss who courted votes. After the war the break-up of the once powerful police and the collapse of virtually all social control left the central government too weak to provide work for millions of demobilized soldiers or to feed the starving homeless. The situation was all the more desperate because the Allied Occupation purged virtually the entire stratum of experienced leaders.

To a sociologist the situation would have been apparent; but the top brass agreed with MacArthur that the time was premature for sociology. Imbued with wartime propaganda, fearful of reactionary risings, they construed the crisis in terms of "rightist" plots to bring back ultra-nationalism. When, therefore, they saw *boryoku-dan* (strong-arm squads) or *guren-tai* (gangs of hooligans), armed with clubs or ancient swords, they did not inquire into causes but, scenting sedition, warned that reactionaries were endeavoring to restore totalitarian control.

With equal naïveté, when Occupationnaires learned that such small businessmen as the proprietors of *tekiya* (canvas-and-bamboo street stalls) had joined protective associations they welcomed these as a cooperative movement. The fact was that such organizations were gangster-dominated.

The oyabun organizations, which in a sense were substitutes for a disrupted family system, and which had developed feudalistic loyalties and peculiar codes of ethics, appeared in the countryside as a landlord-tenant relationship wherein the oyabun, sometimes by hereditary right, controlled the community. Whitney's Government Section and Schenck's Natural Resources Section alike were shocked when too few candidates offered themselves in the Diet elections of 1946, 1947, and 1949. In at least a third of the mayoralty contests in smaller cities one man alone ran for the office; this was the local oyabun, whose right to represent and lead his people was unchallenged by his neighbors. Candidates were even more reluctant to appear at special elections for land-reform commissioner; not only did supposedly downtrodden tenants sympathize with landlords whose holdings were taken away, but in many cases they joined with the oyabun to defeat the purpose of the very laws supposed to liberate them from bondage. Whitney, misunderstanding the situation, tried to cure the evil by reforming political parties and was astonished when the reforms proved to be ineffective.

The oyabun system flourished also in the coal fields of Kyushu and Hokkaido. Mine owners contracted with oyabun for laborers, conducting all negotiations through these leaders, who received pay in lump sums and distributed as much or as little as was necessary. After the war, oyabun received relief goods for the men but diverted much of them to the black market. When Marquat's Labor Division insisted that labor unions replace the feudalistic system the oyabun, in many instances, managed the union locals.

Chaotic conditions in the devastated cities favored postwar oyabun-kobun development. As Kingo Shibayama, boss of the Asakasa amusement district, explained, "The big shots threw up their hands after surrender and did nothing to help the masses escape from their desperate condition; but I went to work to make things better."

Shibayama's assistance took the form of a protection racket whereby tekiya proprietors, in return for a 40,000-yen initiation fee and a 1,000-yen daily security and prosperity tax, joined his stall keepers union. He admitted that his system was "feudal" but added, "The world needs our benevolence and righteousness." The Occupation tried to break the union in February, 1948, by having him arrested for extortion; but no witnesses appeared against him.

The reluctance was typical; but even when victims overcame their fears police and judicial authorities were indifferent. Early in 1946, for instance, Kinnosuke Ozu, whom the Occupation once termed the worst criminal in Japan, ordered tekiya who refused tribute to go out of business and tore down the stalls of any who stood their ground. The American Provost Marshal told the police to protect them; instead, the police chiefs supported Ozu. Nine months later Willoughby's police expert, Harry S. Eaton, finally had him arrested only to find that procurator and judges were apathetic about the case; the former was suspended, and the latter were reprimanded. After ten months' further delay Ozu was convicted; but police, procurator, and judicial officials certified that he was too sick to be jailed. As a reform gesture, Ozu converted his protective association into a "cooperative," in a public ceremony at which the chief of police and the judges who had convicted him certified to his high character.

Even many Occupationnaires accepted Ozu's protestations, "Gangs are democratic" and "I have awakened to the spirit of righteousness."

Ample evidence against gang democracy was in the Occupation files. As far back as August, 1946, Harry Shupack, one of Eaton's investigators, had filed a remarkable report concerning a gang war between Koreans and Formosans on one side and a private feudal army on the other. The prize was control over fifteen hundred black marketers at Shimbashi who had been paying daily tribute to Giichi Matsuda, "Emperor Matsuzakaya V." Matsuzakaya's men had rebelled, and the Koreans and Formosans, claiming extraterritorial rights, had intervened with machine guns. At this point the "emperor" had been killed, probably by one of his own men. His widow, calling herself "Matsuzakaya VI," swore to take vengeance, "regardless of danger and resistance," upon both the rebels and the foreign interventionists.

Perhaps Shupack's story is too fanciful to deserve full credit; but it does reveal the pattern of oyabun-kobun relationships. It shows, also, that Shimbashi police connived at Matsuzakaya's assumption of civic government. He was allowed to levy and collect taxes, provided he gave part of the proceeds to the local treasury; he ran the fire service, held contracts for street cleaning, and controlled the reconstruction program.

This, the Occupation learned, was not only a general practice but was wholly legal, in Tokyo at least. In March, 1943, the Tokyo Assembly had officially recognized stall-keeper oyabun not only as tax agents but also as price and distribution controllers with power to punish disobedience. In January, 1945, moreover, the Metropolitan Police Board had forced all stall keepers to join a Tradesmen's Union (Roten Dogyo Kumiai), in order to tighten the oyabun hold. Shupack reported this situation and recommended that the system be abolished.

So little attention was paid to Shupack's report that in September, 1946, Eaton allowed the Metropolitan Police Board to renew the Roten Dogyo Kumiai's right to monopolize tekiya administration. The oyabun —Kinnosuke Ozu, whom the Provost Marshal was even then ordering the police to control—was to levy whatever tax he desired, paying into the city treasury only as much of the total as he thought fit and retaining some of this, too, as his fee. Ozu was at that time known to control 88 per cent of Tokyo's 45,000 registered street stalls; the Metropolitan Police Board ordinance thus legalized his hold upon the remaining 12 per cent.

None of this oyabun story—neither the Shimbashi incident nor the Ozu grant—was thought sufficiently important for MacArthur to report in his Monthly Summation of Non-Military Activities. The omission was deliberate, as was the suppression of similar material gathered by a member of Whitney's Government Section who in August, 1946, uncovered Usaburo Chizaki's oyabun activities. This Chizaki report, complete with verified data, was suppressed because "the old man must not be disturbed."

Not until nearly a year later did MacArthur show an interest in the oyabun situation. In June, 1947, when Tokyo police were again embarking upon a half-hearted attempt to wipe out gangsterism, a confidential report by Willoughby informed MacArthur that the oyabun system was a dangerous complex; but no public admission was made, and as far as the Monthly Summation was concerned the only peril was that of an organized black market. Whitney's political officers were warned again in March, 1947, that Chizaki had muscled into the newly organized Democratic Party and received documented evidence of Chizaki's relations with leading political bosses in the other parties; but they shrugged the matter aside as unimportant, and ignored revelations that high-placed politicians, including members of the Cabinet, were implicated in rackets. A complete story of Ozu's illegal activities and their connections with the dominant Liberal Party was published by Government Section in its Weekly News Review; but no action was taken, lest wider publicity contradict boasts that all was well in Japanese political affairs.

In July, 1947, however, a rival oyabun in Shinjuku, the Ozu fief, so glaringly defied police control that the Occupation had to take notice. Ken Sekine, a notorious gangster, was being sought on charges of intimidation; but the police could not find him, in spite of clues published daily in the Japanese press. Later Sekine agreed to surrender if the police would go easy on him.

By this time some 970 gangsters had been rounded up. Willoughby's police supervisors reported that nine important oyabun had been arrested, but they did not mention that seven had already been released for lack of evidence, nor explain that at least half the lesser men were also freed immediately.

A general conference of all Occupation agencies to study the oyabun situation was then decided upon, Willoughby's aides conferring first with the Civil Information and Education experts and later with labor specialists in the Economics and Scientific Section.

On September 12 various Occupation agencies pooled their information on oyabun affairs. Much of it, as a matter of fact, had already appeared in the press, and some in the English-language papers which Occupation officials read daily; but heretofore it had been considered to be relatively unimportant. It included the tekiya story, the Hokkaido and Kyushu coal-mine situations, the leakage of goods to the black market, the tax-farming racket, the landlord-tenant relationship, and the unwillingness of police to take action.

The Occupation discovered to its astonishment that virtually all the construction work done by its order, or for its interests, was handled through *gumi*—oyabun organizations that held their workmen in semi-feudal bondage. Approximately three million laborers were thus engaged.

Occupation families lived in gangster-built, or gangster-maintained, houses.

American supply ships, as well as other vessels docking in Japan, were handled by oyabun gangs which not only monopolized stevedoring and transport, but were closely linked with the reactionary militarists of prewar Japan. The Black Dragon Society, of which much had been heard in the days when Japan was plotting overseas expansion, was rooted in the stevedore monopoly.

All gambling, dance halls, cafés, bars, restaurants, theaters, and amusements, as well as commercial prostitution, were under oyabun control.

The Occupation's discovery of this vast nexus came, curiously enough, after some of the oyabun themselves had decided that the time was ripe for reformation. The Ozu and Sekine gangs had turned themselves into pseudo cooperatives whose genuine conversion was more than doubtful, but Yoshiko Matsuda, "Matsuzakaya VI," had already announced in August, 1947, that her group had undergone a change of heart. "Although the profession of my young men," she said, "has been to quarrel and fight, many have clean, pure hearts." Hodennosuke Shinohara, oyabun of a gamblers' organization, echoed her words by saying: "My boys have turned respectable; I hope they will not again fall into evil ways." Similar pious protestations were made elsewhere, but subsequent surveys showed that many of the former gangsters, far from mending their evil ways, had broken into smaller groups of pickpockets, stick-up men, and petty criminals.

These resolutions were dictated by fear, rather than conviction that democracy was desirable. In the year ending August, 1947, 7,962 individuals had been arrested; at least half had been set free without a charge, and the rest had been mildly punished. In Tokyo itself, police raids beginning in July, 1947, netted 1,609 by November. Though Ozu and Sekine were the only important oyabun included, and although only 896 of the 1,609 were actually indicted, the publicity had been unpleasant.

Shupack commented that the general situation remained unaltered, and that the Ozu-Sekine combination retained full control.

By this time Government Section, awakening to the significance of the information it had had for fifteen months, came forth with startling accusations. In an address to a national gathering of public procurators, Colonel Kades, deputy chief, warned that a vast and insidious network of feudal forces was undermining American democratic policy. He admitted that the supposed democracy for which MacArthur had taken credit was merely a façade, and declared that the real rulers of Japan were not the politicians nor the Diet but bosses, hoodlums, and racketeers who together amounted to an underground government. "Unless this is wiped out," he said, "all gains of the past two years toward attaining democratic government responsible to the people will be imperiled, if not extinguished."

Colonel Harry E. Pulliam, chief of Willoughby's Public Safety Division, warned Home Minister Kozaemon Kimura that "the entire political, economic, and cultural life of Japan is at the mercy of the gangster groups." He insisted that the police eradicate the gangs.

Prime Minister Tetsu Katayama, although usually mild and yielding to Occupation pressure, denied emphatically that any dangerous rightist undergrounds existed. "There are," he said, "some dregs of feudalism, but the Government is making war upon them." However, his Crime Prevention Bureau estimated that at least 1,260 gangs were in existence, with 53,051 leading members, and that only 15 per cent of the membership had been caught in raids.

Further raids followed, as many as eight in Tokyo alone from 1947 to 1951, with at least 1,750 to 2,000 prisoners taken in each raid. While the grouping in police statistics of all threat and intimidation cases makes it difficult to ascertain what punishments were inflicted, the number must have been small since convictions for all such cases totaled but 465 in 1949 and 964 in 1950. Only two of the convicted offenders were jailed for as much as three years. Lesser jail sentences were imposed upon 214 in 1949 and 353 in 1950, but two-thirds of the sentences were suspended. Fines of 10,000 yen were inflicted upon 42 offenders during the two-year period; but of the 735 other fines 637 were sums less than 5,000 yen.

Convictions for gambling and allied offenses, usually regarded as gangster-dominated, actually fell off during the period when the Occupation was insisting upon drives against gangsters. Such convictions, which totaled 62,907 in 1948, dropped to 36,553 in 1949 and 26,645 in 1950. Convictions in 1940, the last normal prewar year, had been 67,767.

Not only did convictions for gangster-dominated operations fall in 1950 to 42 per cent of the 1948 level but punishments inflicted were remarkably slight. Of the 26,645 offenders proved guilty only 505 habitual gamblers were jailed, and 174 of these were at once released on suspended sentences. The number of new prisoners admitted to jail for such offenses had so declined in each year of the Occupation that the total in 1950 was but one-fifth the annual admissions during the fifteen-year period prior to the war.

No persons convicted of habitual gambling paid any fine whatever.

So reluctant were the police to take action, and so lenient were the courts, that the Occupation's own prosecutors intervened in the case of Ken Sekine, oyabun of Shinjuku, to charge him with extortion and his associates with illegal possession of a machine gun. He was sentenced to five years imprisonment and to a fine of 75,000 yen; but the sentence was reduced upon appeal to three years, and soon after he entered upon it he was declared, like Ozu, too ill for imprisonment and went free in May, 1949.

The net result of all the highly publicized anti-gang campaigns was therefore virtually nil. The gangs, in fact, grew stronger and took over control at Honjo, Omiya, and Konoso, all close to Tokyo, while the campaign against them was at its very height. Chief Iwasaki of the National Rural Police confessed that the small local forces could not successfully resist ruffian assaults. At Hiroshima the police helplessness became so apparent in the course of six years of civil war between two rival gangs that the police authorities admitted in 1953, according to the Osaka *Asahi,* that the only conceivable solution would be the murder of one or the other of the contending bosses. The Tokyo Metropolitan Police Board reported 7,506 gangster crimes from January 1 to October 1, 1953; an increase of 5,419 over the figures for all of 1952.

By 1953, of course, the Occupation had long since withdrawn; but even prior to its departure it had virtually abandoned the anti-oyabun struggle. Having commanded Japan to end the oyabun system, Occupationnaires assumed that the Employment Security Law of November, 1947, would be a sufficient safeguard. Under this law, however, only 190 persons were convicted during 1950, 34 being sentenced to imprisonment; more than half received suspended sentences and no sentence was for more than two years. None of the 175 fines imposed was more than $30.

Occupation enforcement officials ignored the meager results of this law for oyabun control, if indeed they were aware of its ineffectiveness, and turned attention thereafter to ferreting out subversive tendencies among oyabun followers. Discovery of swords and pistols among gangster armaments stirred fear of anti-Occupation plots, perhaps even of gangster understandings with the Communists.

SEVENTEEN

Democratic Police

Foremost among the accusations leveled against prewar Japan was that it was a police state, not only in the broad sense of being totalitarian but in the narrower meaning that policemen dominated every social, political, or economic activity. The uniformed man in the police box under the Imperial sixteen-petaled golden chrysanthemum crest ruled the neighborhood; the Home Ministry to which he was responsible controlled the Empire's internal affairs.

To destroy police dictatorship, to free the citizen from close supervision over his daily living—so strict that it even dictated when and how he must clean his house—and to loose the stranglehold of Tokyo bureaucracy were fundamental objectives of Occupation policy.

How well were these objectives attained? Recognizing that by orders issued in October, 1945, the infamous secret police system was abolished, the iniquitous military gendarmerie destroyed, and the more obviously evil leaders purged, and that the Home Ministry itself was wiped out in January, 1947, by SCAP directive, how far has police reform proceeded? How, if at all, does Japanese resumption of independence affect the changes introduced by order of the Occupation Forces? The results are both encouraging and ominous.

Police enrollments provide a case in point. While police duties certainly diminished, numbers have increased. Instead of being less policed, Japan was more policed, with 125,000 uniformed men in 1952 against 84,141 on December 7, 1941. In 1941 there were 872 Japanese per policeman; in 1952 there were but 672.

This increase of police strength by 48 per cent over a period when

181

population rose but 20 per cent may not in itself tell the full story. There are, in addition, 120,000 members of a National Police Reserve which, although in reality an army, is theoretically a police force. Much of the increase centered in the larger cities. Disregarding NPR, Tokyo provided one uniformed policeman for every 130 residents as compared to one per 251 in 1941. Osaka, which in 1940 had one policeman for every 493 residents, now has one for every 150 people. But the increase appears in every section of Japan. Whereas in 1940, fourteen prefectures had more than 1,000 persons per policeman, in 1952 there were but two such prefectures. Instead of 1,013 prewar police stations, Japan had 1,565, plus 705 NPR centers.

General Willoughby, who approved, if indeed he did not initiate, the increased strength, never explained why increases were necessary. He intimated however, that abolition of the third degree, of secret espionage agencies, and of other undesirable prewar practices had so reduced efficiency that more men were required to do the work that expert policemen had previously performed. He also declared that only 5.7 per cent of the prewar personnel had been eliminated by SCAP.

Yet on nothing were Willoughby and Pulliam more insistent than in reporting that Japan had had no significant increase in crime. Whereas, they said, Japan in 1932 had shown 1,298,327 offenses against the criminal and penal codes, the 1948 record revealed only 1,586,444 such offenses despite a larger population, postwar dislocations, and a multiplicity of new laws. The crime rate during the period from 1945 to 1950 was, they said, below the 1933–1935 average. They did not show that crimes by women had doubled and juvenile crimes tripled since 1941 or that violent crimes had more than tripled.

Not all Japanese observers accepted the Willoughby statistics at face value. Yoshio Izui, chief of the Criminal Department of the Tokyo Procurator's Office, complained of an "amazing postwar increase in crime" indicating that one out of every thirty Tokyo residents was a criminal. This was, in all probability, an overstatement; but the Willoughby statistics did not cover violations of the economic regulations, where the largest increase had occurred.

Regeneration was slow in reaching the police. Shinnosuke Abe, Japan's most popular press commentator, wrote in *Hassen-mannin* magazine, September, 1948, that the police, far from being democratized and far from having been transformed from masters to servants of the people, had retained their old-time haughtiness. The Attorney-General's

Office protested, in the summer of 1951, against police brutality. Shun-kichi Ueno, head of the Civil Liberties Bureau, an official agency, re-ported a thousand violations monthly against basic human rights, mostly by the police. The shrewdly observant English-language newspaper, *Nippon Times,* remarked in 1951 that, while Japanese police were polite to Occupation personnel, not to Thailanders, Filipinos, or other Orientals, they continued their prewar brusqueness in dealing with their fellow countrymen. Police rudeness toward women led to official pro-tests in the Diet.

National Rural Police officials, disturbed by criticisms, authorized a public opinion poll on public reaction to postwar changes. The survey, compiled after questioning 2,751 adults in sixty-four communities, showed that while 64 per cent believed that police methods had been improved, 12 per cent denied betterment, and 24 per cent were unde-cided. Only 21 per cent believed that policemen in 1951 merited being called "democratized," and 61 per cent desired further changes. Dis-satisfaction was "particularly strong among the intelligentsia."

Much of the failure, if indeed there was a failure, was traceable to the fact that while regulations were easy to issue, enforcement of kind-ness, thoughtfulness, and democratic attitudes was difficult, particularly where enthusiasm was lacking. While Japanese were usually willing to cooperate they were often bewildered concerning what was actually re-quired. Shidehara, an old-school liberal, confessed in 1950 that he had come away from instruction by MacArthur to democratize the govern-ment with only the vague idea that he must dismiss his Home Minister, draft a new Constitution, and free all those jailed for Communism. His inquiry at Government Section had yielded only the explanation that police democratization was required but the Japanese must themselves discover the means of accomplishing that goal, and that the drafting by Government Section of specific requirements would constitute an unde-sired intrusion into Japan's internal affairs.

The guidance to Shidehara consisted chiefly in orders to purge his police of all militaristic and ultranationalistic elements, and of all those who had been instrumental in denying political, social, or economic equality. Later he was told that controls over labor must be taken away from the police. An effort to insure political neutrality by barring police from political activity was forbidden. The new Constitution guaranteed fundamental human rights, equality of treatment, and due process of law but failed to interpret the meaning of the guarantees.

The Occupation's concern with the maintenance of civil liberties, especially of free speech, together with the injunction that nothing critical be said of any of the Allied Powers, including Russia, led some high-placed Japanese to the mistaken conclusion that certain of Mac-Arthur's chief advisers were Communist-minded. This conviction was intensified by the order to release radical leaders from their eighteen-year-long imprisonments. When to this was added the realization that Japanese might criticize their Emperor as harshly as they desired but praising him, or even defending him, was "feudal," various Communist spokesmen professed with impunity that they were MacArthur's special pets.

It was Japan's good fortune—and America's—that the Communists were either too slothful or too confident to take the initiative. The disorganized police, defenseless and leaderless, uncertain of their privileges, and instructed to tolerate many things that previously had been anathema, were helpless. For months after the Occupation, any lawless element might have deposed the Emperor, taken over the government, and functioned at will, provided only that it did not tread on Occupation toes. MacArthur was under strict orders not to interfere with any *coup d'état* that did not imperil Occupation security. Many conservative Japanese leaders were, in fact, certain that this was what Mac-Arthur wanted. Their worry was intensified when MacArthur purged, as dangerous reactionaries, men like Ichiro Hatoyama and Reikichi Kita, who had stood firm against the Reds.

The Communist tide, favored by a press whose larger papers were controlled by radical influences, could not be stemmed by police activity. Even ordinary detective work was handicapped by restrictions upon interrogations or investigations that were not specifically ordered by some responsible government bureau upon matters especially assigned. Happily the Communists, probably concerned that excess activity would precipitate a Third World War, failed to take advantage of their opportunity.

This was fortunate, since the Japanese police had recently lost as undesirables 10,031 experienced officers, chiefly from the Police Bureau of the Home Office or from leading local administrators. Many others must have quit voluntarily, because only 40,993 of the 84,141 policemen on Pearl Harbor Day were active at the end of 1946.

Filling the vacancies was difficult. Applicants with previous police service were not encouraged, and former military personnel were barred.

Low pay and loss of former privileges still further handicapped recruiting. Tokyo experimented with hiring women and recruited 65 high-school graduates in March, 1946, only half of whom remained as long as three years. The experiment was not particularly successful since only 99 of the 223 Japanese cities employing women allowed them to make arrests. Most of the 860 female policemen were actually clerical assistants.

Not only were two-thirds of the police relatively inexperienced; they were for a long time tragically defenseless. Supposedly, by a MacArthur order of January 16, 1946, each policeman was to have a revolver and 100 rounds of ammunition; but as late as June, 1948, Pulliam found but 12,000 revolvers among the 125,000 officers. Many of these weapons, moreover, were useless, and the 12,000 pistols included 197 different models produced by 110 different manufacturers. Cartridges were so lacking in 1950 that recruits were limited to three practice shots during their entire training period, with two additional refresher shots while in service.

Lewis J. Valentine, former commissioner of New York police, was called upon to remedy this confused and inefficient system; but after examining the situation he spluttered angrily, "These people drive you crazy." The absurdity of sword-bearing policemen riding bicycles, the requirement of innumerable reports, the inexplicable communications system, and above all the nondescript uniforms fastened by safety pins caused him acute distress. "Even the cops on the Toonerville trolley," he said bitterly, "wouldn't be seen in some of these uniforms."

Together with Oscar Olander of the Michigan State Police and Frank Meals of the Coast Guard, each concentrating on a special field, Valentine recommended that recruits be better selected, better trained, and better armed, that they receive ample opportunity for promotion, and be better cared for in clothing, food, and pensions. They suggested a strong national police force of 30,000 men, with separate police systems, totaling 95,000 more, for each city of more than 50,000 population. While theoretically decentralized, each of the 118 local forces should be coordinated through national police schools, fingerprint and records bureaus, radio services, and special investigation and detective units.

Willoughby and Pulliam forwarded this plan to the Japanese Government and induced the Cabinet, February 22, 1947, to send it to MacArthur as a Japanese proposal for police reform.

Willoughby was certainly charged with responsibility for police affairs, but the proposal ran counter to Government Section's cherished ideal of a completely decentralized administration. Whitney, therefore, sharply opposed the plan, and interchanges of check sheets within the Occupation delayed reform. Argument, and often tempers, ran high, but in July Willoughby, unwilling to wait longer, circulated the proposal to all Occupation section chiefs for comment. Most of the sections concurred, some with suggestions for amendment, but Whitney flatly rejected the plan. In its stead he suggested a scheme, which he ascribed to Justice Minister Yoshio Suzuki, forbidding centralized police and recommending a separate and independent police force for each town of more than 5,000 population.

Whitney's proposal, approved by none of the Willoughby staff, led to a rebuttal in which Pulliam declared that as Hammurabi, Genghis Khan, Cesare Borgia, and Charles V all had relied upon a centralized police, Japan should do likewise. Willoughby added, after a conference with Suzuki, that the Whitney plan carried no Japanese endorsement whatever but had been imposed upon Suzuki by Government Section. Public Safety Division reprimanded the Justice Minister for accepting it.

Prime Minister Katayama, also rejecting the scheme proposed in Suzuki's name, promised Willoughby to recommend the Valentine-Olander-Meals proposal to MacArthur. This was embodied in an official letter from Katayama to MacArthur, September 3, 1947.

Whitney, nevertheless, continued his objections and argued so persuasively that MacArthur ordered Willoughby to accept the Whitney plans. On September 16, 1947, MacArthur wrote to Katayama to establish an independent—MacArthur's word was "autonomous"—police force in every community of more than 5,000 population. There was no provision for centralization or for compulsory cooperation.

This meant that, instead of a single, nationally unified police with 118 local forces, Japan must create 1,605 small systems, each self-contained and each independently financed. Of these, 23 would be in greater Tokyo, plus a Metropolitan Police Board; indeed some believed that a separate force would be required for each Tokyo and Osaka ward.

MacArthur thus approved the rise in police strength to 95,000 local policemen plus a National Rural Police (NRP) of 30,000 men. The NRP was to guard the countryside, to intervene locally whenever the Prime Minister declared an emergency, and to offer as much integration as possible for fingerprint exchange, laboratory analysis, and centralized records. There was to be no interchange of personnel and no centralized control over the fragmented forces.

Experienced Japanese legislators privately opposed the plan but dared not take an open stand against a bill proposed by General MacArthur himself. The bill therefore passed the Diet, December 17, 1947, and became the Police Law.

The Police Law vested administrative control in a five-member National Public Safety Commission, appointed for five years by the Prime Minister with the consent of the House of Representatives, and directly responsible to him. Membership was forbidden to those with police experience, to those who, prior to Surrender, had been career public officials, and to officers of political organizations. Members could be dismissed (also by the Prime Minister with Diet consent) if they became physically or mentally incompetent, or bankrupt, if they "behaved badly," or "violated official obligations," or if they joined subversive organizations. Similar regulations applied to the 46 prefectural and 1,605 local Public Safety Commissions, each of three members appointed by the governor, mayor, or headman and approved by the appropriate legislative council.

Fears that undue powers had been given the Prime Minister were dispelled by clauses requiring him to report promptly to the Diet any action involving police matters and to obtain its consent to those actions within twenty days.

In theory, police financing was to continue from the national treasury until such time, believed to be imminent, as the prefectures or local communities could pay the bills. In practice, however, the Diet proved reluctant to vote appropriations for police systems which it could not control. Local communities, it was hoped, could defray police costs by taxing amusement enterprises; but, as these were not present in rural regions nor often in the suburbs of large cities, recourse was made to income taxes, to levies upon sewing machines or gardens, or upon electric consumption.

Another solution was available, although socially undesirable. For many years various unofficial groups had voluntarily contributed for police expenses. Sometimes these "police supporters" or "crime prevention clubs" were innocent; more often their support covered bribery or protection of illicit interests.

Although Willoughby, briefed by the Japanese, warned against private subsidies to police, the risk was taken. Thus, in 1947 the Tokyo Police Supporters Association collected 8,000,000 yen, a Crime Prevention Society gave 2,000,000 yen more, and other contributors raised enough to bring the total to at least 15,000,000 yen. Yokohama police supporters exceeded this amount by giving 16,000,000 yen, while in Osaka in 1948 sixty-seven police aid societies, all unofficial, raised 32,-000,000 yen. "This is an unfortunate situation," said Chief Masui of the Police Affairs Bureau, "but we cannot help but rely on voluntary contributions from influential citizens."

Japan's highly organized gangster system thoroughly approved the private financing of the public police; it placed the fragmented, poorly equipped, and inexperienced police forces under heavy obligations. A police chief, receiving a new official residence worth, as at Sakamoto, 1,650,000 yen, as a gift from gangsters would not be likely to prosecute too vigorously a drive against his benefactors. In Chiba, Aomori, and Shiga prefectures gangster organizations, such as the postwar White Dragon Society, boasted that they had bought protection.

Even where the police were honest the tiny forces were inefficient; often they were at the mercy of the gangs. Villages with but a single constable were helpless; cities as large as 10,000 population, having perhaps half a dozen unarmed policemen on duty, were vulnerable to armed attack. A few gangsters wielding swords or baseball bats could easily dominate a town, warned Chief Iwasaki of the National Rural Police. Poor telephone communications, bad roads, absence of police motor equipment, and above all the lack of coordination and cooperation prevented the rush of help from neighboring communities. That the danger was real was evidenced when the Saitama cities of Konosu and Honjo, close to Tokyo, were captured by armed thugs, when Taira in Fukushima prefecture was taken over by Communist mobs, and when in Osaka itself gangsters held the governor prisoner until he yielded to their demands.

Though it was common knowledge that many local Public Safety Commissions were packed with gangsters, few dared to criticize. Japanese, barred from criticizing Occupation policies, not only kept silent but even, on occasion, praised the police for democratic attitudes; they refrained from comments on efficiency.

In September, 1948, the exposé by Shinnosuke Abe broke the ice. The Japanese press thereafter chorused disapproval of the decentralized police as weak, inefficient, graft-ridden, and boss-controlled; they charged that police departments, including the Tokyo Metropolitan Police Board, were riddled by jealousies and nepotism. Some observers believed that this barrage sprang from police inability to catch notorious fugitives and from failure to curb Communism; others said that it was the result of an appeal by Kudoyama town in Wakayama prefecture for permission to surrender its local police as too costly a luxury.

Whatever the cause, the criticism led the dominant Democratic-Liberal Party (now the Liberal Party) to revive the Willoughby proposals. Ministers of State Kozaemon Kimura and Senzo Higai—the latter the former Speaker who was in charge of police affairs for the Cabinet—consulted actively with police and prefectural authorities about revision of the Police Law. After thirty-one prefectures petitioned the Diet to replace the local systems by a centralized police, Yoshida approached MacArthur with a proposal to incorporate the local units into a national police and to create a special centralized police agency.

When news of this move leaked to the press both Frank Rizzo, deputy chief of Government Section, and Chief Cabinet Secretary Masuda categorically denied that letters had been exchanged upon the subject, but they avoided comment upon possible verbal discussion.

So confident were Japanese officials that police reform, previously blocked by Whitney, had Occupation support that Higai, following a House of Representatives special committee recommendation, announced that revision was actually under way. He asserted that cities of less than 50,000 population would lose their independent forces, that the National Rural Police would be strengthened, and that all police would be closely integrated. He averred that Harry Eaton had approved these changes, and had also approved a plan to create a force of 50,000 well armed infantrymen to guard against riots and insurrections.

The disclosure, coming soon after a tirade against Japanese police by Derevyanko before the Allied Council for Japan, caused a furore. Derevyanko had charged that Japanese police, exerting "ever increasing pressure upon democratic rights" had mobbed "progressively minded persons" under the very eyes of the Occupation officials, and that nothing had been done to protect civil liberties. Accusing the police of murdering a union leader—the charge was later proved false—Derevyanko asserted that the Japanese were actively rebuilding an army. The Higai statements, capping the Derevyanko tirade, led the London *Times* to declare editorially that Japan was planning a revival of the hated prewar secret police.

This statement Higai denied; but, unfortunately, he coupled his denial with a statement that "no concrete discussion had been made in the Cabinet" concerning plans to improve the police system—which was undoubtedly an exaggeration. Nevertheless, the time was thought unpropitious to advance important police changes.

Had the Communists been clever they would have held their peace; but instead they chose this very time to threaten the Government with a crisis of serious proportions. With incomparably bad timing they staged riots and demonstrations which advertised the helplessness of local police to resist organized mobs, and which led the Government to extend control legislation designed to curb reactionaries into wider applications.

Higai, accordingly, reiterated a demand that police be reorganized and that special militarized forces be created to guard against the Reds. He was, however, the wrong man to make the suggestion. Whitney, who in 1946 had caused his dismissal as Speaker, distrusted him not only because of his supposed rightist tendencies but also because of his relationship with Eaton. Yoshida also for political reasons disapproved him. When, therefore, Higai's demand became public, Yoshida, professing himself scandalized, suggested that he resign.

Higai protested that he himself had said nothing to the press; that information had leaked from his private conference with Yoshida, but not from him; and that, in fact, his proposals had actually been much milder than police changes suggested by Yoshida and other Cabinet members. He did, however, offer his resignation.

No doubt his protestations were well founded. No sooner had the furore subsided than MacArthur himself sent Yoshida a letter on July 8, 1950, requiring Japan to follow the very policies for which Higai had been rebuked.

MacArthur called for a separate National Police Reserve (NPR) of 75,000 men—later increased to 110,000 and in 1954 to 150,000. This was to be kept under the Prime Minister's personal control, entirely separate from regular police and free from interference by any Public Safety Commission. It was to be armed with American weapons, including, as it later developed, mortars and machine guns, was to be clothed in American-type uniforms, and was to be drilled in army fashion. Both Occupation and Japanese officials carefully refrained, however, from referring to it as a military force, though on May 5, 1951, MacArthur told the United States Senate special investigating committee that the NPR could readily be converted into excellent ground troops.

This statement was officially repudiated before the House of Councilors by Attorney General Takeo Ohashi, who denied any intention of making the NPR a ground force. He admitted, however, that it was "potentially feasible" to do so. In January, 1952, moreover, he boasted that the NPR was better drilled and organized than the defunct Japanese army had been and said that it was "virtually the same as a military organization," the only difference being that it would never be called upon to serve overseas.

By the summer of 1950 it had become obvious that decentralized police forces were costly and inefficient, and that, as able men had little opportunity to advance themselves in local forces, morale was ebbing. Such men as Eiji Suzuki, head of the Osaka Metropolitan Police, and Eiichi Tanaka, who held a similar position at Tokyo, resisted change; and so did the Local Autonomous Federation and the Local Autonomy Police Association. After Whitney and MacArthur left Japan, the Diet voted, June, 1951, to permit local communities, if they so desired, to merge their forces either with each other or into the National Rural Police. Within a month 101 towns voted to join the NRP, none electing to retain independence. By October, 1951, a total of 1,028 towns out of 1,314 had held plebiscites, all but 4 asking the NRP to assume control. An additional 49 towns voted to merge in early 1952. By the end of February, 1953, fewer than 200 of the 1,600 communities retained their local police. Thus, the Whitney proposal had been soundly repudiated.

The overwhelming vote destroyed any lingering belief that decentralization was popular. Recognition that Japanese police work involved more than routine crime prevention and must cope with major political movements, particularly with riots and perhaps civil uprisings fomented from Soviet Russia, led to the conviction that small local forces were entirely insufficient to preserve law and order.

The thesis that strong centralized forces should be restored had already been expressed in July, 1951, by an Ordinance Review Committee, established to examine the desirability of continuing Occupation-sponsored reforms. It had suggested the merging of all security agencies, including local and national police, the Maritime Safety Board (coast guard), the Immigration Agency, and the Special Investigation

Board of the Attorney-General's Office—the Japanese FBI—into a Public Safety Ministry.

Such an amalgamation, combining the police and the army and thus restoring a police state, met strong opposition from democratically minded Japanese. As an alternative, the Cabinet, February 10, 1952, voted to split the forces, merging the NPR and the coast guard into a Security Force. This was to be supplemented by a 6,000-man Public Security Investigation Board to unify intelligence activity. Both Security Force and Investigation Board were to be responsible to a new Security Board directly under the Prime Minister as commander-in-chief.

Instead of waiting for requests by local authority for military help, as, for instance, in the event of riots or uprisings, the Prime Minister was to have power to order military forces into action during any national emergency which he might proclaim, subject to approval by the Diet within twenty days.

The Security Board was to be headed by an Inspector-General. Originally, as suggested by Construction Minister Uichi Noda, this official was to command an integrated land and naval force; but at the advice of Minister of State Ohashi two chiefs of staff were provided—one for ground forces and another for the coast guard.

Despite strong protests by the *Asahi* and the Osaka *Mainichi,* Japan's major newspapers, that this plan gave excessive power to the Prime Minister—*Asahi* said it made him a dictator—the Diet, while delaying passage of formal enabling bills, endorsed the general idea by passing the 1953 budget with appropriations for the change.

Probably Communist clumsiness aided the movement toward concentration not only of military but of police authority. Disclosure of a Communist leaflet, innocuously entitled "How to Raise Flower Bulbs," setting forth a blueprint for disorder, awakened Japan to the need for controlling radicals. Director Mitsusada Yoshikawa, of the Special Investigation Bureau, reported that Communists, having abandoned plans for peaceful revolution, had instigated 38 cases of mass violation, involving 18,000 people and resulting in 1,733 arrests between June 10, 1949, and February 3, 1952. His prediction that further riots were contemplated was borne out when 41 additional attacks upon police occurred in February, 1952, with 91 more in March and 34 in April.

His warning was followed within ten days by Communist-led disturbances in a dozen communities. Armed with spiked clubs, handfuls of pepper and ammonia-filled bottles, rioters seriously injured 20 policemen. The occasion was a commemoration of a supposed Indian Navy mutiny against British rule, but the rioters shouted slogans accusing the United States of turning Japan into a colony.

Simultaneously, 300 Tokyo University students staged a play in memory of a Communist said to have been tortured to death by police. When, during the course of the performance, spectators discovered plainclothesmen present, they stripped the detectives of identification marks, beat them up, and threw them out with warnings not to enter the university grounds again.

These demonstrations not only convinced the Government of the need for a Security Force but also furthered the amalgamation of the remaining independent local police units. Attorney General Tokutaro Kimura promptly moved in the Diet to combine all forces, thus facilitating the transfer of personnel between local units and the National Rural Police, and to place the Tokyo Metropolitan Police Board, a separate unit since 1882, under direct central administrative command.

While this was pending, further riots broke out. At Tokyo Teachers College, students locked up a policeman whom they found copying notices from a campus bulletin board. When Eiichi Tanaka protested, the school authorities cited a memorandum, dated July 20, 1950, from the Ministry of Education prohibiting police from entering college grounds without permission of the institution. Soon thereafter Waseda University students, relying on the same grant of extraterritoriality, seized two intruding policemen. Police reinforcements came up in the latter case, and a club-swinging brawl ensued in which 500 police battled 1,000 students with serious injuries to 25 police, 55 students, and 3 bystanders.

Attorney General Kimura, admitting in the Diet that the police were at fault in entering the campuses—an admission which Tanaka repudiated—apologized in the Diet for strong-arm police methods. He added to his Diet proposal an amendment, however, that the Prime Minister be empowered to dismiss and to appoint the chiefs of metropolitan police forces—an obvious rebuke to Tanaka—thus depriving mayors and city Public Safety Commissions of privileges formerly granted to them. *Mainichi* and *Yomiuri* condemned the move as a dangerous centralization of authority.

Mosaburo Suzuki, Central Executive Committee Chairman of the left-wing Socialists, went further by appearing before the Supreme Court to challenge the constitutionality of all moves to centralize police and to rebuild a Japanese defense force.

The protests, however, were unavailing. Instead of disarming, as the Constitution seemed to require, a movement spread to amend the Constitution by permitting Japan to possess a war potential. No counter-tendency appeared to restore the small local police departments which had been tried and which had proved dismal failures. The threat of Communist civil war proved strong enough to uproot the Occupation experiment with decentralized police, restoring, in effect if not in name, the prewar centralized systems. It was a return to the beginning but with the difference that the Japanese police were neither as efficient nor as powerful as before the war.

After more than a year's careful deliberation the Yoshida Cabinet on February 18, 1953, approved a bill restoring much of the prewar police system. The plan provided:

1. Unification of all fire and police systems under a National Security (or Police) Board headed by a Cabinet minister.

2. Replacement of locally controlled police, except in the six largest cities of more than 700,000 population, by metropolitan or prefectural police responsible to the National Security Board.

3. Transfer of all police and fire officials of the rank of inspector or above from local to national control.

4. Appointment of a national police chief by the Prime Minister and of all metropolitan and prefectural chiefs by the national police chief thus appointed. In each case the nomination was supposedly to be subject to approval of the national, or the prefectural, Public Safety Commission; but this consultation was regarded as merely a matter of form.

5. Reduction of powers of the various Public Safety Commissions and removal of eligibility restrictions imposed under the Occupation.

6. Appointment and dismissal of police personnel by prefectural police chiefs.

Announcement of the Cabinet proposal stirred immediate editorial protest that it meant restoration of a police state, tended toward dictatorship by the Prime Minister, deprived localities of police control, furthered political interference, and perhaps lead to a restoration of prewar thought control. The virtually unanimous press opposition was echoed by the Japan Mayors' Association, the Municipal Police Liaison Council, the Osaka and Tokyo police chiefs, and the Public Safety Commission chairmen of the five largest cities.

These protests had been anticipated and discounted. Both the dominant Liberal Party and the leading opposition party, the Progressives, favored unification, though the latter's president, former Foreign Minister Mamoru Shigemitsu, warned against reviving a police state. As Prime Minister Yoshida and Justice Minister Takeru (Ken) Inukai promised that this would not occur, the way seemed clear toward Diet passage, but internal politics were so confused that action was delayed. In February, 1954, however, Shigemitsu was won over and as Yoshida had made his peace with Hatoyama the major parties were united on the matter. The Cabinet, therefore, voted to support an even stronger police reform bill, abolishing all local forces, including those of the largest cities, and to place them all under central control. A target date of July 1, 1954, was set for ending the last important vestige of the Occupation's police reform.

EIGHTEEN

Painless Punishment

Nowhere had any nation seemed more spectacularly revolutionized; but the astonishing achievement of redrafting political, social, educational, health, labor, and welfare laws was, for the most part, on paper only. The laws enacted, voluntarily or under pressure, read magnificently but all too often were entirely disregarded.

Infraction of the social or welfare laws, for instance, was a misdemeanor only, a nonpenal code offense carrying no more than a three-year jail sentence or a fine of $275; and even these light penalties were seldom meted out. Over a three-year period of intense industrial strain only twenty-six of Japan's 650,000 employers of more than ten men—one employer in every 25,000—violated the rights of labor unions. Even these few offenders escaped easily, the majority being released on reprimand and only nine being fined as much as $14.

The widely heralded Labor Relations Act of 1946, a labor Magna Carta embodying a far more comprehensive code than exists in some American states, developed into a dead letter. Nagasaki, to be sure, jailed two employers for several months during 1948, but no jail sentences were imposed thereafter in any region of Japan. Three full years of careful investigation resulted in 1,337 indictments for wage and hour violations; but only 126 persons went to prison, all but 7 for less than a year, and only 3 persons were fined as much as $100. Of the 41 persons sentenced to prison during 1950, 37 received stays of execution.

Much, also, was claimed for Japanese progress in advancing factory, mine, and marine safety, and Japanese laws for such purposes ranked high in world legislation; but the courts lagged in penalizing offenders.

196

Except for two men jailed three years for refusing to observe the mining laws no one was imprisoned; and violators of any of these laws have not been fined more than $30.

In view of Japan's prewar history and the undoubted continuance of child exploitation it was astonishing that the three-year period reported only forty violators, and that only eight of these went to jail for as much as a year. No one paid more than $30 in fines. Violations undoubtedly occurred, the Labor Ministry reporting in November, 1953, that more than half the "small and medium-size industries" worked children more than nine hours a day. Yet no one was punished for this.

Similarly, while much was made of social insurance programs either the inspectors or the courts were remiss. Neither of the two persons convicted under the Health Insurance Act, and none of the three found guilty under the Accident Compensation Law, paid more than $30. Seven of the twenty-one violators of the Unemployment Insurance Act paid this sum; but the other fourteen were fined smaller amounts. Offenses against the Employment Security Act met heavier penalties, twenty-four of the ninety-one persons convicted going to jail for a year; but all the rest were released on minimum fines.

It is conceivable, though highly improbable, that all labor controversies were settled out of court, and that the newly organized unions achieved astonishing success by direct negotiations. It is also possible, although again extremely unlikely, that Japanese employers, hitherto stiff-necked and "feudalistically minded," suddenly reformed. It is more probable that lawmakers and judges, despite the progressiveness claimed for them, contented themselves with lip service to Occupation-sponsored reforms and applied the new legislation with great reluctance.

Wayland L. Speer, chief of General Crawford F. Sams's Narcotics Control Division, estimated that 15,000 drug addicts were in Japan and, during the three-year period, more than 5,500 arrests were made; yet only nine drug peddlers were imprisoned for as much as three years. Of the 2,014 offenders sent to jail, 1,496 were set free within a few months; of the 807 who were fined, only four were penalized by as much as $150 while 642 went free after paying $14 or less. With less than 40 per cent of the guilty going to jail and only 14 per cent paying fines, the Narcotics Law was broken with comparative impunity. It was extremely probable that Japanese narcotics control officers misled Dr. Speer concerning the fate of peddlers caught dispensing drugs, because he repeatedly announced on Japanese authority that both courts and police were cracking down on offenders, and that the traffic was being controlled.

Yet, by November, 1953, the *Nippon Times* charged that more than a hundred thousand persons were using morphine and heroin, and approximately a million were using *philipon*. Major General P. E. Ruestow, commanding the Tachikawa base, complained that inadequate control laws and lightness of penalties were dangerously increasing drug traffic. Kazuo Ichikawa, chief of the Welfare Ministry's narcotic section, then disclosed that about 11 per cent of all drug peddling discovered in 1952 had been in the neighborhood of American army camps, but that the rate had risen to 16 per cent in 1953.

Medical and educational officers were shocked to learn that swarms of quacks, charlatans, and "healers," most of them without laboratory, clinical, or hospital experience, were treating the sick; they demanded and secured legislation requiring adequate training and interneship. But once the standards were adopted few persons, Americans or Japanese, showed particular concern for enforcement of the regulations. During the initial three-year period ending in December, 1950, only 344 violations of professional standards were found in all the medical personnel. One flagrant medical practitioner went to jail for three years; nine unqualified doctors and a dentist were imprisoned for a year; and fifteen physicians, ten dentists, and a midwife were temporarily detained. All other guilty persons escaped with fines of less than $50.

As far as court records showed, only one lawyer was unethical, being fined $30, and no one broke the laws requiring higher qualifications for lawyers, teachers, priests, librarians or social workers.

Among the 209 persons guilty of malpractice, only 8 went to jail for as much as a year and 47 suffered shorter detentions, all the rest paying fines of less than $20. Adulterated medicine involved 136 convictions, with one imprisonment for a year and eight others for a few weeks, no one paying more than $30 in fines.

Poisoned food sent 93 defendants to jail for three years; but only one of the 6,244 sellers of contaminated food received such a sentence, with 12 receiving a year and 72 shorter sentences. One man was fined $275 for selling impure food, and two paid $150; all the rest escaped on fines of $15.

Of Japan's 47,000 dairymen, all but two were scrupulously clean, honest, and properly certified; the two paid fines of less than $5. None of the 29 violators of the Cemetery Act, the 156 dead-animals disposal cases, the 13 housewives who broke the cleaning regulations, nor the 161 breakers of the hotelkeepers' codes paid more than $20 fine.

Breaches of price and ration laws were, however, more severely penalized. Such categories included 130,350 convictions, from which 6,946 defendants went to jail; but only 25 served more than three years, and only 839 were held for more than a year. While 678 offenders were fined $200 and 4,210 paid $50 each, more than 96,000 convicted persons were freed on paying less than $20.

Japan had 181,187 gonorrhea cases and 188,204 syphilitics in 1949; but only 794 diseased persons were convicted of breaking sanitary regulations over the three-year period, and of these only 4 were imprisoned for as much as a year, 85 others being held for a few weeks. Here, too, all fines were less than $50. Most of the punishments, moreover, fell within the first few months of the new law, the one person convicted during 1950 receiving a suspended sentence.

Contract prostitution had been illegal for more than seventy years, and a new law of 1946 restated that anyone selling a woman into professional prostitution must be punished. Yet 1,466 convictions brought only 229 jail sentences, including 28 of a year or more. The heaviest fines were $30 each, in 78 cases. The frequent and spectacular raids on railway stations and pleasure resorts brought only two convictions during three years, one girl being at once released and the other fined $20.

Under the highly publicized eugenics codes only four convictions were returned, the heaviest penalty being $30.

Show-window legislation was not confined to health and labor matters. To stem the bribery and dishonesty of Japanese elections a Corrupt Practices Act, a model of its kind, was passed in 1948 under strong Occupation pressure. Once it was entered on the statute books, however, the Occupation experts apparently lost interest, the theorists assuming that the law would guarantee clean campaigning, equalize the opportunity of rich and poor candidates, break down political machines, and give the amateur an equal chance with professional politicians. Not only was no effort made to see that the law was properly enforced, but Government Section officers shut their ears to proof that violations were occurring.

Requirements of both the Corrupt Practices Act and the fantastic election laws were so severe that violations were unavoidable. Procurators therefore brought to court only the more flagrant offenders, a total of 8,769 persons being convicted after the 1948 and 1949 elections. Of these, however, 5,840 were freed on fines of less than $30. Two men went to jail on three-year sentences and six were fined $140, the rest were lightly punished. Cases of vote-buying were not seriously regarded, none of the eight persons convicted being jailed and the two heaviest fines were but $70 each.

Following the Occupation the severe restrictions apparently became wholly ineffective, the Supreme Procurator reporting no fewer than 46,-000 offenses in the Diet election of 1952. Most of the violators escaped scotfree, 12,500 being punished in summary court, which meant light fines, while few of the 5,556 who were referred for formal trial received hearings prior to the statute of limitations deadline.

Thus the Occupation-sponsored law, which won plaudits both from Government Section, which drafted the law and whipped it through the Diet and from MacArthur, who hailed it as a triumph of democracy, actually lessened rather than increased punishments. Convictions under the Corrupt Practices Act were far less numerous than before the war, when the regulations were less stringent and the offices to be filled were a tiny fraction of those elected after surrender. In 1930, for example, before the militarists clamped down, and when electioneering was relatively open, 221 persons had been jailed and 12,690 had been fined; in 1928, when alleged infractions were common, 241 offenders went to jail and 7,559 were fined. Four times as many persons were imprisoned, and six times as many were jailed, in 1915 as in the two years 1948 and 1949.

Nor was the explanation convincing that the postwar campaigns were cleaner, and that participants were more careful about law observance. Revelations, supported by sworn confessions both in courts and before special Diet investigation committees, proved that hitherto unequaled sums of money had been spent to buy votes, to corrupt candidates, and to swing the elections. Necessarily the sums legitimately spent would have been greater because of inflation and the higher costs of political manipulation; but the sums spent in the postwar years were far out of proportion to the lessened value of the yen. In spite, however, of the open admissions of wrongdoing, in spite of clear evidence of Corrupt Practice violations, no action was taken to enforce the law.

Americans also found it difficult to understand why, in all Japan, procurators could lodge only 102 indictments for local tax fraud or evasion; it was even more impossible to understand why only 8 were followed by jail sentences of more than a year, or why 33 cases were dismissed without penalty.

Responsibility for nullifying the admirably worded reform legislation rested primarily upon the Diets which classified violations as misdemeanors rather than as crimes carrying heavy penalties; but this was merely a roundabout recognition that Japan's politicians accurately gauged the lack of interest among Occupationnaires. Few observers maintained that Japan's Diet members, whether conservative holdovers from prewar parliaments or less experienced new members, enthusiastically demanded reforms. While in the main they were progressive and, in the Japanese sense, "democratically minded," it was obvious that they were pushed and prodded into passing laws which Occupation people, rather than the Japanese, required. Most of the laws met little resistance; but, on the other hand, few were initially pressed by Japanese. Japanese lawmakers, voting for bills imposed upon them, contented themselves with approving anything which seemed sufficient to appease the Occupation, irrespective of need or of possible effect. If thereafter the Occupation showed no interest, the Diet, having done its duty, did not care.

Nor were procurators overly concerned. Prewar health and welfare measures, while certainly inferior in Western eyes, had satisfied the Japanese; they saw but little reason why such problems, traditionally the province of the family, should now be shouldered on a burdened state. With offices busy on hundreds of thousands of economic cases, particularly black marketing and rationing and similar controls, procurators had neither time nor energy to hunt up trouble in areas for which they were not primarily responsible.

Such cases as came before the courts, moreover, became confused in mazes of interpretation. The majority of the new laws were almost wholly American in principle, reflecting American modes of thought and American ideas of justice; but the courts, staffed by men trained in Continental schools or in Japanese law that was a derivative of French and German ideas, construed the laws in ways unintended by the framers at GHQ-SCAP. The judges were not hostile nor recalcitrant; but, lacking the pragmatic philosophy of American jurisprudence, they often failed to understand the nub of the contentions. Thus, considering the motive rather than the deed, studying the personality rather than the offense and weighing these against the spirit rather than the letter of the law, they ignored precedent and rendered decisions far out of line with what Americans expected.

From this point of view, it was no doubt fortunate that the Occupation paid so little heed to court administration of the law. Dr. Alfred C. Oppler, an extraordinarily well qualified pre-Hitlerite Prussian judge who was legal adviser to Government Section, strove to create and maintain an independent Japanese judiciary, free from subservience to the Justice Ministry and uncontrolled by bureaucratic procurators.

Following the usual Occupation pattern, Oppler advised and guided Japanese jurists; but, unlike many other Occupation officials, even within his own Government Section, he refrained from authoritarianism. In lengthy conferences his staff, probing deeply into basic theories and practices, endeavored to persuade; but when agreement proved to be impossible Oppler consented to compromise that did not vitiate his general principles.

With public attention focused on more spectacular reforms, legal and judicial changes proceeded quietly and, in the main, without publicity. The mistaken general belief that his work was primarily technical rather than high-level policy determination had disadvantages, as Oppler was well aware; but it relieved him from the pressing need felt elsewhere to show quick, steady, and drastic progress toward democracy. After correcting the worst deficiencies of the basic codes and simplifying the more confusing practices, he and his aides proceeded more slowly and accordingly with greater success than was sometimes possible in other fields.

Oppler sensed the danger of imposing American innovations upon a legal system based upon essentially different Continental law. As a practitioner in German courts and as a student of the French legal system he understood the difficulty of hybridizing Japanese and Anglo-Saxon theory. His concern was not to usher in a revolution through court interpretation and procedure, but to clarify the position of the judiciary and to help the judges become, and remain, impartial and efficient.

Relaxation of Occupation controls facilitated his task, especially after General Ridgway, on May 3, 1951, authorized Japan to review and, if necessary, revise legislation already directed by the Occupation. This freedom, together with the failure of social reformers, economic theorists, and political revolutionists to execute laws imposed upon Japan, shifted Japan, even in advance of a peace treaty, from the status of an occupied to that of a friendly allied nation. By permitting the emergence of Japanese ideas and preferences, hitherto suppressed by real or fancied censorship, it confirmed Oppler's contention that free discussion was an essential democratic tenet, and assisted in the synthesis of Western theory and Japanese reality.

Again, as with other successful Occupation reforms, precedent favored Japan's acceptance of foreign theories. However impatiently the Westerner regarded the Oriental's faithfulness to tradition, the existence of a thousand-year-old precedent eased Oppler's task. Because Confucianist ideas had been imported in the period between A.D. 600 and 964, thereby modifying Japanese legal principles, and because European Continental concepts of codes and statutes based on "rights" had been introduced after the Meiji Restoration of 1868, Oppler's innovations faced weaker opposition than would otherwise have been presented.

In all three instances foreign legal importations led to important political results. The Chinese infusion furthered Imperial supremacy over clan lords and set up a bureaucratic hierarchy wherein law was merely a technique to be applied to any recalcitrants who could not be controlled by custom or by moral suasion. Europe's contribution, at a time when the Japanese language had no word for "rights," opened the way for Constitutional monarchy, separation of powers, and civil liberty but had not yet produced them at the time of surrender. Western principles of absolute ownership, freedom of contract, and liability as a corollary of fault had been incorporated into the civil code, and the adoption of the limited company principle had accelerated the development of capitalism.

Upon these foundations, Oppler built a democratic policy wherein the people were sovereign. This, to be sure, had been required by the Potsdam Declaration and the surrender terms, and had been incorporated into a Constitution largely drafted before Oppler's arrival; but the new basic law required wholesale revision of virtually all other legislation.

Although there was no conscious effort to bring Japanese law within the common-law system, reform measures sometimes inadvertently did so, thus producing confusion and, perhaps, inconsistency. Other weaknesses, unavoidable because of the lack of time to harmonize and correlate legislation, also appeared, so that much remained to be revised after peace had been restored—for instance, the grafting of modern American corporation law upon a Japanese-European base; but these were relatively minor flaws when compared with the extensive network of legislation.

Chief among the changes were the revision of the civil code to insure equality not only for women but for younger sons and for others previously subordinated under the patriarchal and primogeniture systems, the introduction of habeas corpus, the right to challenge in court an illegal administrative act, an embryonic form of grand jury, fairer rules of evidence, and the abolition of lese majesty.

Some reforms, while excellent on paper, failed in immediate value. The courts, for instance, received the right, by judicial review, to decide the constitutionality of any law, regulation, or official action; but, as late as 1954, they had made no use of the privilege. Provision for dissenting opinions, which would afford a basis for discussion, reference, and possible later use of precedent, fell afoul of the tabu against unnecessary public discussion; disagreement among judges was considered to be in bad taste.

Similarly, while the principle of state redress for illegal arrest or detention or for improper conviction was reaffirmed, the actual operation fell short of expectation. As against an average of 50 persons yearly who received compensation between 1932 and 1940, only 20 were compensated during 1949. The amounts paid fell from an average of 860 yen in the prewar period to 350 in terms of the much inflated postwar yen. Under Occupation stimulus, more persons were enabled to lodge claims; but of the 3,000 supposedly eligible during 1950–1951 only one-fifth applied, and few of these were successful. Had each of the 600 who filed claims been successful the total budget appropriation for the purpose would have yielded 50,000 yen per capita (roughly equivalent to $140), or about two-thirds of the average sum actually paid during 1939–1942.

While Oppler insisted upon the maintenance of judicial dignity, little successful action was taken until 1952 to uphold court prestige. Following the pattern of leftist trials in other countries, Communist defendants, lawyers, and spectators repeatedly created disturbances which courts were powerless to check. After Chief Justice Kotaro Tanaka officially complained that the Occupation-sponsored Court Organization Act was too weak to cope with this situation, or even to discipline a lawyer who struck a procurator and twice threatened to kill the judges, the Diet belatedly passed a Contempt of Court Act under which the maximum penalty was twenty days in jail or a fine of 30,000 yen (less than $1,000). The Supreme Court, however, was permitted to enlarge the number of its guards from 70 to 200.

Laws, however, were insufficient, much of the difficulty stemming from misunderstandings by judges themselves concerning fairness and justice. Courts could not tolerate open seizures of witnesses or defendants, such as occurred at Yokohama; but Judge Tetsuzo Sasaki of the Osaka District Court, when defendants under trial for rioting regarded themselves as "martyrs," held that they were entitled to special freedoms. He therefore yielded to their pleas and presided over courtroom ceremonies wherein the defendants prayed for the repose of the souls of Josef Stalin, the North Korean war dead, and Julius and Ethel Rosenberg, the American atom spies. Such prayers, and the singing of "peace songs," he said, were comparable to the acts of Western Christians in praying and singing hymns. Another jurist, Presiding Judge Kasematsu, also of Osaka, refused permission for prayers for the souls of atom-bomb victims but added that, if spectators and defendants cared to conduct exercises after he had left the bench, he would not forbid them. A third Osaka judge in November, 1953, jailed twenty-three Communists who insisted on praying for Stalin and the Rosenbergs. Osaka court authorities indignantly refused permission for a Diet investigating group to inquire into these incidents; such an investigation, they declared, infringed upon the rights of the judiciary.

In its zeal to bolster court prestige the Occupation saddled the Supreme Court with a multiplicity of duties ranging from the rule-making power to the collection and publication of statistics. In addition to its own greatly increased judicial activities it was burdened with supervision over the eight high courts and their six branches, 49 main district courts, 232 lesser district courts, and 800 family and summary courts, together with administration of 2,000 judges and many more lesser officials. It was to prepare lists of candidates for judicial appointment and promotion including, originally, its own membership.

These duties, at a time when postwar social and economic maladjustments called for numerous new laws to halt a threatened rise in crime, overwhelmed the Japanese judiciary. Criminal cases alone reached five times the 1937–1941 average; but there were only half as many more judges. Lacking such necessities as office space, telephones, clerical assistance, reference materials or other facilities, judges who had handled an average of 100 cases yearly before the war found themselves swamped with work.

Even with an efficient judicial and legal system such log jams would inevitably have resulted in delays; but Japanese custom increased the dilatoriness. Separation of procurators from police, while essential for preserving democracy, induced them to reinvestigate each case referred to them for indictment. Lawyers, taking advantage of loopholes, sought postponements and delays, so that cases were not tried uninterruptedly but in such scattered sessions that trials dragged on interminably. The Showa Denko corruption case, for instance, continued more than four years, while a famous suit against the Agriculture Ministry for illegal seizure of a village forest-land involved six presiding judges and 40 Agriculture Ministers before the forest was returned, forty-eight years after the original transfer. A similar case, in which 56 Agriculture Ministers had been involved, remained unsettled in 1954.

The dilatoriness was nothing new, since 3,465 of the 101,637 civil cases settled in 1940 had required at least two years in court; but under the Occupation the courts fell steadily behind.

Overburdened though they were, Japanese judges bent over backward not only to preserve their integrity but to decide efficiently. One jurist was popularly, though probably erroneously, believed to have allowed himself to starve rather than patronize the black market as most of his neighbors were said to be doing. In an unprecedented and astonishing action the Supreme Court fined four of its members 10,000 yen each for overlooking one of the numerous minor procedural rules and, when in addition they refused to resign, added a reprimand.

Failing the appointment of enough capable new judges to speed procedure, only the courts themselves had any real power to correct the difficulties. Theoretically the public held the weapon of a recall election over incompetent judges; but the first such vote, taken on five justices in January, 1949, after only a year and a half's experience, found voters not only unprepared and unqualified to pass upon judicial records but almost wholly without interest in doing so. After a very desultory campaign in which the issue was largely ignored by the press, all five justices were approved, Chief Justice Tanaka receiving an eight-to-one vote; but the total vote was only a fraction of that cast for other candidates.

NINETEEN

They Live Longer

Active effort to reform public health conditions developed slowly. While American army officers hurriedly revolutionized governmental machinery, police and judicial methods, school administration, banking and corporate practice, indeed almost every conceivable field of economic and political enterprise, they trod cautiously in matters affecting public health. Elsewhere they rooted out traditional Oriental concepts and philosophies; but, even when they realized the backwardness of Japan's health prevention system, they hesitated to command reform.

The gingerly approach implied no lack of interest in humanitarianism, though certain statements might easily have been distorted into such a meaning. MacArthur himself, in January, 1946, penciled a memorandum that sociological concern with Japanese conditions was premature; his top assistants, speaking too hurriedly and off the record, remarked that public health was a problem only for the Japanese. Unless, the generals declared, conditions grew so bad as to engender civil war, the Occupation Forces would do nothing. Hesitancy arose partly from lack of clear directive from his superiors, the Joint Chiefs of Staff; the United States Initial Post-Surrender Policy informed him merely, in passing, that he might direct the Japanese Government to develop and enforce programs to avoid acute economic distress and to assure just and equitable division of available supplies. Subsequent instruction failed to broaden the commitment.

Thus, in requiring Japan to meet the "minimum humanitarian needs" of its people, MacArthur seemed to be less concerned with promoting public health or social welfare than with safeguarding Allied soldiers

207

against infection. Reestablishment of prewar civil health controls was not primarily designed to prevent widespread disease but to provide machinery whereby Occupation officials could forestall possible civil unrest.

Similarly the confiscation of army and navy stockpiles and distribution of nonmilitary stores to the civilian population afforded immediate and necessary relief to the suffering populace; but the basic purpose was less humanitarian than aimed at complete demilitarization of the remaining Japanese armed forces.

Whether because Japanese administrators were conscious of this fact or because Occupation officials were lax in demanding complete returns, records of both collection and distribution are extremely scarce. Although the Japanese Government was required to submit detailed accounts of the number of persons needing and receiving food, shelter, fuel, medical care, or other relief, as well as the total of all facilities and supplies furnished to them, only 83,502 persons were certified as receiving relief on October 1, 1945. Inasmuch as approximately 4,500,000 houses had been wrecked during the war, disrupting families, separating hundreds of thousands of children from their parents, and leaving millions homeless, the total was obviously far too low. Yet, when on December 1, 1945, the Government submitted an amended list of 8,000,000 persons in need of relief the estimate was rejected as excessive. It was, as a matter of fact, low.

Just as the Occupation had but slight concept of the relief problem to be faced, so also it floundered in estimating the total of relief supplies available. Unquestionably enormous amounts of food and clothing, as well as tremendous amounts of manufactures and raw materials flowed away into the black market; but even those that remained in Government control were slow in moving to relieve suffering. At least 30,000 tons of biscuit and canned goods remained in storage throughout 1945, when food was so scarce that Japan feared starvation. Not until the last week of February, when fruit trees were in blossom close to Tokyo, was the release of blankets and winter clothing authorized; and MacArthur complained two months later that, even then, they had not been issued to persons in need.

Strictly speaking, MacArthur, in so complaining, stepped beyond the narrow bounds to which he was restricted. The Joint Chiefs of Staff in their directive, approved by the President of the United States, had laid down a clear dictum: "The plight of Japan is the direct outcome of its own behavior and the Allies will not undertake the burden of repairing the damage." This had been endorsed by the State, War, and Navy Coordinating Committee, October 1, 1945, in a statement to MacArthur: "The only responsibility on our part for the Japanese standard of living is the purely negative one prohibiting us from requiring for the Occupation Forces goods or services to an extent which would cause starvation, widespread disease and acute physical distress." The basic criterion appears to have been the safety of the Occupation Forces, and the attainment of other objectives in Japan was only inferential.

Not only the Occupation but also the broken and disheartened Japanese Government professed unconcern. Few agencies kept records, and the records kept varied widely. Not until March, 1946, did any Government agency tabulate reports upon the cost of aid; and when a report was compiled, in response to an Occupation demand, it showed that during the month a total of 2,328,815 persons had been aided at a cost of 49,297,874 yen. With the yen then exchanging at 15 per dollar, this figure—which remained fairly constant over the next four months—indicated that the average per capita monthly relief was about $1.25.

This evidence, to be sure, concerns relief and welfare data; but many of the same bureaus also administered health and sanitation matters, where certainly the same philosophies applied. The difficulty of establishing *de novo* the principles and organizations of a democratic society among people who had never known real liberty, of inculcating personal, or even communal, responsibility for health conditions among people who, if they knew the idea at all, looked upon it as an outrageous and certainly dangerous violation of Japan's traditional ideology—the difficulty of either of these in the face of economic collapse was of unimaginable proportions. Army officers were wholly untrained for such a complex task, which held no attraction for them; and some of them, not knowing what to do, having insufficient personnel and no equipment or supplies with which to do it, resented their assignments.

Quite possibly these attitudes were unavoidable. Though Japan stood in sore need, immediate improvement was impossible. The country had sunk so deep into bankruptcy and internal chaos that every condition favored the spread of epidemics. Without penicillin, potent typhoid vaccine, diphtheria toxoid, sulfadiazine, or antisyphilitic drugs, without DDT, and with two-thirds of the meager medical production requisitioned by the militarists, Japan had no ammunition for the war against disease. Her crowded cities, wrecked by fire and bombs, were, for the most part, without water or sewage service. Rats and insects had multiplied beyond control. Even had these conditions been miraculously remedied, little could have been accomplished quickly by an antiquated and never efficient public health administration whose treasury was empty, and whose personnel was not only scanty and inefficient but listless and disheartened.

Colonel Sams, to whom MacArthur assigned the seemingly impossible task of correcting the deficiencies, found Japan's public health situation a mass of superstition, incompetency, and carelessness. No one knew certainly how many medical men and women nor how many hospital beds were available. Statistics seemed to indicate that at the time of Pearl Harbor only 67,512 physicians had been licensed to practice— an average of one doctor for each 1,100 persons; but only 26,842 of these were university graduates, and only 103 had studied abroad. The remaining 41,000 physicians had attended junior colleges where little dissection, clinical or laboratory work had been required, nor had they been obliged to undergo internship or hospital residency.

In contrast to the 67,512 physicians—60 per cent of whom were substandard—there were 75,976 practitioners of such medical arts as acupuncture, moxicautery, and shampoo therapy. The quality of service rendered by these is indicated by the fact that half of them were blind.

At least a third of Japan's villages had no medical care available. Incomes of physicians were so low that only 53,960 of the licensed doctors were in actual practice; the rest—including most of the better trained personnel—devoted themselves to administrative or governmental work. Nearly all practicing physicians eked out a living by selling patent medicines—which brought them into conflict with the pharmacists—or by practicing dentistry. Thus the latter art attracted a pitiful number of desirable students. Of Japan's 26,614 registered dentists, one for every 3,100 people in 1941, nearly all had learned their trade at junior colleges, at night schools, or by apprenticeship. Their operative and prosthetic methods, for the most part, had been obsolete in the West for at least a generation.

While Japan theoretically had a total of 149,992 nurses in 1941, none of these were public health nurses; and perhaps 100,000 could more properly have been classified as receptionists, office assistants, or, at best, practical nurses. A total of 62,741 midwives, of whom few had

had formal training and none were supervised after payment of their fifty cents' license fee, presided over 96 per cent of births.

The 1941 numbers had been small; but war conditions had still further reduced the numbers. In spite of recruits brought in by quick emergency courses, a census of September 15, 1945, showed only 39,269 physicians, 17,438 dentists, and 96,846 nurses available in Japan, with an estimated 20,000 doctors, 4,000 dentists, and 35,000 nurses yet to be demobilized.

Colonel Sams undertook sweeping reorganizations and improvements. He began by ordering a complete administrative adjustment—an extremely complex task involving the destruction of a centralized bureaucracy and the creation of local agencies. To decentralize administration while increasing efficiency posed a problem that was in itself contradictory; yet Sams succeeded by establishing new and improved supervisions. He avoided the customary Japanese error of appointing to leadership men skilled in administrative technicalities and placed in command physicians, dentists, pharmacists, hospital managers and nurses. It was the first time that such power had been assigned to technicians rather than bureaucrats.

To increase the number of medical personnel involved an overhaul of educational institutions and requirements. For this the Occupation asked the aid not only of a United States Education Mission but also of specially created councils chosen from Japanese medical, dental, and nursing groups. This type of consultation also was an innovation.

Standardized requirements of two years' premedical or predental college training, followed by four years' professional study, largely clinical, were set for admission to examination. Candidates for medical licenses were required to take a year's internship, in addition; but this was not required of dentists. Nurses and midwives were licensed upon completion of senior high school, a three years' training course, and an examination.

While the new standards were higher than before the war they were, in each case, lower than the special Japanese councils themselves requested. Both physicians and dentists preferred a three-years preprofessional course, and nurses had asked a mandatory extra year for public health nurses and midwives; but, in view of Japan's limited school facilities, the University Accreditization Association, the final authority, declined to accept the recommendations.

Even without the proposed extra year, professional schools were overtaxed. Of the 39 medical universities and 50 second-class medical colleges certified on September 15, 1945, only 22 qualified under the new requirements; 23 more were added by 1949, but still the institutions operating were but half of the war-time number. Similarly, eight dental colleges (six of them private and five of them in Tokyo) survived the war; but the low quality of their facilities is indicated by the fact that their operating cost per student during 1946 was only 960 yen—about $65. Two of these were disqualified as inefficient, but one additional college was founded during 1949.

Nursing education offers a brighter picture. Under the old regulations, few formal schools of nursing had existed; and, as these had no uniform curriculum, comparisons and statistics are virtually worthless. By October, 1947, however, 739 centers for nursing education had been established where 31,953 girls were undergoing a properly designed course of study. The Public Health and Welfare Section in August, 1948, reported 251,375 graduate nurses in Japan, almost twice the 1941 total, but the Welfare Ministry in March, 1951, listed but 80,000 active nurses. Nor were their working conditions good; the average general duty nurse was working 68 hours a week (of which 12 were in record-keeping and 8 were overtime) for a starting gross pay of 5,000 yen monthly—$14 at the new exchange rate.

With administrative and supervisory reforms under way and better professional education being provided, Sams also undertook hospital improvement. Here the need was extraordinarily great, but no one actually knew the situation. Even the number of hospitals was in doubt. The Health and Welfare Ministry assured Sams that there were 3,335 hospitals with a bed capacity of 356,143 on September 15, 1945—figures which, if true, would have meant that, while 19 hospitals had been destroyed during the war the bed capacity had tripled from the 1941 total of 107,899. Sams in an independent check found 2,796 hospitals with 256,041 beds. But his figures, too, are dubious: his monthly reports disclose 3,224 hospitals in June, 1947, and 3,478 in April, 1948; but the seeming gain of 254 hospitals was accompanied by a loss of 14,814 bed capacity. Sams reported 3,900 hospitals in December, 1946 (a gain of 900 within a month) with 218,014 beds, whereas the Prime Minister's office of statistics noted 2,727 hospitals with 112,581 beds. Lieutenant Colonel Merle Smith, officer in charge of public health for the 8th Army, believed in August, 1949, that there were 3,019 hospitals and 249,042 beds.

Whatever the true statistics, hospital conditions were deplorable. Three-quarters of the 1946 institutions were privately run, consisting usually of nothing more than one- or two-room apartments in private residences where, despite wholly inadequate facilities, physicians were treating serious illnesses and performing major operations. At the outset of the Occupation even the best hospitals were without medication, antiseptics, or sterilizing facilities; they were unheated and without cooking equipment, so that patients depended upon food brought in by their families. Bandages were washed out, for reuse, in cold water. There was no segregation of cases, and patients brought their own blankets and bed linen.

Full recovery has not yet been achieved. As late as 1954, observers were shocked at poor maintenance and at low-sanitation standard wards, lavatories, and operating rooms. Kitchens, however, have been installed; families are forbidden to move into the wards to nurse their relatives; and drugs and antiseptics have become more generally available. Under the new medical service and hospital laws, the private hospitals of less than ten-bed capacity have been reduced to the status of clinics where patients may be admitted for a maximum stay of forty-eight hours. The change in status, together with the transfer of former private hospitals to public control, produced a rise in the number of government institutions and sharply reduced the number of private hospitals but rendered fruitless any effort to use the statistics for comparison purposes.

Development of the idea of decentralization led in 1952 to a move by the national Government to divest itself of 60 of the 99 hospitals currently under its control by releasing them to the prefectures for improvement of local public health facilities. Of the remaining national hospitals, 15 were to be converted into tuberculosis sanitaria while 24 were to be nationally maintained as "model hospitals."

Contrary to expectation, the local authorities did not welcome the decision. Governors complained that the plan would shunt over to prefectural control the less desirable and less well managed institutions, burdening the communities with the expense of raising them to proper levels and ncessitating greater drainage on local finances.

A further change, strongly recommended by Colonel Sams, also failed to win wide acclaim. This was the introduction of a system whereby any physician should be allowed access to patients in any hospital where they might be under treatment. Traditionally, doctors without hospital affiliations had been unable to place their patients in hospital care—a practice which fostered monopolization since unaffiliated physicians were shut out unless they established their own small private establishments. Under Sams's encouragement a new state hospital, established at Tanabe in Wakayama Prefecture, opened its facilities in July, 1951, to any practicing physician. It was hoped that other hospitals would follow the example; but few did so.

Quite to the contrary, under conditions of rising costs and limited facilities, hospitals showed a tendency to reject cases involving open access or charity. The case of a vagrant girl who, burned severely, was refused admission to three Tokyo hospitals—a university, a private and a national hospital—roused considerable indignation but brought no remedial action.

Brigadier General James Stevens Simmons, Dean of the Harvard School of Public Health, described the public health achievements under the Occupation as unmatched in history.

Yet comparisons are dangerous. Sams distrusted Japanese statistics; but, because his Public Health and Welfare Section (PHW) was overworked and undermanned, he had little opportunity to gather correct prewar data. To prove the improvement under the Occupation he fell back perforce upon the late war years, particularly 1943, 1944, and 1945; but these chaotic years were far from satisfactory as an index base. PHW-sponsored activities in more nearly normal times showed remarkable success, but certainly the restoration of peace itself facilitated that success. Thus, for example, Keio University resumed its work in preventive medicine, begun under a Rockefeller Foundation grant in 1929, while teaching, research, and nursing fellowships under the Public Health Institute since 1938 were also revived.

Although certainly the mean death rate for 12 reportable communicable diseases fell from 29.2 per 1,000 in 1945 to 17.6 in 1946, it should be remembered that 1945 had both the highest death rate and the highest morbidity rate in Japanese history. (The morbidity rate, to be sure, rose by 5 per cent in 1946; but, as this reflected more complete and more careful reporting, there is strong probability that there was really less disease in 1946 than in the year preceding.) The war years had been sickly with a 22 per cent increase in both 1943 and 1944 and a further 11 per cent rise in 1945, but it is also true that most of the increase was in filth- and louse-borne diseases whose spread was easier under war conditions.

Use of the 1943–1945 base resulted, therefore, in a sensational index decline when more drugs and better medical attention became available. Dysentery cases dropped from 96,462 in 1945 to 39,249 in 1947. Although water systems were too often contaminated, typhoid fell from a high of 57,933 in 1945 to 17,820 in 1947 and to fewer than 3,000 in 1951. Diphtheria, which had reached 85,933 in 1945, fell to 28,546 in 1947 and to 14,825 in 1949, the lowest since 1927.

These triumphs were in fields wherein the Japanese had themselves accomplished success. For all its weaknesses, the prewar Japanese public health system had held typhoid within bounds, had cut dysentery to 75 per cent of the 1937–1940 peaks and, while diphtheria was epidemic in 1945, had steadily reduced the death rate of that disease from 24.56 per cent of cases in 1926 to 9.12 per cent in 1945. During the war, despite highly unfavorable conditions, the Japanese had wholly prevented cholera, were lessening smallpox, had defeated scarlet fever, and were holding their own against typhus itself.

A potent factor in the postwar victory against disease was the introduction of new drugs, particularly penicillin and streptomycin, and of improved disinfectants and insecticides—DDT was first brought in by the Occupation. In December, 1945, Japan was producing 300 units of penicillin monthly, at a retail cost of 600 yen per 100,000 units; in April, 1951, the monthly output, from 23 factories, had soared to 1,177 billion units and the price had dropped to 30 yen. Streptomycin, first produced in July, 1950, became plentiful enough in August, 1952, to make Japan self-sufficient.

Neither recognition of the work of the rejuvenated Japanese public health service nor the magic of new drugs, important as they are, detracts from the glory due to Colonel Sams's Public Health and Welfare personnel, who spark-plugged the accomplishments, who alternately cudgeled and cajoled the Health and Welfare authorities into remedial action, and who provided essential technical advice.

Thus, when in 1946 the influx of 6,000,000 repatriates from disease-ridden Asia and Oceania brought an unprecedented 32,366 cases of exanthematic typhus—twenty times as many cases as in the entire fifteen years before the war—together with 1,245 cholera patients and 17,954 smallpox sufferers, PHW insisted upon a wholesale inoculation and immunization program. As this recommendation was in keeping with Japanese practice—Japanese physicians more than those of other regions favoring injections as preventives and cures—popular acceptance was readily obtained. Within a few weeks 31,197,945 typhus shots were given, 36,000,000 cholera and typhoid inoculations, and 64,000,-000 vaccinations.

The methods worked successfully. In 1949 only 124 cases of smallpox were reported, and cholera again disappeared. While there were 121 typhus cases in 1949, the disease thereafter became as rare as in the prewar period.

Enactment of a Preventive Vaccination Law now requires compulsory immunization of all Japanese against tuberculosis, smallpox, typhoid, paratyphoid, pertussis, and diphtheria and also, whenever epidemic threatens, against cholera and typhus.

These accomplishments, important as they were, only partially improved the Japanese health situation. Even when the Occupation closed and Japan resumed control over its sanitation, health, and welfare activities, much remained to be accomplished. The problems of dysentery, tuberculosis, and venereal disease were particularly pressing.

Social as well as medical factors complicated tuberculosis control. Certainly the disease was not new to Japan, having been well described as early as A.D. 936 in *Insho,* the earliest Japanese medical text; nor was it rare, since the Ministry of Welfare and the Tuberculosis Prevention Society (founded in 1913) agree that some 1,600,000 persons are currently affected. But, as all classes of the population, from the Imperial Court itself to the lowliest coolie, regard tuberculosis as a stigma upon the family record, cases are so concealed that no one knows the actual extent of the disease. Sams was able in 1949 to identify only 469,504 cases because physicians preferred such misleading diagnoses as "infiltration of the lungs," pleurisy, or chronic bronchitis. A Welfare Ministry survey reported that in 1954 "at least 4,500,000 Japanese were suffering from tuberculosis."

Undoubtedly wartime privations, including malnutrition and exposure, increased both incidence and exposure; but published death rates indicate that the 1915–1920 death rate of 23.1 per 10,000 population fell to 18.7 in 1947, to 16.8 in 1949, to 14.7 in 1950 and 11.1 in 1951. The 1951 figure, however, while the lowest since 1899, does not mitigate the fact that tuberculosis, with 122,000 deaths in 1950, remains the largest single cause of deaths, accounting for approximately 13 per cent of Japanese mortality.

To combat this disease, Japan has 639 sanitaria; but most of them exist only in name, being without full facilities. A total of 294 tuberculosis hospitals, 46 of which are completely equipped, had 137,984 beds in January, 1953, sufficient for the care of less than one-tenth of the sufferers; but only about three-quarters of the beds were occupied. The total, however, represents a 600 per cent increase over the number of beds reported in the 56 public and 146 private sanitaria of 1941. Approximately 530 physicians and 2,150 nurses specialize in tuberculosis work.

Japan has laid great emphasis upon the Bacillus Calmette-Guérin (BCG) inoculation treatment, which was made compulsory under the Preventive Vaccination Law. Such wholesale immunization was not new, 5,025,794 adolescents having been inoculated in 1944 and 3,098,000 in 1945; the pressure of other needs caused little to be accomplished during the first years of the Occupation, but the production of BCG in sufficient quantity, together with the budgeting of 8,300,000,000 yen for tuberculosis control during 1952 touched off a serious controversy. Acting upon the advice of Dr. Taro Takemi, former Vice-Chairman of the Japan Medical Association, and ex-President Taizo Kumagai of Tohoku University, head of the Japan Tuberculosis Society, as presented by the medical section of the Japan Science Council, Welfare Minister Ryogo Hashimoto recommended that the compulsory vaccinations be suspended.

This suggestion, however, angered the PHW authorities, particularly Colonel C. S. Mollohan, Sams's successor, and, in the closing days of the Occupation, they prevailed upon the Diet to overrule Hashimoto and the Council. Hashimoto then pointed out that the law requiring inoculation set no penalty for those who refused to comply, and urged that the compulsion be ignored. When both the Diet and Yoshida refused to support the proposed evasion, he resigned, although he gave other reasons than the BCG controversy for doing so.

The tuberculosis contest had been largely policy and administrative imbroglio, but it also laid bare a flaw in Occupation planning. Much had been hoped from the reactivation of the Japanese health center system, which, under a 1937 law, had resulted in the opening of 134 health centers by the close of 1940. These free clinics, each manned by a minimum of two physicians, a pharmacist, a graduate nurse, and clerical personnel, with additional assistance in larger centers, had offered health education, hygiene counseling, maternal and child welfare guidance in addition to examinations and treatment for tuberculosis and venereal disease. When the Occupation opened, 645 health centers were in full, or partial operation, although many of them had deteriorated and most of them were short of technical personnel.

To guarantee continuance of their activities, the Diet had ordered the establishment of 780 health centers (one, at least, for each district of 100,000 population) and had assigned to them twelve essential public health functions. In thirty-one large cities, activities were supervised by mayors; and prefectural health departments administered the other centers. To guide all centers in proper operations six model health centers were installed.

Full service has, however, never been rendered. By October, 1951, most of the 645 surviving centers had been reactivated, although trained technical and professional personnel were not obtainable in sufficient quantity; and 125 new offices had been created. Complete examination of all suspected tubercular or venereal cases has not been possible—much less, treatment of all illnesses discovered. In 150 health centers eugenic marriage consultation offices were placed in service.

Sams's assault upon venereal disease started with the astonishing assumption that, although it was widespread and there were numerous cases, "Japanese physicians were unfamiliar with the epidemiologic and clinical signs." He complained that the prewar Venereal Disease Prevention Law of 1927 had been so loosely drawn that only prostitutes were affected; that, even so, it was unenforced; that contact tracing was not pursued; and that clinical procedures were not only inadequate but also archaic.

Nevertheless intensive antivenereal disease efforts had evidently been effective, since only 12.69 VD cases were reported among each 1,000 conscripts in 1930 as against 26.57 VD cases in 1914.

Sams required that existing legislation be enforced, that cases be made reportable, and that each prefecture provide adequate facilities for efficient VD control. Although the requirements were promptly embodied in an Imperial Ordinance, compliance was slow; about one-quarter of the prefectures waited at least four years before meeting the obligation, and most of the 780 health centers similarly lagged. Only 56 clinics and private hospitals admitted in-patients.

Further steps included the abolition of compulsory, but not of professional, prostitution—a law that could not be completely enforced—and the passage of a revised Venereal Disease Prevention Act calling for premarital and prenatal examinations. This Act was administered with uneven efficiency and was often the excuse for brutal and callous treatment; but it was credited with reducing VD cases from 386,990 in 1949 to 310,000 in 1950. A previous drop, from 473,822 in 1946, was ignored in claiming success for the new law. Of the 310,000 cases, the Welfare Ministry asserted that one-third were prostitute-derived, and that another 7,535 cases were caused by "other extramarital relations"; but no explanation was given for the remaining 200,000 cases. The Ministry also admitted that its figures were incomplete since the accelerated Japanese production of sulfanilamide, mapharsen, bismuth subsalicylate, and penicillin brought it about that many cases which should have been treated in clinic or hospital were cared for by what it termed "back-door, or self, treatment."

Diseases requiring popular cooperation have been checked but not yet beaten. Reopening of restaurants long closed because of food shortages, hawking of ice candies, jellies, and ice creams, open, although illegal, exposure of foods in markets, and other insanitary practices opened wide loopholes. The Welfare Ministry warned against carelessness in garbage and trash disposal and against insufficient washing of raw foods grown with night-soil fertilizer.

Dysentery, which had increased steadily from 17,135 cases in 1926 to 97,250 in 1939 but had then dropped yearly to 50,188 in 1943, again rose in the two years when Japan was heavily bombed. Japanese and Allied health officials cut the incidence from 95,462 in 1945 to 24,001 in 1949, the lowest total since 1927 and, during the same period, cut deaths from this disease from 20,107 to 7,824. But Tokyo showed a reverse tendency. Dysentery cases in the capital rose from 1,491 in 1945 (the highest in fifty years), to 3,372 in 1949. Nor was this all, the Welfare Ministry reporting 9,402 cases in 1950, and 14,203 in 1951, with the first half of 1952 showing a rise over the corresponding figures of 1951. Most of these cases were in the semi-slum Arakawa and Kita wards.

Much of the blame, according to Dr. I. D. Hirchy, Chief of Sams's Preventive Medicine Division, was attributable to overconfidence in the efficacy of new sulfa drugs.

Whether, as the *Osaka Mainichi* asserted, a parallel increase existed also in parasite infestation is uncertain, since statistics are not wholly reportable. Acting under a Parasite Prevention Law, Japanese physicians had reduced ascariasis from 295,626 in 1938 to 180,552 in 1941, and other parasite afflictions from 76,917 to 47,574; but postwar figures are not available. The *Mainichi* asserted that 80 per cent of Japanese were worm carriers and recommended importation of santonin and hexylresorcinol to combat the situation. It also proposed that flush toilets be installed, and that the use of night soil for fertilizer be abandoned.

TWENTY

Great Land Reform

MacArthur entered Japan with the firm conviction that peasants suffered under an archaic land system cruelly devised to keep them always on the threshold of starvation. Little was generally known concerning Japanese agriculture, only a few trustworthy volumes having been available abroad; but prewar Agriculture Ministry surveys had proved that no tracts under 4.5 acres could possibly return a profit to the average 6.5 member farm family unless women and children worked both in the fields and in subsidiary domestic occupations. Official Japanese statistics had shown that in 1940 only 9 per cent of Japan's 5,479,-571 farm families cultivated this minimum; that two-thirds held only 2.5 acres; and that half of these lived on but 1.25 acres. The average household held 2.9 acres.

By the time MacArthur arrived the war, by draining off farm labor, had reduced even these small holdings so that, in 1946, 94 per cent of farm households lived on less than subsistence-sized farms; 70 per cent were on 2.5-acre tracts, and 40 per cent on 1.25-acre plots.

American wartime propagandists publicized that in 1940 less than a third of Japan's farm land was owner-operated (though this included half of the better rice paddies); that 1,466,866 tenant farmers tilled 27 per cent of the farms and, as hired men, helped cultivate another 42 per cent for the owners. War conditions brought a two-point rise in both owner-operated and tenant-cultivated farms, and the joint owner-hired-man farms fell off in 1946 to 38 per cent.

MacArthur, conscious of the evils of sharecropping, and assuming that similar conditions must exist everywhere, determined to "tear from

221

the evils of the Japanese countryside the roots of legal landlordism." In this his Natural Resources Section chief, Colonel Hubert G. Schenck, supported him, damning "the oppressive bonds of a feudalistic system" whose pernicious tenant farming "long blighted Japanese agriculture and impaired the development of a peaceful national economy." Unless land reform came immediately, Schenck explained, economic instability and malignant social conditions would revive militarism and foment extremism.

Almost as a matter of course, absentee landlordism was assumed; but its extent was certainly exaggerated. Statistics are uncertain, the best available reports appearing to indicate that prior to the war some 24,129 large landowners were nonresident; but food distribution difficulties during the war sent many of them back to the farms, and there were only 17,793 absentees in 1944. After surrender this number sharply dropped to 3,245 in 1946. In only eight prefectures did absentee landlords constitute as much as 0.1 per cent of farm owners.

Many tracts credited to absentees were really public lands, and these were largely mountainous, forested, or otherwise uncultivable. Of more than 38,000,000 acres thus owned in 1930, the national government held approximately a quarter, and local entities slightly more than a third. Far from increasing, these totals had actually dropped by about 10 per cent in 1946, the total acreage still in public hands being for the most part national parks or lands held for conservation purposes.

Contrary to the general impression abroad, shrines and temples, with 356,000 acres in 1930, held but 0.6 per cent of this forest and field land and by 1946 they had added only 119,000 more acres. Shiroshi Nasu noted in 1939 that all but 419,000 of the Emperor's millions of acres were forest.

Commercial company holdings, too small to be noted in 1930, outstripped the shrines and temples, owning in 1943 some 850,000 acres of mountainous, forest, and waste land; but they lost much of this before the war ended, and had only 750,000 acres in 1946. Special corporations, including colleges and a small number of cultural and welfare foundations, doubled their ownership of such areas, from 300,000 acres in 1930 to 600,000 in 1946.

Latifundia, which had not existed since the Meiji land reforms, ranked very high among the supposed injustices. Wolf I. Ladejinsky, for a decade Orient land expert for the United States Department of Agriculture, had warned against "a striking concentration of land ownership" with 50 per cent of all farm households owning less than 9 per cent of the soil while 7.5 per cent of Japan's families owned half the land; but he failed to make it clear that these figures, accepted by Andrew Roth's *Dilemma in Japan*, included 21,000,000 acres of mountain, forest, and waste land. The arable 16 per cent of the Japanese area was far more equitably distributed, only 20,078 landowners possessing more than 25 acres of farm land in 1941; and war exigencies whittled down the total to 12,448 in 1946. These landowners, 0.2 per cent of all farm families, lived for the most part in Hokkaido, tilling relatively poor land, posing no real problem of exploitation of the peasantry.

Virtually none of the larger farm tracts were capitalist enterprises. Following the Meiji Restoration when the Government took over daimyo estates in exchange for national bonds, capitalists had preferred industrial to agricultural investments. Denzaburo Fujita's 10,314-acre plantation, established in 1899, was an outstanding exception.

Writings by such critics as Seiyei Wakakawa, an Okinawan, and Andrew J. Grajdanzev convinced Schenck that rents were highly inequitable, and in the case of paddy rentals should be paid in cash rather than in kind. For these statements also, the bases were misleading. Official yen rents on ordinary fields had indeed been rising during the 1930 decade, but only in exact proportion to the market price of land. Rents on paddy, payable in kind, favored tenants unduly, having gone up 4 per cent while land prices were rising 40 per cent. The war doubled land prices; but yen rents on ordinary fields went up only 50 per cent, and paddy rents actually dropped 6 per cent.

No one would have argued that farmers were leading comfortable lives, even by Japanese standards; but too facile comparison with Western conditions, especially when presented for wartime propaganda purposes, misled observers. Japan was poor, and her farm population worked unceasingly under conditions unendurable to Americans; but the farmers were not serfs, nor had the evils been imposed by capitalists, reactionaries, heartless totalitarians, or Tojo's militarists. The unbearable conditions, moreover, while certainly worse at times of bad harvests such as those of the 1920 decade, showed over-all improvement.

Agriculture Ministry statistics on household budgets, notoriously inaccurate in detail, indicated that during the 1930 decade all farm groups prospered. The average household, which in 1931 lost 7.31 yen, piled up a profit of 1,946.73 yen during the six years preceding Pearl

Harbor—1,168 of this coming during 1939 and 1940, when war prepara-
tions were proceeding feverishly.

Independent farmers, as might have been guessed, won largest shares,
with average gains of 2,316.98 yen during the six-year period as against
2,064.14 for owner-tenant farms; but the supposedly hard-pressed
tenants accumulated 1,462.50 yen. Tenant incomes, rising steadily, were,
moreover, increasingly derived from straight farm operations rather
than from subsidiary occupations.

By Western standards all Japanese farmers lived unbelievably drab
lives, the average payment in 1931 by an average family of 6.5 persons
for amusement being but 3.78 yen, or less than a dollar at current exchange, though part of the 35.49 yen paid out of "ceremonial occasion" may, as in the case of shrine festivals, perhaps be added to the
total. It was not surprising therefore, that, despite official pressure for
austerity, the index of amusement payments rose.

Schenck and MacArthur professed shock that tenants had no legal
guarantee of tenure; leases being verbal rather than written, and law
enforcement being dominated by landlords rather than by tenants, eviction could occur at any time. Yet, as in Japan's conception of social
responsibility a landlord, like other oyabun, was morally bound to
care for his followers, tenants enjoyed security. Irresponsible eviction,
while legally possible, was remarkably infrequent. When crops were good,
as during the 1930 decade, the tenant prospered, and, observing the
letter of his agreement, he pocketed the extra profit; but when crops
were poor, as when typhoons or drought reduced the yield, he looked
to the landlord for appropriate rent reductions. Failure of the landlord
to observe the unwritten oyabun code explained most of the tenant
riots which Schenck attributed to the oppressive bonds of a feudalistic
land system.

Like all other section chiefs and like MacArthur himself, Schenck
faced the necessity of assuring democratic practices within an inde-
terminate period; he, too, hurried action lest the Occupation expire too
soon. Acting under misconception, he gave less heed to real food shortages than to the elimination of fancied agricultural evils.

Even had Schenck been more interested in these problems, he was
hurried into action before he became thoroughly prepared. Within less
than a week after appointing Schenck chief of Natural Resources Section, MacArthur summoned the new Prime Minister, Shidehara, and demanded that agriculture be democratized in accordance with the terms

of JCS 10. As no specific requirements were laid down and no guidance was given, Shidehara sent his Agriculture Minister, Kenzo Matsumura, to ask Schenck's advice.

Possibly, by doing so, Shidehara helped shape Occupation responsibilities. Under Joint Chiefs of Staff directives, MacArthur had no specific authority to meddle in domestic matters unless epidemic broke out or mass disorder jeopardized Occupation aims. Even had he been inclined to stretch his interpretations, as in political, educational, economic, and even recreational affairs, he had assigned no such latitude to his subordinates. Both Schenck's NRS and ESS claimed agriculture, but no decision between them had yet been reached. In sending Matsumura to consult with Schenck, perhaps at MacArthur's own suggestion, Shidehara tipped the scales in NRS's favor.

This, however, did not affect the graver problem of diet and nutrition, then growing to a crisis and involving not only Schenck's NRS and ESS but also PHW. Each of the three groups, while normally eager to enlarge, avoided this knotty difficulty whose solution, however imperative from a humane point of view, promised no spectacular publicity rewards. In promising close liaison with Matsumura's Agriculture Ministry, Schenck made it clear that he was interested primarily in democratic land reform.

Hiroo Wada, an Agriculture Ministry bureaucrat whom the militarists had jailed in 1941 for nonconformity, received unofficial Occupation approval to draft a bill for land reform. Seeing the problem in terms of breaking up the 127,000 farms larger than 7.5 acres, Wada concentrated on the problem for a month and then proposed that all rented land on such farms be sold to the cultivators, and that, in addition, tenants be aided to purchase over a five-year period whatever other rented land owners wished to sell. This, he estimated, would transfer approximately half of the 5,485,543 rented acres, thus creating a theoretical maximum of 1,090,000 new peasant proprietors, each with a 2.5-acre farm.

No one expected that this fantastically optimistic estimate would be fulfilled, particularly as twenty years' operation of a somewhat similar law passed in 1926 had helped but 259,629 newcomers and 245,197 farm families to gain single-acre tracts. The Cabinet, less concerned with breaking up the larger holdings than with returning absentees to their farms, raised to 12.5 acres the maximum to be retained by landlords, which meant that only 50,000 farms would be broken up under

compulsion and those chiefly in Hokkaido. Grajdanzev estimated that
this would have reduced the theoretical maximum to 970,000 new
farmers.

MacArthur, who had voiced no public opposition to the Wada draft,
looked upon the Cabinet amendments as evasive, insincere, and insufficient; on December 9, 1945, while the bill was still under Diet consideration, he demanded that a better land reform program be submitted
within three months. The Diet responded by passing the Cabinet-spon-
sored measure, but MacArthur refused to accept it. Wada accordingly
revised the draft; but Ladejinsky, newly appointed as Schenck's as-
sistant, complained that it did not require long leases, gave no legal
security against eviction, and failed to hold rents below 50 per cent of
annual yields. MacArthur thereupon blasted the proposal as "a deliberate campaign to circumvent the spirit and the letter of the land reform
directive."

Convinced that neither the landlord-dominated Liberals who ran the
Government nor Wada, a leftist Socialist, would draft an acceptable
program, Schenck commissioned Ladejinsky to draw up better plans.
These he sent confidentially in May, 1946, to Wada, Yoshida's Agriculture Minister, for guidance. The contents were kept secret, but in
June Professor W. Macmahon Ball, British Commonwealth member of
the Allied Council for Japan, published parallel proposals. Ball said
that a satisfactory land reform program must include: (1) maximum
ownership of 7.5 acres by any one person, except that in Hokkaido the
limit might be 30 acres; (2) forced sale of all excess lands in exchange
for twenty-four-year government bonds; (3) tenant purchases on long-
term payments with prices to be cut if land values fell prior to full payment; (4) limitation of nonresident ownership to 2.5 acres, with rent
ceilings, written contracts, and periodic revision of rentals; (5) con-
solidation of scattered holdings into more efficient units; (6) completion
of the program within three years.

Ball's recommendations, approved in most respects by a majority of
the Allied Council for Japan, hit landlords severely; but MacArthur's
headquarters thought the program weak. By insistent, though unacknowledged, verbal pressure, the Occupation goaded an unwilling
Diet into passing a more stringent law.

The farm reform bill, enacted October 21, 1946, stripped away farm
lands but not waste lands or forests of the 3,245 nonresidents, and all

but 2.5 acres of operating farmers; but Hokkaido owners retained 30 acres each. For land thus requisitioned, owners received only nominal compensation, at the rate of 3,913 yen per acre of paddy and 2,309 yen per acre of dry farm. For those losing more than 7.5 acres the rates were even lower, being 3,030 and 1,788 yen respectively. Official land prices, regarded as lower than the actual value, were, at the time, 44 per cent higher than even the most generous payments to be made for paddy and 62 per cent higher than for dry lands.

Grajdanzev, shocked at the meager payments, termed them "practically confiscatory"; but, simultaneously, political experts within his own Government Section condemned the Diet for serving landlord interests by setting the rates too high. Some leftists would have preferred outright confiscation without any payments whatsoever.

To many, it seemed that this had been achieved, for the doles were not paid in cash but, as the Occupation had suggested, in bonds, bearing 3.65 per cent interest and non-negotiable for twenty-four years. As inflation was so rampant that land prices tripled within the year, and as commercial loans were bringing 10 per cent or more, landlords received virtually nothing. The owner who sold an acre of paddy at the highest permissible price drew annual interest equivalent to 30 cents, and would cash his bond after twenty-four years for $10.87.

Tenants, on the other hand, received every possible consideration. Purchase prices for expropriated lands were set at the lowest rate given to landlords—the Government subsidizing any loss between the buying price and the top selling rate—and, if they chose to spread their payments over twenty-four years, they paid but 3.2 per cent interest. This, however, was not necessary; in 1947 alone the crop grown on one acre, if sold on the Tokyo wholesale market, brought 6,658 yen, or more than double the purchase price of land. For such rentals as continued, they paid a maximum of 25 per cent of the value of rice grown or 15 per cent of the value of other crops.

MacArthur hailed the law as a gratifying indication of the Yoshida Government's courageous determination to destroy landlordism. It was the same Government he had previously accused of trying to sabotage reform. Schenck and Ladejinsky acclaimed the "peaceful revolution" that measurably weakened militarism, nationalism, and Communism. Others, like Grajdanzev, remained dissatisfied, complaining that non-farming resident landlords, as well as absentees, should have been divested of land; permission to rent out 2.5 acres left, they warned, a "fortress in enemy territory" from which landlords might, in time, regain their lost possessions.

Grajdanzev, like many others, regretted also that farm land reform applied only to arable lands, leaving untouched a three times as great area of forest and *genya* (unwooded waste lands), upon which peasants depended for fuel, grass, and cattle forage. Failure to include forests and genya, he said, left mountaineers at the mercy of feudal landlords who dominated stock raising, charcoal burning, and firewood gathering. Perhaps because of this he was sent home hurriedly; almost simultaneously Andrew Roth was forbidden to visit Japan.

By 1951 the Government had acquired 4,920,365 acres, including 440,192 acres forfeited for nonpayment of taxes. Forced sales, beginning in March, 1947, continued in eighteen stages until 30,000,000 parcels had been taken over.

Purchasing, while comparatively easily accomplished, necessarily involved such vast amounts of surveys and paper work that—as Robert S. Hardie, Schenck's agricultural economics chief, confessed to the Allied Council for Japan—for months, not a single acre was resold to former tenants. Before redistribution could be accomplished, farm lands must be remapped so as to consolidate tracts and allow purchasers, as far as possible, to buy contiguous plots of equal quality convenient to their homes. Thus, although some 4,000,000 acres had been "bought" prior to March, 1948, only 688,148 acres had been released to tenants.

Poor liaison between SCAP sections caused misunderstanding of this lag. Government Section, which strongly disliked Rikizo Hirano, Agriculture Minister during 1947, held him responsible. Though he was a Socialist, some of Whitney's men looked upon him as dangerously reactionary; they preferred Wada, Yoshida's Agriculture Minister, to him. They, therefore, had Hirano purged and followed this action by accusations that "reactionary groups were obstructing land reform for a free and democratic Japan."

Katayama's Socialist Cabinet fell the same day as the Government Section pronouncement, though for a different reason, and was succeeded first by a Progressive-Socialist-Cooperative coalition and later by the second Yoshida Cabinet. Coincidentally, surveys being well advanced, sales increased; and in March, 1949, some 4,410,000 acres had been redistributed. Mark Williamson, chief of Schenck's Agricultural Division, estimated that these transfers included about a third of the cultivated land in Japan. He considered that the retention under tenancy of about 12 per cent of arable acreage was not dangerous; it constituted a healthy guarantee of flexibility in land tenure.

MacArthur, highly pleased with the results of the campaign, marked the third anniversary of the passage of the law by congratulating Yoshida on "possibly the most successful land reform program in history."

The praise may have been premature. Certain gains had certainly been accomplished. The 3,425 large landlords had been eliminated, and no private individual was legally entitled to own more than 7.5 acres except in the northeast, where soil and climate were unfavorable, and in Hokkaido. At least 4,477,000 of the 6,953,000 acres rented just prior to the war had been confiscated for resale, though former landlords retained the more desirable paddy tracts for their own legal use. Peasant ownership had risen from 1,711,404 in 1941 to 3,821,531, while tenantry had dropped from 1,524,290 to 312,364.

Under the Occupation, the percentage of owners among the 6,176,419 farm families had risen from 27 in 1946 to 62, while tenants, who had already dropped from 27 per cent in 1940 to 25 in 1946, were a scant 5 per cent in 1950. Joint owner-hired-man operation, which had risen prior to the war, had now fallen from 38 per cent in 1946 to 33 per cent.

New farm families, while falling short of Wada's optimistic hopes, numbered 478,471—an increase almost as large as that produced by the entire twenty years' operation of the 1926 law. But, although the numbers were large, the increase since 1946 was only 8 per cent while general population was increasing 15 per cent, and the area planted to rice was but 5 per cent greater. After five years of the Occupation the rice area was only 96 per cent of that of 1941.

Special privilege for farmers did not long continue. Kokichi Asakura, of the Bank of Japan, pointed out early in 1948 that, while former tenants had been freed from heavy rentals to the dispossessed landlords, the burden was replaced by heavy taxes. More than 60 per cent of farm income, he estimated, was needed for newly imposed taxation. The Economic Stabilization Board, in an official white paper, reported that, while farm receipts had risen 22 per cent in 1948 over the 1946–1947 mark—after due allowance for inflation—farm expenses had gone up 75.3 per cent; and taxes, 181 per cent.

This tax burden, being locally collected, could not be evaded with the ease with which some former levies had been escaped. In the past, when central agencies collected imposts, local authorities had often looked aside when neighbors understated acreage or underestimated harvests. But when local entities were more and more self-supporting, and dependent upon their own tax revenues, collectors were less lenient with evaders and delinquents.

The central government, contrary to hopes, did not end or seriously reduce the quotas to be delivered; and the percentage rose from 45 in 1946 to nearly 48 in 1948, while newly imposed supertaxes caused collection to rise from 104.4 per cent in 1946 to 106.03 in 1948. Supposedly the extra collections were to be paid at bonus rates, but the practice was soon outlawed.

Following a Joint Chiefs of Staff directive to stabilize Japanese economy by preventing further inflation, MacArthur, in December, 1948, ordered Yoshida to hold down farm prices. Yoshida and his supposedly landlord-dominated Liberals were commanded to sponsor a proposal, the Food Supply Securance Special Measures Bill, to guarantee efficient collection, if not distribution, of staple crops at fixed prices lower than prevailing rates. The quotas to be set were regarded as unwarrantedly high.

Had Yoshida been free to explain that the bill, opposed both by landlords, whose rents were kept frozen, and by independent farmers, whose crops were commandeered at low prices, had been drawn by Occupation order and introduced under compulsion his task would have been easier; but MacArthur forbade him to do so. Leakage of the secret multiplied his troubles. The Opposition, knowing that the bill must pass, but also that Yoshida dared not disown it, violently attacked the proposal, winning credit for themselves and undermining Yoshida's popularity among groups supposed to be his strongest friends.

The opposition grew so intense that, to everyone's astonishment, the Diet failed to pass the bill, in spite of earnest lobbying by Occupation agents. When a second Diet, in 1949, also refused to pass it, MacArthur's Occupation, abandoning all pretense that the democratic Diet was free to legislate as it desired, forced Yoshida to issue a Potsdam Ordinance overriding the highest organ of the state and putting the bill into effect.

To recover the lost agrarian support Yoshida proposed to end Government land purchases, revise face values of bonds already issued, and raise rent ceilings; but Occupation disapproval made it impossible. Marquat also vetoed his plan to decontrol rice, wheat, and barley but allowed a reduction of obligatory rice deliveries to 46.6 per cent of the 1949 harvest. Yoshida wished to permit farmers to sell any rice surplus beyond their own needs on the open market, but Joseph M. Dodge, the Detroit banker who was SCAP's special financial adviser, warned that this would start a vicious cycle. Competitive rice purchases would, he explained, drive up prices, force wage increases, and, by causing higher manufacturing costs, weaken the Japanese economy.

Continued controls intensified agrarian unrest. Landowners, dissatisfied with rent ceilings of 2,286 yen per acre (less than $7 a year) for rice lands, circumvented the law by extorting additional payments in kind, and, when these were refused, illegally evicted the tenants; 325 such cases occurred in Yamagata prefecture alone during 1951. Legal rents were tripled thereafter.

Perhaps the situation was not so serious as to warrant Professor Yasuo Kondo's plaint that farmers were again being exploited; but neither did it justify the Agriculture Ministry's reference in an elaborate report to "epochal reforms" which "should be perpetuated in the memory of posterity."

Almost simultaneously the Welfare Ministry deplored the poverty of farm families. Miss Taki Fujita, chief of the Women's and Children's Bureau, in revealing that 674 farmers in northeastern Japan had sold their daughters into white slavery, noted that this number was but a fraction of the total. Farmers, she said bitterly, "would rather sell their daughters than their land."

They were selling their land also. The Agriculture Ministry admitted 73,000 illegal sales in 1949 and 100,000 more in 1950, when bans on sales were lifted. In 1951, 91,870 more sales were registered; and the three-year total affected about 7 per cent of all landowners.

These readjustments, undermining the spirit of land reform, foreshadowed future reactionary developments. After the first optimistic anticipations of prosperity and happiness, disillusion concerning land distribution had set in. This was strongest, of course, among dispossessed landlords but was felt in other circles also.

Fragmentation, basic evil in the farm economy, was far from being cured; it actually intensified, with farms smaller than the 4.5 acres regarded as essential for subsistence climbing to 92 per cent.

This was not wholly the effect of land reform; it was furthered by new constitutional provisions. Prior to the war, peasant proprietors, fearful of subdividing already pitifully small farms, left their entire estates to eldest sons under the unexpressed but well recognized assumption that the new family heads would guard their brothers against unnecessary loss. Occupationnaires, in the interest of democracy and equality, forbade the practice, preferring that estates be shared among all heirs.

Some effort had been made to evade this subdivision, the Agriculture Ministry reporting in 1949 that in 84.7 per cent of more than 33,000 successions younger brothers had voluntarily surrendered their claims or made special arrangements with the eldest sons; but the new requirements helped cut down the size of farms.

The average size of farms decreased from 2.9 acres in 1940 to 2.6 a decade later. When land reform was complete, the proportion of farmers living on less than 2.5 acres had risen from 67 per cent in 1946 to more than 70. About 23 per cent of Japan's farmers lived, in 1950, on less than 0.8 acre.

The campaign to break up large estates failed of spectacular overall success. Of 127,927 farms of more than 7.5 acres in 1946, 125,170 remained, 98,092 in Hokkaido, and almost all the rest in the northeastern prefectures. Less progress had been made in reducing large farms than during the war years, when the number of farms larger than 7.5 acres had been reduced by 60,535. Nor had the earlier reduction been solely due to emergency war conditions; the scaling down had been consistent for a generation, there having been in 1928 more than 225,000 farms larger than 7.5 acres.

Sociologically, farm reform, however desirable theoretically, had introduced new problems. An Occupation which stressed democracy and fundamental human rights, demanding that they be firmly embedded in the new Constitution, denied to farmers the right to buy and sell at will. Insistence that crops be delivered by fixed quota and at arbitrarily established prices was perhaps defensible in the emergency, particularly as it was a prewar Japanese requirement; but the refusal to farmers of the right to dispose of lands without special permission imposed a modern form of serfdom. Free enterprise, however it may have been abused in the past, was supposedly an Occupation aim; yet farmers had no share in it.

Inability to sell land freely, while glibly explained as a protection against the return of a latifundia that had not existed since the Meiji

Restoration, handicapped the farmer's business dealings. Japanese agriculture, like business everywhere, depended largely upon credits; but when land sales were restricted and farmers had little other security banks were loath to lend. Accordingly, special cooperatives were created for such purposes, under conditions which in theory avoided the totalitarian evils of the prewar agricultural associations; but the cooperatives, in practice, operated along very similar lines. Private moneylenders, exacting heavy interest, became a common recourse.

TWENTY-ONE

Tightening the Belt

Food supply was a more pressing problem which Occupationnaires in 1945 did not overlook, but to which, in their haste to root out totalitarianism, they sometimes gave only secondary attention.

Whatever the cause, and whether or not deservedly, large sections of the people faced starvation. However plentiful the food reserves in rural regions, the breakdown of communications, labor shortages, and depleted coal stockpiles, as well as an understandable postsurrender lethargy, hindered transport of the reserves to city residents.

Other than labor losses, Japanese farmers had not suffered heavily by the war. A few dams had been bombed, limiting light and power output and affecting irrigation systems, and the soil had been seriously devitalized for lack of needed fertilizer; but, even with the inclusion of the catastrophic 1945 surrender year, wartime crops had almost touched peacetime averages. Fruits, sugar, and vegetables were in serious shortage; but, except for 1945, even the lowest wartime harvests yielded more staples than the harvests of the 1920 or most of the 1930 decade. The 1942 rice crop, fourth largest in history, was but 6 per cent below the all-time record.

Farmers, while resenting orders to sell their rice at fixed rather than competitive prices, cooperated willingly to relieve food shortages except in scattered instances, sometimes fomented by radicals. Of course rumors were current that many sold upon the more profitable black market and, to avoid taxation both in money and in kind, underreported their plantings; but the average rice acreage in the five war years stood at 96 per cent of the 1930 decade, and while the 1945 rice planting was the lowest in forty years a general decline had been in progress since 1921. Wartime losses were easily explainable by lack of labor.

Agricultural experts, making a brief, hurried, and doubtless inaccurate survey under difficult circumstances, anticipated a 1945 rice harvest of 8,400,000 metric tons. Such a crop, while the lowest since 1906, would have brought wartime yields per acre above those of any ten-year prewar average. Each Japanese could then have received a pint of rice daily, and this, with legumes, potatoes, other vegetables, and fruit, would have afforded a reasonable though far from lavish ration, larger than that which would have been possible under the domestic farm production of 1930.

Unhappily, disaster struck. Three great typhoons, together with a flood, so devastated the ripening rice that at least 15 per cent of the crop was lost. In addition, storm damage together with continuing coal and labor shortages forced a 50 per cent slash in railway service, preventing food supplies from moving to the cities.

The dark prospect led Finance Minister Keizo Shibusawa to predict that, unless America sent aid, 10,000,000 Japanese would starve. The forecast came at an unfortunate time and probably from the wrong person—many Occupationnaires, fresh from the battlefields, balking at feeding their late enemies. Shibusawa, heir of one of Japan's ten biggest financial families, had not personally exploited his countrymen; but, as a big businessman, one of the Zaibatsu, he had profited by Zaibatsu policies. If therefore, some leftists said, Japan needed food, Shibusawa and his fellow Zaibatsu should open up their granaries and themselves distribute it.

Such critics, more intent on punishing Japan for war crimes than upon relieving distress, waved aside crop failure. The 1945 rice harvest, anticipated at 8,400,000 metric tons, actually totaled 6,445,050 tons, which the Agriculture Ministry said was 38,822,000 koku (one koku is 5.12 bushels) but which the Occupation rendered as 42,967,000 koku. The latter figure, assuming perfect collection and distribution and the highest efficiency in use, would have assured each Japanese just about half a pint of rice per day.

MacArthur, impressed by Shidehara's pessimism, particularly after learning that Tokyo, which had received 8.5 ounces of fresh foods daily in the spring of 1945, was getting but one-fifth as much in August prior to the typhoons, called upon Washington to send 1,600,000 tons of food.

Action followed very slowly. MacArthur himself, assuming that his recommendations would be respected, turned to other matters. His aides, however, failed in their teamwork, and Washington procrastinated. Meanwhile the situation worsened until in November, 1945, each Tokyo resident was receiving but 0.88 ounce of rations daily.

This tiny allowance testified tragically to Japan's inability to feed herself. Economists had long been aware that Japan, far from being self-sufficient, had normally imported more than 20 per cent of her food requirements. Even when she had controlled Korea and Formosa she had annually purchased abroad 2,000,000 additional tons of rice, wheat, beans, and sugar.

During Japan's aggressive years Chinese, Thai, and Cambodian markets closed, and Americans, Canadians, Indians, and Australians reduced their sales or applied economic sanctions. But in 1940 Japanese control over North China became so secure that this source reopened, imports from Indo-China, Thailand, and India suddenly soared to unprecedented heights, and even Australia resumed wheat shipments. Japan's 1940 food imports were more than thirty times the preceding five-year average.

Some Occupationnaires, ignorant of prewar trade trends but deeply steeped in wartime indoctrination, construed this startling increase as solely due to stockpiling for aggressive war. Unfamiliar with the national economy, they could not realize that Japan must import food or go hungry.

Nor did they understand that Japan, whose industries were paralyzed and whose economy was shattered, must buy food in expensive markets with foreign currencies which she did not possess. Less well informed Occupationnaires simplified the problem by believing that Japan, sulking over defeat, was pretending starvation in order to extort charity from her conquerors. This, they contended, was unendurable in a nation which by reckless aggression had brought misery to millions.

Headquarters officials, insufficiently informed of general conditions, stoutly denied food shortages. Colonel Sams, a confirmed critic of Japanese statistics, insisted that Japan consistently lied about food scarcities—a charge in which Edwin W. Pauley's Reparations Commission concurred. Colonel Schenck reported that, after surrender, Japanese army stores contained 3,000,000 tons of rice, or slightly less than half the entire 1945 harvest, and someone assured Mark Gayn of the Chicago *Sun* that as late as June, 1946, the Government, in collusion with the landlord speculators by whom it was said to be dominated, was still hoarding a seventh of the 1945 crop.

If this were true, neither the Occupation's widespread intelligence agency nor the Communists, most eager spreaders of the rumor, were able to discover it, though leftist agitators raided various storehouses, including that of the Imperial Household, where the rice was supposed to be. Whether or not the radicals were correct in the charge that "official inertia, corrupt and archaic supergovernment and plain and fancy politics" were starving the people, as Gayn reported, some top Occupation officers assured correspondents that Shibusawa and other Japanese officials were trying to delude Americans.

Conflicting statements confused the issue. Though Schenck contended that no Japanese was starving, John La Cerda of the Philadelphia *Evening Bulletin* saw hunger everywhere. "It is not an uncommon sight," he wrote, "to see Japanese collapse and die on the street. Passers-by pay no attention to an occasional body." Sams, on the other hand, denied that any one had starved to death and, after checking 1,933 Tokyo families, reported that Japanese food intake was 1,971 calories, or nearly 30 per cent above the 1,572-calories official ration. Tokyo men, he said, ate even more than this, 2,252 calories per day. He tacitly admitted that this was possible only by black-marketing. Actual ration deliveries, he said, were 1,232 calories, the remainder coming from illegal purchases at 7.5 times the official price, or from food smuggled from rural areas in defiance of police regulations. No one could possibly deny that this was true; trains from the countryside, crowded with city people bearing huge bundles of food, showed only too clearly what was happening. Not only the "burnt-outs" of bombed areas but also the more fortunate whose homes had not been destroyed sold off their valuables, including spare clothes, to buy food in an "onionskin existence" possible for the wealthy but not for the poor. Farm women so blossomed in rich kimonos bartered for rice that Robert B. Cochrane of the Baltimore *Sun* airily referred to them as the new "country club set."

Unquestionably speculation existed; but it was illegal, and so no statistics were available. The crisis, nevertheless, was cruelly real. Whatever the cause of shortages, especially among the poor of the cities, the need for quick relief was apparent. Shibusawa's warning was echoed by Commerce Minister Sankuro Ogasawara, who pleaded urgently for immediate delivery of 330,000 tons of food. The amount looked large; but, even if distributed only to the 20,000,000 residents of the 149 cities of more than 50,000 population, it would have meant only 22 pounds per capita. Ogasawara proposed that this initial shipment be supplemented by an additional 600,000 tons before the end of June, 1946; but this was ridiculed as excessive.

With winter approaching rapidly and with transportation disrupted, Tokyo's food reserves fell to a five-day supply. Sporadic food riots, which may well have been Red-inspired, broke out in Hokkaido, and the normally conservative and censorship-conscious *Nippon Times* blazed with a banner head predicting more disorder.

Moved by fear of disorder and consequent threat to Allied objectives, MacArthur resorted to the authority conferred upon him by the United States Initial Postsurrender Policy. He authorized General Walter Krueger of the Sixth Army at Kyoto and General Robert L. Eichelberger of the Eighth Army at Yokohama to release for civilian use large amounts of Japanese army war supplies. Because of pressing emergencies, accurate measurement of the foods thus distributed was not always taken; but official estimates, which were probably too high, ranged from 132,000 tons of beans, 41,000 tons of fish and meat, and 113,000,000 cans of vegetables to a fantastic claim that 30,000,000 tons of food were thus provided.

By the opening of 1946, MacArthur, convinced that famine was actually close at hand, proclaimed that the food shortage was unprecedented in magnitude, and that "mass starvation would be inevitable" unless American help came at once. In thus endorsing Shibusawa's fear, previously too lightly regarded, MacArthur predicted that the ration must drop to 700 calories unless the United States intervened.

Instead of the 930,000 tons for which Ogasawara had asked, or the 630,000 tons approved by the Combined Food Boards in Washington, MacArthur called for prompt shipment of 3,311,000 metric tons as the minimum necessary to guarantee a 1,550-calorie ration, "the minimum needed for limited physical exertion."

To Herbert Hoover, who came to Japan with a Famine Emergency Commission, he said that unless the full 3,311,000 metric tons were at once dispatched mass starvation would ensue, and civil unrest break out. The choice, he said dramatically, was more food or more troops to quell disturbances.

To many the demand for 3,311,000 metric tons seemed wild exaggeration; yet MacArthur's estimate was valid and even conservative. As long ago as 1926, when Japan's population had been only 60,000,-000, she had imported more than 2,000,000 tons of food; in 1946, with 75,000,000 population but without the millions of tons of food formerly produced in Korea and Formosa, rice importations must inevitably increase heavily. That MacArthur was understating the need became plain when, in 1950 alone, Japan imported approximately the same amount of food as in the combined nine years prior to 1940.

MacArthur's demands were not fully met. Not until March, 1946, were any shipments sent; and during the year Japan received only 800,000 tons of wheat, peas, beans, and corn.

Sending the corn helped reduce American surpluses but had unexpected consequences; wheat and dried legumes were familiar commodities but Japanese housewives did not know how to use cracked corn. To eat the dried, flinty grains raw was manifestly impossible; pounding it into coarse meal for stewing yielded an unappetizing dish. A young, eager American dietitian, working with the Occupation, rushed to the rescue and induced the press to publish a recipe that called for generous quantities of sugar, cream—at least a cupful—eggs and butter, not generally available, and for baking the mixture at 350 degrees for about forty-five minutes. But Japanese kitchens had no ovens comparable to those in the United States, and even if such ovens had been available closely rationed fuel supplies were far too scanty for the operation; and so the suggestion brought ridicule and anger.

Another faux pas was the distribution of two weeks' full rations in the form of brown sugar, the Japanese apparently being expected to live during that period on sweets alone.

Other well intentioned food experts, Japanese as well as foreign, often counseled change of diet. Japanese people, they said, ate too many carbohydrates and too little calcium; deficiencies of essential needs induced beriberi and other diseases.

The fear of beriberi was apparently exaggerated. Since this disease was not reportable the prewar morbidity rate is unknown; but fatalities dropped steadily from 15,407 in 1930 to 7,179 in 1940 and—despite the almost complete dependence on rice during the war—were but 8,596 in 1947, not enough to rank among the twenty-five most serious diseases. The figure dropped to 3,952 in 1950. Because a more varied diet would improve the national health, the food experts recommended diversified farming. Professor Seiichi Tohata of Tokyo University, one of Yoshida's agricultural advisers added that westernizing food habits, by eliminating a one-crop rice economy, would enhance initiative and originality in Japan's rural population.

Custom and tradition, as well as long, successful experience in rice planting, would, in themselves, have barred a speculative shift to relatively unknown farming practices. Small farmers, whose margin of profit was razor-thin at best, dared not experiment. More importantly, the growth of population on limited arable lands forced reliance upon those foods which, like rice and wheat, yielded the highest food quantities per acre.

This involved problems of land maintenance. Farmers who, in 1931, raised an average of 38 bushels of rice or 32.6 bushels of wheat per acre were assuredly efficient, the averages being one and one-half times those of the United States and fully double those of any other Oriental nation. Rice yields, moreover, had risen almost uninterruptedly since the Meiji Restoration.

Such crops had gravely depleted the soil. By Grajdanzev's estimate that each koku of rice used up annually 18 pounds of nitrogen, 11 of potassium, and 2 of phosphate the small 1945 harvest further exhausted no less than 386,700 tons of nitrogen, 236,000 tons of potassium, and 43,000 tons of phosphorus, plus 15 per cent more that had been washed out by the storms.

Part of this could be restored by applications of dried fish, night soil, and green manures; but Japan needed an additional 4,000,000 tons of commercial fertilizer to replenish her depleted soil. Prior to the war, in the 1936–1940 period, her annual production of ammonium sulphate equivalents had averaged 1,800,000 metric tons, and, in addition, she had imported 2,000,000 tons of fertilizers from the United States, Germany, Chile, and the Pacific islands.

At the time of surrender, Japan had 30,000 tons of fertilizer stockpiled and a manufacturing potential of only 400,000 tons. As nothing was arriving from abroad, Shidehara asked MacArthur to allow 350,000 tons of phosphate rock to come in from Pacific islands formerly under Japanese mandate.

The amount, requested for overworked fields that had not been properly fertilized for five years, was far below the prewar normal import of 1,098,000 tons; even so, it could not be supplied, total importation between September, 1945, and July, 1946, totaling but

12,000 tons. No nitrogenous or potassic imports whatever arrived during that period.

Farmers labored earnestly to overcome fertilizer shortages and, by intensive cultivation of the lowest acreage since 1897, succeeded in raising 61,386,000 koku, nearly twice the 1897 harvest and half a million koku above the 1940 crop. The average yield per acre was second only to the record bumper crop of 1933.

More American imports were, however, needed, and 1,089,190 tons arrived between April, 1946, and March, 1947, half being wheat; but this was insufficient, and by July, 1947, Bruce F. Johnston, chief of Food Branch, ESS, estimated that the ration must be cut to 997 calories. MacArthur privately told a group of publishers that unless 600,000 tons of food arrived immediately "millions of Japanese would face starvation."

This, at least by implication, suggested that Washington had been at fault in failing to honor MacArthur's previous requests; but a Department of Agriculture food commission had already taken SCAP's headquarters to task, in a report signed by Colonel Raymond L. Harrison, for doing nothing but exhort farmers to work harder and the government to enforce its rules more diligently.

Certainly the imputation did not apply to Schenck's Natural Resources Section, which, while patiently feeling its way during the opening of the Occupation, operated with increasing speed and sureness. Well aware that crop deficits required food imports at the expense of American taxpayers, and suspecting underreporting by Japanese farmers, Schenck in 1948 set up an improved reporting system within the Agriculture-Forestry Ministry to replace the unreliable methods begun in 1878. Mark Williamson claimed that this would prove that farmers had failed to report a million acres of land, 7 per cent of the national farm acreage; but his statement was not borne out by official 1950 cultivation statistics, which showed only an insignificant increase over 1945's abnormal low.

Legislation enacted on Schenck's advice after July, 1948, provided agricultural advisory service, under which 6,000 local farm agents were appointed and 666 experimental farms established for soil surveys and other scientific aid.

Little of this program was actually new, Japan having long practiced similar activities; but Williamson and other Schenck experts contributed new techniques. Hybridization and back-crossing improved seed quality, grading and certification guaranteed uniformity, while more powerful insecticides and field dusting by American planes reduced plant disease loss far below the 12 per cent prewar yearly average. Such methods enhanced production, rice crops increasing from 58,652,-230 koku (9,082,064 metric tons) in 1947 to 66,439,200 (9,967,550 metric tons) in 1948; they fell slightly thereafter, but the first five-year postwar average was second only to the exceptionally heavy crops of 1936–1940.

This meant that Japan must import 900,000 tons of rice or its equivalent annually, exactly the amount Ogasawara had estimated in 1945. It also meant, as Shigeo Maetani, chief of the Food Board, reported in 1954 that Japan must spend huge amounts of foreign currency for food. Japan, he said, had thus spent $246,000,000 in fiscal 1951, $390,-000,000 in fiscal 1952, and $560,000,000 in fiscal 1953.

TWENTY-TWO

What Japan Eats

The benefits of the Schenck program became evident during the 1953–1954 crop deficiency. Although floods and early frost reduced the Japanese rice harvest to the lowest level since 1934, the northeastern Tohoku area, usually the worst sufferer in famine years, gathered an almost normal crop.

Joint efforts by Schenck's NRS and the Agriculture-Forestry Ministry brought this fortunate result. As early as 1936, Minoru Tanaka, working at the Ministry's Fujisaka Agricultural Experiment Station in Aomori prefecture, began work on a short-stalked rice tentatively named Fujisaka No. 5, which seemed to be cold-resistant. The war delayed developments, but, by 1946, Tanaka had fixed the strain though the Ministry lacked funds for distributing it. Three years later, NRS took up the project, supplying seeds to much of the Tohoku area. The success of Fujisaka No. 5 in weathering the adverse conditions of 1953 saved Tohoku farmers from much of the distress usually suffered during such unfavorable seasons.

Not every one gave Schenck's office undivided credit for inspiring gains. Shinkichi Katayanagi, head of the Japanese Food Boards, believed that abolition of black-marketing was responsible. But, whatever the cause, larger harvests increased the staple ration of rice or its equivalent in wheat, barley, or potatoes from 12.23 ounces to 13.38 ounces, or, approximately, from 1,250 to 1,350 calories.

Need for American imports was not, however, ended. The fiscal year ending in March, 1948, had seen a total importation of 2,257,074 tons of wheat, corn, sugar, and barley; and the twelve months following, a total of 2,186,002 tons. Thus, between surrender and April 1, 1949, America contributed no less than 5,561,008 tons of food. Importations thereafter averaged slightly less than 2,000,000 tons yearly.

Increased farm production, with a 20 per cent over-all rise in food-crop harvests from an average of 26,177,000 metric tons in the 1930 decade to 29,318,000 tons in 1949 and 30,947,000 tons in 1950, while the population rose but 15 per cent, reflected a very rosy light. Mac-Arthur boasted that, with Japan's harvests at an all-time peak, living conditions were improving.

Statistics were somewhat misleading. Total food production had undoubtedly risen, and staple crops even more rapidly, from 16,743,000 metric tons in the 1930 decade to 21,647,000 tons in 1950—an increase of 30 per cent; but nutritive values had not kept pace. Most of the staple-crop increase was in sweet potatoes, which had doubled over the 1930 decade average. Rice had risen but 4 per cent, other grains 3 per cent; fruits, 3 per cent; and vegetables, 2 per cent. The actual harvest, which had averaged 14,903,000 metric tons in brown-rice equivalents (BRE) during the 1930's had risen to but 15,830,000 in 1949 and 16,606,000 in 1950. While population had risen 15 per cent, the BRE index had risen only 11.5 per cent.

Further analysis revealed that fruit increases were wholly due to apples, all other commercial fruits showing heavy losses, and that colored vegetable gains were due to burdock, carrots, onions, and tomatoes.

Crop increases, therefore, failed either to raise Japan's caloric intake or substantially to reduce need for food imports. Mosaburo Honda, Food Board chief in 1951, estimated that on an average 13.5 ounce ration, Japan must continue to import at least 2,700,000 metric tons BRE at prices requiring her to spend for essential food alone at least one-third of the foreign exchange derived from exports.

Steady improvement in the fertilizer situation had prevented import needs from rising even higher. By 1950, Japan had virtually recovered its 1936–1940 production of ammonium sulphate equivalents and was manufacturing 70 per cent of its prewar superphosphate equivalents. Potassic imports had passed the prewar level in 1949 and slightly exceeded them in 1950. Imports of nitrogenous fertilizer in 1950 were at 88 per cent, and of phosphate rock at 70 per cent, of the 1936–1940 levels.

Part of the recovery, however, was countered by the failure of peasants to utilize all the fertilizer available. Price increases were doubtless partly responsible, but the transfer of lands to new owners less familiar with scientific farming methods may have contributed to the failure.

Heavier fertilization provided no final cure for Japan's sick farm economy; the problems resulting from dependence upon rice still awaited solution.

Other crops received minor attention, being grown as side interests, for the most part upon land not well suited for rice.

The diet therefore became one-sided, lacking in balance; it filled the stomach but failed to give necessary nutriment. Although this was not a recent development and was not peculiar to Japan, it came increasingly to public attention with the development of dietary science.

Occupation specialists, especially those attached to Sams's PHW, stressed the need for balanced diets and recommended that upland fields, less profitable than paddies for rice growing, be converted into garden patches or used for large-scale dairy farming. This, however, was not so easily accomplished as armchair theorists assumed.

Two American 4-H kids knew the slimness of Japanese food supplies. Barbara Buffington of Kansas and Gerald Grooms of Ohio spent the summer of 1953 in an exchange project whereby they lived on Japanese farms in the Japanese manner. "We wanted to live like Japanese," they said, "but, to be honest, we would have starved to death if we had taken the same food that they ate."

The paucity of Japanese food resources was hidden from top Occupation brass by their disregard of sociological considerations and their failure to create a unit specially concerned with standards of living. More familiar with the Westernized capital than with the rural areas, and seeing only the more prosperous portions of the major cities, they could not realize the narrow margin of subsistence.

No media regularly conveyed this information, save in the most abstract, impersonal manner. Few of the English-language periodicals upon which the brass relied for knowledge translated the articles that appeared from time to time in the Japanese press, and the army-managed *Stars and Stripes* avoided the food topic so sedulously that some readers suspected that it was under orders to do so. When news items concerning short rations appeared in English they were almost invariably couched in terms of Japanese weights and measures not readily comprehensible to those accustomed to avoirdupois. MacArthur's Statistics and Reports Sections, which might have clarified the matter both for the top brass and for the foreign public, deliberately avoided any use of customary American weights and measures—because, as its chief explained, American law required all official documents to use the metric system exclusively. Few Occupationnaires quickly understood food shortages when expressed in grams, or land areas in hectares, and many older officers were baffled even by calories; and on that account the majority gave hungry Japanese the impression of callousness and indifference to suffering.

In some ways, improvement of the food situation actually worsened understanding. Occupationnaires who saw well stocked markets on main traffic arteries unconsciously supposed that there was a similar display of meat, eggs, fruits, and confectionery in rural districts; lacking first-hand knowledge of farm living conditions, they did not guess that these were luxury foods which farmers seldom ate. Supplied with ample milk and finding ice cream abundant at all snack bars, they did not realize that these were almost wholly absent from the average Japanese table.

Japanese milk production had never been high. Sams, discovering in 1946 that it was rationed to infants, expectant mothers, and invalids with medical prescriptions, urged an increased supply; but as late as 1953 only 175,000,000 gallons yearly was available, barely enough to supply a pint per capita monthly. Butter production in 1953 was less than two ounces yearly per capita; cheese, but one-tenth that amount.

The diet was almost exclusively grain, of which the average Japanese ate 13.1 ounces daily in 1953; of this, 10.6 ounces was rice, the remainder being about equally divided between barley and wheat. Animal foods other than fish constituted less than 1 per cent of the total intake, the totals being absurdly small and showing no change from the amounts consumed in 1934–1935. The consumption of beef in the 1930 decade was less than two ounces per capita per month, and that of pork was even less. These tiny amounts doubled during the next decade but fell back during the war and have not increased since. Less beef was consumed per capita in 1953 than in 1934, though the consumption of pork has risen, though only to 2.1 ounces monthly. Mutton was virtually unknown, only 51 tons being marketed in 1951; but 12,612 tons of horse meat was on sale, equal to one-fifth of the pork supply and one-sixth of the beef supply.

Edible wild life added little. The bag was relatively good in 1950, though lower than in 1933; yet had the game been equally divided each rabbit would have been shared by 145 Japanese, each wild duck by 270, and each deer by 27,000. In the open season for sparrows and thrushes, 3,000,000 were shot, one small bird for every 27 persons.

Eggs also were extremely scarce: Japan in 1936 had had one hen per capita, and war exigencies reduced the country to 15,369,000 chickens in 1946—less than one-third the prewar averages. The number increased thereafter but an official census in 1953 reported 47,000,000 chickens, slightly more than half a chicken per capita. Eggs were more abundant also, especially in the cities; but the total supplied only a little more than one egg weekly.

Virtually all Japan's animal protein came from the sea. The annual salt-water catch, though heaviest in the world, totaling 4,846,858 metric tons in 1950, yielded only six ounces daily per capita—an average considerably above that of 1946 but below that of 1933, when the population had been considerably smaller. Prior to the war, moreover, Japan had drawn an additional fish supply from northern Kurile Island and Soviet fishing grounds denied to her later.

While yellowtail, cod, flatfish, horse mackerel, and sea pike all registered substantial postwar gains, none yielded a large total; cod, the most important fish in the group, constituted less than 5 per cent of the 1951 catch. Sardines, normally a quarter to a third of the total catch, dropped off 30 per cent from the 1936 catch; and only half as many herring were caught as during the war years. Seaweed, a highly important item in Japan's food economy, fell almost 70 per cent below the prewar averages.

Foreign experts, among them Occupationnaires, suggested diet improvements through better utilization of the 3,553,775 acres classed as pasture land. Though 40 per cent of this was forest and much of the remainder too hilly to be cultivated, 1,677,615 acres, as late as 1949, were registered as grazing land and another 1,676,160 acres as mowing areas. Little of this was farmed, and each of the 316,922 animals roaming the grazing lands had an average of 5.3 acres upon which to feed. In Hokkaido, where 40 per cent of the grazing lands were located, each horse or cow enjoyed 10 acres of pasture.

Even where the pasturage was not too mountainous nor too barren, the grasses were unsuitable. Unfavorable climate, moreover, prevented proper drying or storage of such fodder as could be grown.

Nevertheless, experts considered that livestock could be increased, especially as draft animals had grown in numbers yearly since 1917. Though horses had declined, the number of cattle rose even during the war years, reaching a peak of 2,670,000 in 1952.

The increase also applied to milch cattle, which numbered 150,627 in 1930 and reached 265,623 in 1944, or one for every 274 persons in Japan. Postsurrender shortages of millet, beans, and bran, the fodder supplied to most stall-fed cattle, reduced the total to 163,000 in 1946, the lowest since 1930. The situation somewhat improved thereafter, but as late as 1952 Japan had only 275,590 milch cows—one for every 324 persons, as compared to one for every 6.5 Americans. The Occupation had planned to restore the prewar livestock totals.

Long before Pearl Harbor, elaborate plans had blossomed for increasing both pasturage and farm land through irrigation, drainage of swamps, or reclamation of under-water land. Usually complete even to details as to man hours, number of trucks required, and bushels of rice to be grown upon the added lands, the plans were largely on paper, and were not invariably successful when put into effect. In 1930, a net of 31,477 acres was added, 77 per cent of it in fields rather than paddies; but in 1940, despite a gain of 76,067 acres (70 per cent in fields), 86,170 acres were devastated or abandoned, leaving a net loss of 10,-543 acres for the year.

Reclamation proceeded even during the five war years, a total of 303,732 acres being added; but so much land was ruined by flood or abandoned as unprofitable that there was a net loss of 612,167 acres. Mark Williamson credited almost all this decline to the construction of airfields and other military uses; but further land losses during 1946 and 1947, at almost the same rate, indicated that natural catastrophes were at fault. The great loss in 1945, for instance, was easily attributable to typhoon destruction.

Within two months after surrender the Agriculture Ministry produced, and Natural Resources Section approved, yet another comprehensive plan—to reclaim 3,875,000 acres within five years. Upon this land, 40 per cent of which would be in Hokkaido, 938,000 families could be settled and 83,914,600 bushels of rice would be produced annually. Successful completion of the project would thus increase the average rice harvest by 27 per cent.

As usual, results fell far short of plans. The Agriculture Ministry took over 491,000 acres of military-owned land and 1,627,000 acres of state forests and genya, and bought 1,393,000 acres of privately owned waste lands. Of the combined total it proposed during 1946 to make 425,000 acres fit for cultivation. Slightly less than a third of the goal was reached, but losses by fire or flood were almost twice as great, so that 1946 showed a 63,223-acre deficit. During 1947 another 75,602 acres was lost. The losses were within 10,000 acres of all gains made during 1948, 1949, and 1950 even if no land whatever had been devastated or abandoned during the latter three-year period. The cultivated land area in 1950, while apparently 700,000 acres larger than that in 1945, had actually a smaller part planted to food crops or used for pasturage than in 1945. The area under tillage was smaller than that in 1920, and the food crop, as expressed in brown rice equivalents, was only 10 per cent higher. A total of 131,301 new settlers and of 512,522 who added acreage bought a fifth of the lands taken over, including half the former military land.

For these results the government paid 5,763,114 yen.

Undismayed by failure, the Flood Prevention Council in 1953 announced new reclamation projects; among them, ninety-nine huge multipurpose dams, notably to the Owari district and on the Tone River, which would raise the rice harvest by 2,000,000 bushels yearly; drainage of Hokkaido swamps to permit growth of another 3,800,000 bushels; and dredging of Tokyo Bay to provide 250,000 acres of land for city expansion. To this was added a ten-year afforestation project, and improvements on 1,234 of the nation's 6,000 rivers. The entire cost was estimated at 1,864,000,000 yen. The Government agreed in 1954 to pay 34 yen per acre for mountain and forest lands taken over under this program, or 4 yen more per acre for infertile land than the occupation allowed in 1946 to be paid for fertile paddy land.

TWENTY-THREE

Flowers of Yedo

From ancient times the glare of fire by night has colored Tokyo skies; its ravages in that town of wooden frames and paper walls gave rise to the old poetic imagery of Yedo Flowers. The *kaji*-man with his long pole and jingling rings remains a feature of the Tokyo streets. The leader of the fire brigade who holds his brigade emblem high above the crowd that gathers to bewail, though not to help; the acrobats who every January balance on their ladders; the long cloaks and the black helmets of the firemen, are picturesque additions to the scene. Often, however, the fire departments have been far more picturesque than practical. More has been done to prevent fires than to extinguish them. The Tokugawas decreed banishment to persons who carelessly permitted fires, only to suffer embarrassment when the first offender thereafter was a daimyo so powerful that they dared not offend him, therefore they commuted banishment into a fine, lending him the cash to be repaid "30,000 days beyond eternity." Arson was a capital offense, and criminals who were not daimyos were executed for it; heavy penalties were set for persons who caused loss of property to others. Houses must be cleaned of rubbish and fire hazards. But no separate and efficient fire extinguishing system was created, each daimyo and each great householder setting up his own brigade, which operated only for himself. In cities, volunteer fire systems, social groups in the main, refused to stir beyond their private territory.

Japan began her fire departments in Yedo in 1658. Two-thirds of the city had just been destroyed by a disastrous three-day conflagration—poetically remembered as the Furisode Kaji, or Fire of the Long-Sleeved

250

Kimono, because of a burning garment that supposedly set off the catastrophe—in which 28,000 people perished. To prevent a repetition of the calamity, the Shogunate organized an official corps of several hundred carpenters and ladder men and placed them, to their disgust, under samurai control. Members of this *machibikeshi,* Town Firemen's Corps, may not have been expert firefighters, because they specialized in tearing down adjacent structures rather than extinguishing blazes; but they added a decidedly picturesque touch in their heavily padded costumes which they wore dripping-wet. Probably they fought their officers, quaintly garbed in bright embroidered cloaks and golden helmets, quite as efficiently as they fought fires, and certainly they warred with rival companies who dared invade their territory.

Neither the unpredictable machibikeshi nor the Shogun's orders forbidding thatched roofs and requiring a water-filled tub at each front gate prevented other fires from ravaging the city. In 1667, the Yaoya Oshichi, Fire of the Grocer's Daughter, deliberately set, it was said, to cover her liaison with her lover, raged through Yedo. For this the girl was ordered to be burned alive; but she became an idol of the courtesans. Other great but less romantic fires broke out in 1703, 1772, and 1855—the last one, following an earthquake, killing 10,000 people and wrecking a third of the city. The great fire of 1923, after the Kanto Earthquake, killed 190,000 people—40,000 of them in one crowded mass at the Honjo Clothing Depot—and rendered half the population of Tokyo and Yokohama homeless.

Learning by experience, the police, to whose administration the fire service was entrusted, imported twenty-four modern fire engines from Germany and the United States, created a fire ambulance corps, and founded a Water Firemen's Corps. Much of this improvement was, however, on paper only. Actually, upon the outbreak of the war, Tokyo had but 80 per cent of its authorized force of 12,000 firemen and only 1,116 pieces of apparatus of any kind. One of the five ladder cars possessed in 1920 had been too badly damaged for further use, and it had not been replaced. The other fire-fighting equipment was of poor quality, and the men had not been properly drilled and disciplined. More men were recruited for fire fighting during the war, but materials could not be greatly increased or improved.

When Allied forces occupied Japan, the fire service was a stepchild of the police. The hierarchy of police officials, whose chain of command stretched from the Home Ministry to governors and chiefs of police, looked down upon the firemen. Regarding them as less worthy and less dignified, top police career officials denied to able fire executives a fair share of honors and promotions. A legend, which may have been untrue but was widely enough held to be passed on to Occupation leaders, said that police officials not bright enough for promotion were shunted into fire service.

This system guaranteed unity of direction but not uniformity of operation. Instead of one coordinated fire department, presurrender Japan had three independent services, exclusive of the fire departments of the Army and Navy. The most efficient, a Government Fire Service, Kansetsu Shobo, supported by taxation of all Japanese, operated in thirty-six of the largest centers—thirty of them having been added during the war. Authorized personnel tables called for 70 marshals, 1,558 chiefs and 28,550 men; but only 20,247 were found on duty when the Occupation assumed control. Officers in the Kansetsu Shobo above the rank of sergeant drew pay from the national treasury, which provided 60 per cent of the pay for rank and file, prefectures paying the remainder.

A second force, the Regular Fire Service, Jobi Shobo, operating under prefectural or local police control in the remaining urban centers and the larger towns, was paid from local funds. The 250 fire brigade stations of this service employed approximately 18,000 men.

About 12,000 unpaid volunteer fire guilds, with 2,500,000 members, also under police supervision, cared for the rural areas. Thus the smaller areas and the entire countryside not only supported their own fire service but also contributed, through general taxation, to the Kansetsu Shobo in the thirty-six privileged cities under national fire protection.

All were seriously undermanned. More than half of the thirteen Kansetsu Shobo districts had less than 1,000 authorized strength, the exceptions being Tokyo, Osaka, and the prefectures including Yokohama, Nagoya, Fukuoka, and Kobe.

Tokyo with about 28 fire-fighters per 10,000 population, and Osaka with 23, led Japan. Most of the other districts had 10 to 20 per 10,000, but Kyoto, Niigata, and Yamaguchi had fewer than 10.

Japanese equipment was substandard. Reports to the Occupation declared that Japanese departments had 4,815 heavy pumpers of 400- to 500-gallon capacity per minute under 100 pounds pressure; but investigation showed that most of these were really 400-gallon pumpers with poorly designed Japanese engines mounted on imported chassis. Of the supposed 4,815 heavy pumpers, 2,027 were in the Kansetsu Shobo; 2,192 were owned by the volunteers, and 596 by the Jobi Shobo. In addition there were 317 smaller pumpers of 250 to 350 gallons, of which volunteers owned 291, the Jobi Shobo 19, and the Kansetsu Shobo only 7.

These pumpers, however, proved largely non-existent. Occupation fire experts located only 1,994 heavy pumpers including 751 at Tokyo and 674 at Osaka—all in the Kansetsu Shobo. Only ten engines of any kind were found north of Tokyo on the main island; only ten more on the large southern island of Kyushu; and none whatever on the main island south of Hiroshima. Two of the thirteen districts, Yamaguchi and Fukuoka—the latter having responsibility for the great Yawata Iron Works—had no Kansetsu Shobo engines of any kind.

The average for the four major industrial areas, Tokyo-Yokohama, Osaka-Kobe, central Honshu, and northern Kyushu, was 1.8 heavy and 4 smaller pumps per 10,000 population. Osaka led Japan with 4.8 engines per 10,000 population; Tokyo and the Nagoya and Kobe districts had 3 each per 10,000. Hiroshima, Saitama, the great northern island of Hokkaido, and the prefecture including Yokohama were the only other Kansetsu Shobo districts with as many as 1 engine per 10,-000 population.

Such engines as existed were antiquated: those belonging to the Kansetsu Shobo averaged ten years old, and those of the Jobi Shobo about fifteen years. Some of the 24 fire engines which Tokyo had bought from the United States, Germany, and Great Britain in 1924, were still in service; and so were a few of the 20 engines, 25 hose carts, and 5 ladder cars imported in 1920.

While Tokyo boasted 1,116 pieces of fire apparatus including 4 ladder trucks and 13 fireboats, the greater portion of the apparatus consisted of hand pumps and trailers. Kansetsu Shobo fire companies and volunteers relied heavily upon trailer pumpers; the former had 939, and the latter, 11,794. Other light equipment was carried upon motorcycles: volunteers used 581 of these; the Kansetsu Shobo, 38; the Jobi Shobo, 33; and there were 203 trailers. The volunteers reported 25 fireboats; but these, unlike the Tokyo craft, were launches carrying light equipment.

All the motorized fire-fighting equipment in Japan operated on a monthly gasoline ration of but 2,321 gallons, motor oil also being closely limited. Largely for this reason, fire companies almost never voluntarily answered calls from outside their own immediate neighborhood, but waited instead for specific central-office instruction before crossing into other areas.

This custom was furthered also by the inefficiency of fire detector systems. Even prior to the war only twelve cities had installed a total of 4,295 fire-alarm boxes; but when war came, Kyoto, in a burst of patriotism, dismantled its entire system and turned the metal in for scrap. Fire raids wrecked 2,000 of Tokyo's 3,000 boxes. At the end of the war only one city system, that of Ashikaga in central Hokkaido, was in operation. In the absence of alarm boxes, men stationed on fire towers—hinomiyagura, first used in 1718—shouted alarms whenever smoke was seen.

As if these deficiencies were not in themselves sufficiently serious, fire fighters suffered further handicaps. Water supplies were inadequate, limited to the drinking water furnished to the cities through 3.5-inch mains. This, when available, was delivered to the fire through 2.5-inch unlined hose of untwisted linen yarn. The hose provided by the single Japanese manufacturer was supposed to have a minimum resistance of 400 pounds pressure; but tests showed that this was also in fact the maximum, hose bursting at exactly 400 pounds pressure. As another serious difficulty, the carbon tetrachloride extinguishers were found to be completely empty when the war closed, with virtually no chemicals available for recharging. A foam substitute, a lactoprotein derived from soybeans, was under experimentation.

Under such conditions, marked operational inefficiency might have been expected; yet Japan, despite its greatly increased number of wood, straw, and paper buildings, maintained a surprisingly low fire incidence. The number of fires, which had totaled about 18,000 annually during 1911–1913, did not rise appreciably during the 1920 and 1930 decades, and dropped to a 15,000 average during 1941 and 1942, and to 12,483 in 1944. The houses wholly or badly burned fell from an average of 44,000 during 1911–1913 to 30,000 during the 1930 decade and 29,000 during 1940–1944. When fires did occur, however, the loss grew heavier, rising from 31,000,000 yen a year in 1911–1913 to 69,000,000 in the 1930's and to 177,000,000 yen in the first four years of the 1940 decade.

Japanese explained that primary reasons for the low fire incidence were the requirement of periodic house inspections and the severe punishment for persons causing fires. In 1907–1935 the annual average of convictions for carelessness in this regard was 537, with the usual penalties ranging as high as three years' imprisonment or a fine of 3,000 yen. One or two arsonists annually were sentenced to life imprisonment, and two in 1937 were sentenced to death.

In view of the common use of open fires for cooking and heating in tinderbox houses—the cause, according to Japanese fire officials, of at least half of all fires in the country—strict supervision and punishment was deemed to be a proper deterrent. Careless use of matches or cigarettes and improper electrical wiring were each held responsible for 10 per cent of fires.

Pressed by Occupation authorities to modernize the fire service quickly and thoroughly, the Japanese Government promised major equipment changes in November, 1945. The Fire Branch of Willoughby's Public Safety Division had disapproved the old 400-gallon heavy pumpers, recommending a new, streamlined 120-horsepower model that would deliver 750 gallons per minute, equipped with fog nozzles and machine foam equipment. Regardless of the fact that Japan produced none of these and, in fact, manufactured no heavy pumpers whatever except the discredited 400-gallon 1937 model, the Japanese agreed to make the change.

Rural districts, until then without heavy pumpers, and in only a few cases with small gasoline pumps, were to have at least two of the former and ten of the latter for each 10,000 population. The rural population was then estimated at 51,389,000, so that the commitment was for 10,-276 heavy pumpers, more than twice the total owned by Japan, and 51,380 light pumps, or triple all the fire equipment in Japanese possession.

The four major urban concentrations, already equipped with 1.8 heavy and 4 light pumps per 10,000 population, were to have five of each type, which meant another 4,075 for Tokyo and Osaka alone, plus another 4,785 of each type for the other city areas. Although Japanese cities are predominantly of two-storied residences, each urban district was also to have 1 ladder truck for each 10,000 population, or approximately 2,100 to supplement the 3 in Tokyo and the 1 in Nagoya. A more feasible supplementary program called for the conversion of Japanese army trucks into hose carts, wrecking trucks, searchlight trucks, and ambulances.

Gasoline and motor-oil rations were to be increased sixfold, and six-inch fire mains, independent of the portable water system, were to be installed to deliver river water for fire fighting.

The plan did not explain where all the equipment and the gasoline were to be obtained, although presumably they would be imported from the United States, nor how their purchase or the cost of installing new mains would be financed. Tokyo did find funds to buy three of the recommended streamliners, each of which did the work of three old-style pumpers at a cost only one-third more than that of the 400-gallon model. Nagoya, Kyoto, Osaka, and Yokohama also were to have one of these. The United States Army lent Tokyo, and did not expect to recover, nine 500-gallon pumpers, two three-quarter-ton trucks, and two quarter-ton weapons carriers; but elsewhere the program lagged. In 1950, four and a half years after the plan was announced, the National Fire Board estimated that, while Japan had 3,753 large-sized engines, at least 78,652 more were required to equip the 16,000 fire brigades. It set the cost at 94,383,000,000 yen, or $262,000,000.

Tokyo's forty-three fire battalions owned in 1950 a total of 436 fire-fighting cars of all types, together with 8 ladder trucks, 3 chemical trucks, 18 ambulances, 5 auxiliary cars, 11 boats, 104 motorcycles, and small miscellaneous rolling stock.

The announcement typified the half-truths and deliberately misleading statements that frequently were issued to give an appearance of greater accomplishment than had been attained. The equipment no doubt existed; but in 1953, Tsuruji Okawa, head of the Tokyo Fire Brigade's mechanical department, confessed that the ladder trucks included the four antiquated ladders imported in 1920; the other four were medium-sized only. Not one, he said, carried ladders long enough to mount much more than halfway up the new office buildings that were being erected in Tokyo; and all needed repairs so badly that he doubted if they would be operable in the event of a serious fire. Tokyo, Okawa said, needed 20 new and large-sized ladder trucks.

At least 80 per cent of the pumpers, Okawa declared, had one-third horse-power pressure, and lack of better water supply prevented stronger pumps from being used: if the pressure were increased, 90 per cent of the hose would burst. At least 60 per cent of the hoses in service had been patched, he said, an average of fifty times each. Ogawa and his associates estimated that proper standards could not be met for at least a decade.

Personnel had undoubtedly improved in quality. George W. Angell, as the Occupation's Chief Fire Administrator, insisted upon regular drills and supervised so rigidly that efficiency greatly increased. Numbers, however, did not greatly increase. Though Tokyo added 7,500 firemen during 1946, most of them were replacements for men dismissed for militaristic or ultranationalistic activity; and many others were reservists. By 1952, the Tokyo fire force numbered 6,344 regulars and 16,000 reserves. At the close of the Occupation the national Government Fire Service numbered 20,837, which was 4,000 short of the authorized maximum and only 590 men more than had been in service when the Occupation started. The forty-four groups of the Regular Fire Service employed 16,000 men, and the 16,000 volunteer fire brigades—an increase of 2,000 over 1945—enrolled about 2,000,000, two-thirds of the membership in 1939.

The National Fire Board pleaded consistently for more money with which to buy equipment. Japan, it said, was defenseless against a major conflagration. As a beginning, it asked for 250,000,000 yen in the 1953 budget to equip the seventy cities of more than 100,000 population each with modern alarm systems and to buy 330 engines; but it could not get the necessary funds.

Meanwhile, disastrous conflagrations had swept Japan. On April 13, 1950, the greater portion of the resort city of Atami, usually overcrowded with vacationers, was wiped out. Its 35,000 regular population should have had, under the government plan, 30 engines; but its 78 fire fighters, including 57 volunteers, actually had 9 engines, 3 motorcycles and 2 hand pumps, and these were not in good condition. Two weeks after the fire, the entire Atami volunteer corps resigned in disgust.

The Atami fire was but one of a series of conflagrations. During the seven years since the hostilities six other large fires, in addition to three caused by earthquakes, destroyed more than a thousand homes each. At Iida in 1947, and at Tottori in 1952, more than 4,000 houses were lost.

Money losses also mounted. The great Tottori fire, April 17, 1952, the largest since the burning of Shizuoka in 1940 and of Hakodate in 1933, cost more than 15,000,000,000 yen. Atami's loss was about 3,000,000,000 yen; that of Atsumi in 1951 about 1,500,000,000; and the Wakayama disaster in 1946 cost still another 1,000,000,000 yen. These, of course, were the largest and the most spectacular fires; but every year saw a heavy toll. A three-billion-yen loss in 1946 tripled to ten billion in 1947, rose to thirteen billion in 1948 and to twenty-six billion in 1949. The toll fell under twenty-two billion in 1950 and 1951, but reached its peak of thirty-eight billion in 1952. Even with proper allowance for inflation the increase over the 1930-decade average annual loss of 60,000,000 yen is impressive. More than 400 people were killed in fires in each year after 1945.

Tokyo's picture was somewhat brighter. Though the number of fires did not perceptibly diminish after surrender, with more houses burned than were built in some years, notably 1946, new safety measures proved to be effective. In March, 1948, the Tokyo Assembly required theaters to eliminate fire hazards by restricting the size of audiences, forbidding aisle congestion, requiring adequate exits, installing fire extinguishers, and fireproofing curtains and all cloth fixtures. These requirements did not prevent the burning of two of the largest midcity theaters, Subaru-za and Yurakuza-za, in 1953 but did prevent loss of life.

Tokyo's 177 fire towers substituted for the former polar coordination method of locating fires, the azimuthal system—an improvement that made it possible to spot locations more accurately, reducing errors from as much as half a mile to a maximum of 500 feet and an average of 60 feet. Coupled with this was installation of an improved telephone system and a special switchboard linking all fire stations, towers, alarm boxes, and police offices. The use of a telephone fire-call number, 119, and the resultant speedy service not only hastened the dispatch of fire battalions but reduced burned area per fire by about 40 per cent during 1949. This coordination, and the abolition of strict ward boundaries in which fire companies could operate without special orders brought about the concentration of thirty-four fire companies at the great Shimbashi market fire in January, 1951, within a period when, under the old system, one company alone could have reported.

Another innovation, perhaps of less value, followed the passage of a new Fire Defense Organization Law in 1947. This separated the fire service from the police, thus affording a necessary equality of the services and promoting morale, and also decentralized all fire services. Small communities and the rural areas were thus freed from further need to support the Kansetsu Shobo, and city residents had to pay the entire cost of fire protection.

For many urban districts, at a time of financial stress upon limited local resources, the enforced decentralization proved heavy. In September, 1948, therefore, Chofu, a town of 20,000 near Tokyo, disbanded its 32-man, 3-engine fire department as too costly, and relied instead upon a volunteer system. Ten other towns in the same region immediately followed.

Decentralization occurred, moreover, at a time when there appeared to be a concerted arson movement which many observers believed Communist-inspired. Beginning with a series of market fires—six at Shimbashi between February, 1947, and January, 1951, and fifty in various parts of Japan within the first eight months of 1947—clusters of fires broke out under highly suspicious circumstances. Four huge fires within seven days in April, 1951, at Atsumi, Sendai, Yamagata, and Ogikubo in Tokyo—the last three on the same day—centered suspicion on arsonists. Arson, though not for political reasons, also explained the destruction of the 552-year-old Kinkakuji, or Golden Pavilion, at Kyoto in July, 1950. Three years later, the ancient Izumo Shrine was also badly damaged by fire whose origin was never clearly determined.

Yoshibumi Tajima, chairman of a committee of inquiry into other mysterious fires in Fukui, Yanago, and Takefu cities, reported to the House of Representatives in February, 1950, that "a certain political party" acting in conjunction with Communist-inspired North Koreans had been responsible.

A more reassuring development, following an intense campaign by the National Fire Defense Board established on March 6, 1948, against carelessness, flimsy construction, and lack of efficient fire protection methods, was noticed after an earthquake at Imaichi, near Nikko in Tochigi prefecture. Invariably in the past when an earthquake devastated a town as 80 per cent of Imaichi was destroyed in January, 1950, overturned fire boxes, live wires, and other hazards set off destructive blazes. But at Imaichi, even while the ground still quivered with afterquakes, the Imaichi police inspected every house to make sure that the fleeing inhabitants had extinguished all fires. The people of the town had, they found, profited by the experience of a fire of March, 1949, which had burned ten houses; not a single fire was burning, and not a single electric switch was on.

The incident was well publicized to indicate that alert citizens, even living in an overcrowded concentration of flimsy wood and paper structures, and even in the general postwar letdown of economic and social conditions, could, if they desired, observe proper fire prevention and fire-fighting methods.

TWENTY-FOUR

Cities Beautiful

On the very day, August 15, 1945, that Japan decided to surrender, Tokyo municipal authorities began drafting reconstruction plans. Their task, as well as that of similar groups elsewhere in the nation, was stupendous. Of the 1,650,000 prewar houses in the capital, 674,000 had been wrecked; and a hasty survey showed that the other 118 big cities had lost 1,585,000 dwelling houses. More than half of Tokyo was rubble, and four-fifths of her factories and industries had been destroyed; in other towns the damage was proportionate, and in some it was relatively larger. Public services—transportation, electricity, gas, telephones, water supplies, and such sewage systems as existed—were hopelessly disrupted.

Even under the best conditions reconstruction would have been difficult; after the devastating war the lack of labor, money, and materials made it a hopeless prospect. Occupationnaires shrugged off responsibility; Japan herself had brought on the war and must suffer the penalty.

In fact, the Occupation made the project more difficult. MacArthur's men required housing. In the first six months after surrender, they requisitioned quarters for 300,000 troops, hotel accommodations for 9,500 male and 1,500 female civilians in the Tokyo-Yokohama area alone, commandeered housing for 700 families, and appropriated the best 485 houses for its officers. All these were put into first class western-style condition and equipped, at Japanese expense and Japanese labor using scarce Japanese materials, with every conceivable modern comfort.

260

This was merely a beginning. In February, 1946, when the War Department announced that "dependents" would be sent to join their men in Japan, more goods were requisitioned. Before the peak had passed, in December, 1949, Japan had built 2,664 new houses in the Tokyo region, had reconditioned 594 apartment buildings and turned over 602 dwellings. By 114,880 procurement demands, requisitions covering every need from mansions to daily supplies of cut flowers, it had commandeered a third of Japan's iron and cement, a fifth of its steel, and a tenth of its lumber and glass. It had staffed the houses with maids and houseboys, at the rate of five servants per general and three or four per colonel, given 26,748 servants to the troops and brought in 238,450 other Japanese employees to do the army work. The 1,261 families billeted in new houses at Grant Heights outside Tokyo had two huge water reservoirs, holding 840,000 gallons of water; Tokyo had five big schools and 45 recreation facilities, including athletic fields, gymnasiums, and stadia for troop athletics. Yet the Occupation warned dependents en route to Japan that they must be prepared to face frontier conditions.

The Occupation commandeered so lavishly that at the end of 1949, while the Occupation was still in full swing, 1,500 buildings were found to be surplus. The army then turned back 281 office buildings, 400 factories and warehouses, and 95 hotels.

To make life easier for Occupationnaires, 634 railway cars, and 128 interurban trolleys were taken over. In these, the Occupationnaires traveled (free until August, 1947, and thereafter at a cent a mile)—430,358,000 miles during 1947 alone; they made 234,615 sleeper trips at $2 per berth and vacationed in half a hundred swank resort hotels at 50 cents to $2 a night. In the same year freight cars carrying 3,368,469 tons of materials for Occupation use traveled 47,452,000 miles.

All this drained Japanese resources and delayed rehabilitation. This was to be expected; the needs of the army of Occupation necessarily came first. As long as Occupation interests were not imperiled, as long as epidemic did not threaten nor widespread distress invite rebellion, no Occupation section was concerned. Japanese officials were not really aware of this indifference until, after numerous rebuffs to requests for help, they heard, in late October, that the Occupation would do nothing.

The delay could not be laid at the door of the Occupation. No one in any staff section had, at any time, held out hope that Americans would aid Japan to rebuild; but the habit of relying upon Occupationnaires for leadership and guidance had been so thoroughly drilled into officials that they foolishly assumed that the same practice would be followed in reconstruction work as, for example, in reorganizing government, education, industry, and public safety.

Tokyo planners had been daydreaming of fireproofing and zoning, of cultural centers and decentralization of business areas, of parks and green belts, of lowland drainage and slum clearance. Most unrealistically they thought of building 808 miles of wide, new highways, of digging subways to replace surface transportation, of tearing down the Yamate elevated line, of replacing 2,200 wooden bridges with steel and concrete structures and of modernizing 2,000 other bridges within the city limits. They did not think of costs.

The national government was little more realistic than the Tokyo utopists. It, too, had waited for an Occupation lead; but on November 5, when winter came close and shelter became imperative, it established a Reconstruction Board to supervise erection of 3,000,000 houses. Following the wartime and Occupation practice, it set up a quota system whereby labor and material would be rationed to those in greatest need.

Black-marketers and racketeers had not waited for official permission, nor had thousands of impatient landowners. In Tokushima prefecture, for example, 20,648 houses had been finished, and many more were under construction before the Reconstruction Board announced that building might begin. This was honest construction; in the larger centers, especially the major cities, materials intended for essential housing had already been diverted to construction of brothels, cafés, movie houses, and nonproductive enterprise. Legal proceedings could have been taken against them; but too many important politicians were involved, and the violators went unscathed. From time to time, as offenders fell out with the party in power, belated suit was brought and punishments were inflicted; but such cases were rare.

The housing program limped badly. Schedules called for the completion in Tokyo of 65,000 two-room dwellings (one room ten by eleven feet, and the other six feet by nine) before February 1; but only one-seventh of the number was finished on time. Osaka built but 1,296 of the anticipated 29,000 houses. MacArthur was told, and therefore certified, that after a full year of Occupation Japan had rebuilt 15 per cent of her wrecked buildings, and that at the end of the third year 324,000 more dwellings had been replaced, two-thirds in the rural regions. By this estimate, which was guesswork, Japan in August, 1948, had not recovered as much as half of her war losses. At least 3,000,000 more dwelling houses were urgently required.

The need has not been satisfied. According to the Construction Ministry, 3,500,000 houses were built between surrender and 1954; this more than equaled the number destroyed in the 119 major cities, but Japan's housing shortage remained at least as acute as when the Occupation started.

War loss was not the only factor in the shortage. Each year typhoons, fires, and floods have taken a heavy toll. According to the Construction Ministry, 485,000 houses were lost between 1945 and 1953; another 550,000, it said, had "crumbled with age." Meanwhile, Japan had gained more than 6,000,000 people—approximately 1,200,000 families—who needed housing. The Ministry declared in 1952, and again in 1953, that Japan still needed 3,160,000 houses, plus an additional number to replace annual losses through disaster or decay. The Statistics Board of the Prime Minister's Office reported as late as 1952 that 1,300,000 Japanese were living in tents, air-raid shelters, or dugouts.

Tokyo's situation was particularly critical. The Metropolitan Statistics Board announced in June, 1953, that 7,090,000 people were living in 1,119,554 houses—which meant that a population greater by 412,000 than that in 1941 was housed in 470,000 fewer dwellings. The city has been growing at the rate of more than 330,000 people annually, or about 60,000 households; but only 34,000 new houses were completed during 1952. Governor Seiichiro Yasui has repeatedly urged remedial action to benefit the 520,000 families living in exceptionally congested conditions.

Unhappily, the problem is not new. Oriental cities have always been congested. Heavy competition for scarce land has driven up the price of building lots, thus holding down lateral expansion, while lack of structural steel and scarcity of brick and building stone limited vertical growth. Cities in Japan therefore became congeries of wooden houses, unplanned and chaotic, where fire hazards were high and disease rates soared. As late as 1923, Tokyo was 91 per cent wooden, having 326,241 wood structures as against 6,943 brick buildings, 1,689 stone houses, and 232 concrete dwellings. Next to wood, the most common building material was earth, there being 22,658 earthen "buildings," according to the Tokyo Municipal Statistics Office. The heavy growth between 1923 and the outbreak of the war continued the emphasis on wood. The pressure on land resulted in a tangle of narrow, twisting lanes, unfit for traffic even in ancient times for sedan chairs and, wholly impassable for motorcars.

In the confused state of local governments cities were unable to relieve their strangulation. Until 1932, Tokyo governed only 34 square miles, one-seventh of the urban area, and this urban area was itself but a third of the mainland area of Tokyo prefecture, most of which was satellite, and all of which was economically but not politically linked with Tokyo city. Costs of civic improvements shared by the entire prefecture fell upon a relatively few central city property owners or upon the middle-class or semi-slum residents while richer suburbanites enjoyed the benefits but paid no share. Inequalities were accentuated by a grossly unfair tax system which assessed private park lands at low farm rates.

Twin laws passed in 1919 allowed the six largest cities, and later forty-three other communities, to increase land taxes 12.5 per cent and to levy a special 40 per cent surtax on certain prefectural taxes collected within city limits. The proceeds were to be spent for street improvement, for sewage disposal and waterworks, and for the acquisition of park lands. At the same time zoning was legalized, fireproofing became compulsory in central city districts, and buildings were limited in height to 50 feet if of wood and 65 if of stone.

Much of this was show-window legislation to indicate that the West had no monopoly on city planning or on progressive social thinking. The business sections of Tokyo and Osaka, where land was largely owned by a few great corporations, blossomed with impressive steel, brick, and ferroconcrete structures; but little was accomplished elsewhere. To the dismay of low-taxed suburbanites, the laws allowed large cities to merge with neighbor communities. Osaka expanded in 1923 from 768,560 to 2,144,809 population, and Nagoya from 429,927 to 1,252,983. Tokyo, facing stronger opposition from influential political and industrial personalities, delayed until 1932, when it absorbed eighty-four towns and villages within a ten-mile radius of Tokyo Central Station. The move had been contemplated at the time that Osaka and Nagoya expanded, and had been approved by Professor Charles A. Beard, who in September, 1922, had begun a six months' survey of city needs; but the Great Earthquake of September, 1923, had caused action to be postponed.

This earthquake destroyed some 400,000 houses in the seven prefectures most severely affected. Of 2,287,500 families living in the area,

694,621 lost their homes. In Tokyo, where, as Mayor Hidejiro Nagata phrased it, half the city had become "a veritable desert of smoldering embers and ashes," the burned-out area included the downtown district and much of the better uptown residential section; the city lost 250,000 houses.

Almost invariably in Japan, such catastrophes excite grandiose dreams of city betterment. In 1923 the Tokyo leaders dreamed of reconstruction on a wide and extraordinarily expensive scale; but because, as in 1945, money was lacking and materials were scarce the city dawdled. Jerry-built shanties of waste materials sprang up amongst the rubble—the violation of the highly touted zoning and fireproofing laws being at first ignored and then legalized by a year's suspension of the regulations. All these shacks, presumably, were to disappear within five years; but when, in 1927, their number had not appreciably diminished an extension was granted. This relaxation became a precedent justifying evasion of the building codes in the postwar emergency.

Public housing lagged, but dreams of betterment continued. Scarcely had the earthquake shocks subsided before Home Minister Shimpei Goto, who had invited Professor Beard to Tokyo, proposed to put the Beard recommendations into practice. An Imperial City Reconstruction Board drafted a seven-year program to replot and readjust the burned-out area, to build fifty-two trunk highways, each at least twenty-two meters wide, with an equal number of eight-meter-wide feeder roads, to widen and straighten streets and to make firebreaks. The cost was estimated at 800,000,000 yen, or about $200,000,000, which, it was expected, the national government would pay.

Little came of the project, though some firebreaks were built and several trunk highways, useful for the military, were constructed. Japanese outside the capital did not share the opinions of the Tokyo Construction Bureau which had announced with a certain amount of smugness, "It is no exaggeration to say that the future of Japan depends upon the reconstruction of its capital." The plan, however, remained and became the basis for Governor Yasui's postwar recommendations for rebuilding Tokyo.

The Imperial City Reconstruction Board, after being quietly reduced to a bureau of the Home Ministry, with some of its functions transferred to the Welfare Ministry, paid more attention to housing than to city planning. In 1939 it directed the construction of thirty apartment houses in the major cities to care for low-paid workers and instructed twelve prefectures, where the need was greatest, to carry out a three-year program of providing 30,000 family houses and 200 dormitories, each with room for 200 bachelors. Land and materials would be supplied at Government expense, largely by use of timber from state forests, and the Finance Ministry would lend 30,000,000 yen at from 3.2 to 4.2 per cent interest. Two years later, in 1941, further legislation authorized a five-year construction plan for 300,000 houses. This, of course, was interrupted by the war, but, even in the so-called normal years, little actual gain had been accomplished. During the three years 1936–1938, for instance, Tokyo had built 86,308 houses; but fires and deterioration had destroyed 53,940, so that the net gain was too small to care for population growth, much less to relieve congestion.

Though the Occupation had no responsibility for housing improvement, American sociologists in Tokyo suggested that reconstruction include slum clearance and provision of sufficient housing. Governor Yasui, reviving the Beard plans, replied that Japan must set an example to the world and that wide boulevards and impressive public buildings would attract more visitors than low-cost housing, and therefore bring more profit. He urged the Tokyo Assembly to vote appropriations to rehouse 4,200 shanty dwellers living just behind the swank Imperial Hotel or on embankments near the palace, for these were visible to tourists; but he showed warmer interest in the building of a 2,000,000,000-yen cultural center and auditorium. He proceeded to widen roads leading to Shibuya and Shinagawa, where foreigners traveled, but did little to improve Tokyo's innumerable narrow, unpaved lanes.

Except for relocation of the shanty dwellers, slum clearance made little progress; it may, indeed, have retrogressed. In 1925 the Home Ministry had reported the existence of 217 slum areas and, aided by Toyohiko Kagawa's Social Work Investigation Society (Shakai Jigyo Chosa Kai), had brought about the passage of an act empowering the Government to pay half the cost of clearance. Eight years thereafter, Tokyo alone had 185 slum areas.

Failure had lain inherent within the terms of the law. A builder pledged himself to use only 60 per cent of his land for housing purposes, leaving 40 per cent for greenery and breathing, to use at least 10 per cent of wall space for windows, to install modern plumbing, and to observe other regulations that would give his houses higher standards than those customary elsewhere in Japan; but the law was loosely drawn and enforcement provisions were inadequate, so that contractors took the subsidy and then failed to comply with regulations. In Tokyo,

Osaka, and Nagoya, both public and private contractors violated the law with impunity.

At least a fifth of Tokyo's population in 1953 had less than 36 square feet of housing space per capita. This, too, was a long-standing condition, not confined to Tokyo. Of 3,169,000 urban families in 1930, 2,-609,000 had been found living in one room, often smaller than ten feet by sixteen; of 9,389,000 rural families, 4,987,000 had but one room. The average Japanese house had 3.4 rooms per family and 1.46 persons per room. Still earlier, in 1919, Home Ministry investigators had discovered that 85 per cent of Osaka city residents and, more surprisingly to foreigners, 96 per cent of suburbanites, had less than three mats sleeping space, the six by nine feet regarded as the hygienic minimum. For this small area, white-collar workers paid a quarter to a third of their monthly salaries.

Housing scarcities, increased congestion, the always impending threat of disease, and crime and other social maladjustments did not complete the roster of critical civic problems. These were dangerous enough, and it was a tragic commentary that only the disastrous earthquake of 1923 and the more calamitous wartime bombings and fires had spared Tokyo from their serious effect; but more shortages were being felt. The Construction Ministry agreed that Japan must build at least 60,000 houses a year for twenty years; yet budget provisions gave it only enough funds for 25,000 houses in the first year of the campaign. In 1953 the major cities had been less than 70 per cent rebuilt since the war, and there was little prospect for quick recovery.

Tokyo was in dire straits in 1954. Transportation was clogged, the 929 trams being almost invariably jammed to capacity; the water supply was low, a 68 per cent increase in consumption since 1940 so overtaxing the reservoirs that rationing was needed; the schools, only 43 per cent restored, were inefficient; the streets were so run down that estimates called for 50,000,000,000 yen to be expended annually on upkeep. Even the relatively small provision of a half-pound of staple food daily per person overtaxed the railways by requiring them to bring in 572,000 tons annually.

Yet the only remedial plans considered were revivals of the post-earthquake schemes that had been proved unworkable. In June, 1950, a Capital City Construction Committee of Cabinet members, Diet representatives, Governor Yasui, and Tokyo assemblymen began almost precisely the same program in almost the same manner as the old Imperial City Reconstruction Board.

The Capital City Reconstruction Committee, like its predecessor, looked to grandiose city planning rather than to essential betterments. It, too, looked upon its work as one of national rather than local interest; it, also, dreamed of windfalls, such as the transfer of "idle state property" and national subsidies, rather than self-liquidation projects or local taxation.

Much was done to improve Tokyo—but by private rather than public enterprise. More than a hundred massive new buildings changed the appearance of the central city, and thousands of new, well built modern houses sprang up in the suburbs; but the slums remained virtually untouched. In the few instances where housing projects were completed, such as Shibuya and Takadanobaba, the work was shoddy; and repairs were needed almost as soon as the structures were thrown open to occupancy.

Early in the Occupation, excuse was made that procurement demands, by drawing off labor and materials, had prevented progress; but delays persisted after Occupationnaires ceased to make demands.

The real hindrance was not the Occupation but lack of originality. Establishment of a Housing Loan Corporation with a 15,000,000,000-yen fund to subsidize home builders under weak enforcement terms no better than the prewar laws, and the passage of Building Standards Acts repeating the zoning, fireproofing, and other advanced requirements of earlier laws, looked well on paper and testified to Japan's modernism; but, once they had been passed, the regulations were ignored.

Tokyo authorities, in 1949 as in 1923, mapped ambitious plans to make Tokyo "a city of sun and fun, a city of fellowship, with no surface traffic, a city of high productivity and of self-sufficiency in food, a city of culture, an incombustible city." The lack of realism was evident when they further planned that a city of over 7,000,000 people should somehow be reduced to one of 3,500,000 as an optimum and, in no case, to more than 5,000,000.

Small wonder that the shrewdly observant *Nippon Times* complained that the surveys that were so numerous, and the plans that were so beautiful, were wholly impracticable. The city fathers had their opportunity, it said, in 1946 as in 1923, when most of the city had been leveled; but, each time, they had allowed helter-skelter and haphazard jerry building, regardless of fire laws, zoning, safety, congestion, and convenience. The chances had been wasted, and only the opening of one small stretch of new subway, in 1954, indicated progress.

TWENTY-FIVE

Red Flag Waves

Communists scored heavily when MacArthur required democracy without defining its meaning; his policy of pretending that the Occupation sought only to revive and strengthen Japanese democracy played directly into Communist hands. His farcical denial of interference with Japanese domestic affairs provided Reds with ample ammunition; they blasted America for hypocrisy and asserted, at the same time, that democracy, popular rights, progressivism, freedom, and civil liberties all were synonymous with Communism, and that only Communists would bring them to Japan.

For months, no high-placed Occupationnaire corrected these distortions; indeed, the brass, by its very real concern for free speech and equal rights, mystified Japanese who, as the brass itself well knew, had never known such privileges. Early in October, MacArthur ordered the release of 276 long-imprisoned Communist leaders, whereupon John K. Emmerson of the State Department and Dr. E. Herbert Norman, later Canadian Minister, hurried to the jail to interview Kyuichi Tokuda and Yoshio Shiga, the two top Reds. According to Eugene Dooman, former counselor of the American Embassy, this action, taken merely for the purpose of understanding the true political situation, gave rise to Communist propaganda that MacArthur was their friend. Transfer of the Reds to Tokyo in an official SCAP staff car supported the rumor.

MacArthur's demand that Shidehara encourage the formation and activity of labor unions, hitherto regarded as tools of radicalism, also helped the Communist cause. Within two months Red agitators, many of them Moscow-trained, infiltrated 508 hastily organized labor unions and drafted platforms echoing the Moscow line. When such old-time labor leaders as Komakichi Matsuoka of the Japan Federation of Labor protested, the Reds, often with the approval of proleftists within Government and Economics Sections, demanded that they be purged as labor bosses, rightists, and former leaders of totalitarian labor fronts. With Labor Division's sanction, if not by its inspiration, leftists founded a radically minded National Congress of Industrial Unions which, six months later, included 1,094 unions and 1,600,000 members.

Few of these were Communists, but Yoshio Shiga boasted to Government Section that most of them were Communist-minded. In the early days of the Occupation, Communists made no secret either of their intention or of their plan to sovietize Japan through labor unions. Shiga, like other Reds, frankly reported such matters to what he obviously considered as a friendly Occupation.

As early as March, 1946, Satomi Hakamada, Moscow-educated chief of the Communist Party Control Department and the Labor Organization Committee, and later head of the Young Communist League, said that a handful of disciplined party members directed union policy. Five Communists, he said, led 11,000 teamsters, fourteen members ruled 10,000 printers, 110 Communist newspapermen dominated 23,000 members of the Newspaper Workers' Union. Similarly small minorities bossed other unions, particularly in transportation, communications, electricity, heavy industry, teaching, and government service.

Light on this technique reached General MacArthur directly through Marquat's Labor Division, Willoughby's Allied Translator and Information Service, and Whitney's Government Section. Shiga himself certified to Whitney's political expert that the infiltration was official Communist Party policy; but the naïve major then in charge of such matters underestimated the revelation or thought it meaningless, and no effective steps were taken to offset Communist influence.

Similarly, though Kyuichi Tokuda, immediately after his release from prison, incited workers to seize control of public information media, transportation, communications, and key productive enterprises, the Occupation saw no peril. At Tokuda's instigation, employees usurped control over manufacture and sale of products, paid themselves out of the proceeds, and withheld from owners any voice in management. According to Richard L-G. Deverall, MacArthur's Chief of Labor Education, their activities were sponsored and largely led by leftists in American army uniforms who used Occupation prestige to foist Communism upon Japan.

Had MacArthur or his Cabinet of section chiefs been seriously concerned with other than military aspects of current problems, had they been more experienced with Communist method, more willing to listen to advice, or more interested in public welfare, they might at once have blighted budding Communism; but, viewing their mission as one of security alone, they at first stood aloof. SCAP's only published comment when Japanese protested against plant seizures was, "These are matters for the Japanese courts to decide," although later, after 50,000 Tokyo municipal workers had attempted to take over city government, MacArthur broadened his interpretation of his mission. Primary responsibility for his lethargy in organizing effective counterpropaganda against Communism rested upon SCAP staff sections who either did not understand the situation upon which they were supposedly expert, or failed to make the situation clear to their superiors. Marquat's Labor Division, for instance, trusting union leaders who concealed their Communism, consistently reported their activities as healthy, democratic, and progressive. Amateurs within Government Section, misinformed by suave Communist apologists and ill advised by high-ranking leftists whom they trusted, regarded the Communists as just another political party instead of as a highly trained and militant international conspiracy.

From the very beginning, MacArthur's agents had deprived themselves of help from the press by an ill considered blast at the vernacular newspapers within the first week of the Occupation for anti-Americanism in publishing a few minor items that alleged misconduct by a handful of drunken soldiers. These bulletins, usually tucked away in an obscure corner of the page, had been more than counterbalanced by longer and more favorably displayed articles enthusiastically praising the Occupation forces; but MacArthur's press advisers, disregarding the extraordinarily friendly and cooperative material, angrily attacked the press for disparagement.

The press, thus rebuffed, and taught by years of militarist censorship to avoid even the appearance of objecting to authority, retreated into its shell. In the absence of a smoothly operating information service, the pro-Allied material that it published came, all too often, from Communist sources. The Communist core within newspaper unions gave all such propaganda the best position, with huge headlines. General Ken R. Dyke, then head of CIE, was no Communist, but he offered no hindrance. Japanese, who did not understand his policy of fair play and freedom of opinion, believed that he, too, was a Red.

Dyke's honest zeal for a free press immeasurably helped the Communists; tireless and devoted fellow travelers misused his fair-mindedness to demand that the press report all Moscow publicity prominently and in detail. Papers which demurred met trouble, agitators rushing to CIE to accuse them of reactionary tendencies. During wartime at least, as a necessity and a patriotic duty, every journal had published militarist propaganda; but now the fact of such publication was taken to be proof of antidemocratic bias, and every editor or publisher had the choice of following the Communist line or risking Occupation punishment. True democrats allowed a free press to function, but Soviet sympathizers blackmailed it into submission.

As in the instance of the purge, strict justice would have required that both sides of the story be heard if charges of reactionary tendencies were lodged, and that condemnation be recorded only after irrefutable proof was offered and all extenuating circumstances were weighed. But, again, the Occupation lacked both time and men to mete out justice. In too many cases, mere accusation was sufficient to purge accused persons from continued public activity.

Almost immediately after surrender, Colonel Don Hoover, MacArthur's press officer, lost his temper when the press used the word "negotiations" in referring to exchange of messages between MacArthur and the Government. Japan, he stormed, was a defeated country; her surrender had been unconditional, and so there could be no "negotiations"; and if the press repeated the offense more suppressions must result. He closed down a little provincial sheet for reasons which were unannounced, but which were generally believed to be a misuse of the blacklisted word.

Dyke's demand for publication of propaganda which Japanese had been taught to regard as either Communist or subversive, like Labor Division tolerance for red-flag demonstrations, Government Section insistence that the Emperor be attacked, and G-2 purge officials' implacable hunt for "reactionaries" strengthened the misconception that the Occupation endorsed Communism.

Communist Party publications basked in special CIE favor. While newsprint was so parsimoniously rationed that major papers were forced to reduce their press runs, *Akahata*, the party organ, with a 3,000 circulation in October, 1945, received a paper allotment for 300,000 copies.

This ample supply permitted it to increase its circulation while other papers had to reject subscribers. At least five other Communist journals enjoyed newsprint rations five to ten times as great as party membership required, newsprint being denied to organs of other political parties.

The Occupation stood by quietly while Katsumi Kikunami, a Communist who concealed his affiliation, professed that Labor Division sponsored his formation of a press and radio workers union, and that CIE guided its policies. Kikunami told newspaper owners that, because they had been militaristic, Robert Berkov, CIE press and publication unit chief, had demanded that they denounce themselves as reactionary, resign their control, and turn over to the union all direction of their papers. This, he said, was what Berkov meant by press democratization.

The report was false, but proprietors who appealed received short shrift. The president of *Hokkaido Shimbun* was informed, when he complained, that union agents were misrepresenting Berkov's intentions, that this was none of CIE's concern. Most proprietors, including all the major newspapers except *Yomiuri,* therefore, complied with Kikunami's demands. Matsutaro Shoriki of *Yomiuri,* who refused to do so, was jailed as a war criminal, but after the union took over his paper the Occupation dropped the war-crimes charge. *Yomiuri* thereafter remained one of the most vociferous pro-Soviet journals.

Other vernacular papers, particularly in Tokyo and Osaka, servilely echoed the Moscow propaganda line. A Press Code had been issued on September 19, 1945, but its provisions forbidding destructive criticism of the Allied Powers took precedence over clauses requiring strict adherence to truth and forbidding coloring or slanting of the news.

MacArthur's headquarters thoroughly understood and tolerated this situation. The daily news summary published by Willoughby's Allied Translation and Intelligence Service faithfully reported current pro-leftist news and Communist editorials. Civil Censorship circulated thousands of mimeographed copies of intercepted letters wherein Japanese civilians protested vigorously against Communist propaganda. But while SCAP cracked down on letter writers who criticized the Occupation, or on editors who said that censorship by MacArthur had replaced that of the Japanese militarists, such action as it took against the ultraradicals was tardy.

Berkov and Lieutenant Colonel Daniel Imboden, his successor as chief of Press and Publications Unit, CIE, protested that they lacked authority to restrict the Reds. Their duties, they explained, were to expedite press freedom, to make clear to Japanese the truth about their war guilt and defeat, and to explain militarist misdeeds and Occupation aims, and beyond this they had no right to act.

Censorship chiefs disclaimed responsibility, asserting that they merely administered policy imposed by Washington. Walter Simmons of the Chicago *Tribune,* however, insisted that censors protected the Reds by scissoring comment critical of Communism while allowing free publication of anti-British, anti-French, and anti-Chinese news. This pro-Moscow line, he said, was particularly evident in the army-managed *Stars and Stripes,* where Communist-minded soldier-reporters consistently threw out incoming agency news unfavorable to Russia but ran daily commentaries frankly paralleling the Communist line. Officers supposedly in charge made no effort to inspect the incoming file nor to check on the accuracy of columnists. William McGaffin of the Washington *Star* added that certain of the censorship officials, while they were not themselves pro-Russian, were oversolicitous of Russian sensitivities.

Dyke's CIE division chiefs outlawed plays featuring swordplay, death, or revenge, thus paralleling the prewar Education Ministry censorship of *Hamlet,* copied the prewar Japanese police by prohibiting sales of popular phonograph records, among them "China Night" and "Moonlight on the Ruined Castle" and censored paper-doll exhibitions for children but hesitated to ban pro-Communist news items. Don Brown's Information Division, in charge of translating and publishing American books, moved so cautiously that although Marx, Engels, Lenin, and Stalin flooded the bookstalls, he licensed for publication only three American books of general interest within the first fifteen months of the Occupation.

Official CIE publications, notably on press, radio, and movie development, favored the Communist line, attacking conservatives as rightist, feudalistic, or reactionary while hailing radicals as progressives, liberals, and democrats. Plays and films produced by leftist groups received extravagant praise as artistic triumphs.

Constructive leadership was notably absent in SCAP's treatment of the motion picture problem. CIE, absorbed like other sections in uprooting evil militarist and nationalist influence, missed an opportunity to explain the meanings of democracy. After the banning of 236 propagandist films by Major A. L. Dibella, whose Press, Pictorial, and Broadcast Division of Civil Censorship was apart from CIE control, movie makers flocked to CIE for guidance. David W. Conde, chief of CIE's Motion Picture Division, however, contented himself with urging them to film "the democratic way of life," giving no specific suggestion but allowing movie men to draw their own deductions.

Necessarily, they scanned propagandist documentaries hurriedly imported but found them uninspiring and unsuitable for Japanese consumption. They studied also the American commercial films newly licensed for showing in Japan but these—*Call of the Yukon, His Butler's Sister,* and *The Ware Case*—gave little clue to CIE desires. They took the fourth picture, however, *Madame Curie,* as indication that SCAP favored fellow traveling.

Leftists who had infiltrated the movie workers' union insisted that CIE required a purge of "warmongers, reactionaries, and rightists," meaning thereby all who had previously managed or directed pictures, and that radical films be immediately filmed.

Though Conde, under instruction of Nugent, his chief, gave no inkling of what "progressive" and "modern" implied regarding films, the hard Communist core within the movie workers' union supplied interpretation. Under the guise of antimilitarism they produced *The Dark Age,* discrediting the warmongers and reactionaries who had retarded Communist development. In *Women's Victory* they celebrated equal rights but gave all credit to the radicals. In *Builders of Tomorrow* the Communists who ruled the Toho union openly predicted the coming of the Soviets.

SCAP offered no objection; on the contrary, CIE movie experts hailed the Toho film as a masterpiece produced by democratic artists. The general public, noting MacArthur's apparent unconcern as Communists turned newspapers into party organs, used studios to film Red propaganda, and filled the air with pro-Russian broadcasts, could only suppose that he was Communism's friend.

Sanzo Nosaka, fresh from Yenan in January, 1946, perceived that the Occupation worked inadvertently for Communism. Without effective interference from MacArthur, Reds had captured the press, radio, movie, and stage and had permeated schools, labor unions, and farm cooperatives. Big business, political parties, and neighborhood associations still remained outside the Red domain; but these were being shattered by determined Occupationnaires within Government and Economics Sections.

Stars and Stripes, the army-managed daily paper, itself hammered propaganda home. Showering praise upon Nosaka as a democratic hero and clamoring for a united front against a non-existent reactionary enemy, the paper sponsored a mass meeting at which Nosaka explained Communism to army officers. Barney Rubin, *Stars and Stripes* columnist who presided at the meeting, held in MacArthur's headquarters building on the same floor and within a few yards of MacArthur's private office, made no secret of his admiration for Nosaka and his ideals.

Rubin and his colleagues, whose writings carried the stamp of Occupation approval, used *Stars and Stripes* to demand purging of prewar anti-Communist leaders, confiscation of big business, landed estates, and "unused mansions," and suppression of the "rightists." Apparently without objection by either military or civilian brass they relentlessly attacked Toyohiko Kagawa, the prewar social worker who had become hopelessly bewildered in trying to reconcile peace, patriotism, and Christianity. By going unchallenged, these editorialized news items, colored in violation of the Press Code imposed upon Japanese, convinced Japan that MacArthur endorsed their opinions.

Incautiously, however, Rubin went too far by accusing the Emperor of war crimes, punishment for which was forbidden by JCS directive, and was promptly banished to Okinawa. The press furore set off in America by fellow travelers who called the transfer a fascist suppression of press freedom, confirmed Japan's belief that America was pro-Russian.

Under such circumstances, Nosaka urged, direct action was unnecessary; with the Occupation playing the Communist game, the party should itself concentrate upon becoming lovable. This did not imply large enrollments. Nosaka preferred a small cadre of dedicated party workers to a mass of undisciplined fellow travelers and therefore was content that the party, which upon its revival on November 8, 1945, had listed but 1,000 members had grown to only 8,132 in 1946.

Shiga the doctrinaire and Tokuda the direct actionist, while agreeing with Nosaka upon the desirability of a manageable élite, looked askance upon his gradualism, his reliance upon parliamentary action, and, above all, his willingness to work within the Occupation framework. These qualities which endeared him to Whitney's political experts did not conform to their conception of Marx-Stalinism, which they contended, required labor offensives, strikes, demonstrations, and sabotage. Their objections caused Nosaka to join an attack against Prime Minister

Shidehara's official residence in April, 1946, and to foment noisy food riots a month later.

These disorders jeopardized Occupation collaboration. MacArthur, calling out the military police and alerting other troops, warned against mass violence. George Atcheson, Jr., his deputy on the Allied Council for Japan, pointedly declared that the United States opposed Communism anywhere. Nosaka, however, hurriedly reassured Government Section of Communist good intentions, and so healed the threatened breach that continuing labor unrest, including delays in coal production, interruption of essential services, slowing down of food rationing, and paralysis in tax collecting failed to stir MacArthur to public condemnation of the Communists inspiring the movements.

So timorous was the Occupation that MacArthur's defenders privately explained that he had been forbidden to mention Communism by name. In September, 1946, the rumors ran, the State Department had "slapped him down" for even referring to the "extreme radical left." Whatever the truth may be, MacArthur, and most of his subordinates, while referring frequently to "disorderly minorities," alien philosophies, and foreign influences, sedulously refrained from using the words "Communism," "soviets," or "Russians" until the Occupation was well established. As late as 1954 MacArthur refused to comment on the reasons for his silence.

Richard L-G. Deverall, in fact, asserted that "a certain SCAP official" told him in August, 1948, to go home "on the specific ground that SCAP did not support anti-Communist activities." This may have been an isolated case since, simultaneously, Major Cecil G. Tilton of Government Section was touring Japan warning against Communist influences; but the Tilton lectures, delivered on the Eighth Army's information and education program rather than as official SCAP pronouncements, centered primarily on the dangers of Soviet military aggression rather than upon the Communist menace within Japan.

Unattached American observers, as well as Japanese, seeing SCAP's apparent unconcern over the internal menace, credited the leftist core with too great power; but the Occupation's hasty set-up offers a more likely explanation. In its origin, SCAP, while entrusted with civil government, was essentially a military organization, conceived for security, to safeguard Occupation objectives, and to watch but not to direct government activity. Staff section chiefs as military men confined themselves to their own field and, despite their ambitions to enlarge their empires, carefully avoided dangerous areas not specifically entrusted to them.

Much of this tolerance is traceable to surprising success by Sanzo Nosaka and Yoshio Shiga in duping the political amateurs within Government Section. They concealed the fact that the Russian Liaison Mission, with its staff of several hundred members and its Soviet-Japanese Friendship Society headed by Lieutenant General Kuzma Derevyanko, the Mission chief, were actively guiding, supporting and perhaps financing the Japanese Communists at the time. Instead, they assured the major in charge of political party liaison that the Japanese Communist Party, like Mao Tse-tung's faction in China, consisted of nationalist agricultural reformers who had no current connection with Soviet Russia. In any contest between Russia and the United States, they said, Japanese Communists would support democracy—a statement which they allowed the major to suppose meant the American rather than the Soviet side.

These assurances seemed to the major to be confirmed by certain Communist Party theses adopted on February 24, 1946. In full conformity with the Shiga-Nosaka promises already made to Government Section, the program included:

(1) The Communist Party must become beloved by the masses.

(2) Japanese Communists reject the idea of an early revolution by force but believe in peaceful reformation through political action.

(3) Japanese Communists, sincerely interested in general welfare, are nationalists and patriots.

(4) The Japanese people will decide for themselves whether to retain the Emperor, after democracy has matured.

(5) All democratically minded people should unite in a democratic front for common action against the national economic crisis.

This program, paralleling the initial policies of Mao Tse-tung in China and of Lenin himself in Russia except for the Emperor clause, precisely followed a pattern laid down at Yenan in 1944 by the Japanese People's Emancipation League. This Yenan Manifesto, drafted by Nosaka, who then called himself Susumu Okano, had been endorsed by liberals within the State Department and was well known to Emmerson but not to Government Section. Having no liaison with the State Department and having held aloof from the Office of War Information which also received the Yenan Manifesto, Government Section assumed that the 1946 Communist Party platform reflected its own efforts in softening Communist policy.

Nor was it in the least suspicious that Shiga and Nosaka, who frequently dropped into Government Section offices, soft-pedaled mention of their belligerent and fiery colleague Kyuichi Tokuda, who came only when commanded to appear. The deluded major explained that his absence was due to defeat: internal strife within the party had led to Tokuda's eclipse and the triumph of the mild and scholarly Shiga-Nosaka faction.

Thus MacArthur, whose information sources concerning Red political activity were remarkably untrustworthy, opposed Communism as an aggressive force elsewhere but benignly permitted its growth as an independent reformist group within Japan. Atcheson referred to American disapproval of Communism as a philosophy but made it clear that in Japan Communists, like all other political parties, enjoyed full and equal freedom for peaceful development. This was, of course, precisely what Nosaka and Shiga desired. It also was the line proposed by Andrew Roth in *Dilemma in Japan*.

Naïve Occupationnaires, accepting Nosaka's public promises at face value, closed their eyes to subsequent abuses. Close espionage over the public and private life of Occupationnaires resulted in some instances in blackmail threats unless victims cooperated with the Reds, gross misrepresentation of Allied purposes, sabotage of regulations; and the leakage of information through unauthorized channels helped Communists discredit the Occupation.

Unless Red demonstrations endangered security, the Occupation offered no objection. Professing neutrality and lack of desire to interfere with Japan's internal affairs, it granted little effective aid to those who fought against the Reds. CIE allotted tons of newsprint to Communist newspapers and magazines and turned aside when much of this was diverted into the black market; thousands of copies of elaborate, fine-paper brochures were published in both Japanese and English, on natural resources and wild life, cultural progress, recipes for cooking foods that Japanese could never buy, and Occupation activities; but during the first two years of the Occupation, Deverall complained, not one pound of paper was allotted to pamphlets telling how to develop democratic trade unions, combat Communism, or form healthy political parties. All such matters, he was told, were Japan's domestic concern. For such purposes, the orders read, "No paper can be used, no printing

employed if it is to be in the Japanese language and for the Japanese."
Deverall, forced to limit even his mimeographs to two hundred copies,
learned that "a pink insider" had forbidden Japanese even to reproduce
SCAP pamphlets.

Soviet Russia made no such mistake. Her Mission used twenty
attachés, well equipped with film strips, movies, and abundant "literature" for liaison work with labor unions. To counteract them, SCAP
assigned two labor education experts to serve 7,000,000 unionists in
every part of Japan but gave them virtually no assistance. Volunteer
donations from such agencies as the American Federation of Labor, the
Congress of Industrial Organizations, the United States Chamber of
Commerce, National Association of Manufacturers, and various schools,
universities, and churches helped overcome this shortage. Much assistance came also from Military Government officers outside the SCAP
organization.

Under such difficulties, Communist misconceptions found ready acceptance among people who did not carefully analyze propaganda.
Government Section showed no alarm, reassuring itself by pointing out
that Communist membership although doubling during 1946, reached
only 16,947 in 1947. It ignored the possibility that many others, not
enrolled, might be tainted by Communist ideas. Soothed by this complacency, MacArthur's men disregarded the Communist teaching that
Japan's current woes sprang solely from the Occupation.

TWENTY-SIX

Communist Suicide

Communism as a wide, integrated field was No Man's Land. Whitney viewed it purely as a political movement; Marquat, as it concerned labor unions, strikes, and production; Dyke, and later Nugent, as it affected education, culture, and publications; Willoughby, as a matter of security. These chiefs and their subordinates were often at odds with one another and their liaison was weak at best, so that the highly drilled, coordinated Communist movement faced a divided Occupation whose components were usually unaware of the widespread nature of the movement they opposed. When MacArthur's historians compiled the exploits of the Occupation, they found neither sources to consult concerning Communism nor any staff section competent to supervise the product.

Nor, had the task of supervising Communism as a broad general movement been assigned to anyone, were Occupationnaires sufficiently well equipped to match the wide resources upon which Communists could draw. Red leaders trained in Moscow, hardened by long campaigning, and guided by experts faced young, inexperienced, and isolated occupation personnel. Nosaka and Shiga easily outmatched the theologically minded amateur surgeon whom Whitney assigned to supervise them; disciplined labor leaders ran rings around a well-meaning high-school history teacher on Marquat's staff; skilled dialecticians, veterans of verbal battles against the prewar Education Ministry, baffled the small-town publishers and naval lieutenants upon whom Nugent relied. And, perhaps above all, the Communists took full advantage of the Occupation's earnest desire to play fair with them and to give them the benefit of any doubts.

The anti-Communist crusade repeated tactical and strategic efforts made elsewhere by the Occupation. Democratic propagandists, ignorant of actual conditions, appealed to Japanese by the same arguments, often in the very words, that would have been employed in warning Americans against the Reds.

Thus, Occupationnaires warned a people who had never tasted freedom, who knew nothing of justice in its Western sense, who had been taught that individuality was evil, and who had not generally accepted Christianity that Communism periled all these privileges. Japan remained unmoved by revelations of Russian atheism, of disregard for private citizens, of impotence of representative governments, and of suppression of free speech, free press, and free assembly; these evils, shocking to Americans and no doubt shocking, years hence, to Japanese as well, had not yet stirred the Japanese to anger. Men in military uniform, who cherished caste and special privilege, and who only recently had plastered the Japanese Empire with off-limits signs against both Japanese and their own subordinates, proved to be ineffective agents in condemning Russia as an undemocratic land.

Occupation officers whose treatment of Japanese officials had been high-handed, and whose contempt for Japanese laws and customs had been unconcealed, failed to convince Japan that Russia set up puppet governments in all her satellites, and that Russian domination meant the importation of an alien culture. Many Japanese saw little difference between the Allied Occupation of Japan and Russia's activity in North Korea.

In fact, as Orientals conscious of a special Eastern heritage, many thrilled at hearing that the Chinese and North Korean armies had driven back Americans. As Japanese, they entertained contempt for the military prowess of both Koreans and Chinese; but the victory, however temporary, proved to them that Asians were capable of standing firm against the whites. Political observers construed the subsequent surge in Communist membership in the Japanese Diet as due to pride in what the Asian Reds had done upon the Continent.

Communist propagandists skillfully exploited the opportunity thus provided. Alleged lack of culture among Americans, as evidenced on the GI radio, in the movies offered to Japan, in comic books and even in the cowboy suits and pistols worn by little boys of the American community might have been laughable arguments had they not been so convincing to Japan. The tawdriness, drunkenness, and vice surrounding army camps, the lack of any effort to appreciate Japan's special culture, and the almost insulting assumption that everything American was good and all things Japanese were feudal worked to Communist advantage.

Not that these accusations were true nor that Communists were wholly free of criticism. Soviet troops stationed in Japan had been overbearing, grasping, and contemptuous; their treatment of Japanese employed in billets had been notorious, and their insistence on Russian superiority had been as constant as it had been loud and boorish. But most of the Soviet troops had been withdrawn or voluntarily segregated; drunken Soviet officers no longer staged night parades in the Dai Ichi Hotel corridors chanting "On to Budapest." Red excesses had been forgotten as time had passed, but GI's continued to walk hand in hand with *panpan* on the Ginza or sprawled, bottle in hand, on cushions of crowded cars of the Keihin, Chuo, and Yamate lines.

Red propagandists, pointing to concrete instances while Americans talked vaguely concerning matters unfamiliar to Japan, registered success. Even conservative Japanese echoed Soviet propaganda that the United States was turning Japan into a military base, forcing Japan into the status of a colony, confiscating good rice-growing land for unproductive recreation, mulcting Japan of taxes. No such charge was true, but Americans were clumsy in rebutting the untruths.

Luckily for Americans, Red propagandists also blundered: they may have been too sure of victory. In 1950, hundreds of repatriates returned from Siberian internment, among them unquestionably scores of Russian agents. Had these entered quietly, they might have fanned out quickly through Japan, widened the propaganda field, and exerted almost irresistible influence; instead, at Moscow's order, they kidnaped ship captains, held sit-down strikes in railway stations, rioted, and, to the amazement of all Japanese, scorned their parents and families, while they visited local Communist headquarters as though they were shrines.

Moreover, Kyuichi Tokuda urged Soviet authorities in March, 1950, not to return repatriates unless they were convinced Communist Party members—an act for which Lieutenant Colonel W. R. Hodgson, British Commonwealth member of the Allied Council for Japan, termed him "a heinous traitor."

Soviet treatment of repatriates, Red encouragement of violence, plagues of unnecessary strikes, and multiple evidences that Japanese Communists who talked so glibly of American colonization were more servile to Russia than loyal to Japan undermined the effectiveness of the anti-American propaganda.

Stupidly, moreover, Communist propagandists stressed issues upon which they were at least as vulnerable as Americans. They roused Japan against American occupation of Okinawa at a time when Russia held the Kurile Islands; they raged against American purging and censorship at the very times when the press was filled with tales of Russian thought control; they called Americans militarists and disturbers of world peace while Russian planes were flying over northern Honshu; they complained against American intervention in Japan's domestic affairs at the time when Cominform agents were demanding that Nosaka be punished for deviationism.

Soviet inconsistencies and blunders, together with the ineptness of Japanese Communist leadership, won the battle for the democratic cause. This was fortunate since the Occupation, having freed Communist leaders from captivity and having nursed them into prominence, had given Communism a start which, without Soviet assistance, it would have been difficult to overcome.

Tolerance for Communist propaganda multiplied MacArthur's burdens. Red leaders, from whom gratitude might have been expected, misrepresented Occupation purposes, distorted facts, and lied about their benefactors. SCAP received no commendation for democracy—all gains being credited to pressure by "the workers" under Communist inspiration—but was blamed for ills resulting from militarism and from war devastation. The columns of *Akahata* and of other Communist publications thundered condemnation of American imperialist aggression. The United States, they said, was turning Japan into a colony and was using the country as a gigantic military base. American soldiers were violating Japanese girls and, by vicious example, were corrupting Japanese school children. The growing corruption in Japanese government and business flowed directly from foreign capitalists who exploited Japan for selfish interests. At the very time when the United States was sending tons of food to aid Japan, *Akahata* reported that America was starving Japan by draining off its rice.

Yet, while this was well understood by Occupation sections, no one was specifically assigned to counteract the evil propaganda. Each section, closing its eyes to matters affecting other departments, waved aside the propaganda as unimportant.

Luckily for the world, Communism muffed its opportunity. Working by the book, bound by dogma, the Reds lacked elasticity. Because the Occupation failed to follow Marxian patterns, neither Japanese Communists nor their Moscow overlords took full advantage of undoubted opportunities. Unorthodox tactics might readily have won Japan for Communism, but Japanese leadership faltered and erred when at the door of victory.

Someone within the vast Communist apparatus blundered badly; its heads could not exploit their almost incredible good fortune. Elsewhere Communists schemed for years first to foster, then to dominate, a labor movement in key industries; in Japan the Occupation handed over intact hundreds of leaderless unions, well financed and numbering millions of docile followers. Elsewhere, infiltration was a slow process; in Japan, Communists moved in en masse to rule communications, transport, electric power, education, press, and heavy industry. Elsewhere, as in prewar Japan, Communists fought guerrilla wars against the ruling class; in Japan after the war the Occupation looked on benignly while Communism defied a helpless government. Yet the Communists threw all these great advantages aside.

Factional disputes no doubt played a leading role in Communist failure to exploit advantages. From the very opening of the Occupation, Tokuda and Shiga, heading a Prison Faction which sought to lead postwar Reds along lines laid down in 1930, sniped at more opportunistic colleagues who, as Lieutenant Colonel Jack P. Napier, SCAP's officer-in-charge of such affairs, declared, "valued personal freedom above principle." Later Tokuda joined hands with Nosaka, who brought the latest propaganda line from Moscow, against Shiga who attacked them both as bureaucrats.

Such differences reflected no variance in theory. Too well disciplined to differ on essentials, all Communists agreed on opposition to "American Imperialism," on antagonism to any non-Communist government, on unquestioning obedience to Kremlin interpretations of what Marx, Lenin, and Stalin had laid down as gospel. But there was disagreement on emphasis and timing: Shiga, for instance, held that the Occupation was the Red's worst enemy, while Nosaka recommended that Prime

Minister Yoshida be first deposed from power, and the fiery Tokuda clamored for direct and drastic action.

Communism won its goals too fast; its leaders failed to realize their strength. In growing labor movements, frequent minor strikes discipline the workers, flex the muscles of the unions, and convince the wavering that workers are prepared for common action. Japanese leaders, unacquainted with the power they directed, thought that such annoying gestures were needed also in Japan; that halting transport or shutting off electric power according to preannounced schedules would impress the public with labor's strength. But the unions were so strong in Japan that nuisance strikes became synonymous with strikes of an industry as a whole; and the public, unduly impressed by labor's strength, recoiled against the menace of a general strike.

A Russian intelligence service competent to observe, analyze, and report psychologies and developments should have warned that power politics would only invite trouble. Observers free from obsession by theory could not have overlooked important changes fatal to Soviet ambitions.

Unhappy experience had matured Occupation judgments; but, more than this, the Occupation had been slowly shifting toward the center. For various reasons, proleftist officials active at the outset either had mellowed or had been replaced. Many had gone home because their work was done, because their leaves of absence had expired, or because their radical affiliations had become apparent. Willoughby's running feud with Whitney and Marquat had inspired searching personnel screenings which had sent home a number of supposedly radical attachés. Unfortunately for Communist ambitions, civilians chosen for merit came to replace marplots or army men transferred to sinecures, and they were not as unskilled, as naïve, or as radical as those who had opened the Occupation.

Changing American policy toward Communism, while not formally acknowledged in Japan, was reflected in steadily increasing impatience with recurrent nuisance strikes, especially in public service industries. MacArthur and Marquat, his general most concerned with labor matters, carefully refrained from identifying these strikes as Communist-inspired, but thundered against strikes "called for obviously political rather than economic ends." Marquat vetoed a coordinated communications strike in March, 1948. Stretching interpretation of the JCS directive, he arrested a telephone repairman who refused to restore communications between Tokyo and Osaka; he charged that the interruption violated Occupation objectives because the British army newspaper, *BCON,* was unable to secure news quickly.

Railway sabotage became so annoying that in July MacArthur commanded Prime Minister Ashida to refuse to public service employees the right to strike. Labor Division Chief Paul S. Killen, regarding this action not only as a breach of fundamental labor rights but as a violation of the JCS directive concerning union privileges, immediately resigned.

Communists promptly exploited the legitimate outcry against curtailment of labor liberty. Labeling MacArthur as an insincere democrat and a hypocrite, they charged that Americans were enslaving Japan.

This vilification campaign, accompanied by ugly charges that some Occupationnaires took bribes, carried tremendous weight. The Occupation's indifference to Japan's national pride intensified the feeling that America was treating Japan as a subject race. All Japanese saw, and most of them resented, the special privileges accorded to Occupationnaires in railway and bus transportation; they protested the exclusion of Japanese from choice restaurants, hotels, beaches, and movie houses. Army regulations that had been drafted for protection of the servicemen were taken, by Japanese at least, as implying that Americans thought Orientals inferior.

Two eminently conservative college professors, a sociologist and an economist, recognizing the dangers of inhumane, thoughtless, and insulting army regulations, braved official discipline in a memorial which they addressed to Douglas MacArthur himself—in no sense, they stated, out of insubordination but rather from their fear as experts on social relations that undesirable psychological reactions would ensue. No reply came from the Supreme Commander; but his chief of staff, Major General Edward M. Almond, assured each professor privately that effective measures were in progress to remedy the situation.

Nothing was, however, done for months thereafter. On the other hand, American military police and Japanese policemen continually rounded up unaccompanied women, as well as women associating with GI's (though not with officers or civilians) and ordered them subjected to physical examination. As far as Japanese could see, soldiers escaped inspection or punishment.

A genuinely free press imbued with public spirit might have offered an adequate corrective through publicity; but censorship, unacknowledged but none the less effective, strictly banned all comment derogatory to the Occupation. As any questioning of Occupation wisdom was to court disaster and any defiance of Occupation order was unthinkable, publicists wrote and spoke guardedly. Researchers avoided studying the effects of Occupation-sponsored measures or suppressed hostile findings. All newspaper items necessarily were optimistic and approving, thus lulling Americans into false complacencies.

By denying a legal outlet to honest opposition and by classing sincere liberals with Reds, the Occupation restored to Communism the undue advantage which the Reds had thrown away. It conferred upon Communism the role of defender of independent Japanese democracy and honest pacifism.

Only Reds, exercising rights of free speech denied to their "rightist" adversaries, spoke freely, so that even conservative Japanese, noticing that only Communists stood publicly for Japan's right as a free nation, unconsciously identified "racial independence" and "restoration of sovereignty" as Communist monopolies. Criticism of the Occupation therefore redounded to Moscow's credit.

Thus, increasingly, MacArthur's men, identifying all criticism as leftist, committed the same error as Japan's prewar militarists. Sometimes, Occupationnaires correctly identified Moscow inspiration; but the accusation of following the Communist Party line could not have been made by any fair-minded person, as it was made by Occupation leaders, against the New York *Herald Tribune*, the New York *Times*, the *Christian Science Monitor*, the Baltimore *Sun*, *Fortune*, *Newsweek*, and the *Saturday Evening Post*.

Thoughtful Japanese, as well as Americans, spotted the falsity of such interpretation; yet the topsy-turvy reasoning attracted followers. Many students swallowed the party's promise of an academic freedom unknown in Soviet Russia. Under extremist leadership, originally spawned under Occupation protection, trade unionists continued political strikes and demonstrations. Red newspapermen, exercising a liberty never tolerated by the Kremlin, revived the lie that Japan had become an American colony; they accused Americans of profiting by the misery of Japanese. While silent on Russia's occupation of the Kurile Islands and Communist delay in repatriating Japanese war criminals, they blasted the United States for garrisoning Okinawa and maintaining bases in Japan.

So cleverly did Communists play upon the themes of race, pacifism, and patriotism that their Rightist enemies, whose prewar propaganda was reflected in the slogans, echoed the tune. Colonel Masanobu Tsuji, Tojo's master strategist, seriously proposed that Tokuda and Nosaka be sent as Japanese ambassadors to Moscow and Peiping.

MacArthur's information sources, purged of leftists, fully informed him of these abuses of democracy; but, for various reasons, he postponed corrective action. Subordinates apologized by hinting that some higher power, probably in Washington, had tied his hands; but, more probably, their own exaggerated assurances that Japan had become truly democratic had lulled him into thinking that action was unnecessary. Servile flattery that he alone created policy, designed and executed decrees, and judged results had captured the Supreme Commander's imagination. Told only in the past that everything worked smoothly, he could not now believe evidence contrary to the comforting reports.

MacArthur was not alone in accepting this myth of infallibility. So successfully had the roles of his military and civilian superiors been minimized that when, smarting under criticism for having wrecked a cyclotron, he answered truthfully in 1945 that he had done so under orders, critics mistakenly assumed that he was trying to shift the blame for mistakes.

Perhaps the disturbing news of Communist perversions caught the Supreme Commander off guard. Possibly he had no remedy. Quite conceivably while most of his advisers had matured and grown conservative, leftist remnants interceded for the Reds.

This was the popular belief among the Japanese, especially in conservative political circles. Yoshida's Cabinet, for example, emphatically held that Communists controlled MacArthur's policies.

As late as April, 1953, the highly influential *Mainichi* echoed these suspicions, suggesting that the United States Congress investigate Communist infiltration into SCAP headquarters, and recalling that fellow travelers and extreme New Dealers had imposed upon Japan policies which were too radical for America, and that MacArthur assistants had inspired Communist and extreme leftist activity.

Few Occupationnaires were conscious Moscow agents; but many of them, fresh out of college, were ridden by theory and burning to establish Utopia in a hurry. They had gulped wartime propaganda enthusiastically and uncritically, and firmly believed that everything Japanese had been part of a gigantic totalitarian plot to enslave the people, and that wholesale reformation was imperative. To them Japan was a vast social laboratory. Sometimes their theories paralleled Communist programs; often the Communists, to increase confusion, supported the innovations. But almost always Occupationnaires worked independently, sometimes even in secrecy, laboring at cross purposes, counteracting one another's efforts.

While SCAP thus floundered, the Communists, under militant leadership and following precisely drawn blueprints, capitalized on popular disillusion and governmental weakness. Appealing to an understandable resistance against alien occupation and to racial pride, they infiltrated labor, student, cultural, peace, farm, and informational organizations. Trained organizers, well schooled propagandists, and persuasive leaders took control of women's organizations, neighborhood meetings, mass demonstrations, festivals, and other gatherings. So many parent-teachers' associations for example, were Communist-led that the PTA became known as "red-headed cranes."

These practices, taken in conjunction with Red successes in China, annually doubled Communist membership. Registered enrollment rose from 8,132 in 1946 to 16,947 in 1947, 37,612 in 1948, and an all-time peak of 93,935 in 1949, and there were additional thousands of unreported fellow travelers. Many observers were impressed by the steady rise and took alarm, failing to realize that the enrollment was scarcely more than one in a hundred of the total population even when it was at its peak.

Much of the increase, moreover, lacked permanence. Some of it reflected Nosaka's adroit pretenses of pacifism. "We will not," he said, "take part in any war under any circumstances"—a pledge which many people took at face value, without considering that Japan possessed no war potential, and therefore neither the Communists nor any other party could possibly participate in war. Nosaka also promised, "Our foreign policy is one of equal friendship toward all democratic, friendly nations"—which sounded well until Communist definitions of democracy and friendship were analyzed. Registrants thus tricked into Communism were not likely to remain loyal after discovering the trickery employed.

Nevertheless, the Communist vote, which in 1946 and 1947 had hovered at 3.8 per cent, shot up to 9.6 per cent in the Diet elections of January, 1949. Communist candidates received 18 per cent of the total vote in crowded Tokyo and 20 per cent in industrial Osaka. Instead of the six Diet seats they had won in 1946 and the five in 1947, they carried thirty-five in 1949.

Some observers regretted General MacArthur's complaisance with these results; but the truth was that many voters, rejecting Communism as a theory and accepting Americans as friends, had cast protest ballots against corrupt and ineffective conservative candidates. The artificiality of the high vote for Diet candidates stood out sharply in local elections held during the same year, in which the Communists won but eighty-one assembly seats as compared to 431 seats captured in 1947. Moreover, only one of the successful candidates won in a prefectural contest, and five in cities; the other seventy-five were elected to represent towns and villages.

Some of the change resulted from sharpened awareness of Japan's dependence upon the American military strength. News leaked out in February, 1949, that Secretary of the Army Kenneth C. Royall had privately admitted that Japan would be untenable in the event of a Russo-American war, and that the entire Far East might be more a liability than an asset from a military standpoint. Japanese, panic-stricken at the possibility of being abandoned to Russian aggression, asked for assurance of support and received a promise that America would defend Japan in the event of a Russian attack, though MacArthur at first waved the rumor aside as the work of a "traitor." This was far from being a complete commitment but underscored Japan's helplessness. Japanese might not like Americans, but few desired Russian imperialism.

Nosaka's lovable policy might have overcome difficulties; but Tokuda and Shiga would not wait. Calling upon captive labor unions for strenuous support, they threatened stoppages of industry, transportation, and communication. By "wall newspapers" prominently displayed in railway stations, ration centers, and places of public resort, they spread wholly false rumors of Allied "crimes." Enlisting small bands of students, they turned schools and universities into hotbeds of propaganda.

As early as February, 1949, a report by Captain Paul Dupell, a Tokyo military security officer, that Red agitation was mounting in the colleges convinced CIE that active counter propaganda was essential; but when Dr. Walter Crosby Eells went to Sendai to warn against Communist penetration a small Communist cell, headed by a Red professor, raised such a clamor that he could not speak. Cells in other universities, carrying on a coordinated campaign, rioted violently under the cry,

"No more Eells." In June a Communist mob, protesting against lay-offs of surplus city employees, attacked the Tokyo Municipal Assembly, and one of the leaders fell to his death from an upper window during a scuffle. This accident, which Communists promptly magnified into the murder of a martyr, set off further demonstrations.

Before the summer closed, Communists had seized a police station, wrecked a train, killing six passengers and injuring thirteen, overturned a locomotive, killing or injuring three other victims, and rioted in Tokyo, Yokohama, Chiba, Shizuoka, and Niigata. The unsolved death by decapitation of the president of the National Railways was popularly credited to Communist murder.

Tactically, Tokuda and Shiga blundered by unleashing Communist violence. Japanese business and government officials, openly instigated by the Occupation, had dismissed hundreds, if not thousands, of excess employees. Skillful propaganda could have used these mass discharges, especially of Communists, as a telling, if highly biased, proof of harassment of the Reds; but Tokuda and Shiga, by demanding speedy retaliation, threw away public sympathy.

Belatedly, the Occupation turned tough. *Akahata* lost three-quarters of its preferential paper ration, Kyodo News Agency, hitherto over-friendly to the Reds, received a stern warning to report news more fairly. Dan Imboden rebuked the leftist-mindedness of the Reporters' Club, which CIE had been coddling. Men who posted lying wall newspapers went to jail.

Similar policy reversals took place in labor union matters, and pro-Communist leaders were cast aside for moderates. Robert Amis, new chief of Labor Division, in reversing former practices, not only enforced the FEC directives of December, 1946, that forbade employers to finance unions but ordered the Government to cease paying 8,500 union officials who, in the comfort of well heated offices, gave their full time to union duties but rendered no public service.

Collapse during 1949 of the gains won earlier by superior organizational skill disrupted the party, Shiga going so far in December as to attack Nosaka for "bourgeois nationalism." While party discipline hushed up within Japan all mention of the disruption, Shiga's attack brought echoes from headquarters. Early in January, 1950, the official Cominform news organ published in Bucharest, but dictated from Moscow, charged that Nosaka tolerated the Allied Occupation and was weak-kneed toward the Emperor. Nosaka hastily recanted, opposing the

Emperor system and calling for direct action against Western democracy. New sabotage, strikes, and riots followed.

No Communist course could have pleased the Occupation better. Hitherto the Communists had appealed to national pride; now they showed themselves to be slaves of the foreign Cominform. Heretofore they had turned to their own purposes Japan's understandable dislike for alien troops; now their demonstrations proved that such troops were necessary for law and order. Previously their soft, and often apparently reasonable, words had persuaded many waverers; now they so distorted fact that the falsity of their propaganda stood out. Clumsy Communist propaganda boomeranged.

TWENTY-SEVEN

War on the Reds

By 1950, even the blindest both in Tokyo and abroad saw the need for vigorous defense against Communist defamation. Washington cut away the gag imposed upon MacArthur and allowed him to speak forcefully without need of softness, caution, and circumlocution. In Tokyo, the days of delusion had passed, and no one mouthed tolerance nor spoke of civil liberties for Reds. Old-line bureaucrats climbed back to administrative power and clamored for curbs, which the Occupation increasingly favored but dared not publicly approve as long as Russia was ostensibly a friend and ally. Section heads usually held their tongues; but they did not check Amis of Labor Division, Napier of Government Section, Imboden of Press and Publications, or Eaton of Police Branch when these subordinates quietly suggested purging Reds from government employ. In schools alone, 246 were forced to resign on twenty-four hours' notice.

Whitney's Government Section, whose earlier purges almost pointedly had ignored Communist dangers in governmental circles, grew suddenly aware of Red dangers. When various ministries proposed to fire Communists under guise of a retrenchment program to cut expenditures, Napier assured them that Government Section would offer no objection. Some Japanese officials, indeed, asserted that Napier himself had inspired the action; but the charge was an exaggeration, as both he and Whitney denied that policies had been reversed or any government action had been dictated.

Whatever its origin may have been, the purge was effective, nearly 11,000 government employees being removed in the autumn of 1949 and the succeeding winter and spring. As in the earlier SCAP-directed political purge, many others "voluntarily" retired. The Communist purge, moreover, was not bound by even the vague generalities of the political purge; it was conducted on a personal basis, and the victims faced no charges which could be disproved and had no opportunity for a hearing, much less reinstatement, in the event of miscarriage of justice.

After the governmental purge of Communists, public information media answerable to Nugent instituted a similar housecleaning, in which nearly 700 persons were dismissed. When former *Asahi* newspapermen protested that the action violated the Labor Standards Act as well as the Constitutional provision of free speech, the Fukuoka Court rejected the complaint, asserting that even fellow travelers were obliged to obey Communist Party plans for violent revolution, and therefore civil liberties should be denied to them.

Industries affiliated with other staff sections copied the example. Banks, chemical firms, mines, transportation companies, heavy industry, life insurance, transportation, manufacturing, and other fields responsible to Marquat's Economic and Scientific Section purged more than 9,000 employees.

Napier, admitting that the Communist purge "militated against the livelihood of 22,000 people," and that it was undoubtedly based on SCAP's "moral support," insisted that millions of Japanese benefited by the purging.

Whitney, whose Government Section had been so grievously victimized by Communist advisers, rejected Communist opposition. When politicians and newspapermen protested the purge, he called in a spokesman for the party and stormed angrily:

"The Supreme Commander has fed you, clothed you and your families, and protected your right to organize as a lawful political party. He has literally saved Japan from the brink of impending disaster. Have you no intelligence or gratitude?"

The outburst, characteristically couched in Whitney's angriest style, mirrored his resentment; but the Communists, torn by dissent resulting from Cominform displeasure, dared not heed. Shiga pressed for drastic action, and the party tried to dismiss him as a Trotskyite; but he recanted in good time, and it could not do so. Tokuda, to save his prestige as advocate of direct action, advised disorders.

Thus, the Communists, protesting against tax-reform plans suggested

by the Occupation, staged ninety-two riots at tax offices, with 5,686 participants in January, 1950; eighty-one riots with 9,242 demonstrators
in February; and four hundred and sixty-four riots involving 103,702
people in March. Other riots occurred at labor exchanges, on campuses,
and at mills and mines.

Tokuda, seizing the opportunity to discredit Nosaka while obeying
the Comintern, again demanded in the Diet that the Emperor be tried
for war crimes. Party rifts were patched by a Draft Thesis calling for
immediate withdrawal of American troops, world disarmament, prohibition of atomic weapons, support of Russia, Red China, and North
Korea, and the taking over in Japan of a "democratic popular front"
under Communist leadership. The obvious subservience to Russia led
MacArthur to denounce the party as "an avowed satellite of an international predatory force and a Japanese pawn of alien power policy,
imperialist purpose and subversive propaganda."

Anti-Americanism flared glaringly on Memorial Day, 1950, when
Communist demonstrators stoned American soldiers in the only antiforeign violence shown during the first four years of the Occupation.
When an American court-martial immediately sentenced eight offenders
to jail terms upwards of ten years, the Communists retorted with charges
of oppression, enslavement, and colonialism.

The United States Army further roused Communist anger by cancel-
ing a projected meeting to commemorate the labor demonstrator who
had been killed a year before while storming the Tokyo Assembly. A
hastily called gathering defied the ban and adopted an "Open Letter
to MacArthur," complaining of American fascism, colonialism, brutality,
and violation of civil liberties. The Tokyo police, following American
guidance, immediately called off all parades, demonstrations, and rallies.

All this took place on the eve of election for members of the House
of Councilors; but Red hopes that violence would breed votes fell flat.
The Communist percentage, which had been 9.6 in January, dropped to
4.7 nationally and to 5.7 in local elections.

After the election MacArthur purged the editorial staff of *Akahata*
because of "licentious, false, inflammatory and seditious" writing.

This thoroughly justified action was accompanied by a less well advised campaign against circulators of the "Open Letter." Had the manifesto been ignored, little would have come of it; but, by raiding Communist offices throughout Japan and threatening to court-martial any
one found with copies in his possession, MacArthur's agents gave the

pamphlet extraordinary publicity. It was the very method of suppression followed by prewar totalitarians against whom the Occupation had complained. Four Supreme court judges officially stated that the SCAP orders concerning *Akahata* were "far worse than the censorship system as prohibited in the constitution and are apparently depriving the people of the freedom of speech and publication in violation of the constitution."

Although, with the nearing of peace, responsibility increasingly lay with Japanese enforcement agencies, the Occupation might have done more to aid democracy. Instead, having become violently anti-Communist, it permitted revival of espionage while reiterating warnings that Japan must not revert to totalitarianism. Police spies, stool pigeons, and other informers within Communist ranks reported projected outbreaks. The Occupation, pretending lack of desire to interfere with Japan's domestic affairs, offered no protest at the recurrence of a system it had boasted of abolishing.

Anxious also to avoid conflict between Japanese mobs and American troops, Occupation leaders carefully withdrew personnel from the scene of coming disorders but at the same time permitted excitement of public apprehension. Pleading inability to censor the press, at the very time that Communist periodicals were being heavily censored and suppressed, Nugent offered no criticism when scare headlines cited State Ministers and high police officials as predicting bloody riots.

Such warnings, while unnecessarily exaggerated, kept innocent people from wandering into perilous areas; but reckless and often unsubstantiated accusations that Communists, especially Koreans and Chinese, were engaged in campaigns of murder, arson, sabotage, and other crimes, violated the Occupation's own Press Code. Precisely as irresponsible press accusations had poisoned people's minds prior to the war, so a sensational press during 1951 and 1952, with the connivance of government leaders, besmirched labor, students, liberals, reformers, and other nonconformists while it was blackening Communist reputations.

In addition to the *Akahata* expulsions MacArthur purged twenty-four Communist central committeemen, charging that they had "sought through perversion of truth and incitation to mass violence to transform this peaceful land into an arena of disorder and strife as the means of stemming Japan's notable progress along the road of representative democracy and to subvert the rapidly growing democratic tendencies among the Japanese people."

Japan's top Communist leaders then disappeared, 25,000 Japanese policemen and the entire Occupation intelligence network in a three years' search unearthing only two fugitives and these relatively unimportant.

Akahata, however, was unrepentant. For perverting the truth of the North Korean aggression it was suspended for thirty days and was thereafter closed. MacArthur continued to uproot the entire Communist press, banning 1,791 "publications" within ten months. Only 24 of these were newspapers, the rest being cell organs, mimeographed sheets, or fly-by-night circulars; but neither MacArthur nor the police drew any distinction in reporting the extent of illegal publication.

Chief among the 24 Communist organs were *Naigai Hyoron* (Domestic and Foreign Review) and *Heiwa no Koe* (Voice of Peace), papers which, quite obviously, were *Akahatas* in disguise. Acting upon Occupation instructions, therefore, Toshio Yoshihashi, chief of the Attorney General's Special Investigation Bureau (the Japanese FBI), revived the prewar militarist practice of nation-wide raids. During 1951–1952 his bureau, working in conjunction with national police, raided no fewer than 4,000 offices and distribution centers, confiscating thousands of copies of the "Open Letter" or of the proscribed papers and arresting hundreds of suspected plotters.

The legal basis for such raids was weak. Constitutional bans upon a national military potential and upon interpretation of treason as anything other than armed insurrection had sharply cut away police authority to interfere. Jurists, however, noticed that the Occupation had thrown aside all pretense of press freedom, MacArthur in 1950 having forced the government to issue an Imperial Decree, No. 542, and a Cabinet Order, No. 325, forbidding criticism of any Occupation action or edict. He stifled discussion as to whether these restrictive orders were themselves constitutional.

Had not the Communists also lost their heads, the illegality of such action might have recoiled against the government, if not against the Occupation; but terrified or hothead radicals wasted this opportunity also. Some counseled armed resistance. Discovery in *Heiwa no Koe* offices of a few swords, homemade daggers, a sheaf of bamboo spears, and especially a few revolvers stolen from Occupation forces convinced the Occupation that insurrection was imminent.

Had Nosaka's advice of a lovable party been followed, few thoughtful persons would have been convinced that such weak "armament" portended evil to the state. Creation of a small classic-type party, capable of concentrating force at weak points, using infiltration tactics, magnifying petty irritations into "abuses of the Occupation," painting anew the horrors of atomic warfare would have won followings among students, workingmen, intellectuals, and perhaps among farmers also.

Instead, Communists once more showed bad judgment. Trusted party members, returning heavily indoctrinated with Communism as repatriates from Siberia, boasted loosely of "liberation armies" waiting to invade from Russian soil, and wondered why assassination squads had not wiped out American leaders and their Japanese cat's-paws.

Loose-tongued party officials, far from discouraging such ideas, kowtowed to the Comintern by apparently endorsing them. Kanichi Kawakami told the Diet that Prime Minister Yoshida was "a destroyer of patriotism," that the Government followed "militaristic, colonial, and slavish policies," and that the Opposition was headed by reactionary warmongers.

Probably few would have heard of this attack had not Occupationnaires matched the Communist bad judgment. A sensitive Government, with full approval of the angry Occupation, demanded that Kawakami retract or be expelled. His choice of the latter alternative did not satisfy Occupationnaires, who soon after had him arrested for circulating leaflets opposing their policies.

Many anti-Communists believed that such outbursts betrayed Communist despair at loss of membership, and attachés of the Attorney General's office happily pointed to a steady loss of registered cardholders from 62,000 in March, 1951, to 53,000 in November, and to 45,000 in July, 1952. These figures represented only avowed members, with no allowance for members who, like the leaders, had gone underground or for many who, while sympathetic, held no cards.

A certain degree of internal unrest also reassured Communist enemies. Tomin Suzuki, who as editor of *Yomiuri* had been active in the 1946 capture of that paper by the Reds, had grown disgusted with the "feudalism and power politics" practiced within the party. Terming it "a gang of gamblers," he complained that prestige depended upon the number and length of prison terms which had been served. Inosuke Nakanishi, a Diet member, also seceded, alleging that the party was undemocratic and "overmilitaristic."

These, however, were exceptional cases, the party being far too closely disciplined and too responsive to its Cominform and Moscow masters to indulge in mass secession. Nosaka and Shiga having kissed the Comintern rod, few lesser leaders dared rebel. Tokuda's fanaticism became accepted Communist policy.

Aping Moscow's example, Communists circulated a secret circular, "How to Raise Flower Bulbs," in which, like daydreaming and impractical teen-agers, they called upon youths to organize small "nuclear self-defense corps" of five to ten members, each corps under a military and a political commissar, and "risk their lives" in taking over for Communism schools, factories, and farm villages. Spiked clubs, bamboo spears, pepper-filled paper bags, rocks, and ammonia-filled beer bottles were to be preferred weapons in a campaign of violence. Students, day laborers, Koreans, factory workers, and the unemployed were enlisted for the struggle.

Terrorism ensued. More major violence had flared in 1951 than in 1949 and 1950 combined; but the 22 cases of 1951 increased to 77 in February and March, 1952. Excuses were flimsy—the February outbreaks being timed to commemorate an alleged mutiny, six years before, of the Indian Navy against British colonial rule, and the March riots to protest a conscription order that had never been issued.

On May Day gangs of young men hurled acid and fire bombs at Osaka, Sapporo, Sendai, Hiroshima, Fukuoka, and Nara. At Tokyo 6,000 rioters, headed by Mrs. Anna Rosenberg Fujiwara, who had given up her American citizenship in 1947, injured 1,402 persons, including 759 policemen, and wrecked American-owned motorcars. Other riots during May and June culminated June 18 in attacks on 68 Kyoto and Tokyo policemen. In celebrating the anniversary of the outbreak of the Korean War, Osaka rioters injured 30 policemen.

Hundreds of arrests followed; many were released for lack of evidence, but 900 indictments were returned for May Day rioters, and undetermined scores of others for disorders elsewhere. In addition, 1,420 persons went to trial for violating Cabinet Order No. 325.

In trying such cases, prosecutors carefully evaded basing charges upon sedition, rebellion, or violation of the Imperial Decree, because these would raise ticklish questions, especially of lese majesty, of which the Occupation disapproved; instead they concentrated upon breach of the peace, rioting, and the breaking of the Cabinet order.

Communist lawyers retorted by appeals to national patriotism. Copying the prewar tactics of political assassins, they excused their clients who, they said, had acted from high motives to liberate Japan from foreign oppression. If this failed, they turned trials into political demonstrations, waving Red flags, singing Communist songs, intimidating the court and witnesses, even on some occasion striking the judge and kidnaping the defendant. Since the Occupation had denied Japan any law strong enough to punish such offenses, the tactics often proved effective. After the enactment in July, 1952, of a Contempt of Court Act, innumerable delays so postponed trials that offenders were rarely seriously penalized.

Delays served Communism's purpose well in cases growing out of Cabinet Order No. 325. Communists who had strongly opposed the Constitution as a Fascist document now clung to it as the guardian of freedom; its provisions, they insisted, outlawed the Occupation-sponsored decree. Eventually, in July, 1953, the Supreme Court upheld the Communist contention, dismissing all 1,420 defendants charged with violation of the Cabinet order. Thus all "Open Letter" and *Heiwa no Koe* offenders went free, as did Kawakami, the former Diet member.

The Supreme Court decision also released seven Communists who, after once having been convicted by an American military court for espionage, had been freed when the Peace Treaty was held to have invalidated all court-martial sentences of Japanese. They had been at once rearrested and convicted for violating Cabinet Order No. 325 but were again rescued from jail by the Supreme Court decision.

The decision also avoided the necessity of trying twenty-three Reds who had been indicted in March, 1952, on the curious and never sufficiently explained charge of "trespassing, felling trees by stealth, anti-Occupation activities and intimidation."

Fears that the order might be outlawed had already caused the Government to consider reenacting regulations which the Occupation had found effective, but which had expired with the signing of the Peace Treaty.

After the Peace Treaty there were no ordinances to control subversion. To fill the vacuum, the Liberal Party, drawing partly upon Occupation practice and partly upon prewar peace preservation laws which MacArthur had condemned as totalitarian, proposed an antisubversive bill. Under the suggested terms, a Public Security Investigation Board, operating with 6,000 agents, would prevent sedition, hunt down sabotage, control and if necessary abolish political organizations, and arrest offenders who performed acts harmful to any American armed forces remaining in Japan.

Such a board, wielding wider powers than the Special Investigation Bureau which it replaced, would be empowered to prohibit mass meetings or other collective activities, to suspend or forbid publication of newspapers and magazines, to break up undesirable organizations, and to exercise many purge powers previously held by SCAP.

No postwar Japanese proposal was so vehemently or so unanimously assailed. Labor unions of every political type demonstrated against it in five nation-wide coordinated strikes. University students held mass meetings in opposition. Every major newspaper condemned the antisubversive bill as more dangerous to democracy than the prewar Peace Preservation Law. Hideo Ono, president of the Japan Journalist Academy, Masamichi Royama of Tokyo University, and the Japan Newspaper Editors and Publishers Association agreed that the proposed law was dictatorial, contemptuous of political freedom and was a blow to civil liberty. Under the loose terms of the draft, they said, even simple factual reporting would be impossible. *Asahi, Mainichi, Yomiuri,* and *Jiji Shimpo* unitedly protested that the antisubversive bill would revive the worst features of the prewar Home Office and the special secret police. Its vagueness of phrase, in reinstituting "instigation" as a crime, increased the alarm, for prewar law-enforcing agents had so misused instigation that MacArthur's lawyers had dropped the offense entirely from postwar legislation.

Vague as the prewar definition had been, the proposed draft was even looser. Though the Occupation conveniently closed its eyes to this threat, Japanese scented dangers to the democracy which the Occupation had introduced. They questioned the proposal that actions of an irresponsible minority might condemn a law-abiding organization, and they demanded clearer explanations as to what lengths would be permitted the new investigation board in its investigations.

Had Communists been content to wait quietly, legitimate opposing public opinion would, in all likelihood, have defeated the proposal; but once more the Reds were too impatient. Choosing the very moment when the antisubversive bill was up for debate and vote in the Diet, they staged their violent and purposeless May Day riots.

No more convincing proof could have been offered that an antisubversive law was necessary. The Liberals, who had already agreed to exempt labor unions and to define "instigation" more carefully, cited the riots as yet other instances of the two hundred assaults upon police, law-enforcing agents, and tax collection agencies which had occurred within a year. The general public, formerly opposed to the proposal, changed its mind, and the bill was passed in spite of a long and annoying filibuster by the Opposition parties.

Attorney General Tokutaro Kimura, whose office was thereby transformed into the Justice Ministry, and former Supreme Court Justice Goichiro Fujii, appointed as director of the Public Security Investigation Board, both promised that they would not distort the law to control free speech or to restrain legitimate organizations. Fujii definitely pledged that he would not introduce thought control, but Chosaburo Mizutani, a left-wing Socialist, continued to predict that the new agents would become more dangerous than the wartime secret military police.

The Antisubversive Act was unnecessary, as it happened. Kremlin policy suddenly reversed, ordering Japanese Communists to resume the Nosaka policy of a lovable party. Though the investigation board, the police, and various other law-enforcing agencies continued to predict bloody uprisings, the Communists remained calm during the remainder of 1952 and all of 1953.

However, the circle had been completed. Japan, after having tasted civil liberties while the Occupation flirted with the Reds, reverted to totalitarian possibilities when the Occupation and Japan moved to the right. There was, of course, no connection, but many Japanese mistakenly assumed that only leftist policies favored true democracy.

TWENTY-EIGHT

Trumpets Bray

The anti-Communists campaign illumined the inability of the military to use propaganda properly.

Top-brass Occupationnaires used power, not persuasion. By clever footwork they could have danced rings around the clumsy Communists, who in their excitement often tripped over their own feet; but demigods could not be agile. Dignity and aloofness called for solemnity, not lightness. MacArthur and his men issued manifestoes by the score, but only the more devoted readers groped through the wordy underbrush. They spoke on every possible occasion, but because they spoke for the ages they spoke in such magniloquence that hearers failed to grasp the simple meaning. They made monsters out of gossamer and squashed them with triphammers. People read and listened to the lies of Communists because the Reds, for all their falsity, were exciting and interesting; the people yawned at Occupation press releases.

Quite possibly, the firing of MacArthur did more to save democracy than most of his official pronouncements ever did. Regardless of his merits or his faults, his successes or his failures, the justice or injustice of the way he was dismissed, the fact remains that many Japanese, rightly or wrongly, had come to question American sincerity. Communist slanders and distortions had burrowed into Japanese minds and certain Occupation practices, however justified they have been, had grated on the nation's nerves.

Occupationnaires preached democracy, equality, and the dignity of human beings; but the army's fixed caste system, both against Japanese and against its own subordinates, advertised aristocracy, discrimination,

304

and the insignificance of individuals. The Occupation talked about the sacredness of constitutions, fundamental laws, and civil liberties but, on the plea of emergency and security, flouted all of them. MacArthur, in particular, insisted that the military must be subordinate to civilian power; yet, to Japanese at least, he stood as symbol of military, not civilian, power.

Increasingly, Japanese, far from accepting Occupation statements at face value, had begun to distrust them as meaningless, repetitious, or untrue. They listened politely and with straight faces; but privately many of them scoffed at oft-repeated assurances that militarism was dead.

Then, on April 11, 1951, President Truman suddenly relieved MacArthur. Feelings changed abruptly. The action may, or may not, have been necessary; it may, or may not, have been fair, but, it did, as nothing else could possibly have done, convince Japan that Occupationnaires had told the truth when they said that the military was the servant of the civil power.

"Had we done that to Tojo," said Yukio Ozaki, "there would have been no war."

Within the Occupation circle, the replacement of MacArthur brought important changes. His successor, Lieutenant General Matthew B. Ridgway, ended the isolation policy. Section chiefs did not relish his unheralded arrival at their offices at eight o'clock in the morning to make inspection tours, but their subordinates and the forces in the field felt, for the first time, that their services were recognized. New blood replaced men who had grown stale. The atmosphere grew clearer.

A minor casualty, unimportant in comparison to much vaster projects but typical of the change of emphasis, was the passing of the Great MacArthur History.

Half a hundred high-priced men and women, a majority of them receiving more than $5,000 and some as much as $10,000 yearly, had concentrated for six years on writing the Occupation history. Total salaries alone ran high as $1,000,000; and, with housing, Japanese assistance, equipment, and facilities added, the total cost probably exceeded $3,000,000. The entire staff knew that the purpose was to glorify MacArthur.

Yet, little was done. No final, comprehensive report was published, nor any material whatever of sufficient quality to justify the heavy costs. Early in the Occupation a Monthly Summation of Non-Military Activities was edited from data wholly supplied by interested staff sections; but even this was halted during the last four years of the Occupation.

The failure was not due to oversight nor to the difficulties of the task but to inefficiency and perhaps to sabotage. On September 8, 1945, a week after surrender, Adjutant General C. J. Engle called upon Mac-Arthur to provide "a full and complete separate history" of the Occupation Force in Japan. This was to summarize administrative organization, policies, major problems, and accomplishments, was to expound the lessons to be learned from Occupation experience, and was to be a guide for future occupations. It was to draw upon all available sources, both Allied and Japanese, including official reports and interviews with key personnel, and was to add such explanatory comment as might seem appropriate. No target date was set, but it was understood that the report would be presented without undue delay.

This comprehensive report on civil activities was to supplement an official military history of the campaigns in the Pacific. MacArthur had already been asked four times since 1943 to prepare this military report, but he had shown little enthusiasm for doing so. Some of his reluctance was certainly attributable to the pressure of military operations; but MacArthur also resented the Adjutant General's requirement that it be done under the technical supervision of the Historical Branch of the War Department General Staff, which must be fully informed of progress, and which must approve the final draft. This was not MacArthur's idea. As it was an order, he did not disobey; but he evaded the required liaison. Although politely replying to all queries and even permitting Historical Branch personnel to examine his files of official correspondence—all of which was also available at Washington—he volunteered little information, pursued his own methods, and set up an organization to draft his own definitive reports. He proposed to include not only events in the Pacific but also causes of the war, comments on Japanese politics, and accounts of diplomatic activity with which he himself had not been engaged. His editors proposed omitting mention of the other Allies, minimizing the work of the Marines, casting the United States Navy in the role of ferrymen, and eliminating the Battle of Midway as non-essential. The war in the East was to be so centered on the Supreme Commander that the official title was to be "MacArthur in the Pacific." The report as thus envisaged might well serve as a military autobiography for commercial publication.

The work moved slowly. Although completion had been confidently anticipated by April 1, 1946, it was not until seven months later that MacArthur received a preliminary draft. This he rejected; but he turned the 695-page manuscript over to Major General Charles A. Willoughby, who threw away more than half of it, rewrote 298 pages and added 187 new pages of his own. MacArthur also rejected this, whereupon Willoughby, in his own words, "hastily assembled a crew, neither trained [n]or experienced as writers or historians," and, with the able assistance of Professor Gordon W. Prange of the University of Maryland, projected a three-volume history of wartime operations, which Prange, at least, hoped would win a Pulitzer Prize.

Prange received every possible facility. By Occupation order, university, public, and private libraries stripped their shelves to send to his offices in the Nippon Yusen Kaisha (NYK) Building, all books, magazines, newspaper files, manuscripts, or other material which might conceivably prove helpful. Japanese political and service personnel were dragged to Tokyo to be cross-examined on their activities. Government officials were commanded to supply documents, and if they were suspected of evasion their homes and offices were searched.

A corps of artists, mapmakers, and illustrators, headed by the sculptress Mitsuko Araki, wife of a Tokyo University economics professor, drew hundreds of multicolored charts, diagrams, maps, and historical pictures to clarify the progress of campaigns. Mrs. Araki, a charming and remarkably sagacious social leader with strong political ambitions, had been a familiar figure in German and Italian diplomatic circles; but Willoughby, who placed high confidence in her integrity, relied heavily upon her advice. He not only gave her access to his own offices, but entrusted her with delicate technical and financial responsibilities relating to the history.

To supplement the "hastily assembled" group of Americans Willoughby recruited some two hundred Japanese and placed them under the nominal supervision of Professor Araki. At least fifteen of these were top-ranking army and navy leaders, some of whom had planned the war and most of whom had held posts of extremely high importance. Lieutenant General Seizo Arisue, for example, had been the General Staff's intelligence chief, holding a post comparable to that of Willoughby himself. Lieutenant General Torashiro Kawabe, deputy chief of the army General Staff, had been Japan's chief representative at the Manila Conference to arrange surrender details. Colonel Takushiro Hattori, longtime chief of the Operations Section, General Staff, had been Hideki

Tojo's confidential military secretary; and he made no secret of his intention to revive Japanese militarism. The Navy representatives, headed by Rear Admiral K. Nakamura and Captain Toshikazu Omae, who modestly referred to himself as "The Japanese Navy's No. 1 thinker," were equally distinguished.

This NYK group, none of whom was a historian or writer, combed Japanese records to prepare an official Japanese version of the war events. Supposedly their work was secret, publicity being so frowned upon that Willoughby flatly denied to Frank Kluckhohn of the New York *Times* that any such history was in preparation. Hattori carried the deception so far as to withhold from use, perhaps even from Willoughby's knowledge, certain documents, such as confidential war diaries, minutes of General Staff meetings and of Imperial conferences, which had generally been supposed to have been destroyed; he did, however, release during 1949 an almost complete file of Army orders and directives not previously available.

Because of the secrecy under which the NYK group operated, certain observers, among them an American civilian nominally in charge of the operation, considered the Japanese activity to be a cover to conceal General Staff collaboration with the American Occupation Army. Professor Araki himself encouraged this belief, boasting of his expertness in detecting Communist influence and in organizing counterintelligence work against it; he professed neither ability in nor interest concerning the historical tasks to which he was nominally assigned.

Hattori and his professional colleagues, however, pursued their work so vigorously, in the effort to ascertain why Japan had failed, that, a year after the signing of the peace treaty, he produced a four-volume Complete History of the Greater East Asia War (Dai Toa Zenshi) covering its causes, preparation, and development and using data not included in the manuscripts prepared for Willoughby and MacArthur.

Suspicion that the war history was not the major interest of the Arakis and of the General Staff officers with whom they worked was strengthened by the special treatment granted them. At a time when Occupationnaires were strictly forbidden to transfer to Japanese any food, clothing, or other commodities brought to Japan in American carriers, the former enemy war leaders received, in addition to extraordinary high pay, meals, lodging, liquor, cigarettes and other luxuries; and Mrs. Araki, in view of her status, was exempted from the rule banning Japanese women from military-owned vehicles, and received a jeep for private use. Willoughby closed his eyes to the strict military organization, maintained along traditional Japanese service lines, within the NYK establishment.

Contradicting Willoughby's assertion that no historical project was undertaken, Prange and the NYK group completed three manuscript volumes of war history, including some twelve hundred double-column eight-by-twelve-inch pages of beautifully printed page proof. These contained forty magnificent color plates of historical scenes executed by leading artists under special commission from Willoughby and Mrs. Araki; there were also some three hundred and fifty operational maps in color.

Completion came at about the time that MacArthur was relieved of duty and, according to Japanese experts of the NYK group, a military aide, hastily dispatched to the printing plant, hurriedly gathered up five sets of page proofs and then commanded that all other copies be destroyed, the plates broken up, and original material be trucked to a secret storage house in Tokyo. Clarke H. Kawakami, chief of the American staff assigned by Willoughby to work with the NYK group, repeated the rumor although not personally vouching for its accuracy; but neither he nor Prange denied the story. The military history, which Prange reported as having been delivered in complete form to General Mac-Arthur in December, 1950, was never published.

While this military history provided a general pattern, the Occupation history received even less attention. MacArthur did not welcome the assignment; he proposed to confine it to a bare outline, and when Washington overruled him, created a Statistics and Reports Division (SRS) to prepare the Non-Military History in its spare time. MacArthur gave SRS only the vaguest direction and thereafter ignored it. At no time did he evince to the staff the slightest interest in anything that it was doing.

Willoughby's hastily assembled crew was poorly qualified; but Statistics and Reports Section, later termed Civil Historical Section (CHS) was hopelessly inadequate. The chiefs of section, five in succession within six years, were neither writers nor editors; none was a scholar, and all were innocent of interest in history. The first chief was a former automobile factory foreman who applied assembly-belt technique to writing history; he drafted time schedules and set fixed numbers of paragraphs as daily stints. He and his successors were unhappy at being sidetracked into blind alleys that would not, they thought, lead to promotion. One chief, transferred from a drillmaster's job, threw up his hands and for six months gave no directions, held no conferences with his division heads nor with historians, and offered no comments; he spent his time secluded in his office reading western adventure stories.

Such were the chiefs to whom the writing of a comprehensive Occupation history was entrusted, a history which would summarize policies, problems, activities, and results, and which would be supported by a series of fifty-three specialized monographs covering every phase of Japanese economy, social institutions, and political development.

The list of monographs was curiously uneven. One college girl undergraduate was to write a monograph on the Trials of Major War Criminals; another monograph seemingly of equal importance, was on Wild Life Conservation. Political Party Development was balanced by Petroleum; Constitutional Reform, by Fertilizer; Public Health, by Arts and Monuments. Organization was chaotic. Legal Reform was separate from Judicial Reform; Elections (which covered the election laws but not the actual elections) had no connection with Political Parties nor with Reform of Legislative Process (which meant only the Diet's procedural rules); Fertilizer had no connection with Agriculture, nor Agriculture with Rural Land Reform. Public Finance was distinct from Local Government Finance as well as from Imperial Household Finance, and all three were removed from Money and Banking. The Purge was broken into Political and Economic, with seemingly no provision for military, educational, press, or diplomatic offenders. The breakup of big business was to be described in two separate and competing monographs. While full-length monographs were planned for Radio Broadcasting and for Theater and Motion Pictures, the population problem was to be discussed only in passing as part of Repatriation. Civil Liberties were buried in Police Reform, and Women and Children were incidental to Legal Reform.

To collect, analyze, report, and comment upon all phases of postwar development, CHS had a staff of about forty-five white and Nisei personnel. Of these fewer than a quarter were college graduates, and fewer than half a dozen had graduate degrees. Of the three doctors of philosophy originally on the CHS staff, one was transferred, and a second, an editor, college professor, and banker, was condemned as incompetent. The judgment came from a supervisor who had failed to complete freshman year in college. The third, with a degree in education, became the economics specialist.

Later additions represented so strange an assortment that other Oc-cupationnaires referred to them as SCAP's "displaced persons." A spe-cialist on ancient Greek inscriptions became the CHS authority on Japanese public health. A prize-fight manager wrote on fisheries; a gentleman whose chief interest was in South America undertook the analysis of the Japanese purge; a writer of children's books surveyed half a dozen widely assorted technical subjects—but the colonels in charge forbade him to talk to Japanese, to go on observation tours, or to consult even SCAP publications. One historian became so annoyed at interruptions from the chief in the front office that he threatened to go to law to prevent interference; another arrived at his desk with a service revolver and announced that he would shoot the next man who edited his work.

During the first two years the writing divisions were headed by super-visors who had neither writing nor research experience, had no college degrees, and quite frankly distrusted persons who thought such experi-ence desirable.

Such executives honestly believed that all that was necessary was to copy material verbatim from some easily available reference book, or to write from dictation, without questioning, verifying, or seeking to amplify, anything that men in authority told them. They said frankly that research was a waste of time, indulged in only by people who hated to write, that desire to investigate betrayed sympathy with prewar mili-tarists, and that study of results might discredit Occupation claims.

Since for many months no one explained the scope, methods, style, or presentation of material, and since CHS direction was in the hand of inexperienced, if not uninterested, officers, the young and untrained staff, bewildered by the complexity of their tasks and uncertain what was expected of them, floundered helplessly. A half-dozen, including the Ph.D. in education and a high-school history teacher, tried earnestly to follow directions but found that the CHS library had few books to supplement the *Encyclopaedia Britannica* and a dictionary. No works on Japanese history nor on economic, social, or political developments were available. SCAP publications were on hand; but there was no subject index and the shelves were forbidden ground for historians.

Historians were expected to gather their material from the staff sec-tions primarily concerned; but, even here, policy was uncertain, contra-dictory, and confused. Historians were bitterly rebuked for becoming friendly with associated sections; such fraternization tended, it was said, to destroy objectivity. At other times, the same historians working on the same subject were criticized with equal severity for not submitting the monographs, page by page, for associated section comment. With astonishing naïveté, CHS section chiefs, all colonels drilled in the strict caste system of the army, expected their historians, mostly middle-rank civilians, to require the colonels and generals of other sections to deliver whatever information was needed. If this were not done, one colonel suggested, the historians should proceed to search the files—a practice which, if applied to G-2, the section then concerned, would certainly have led to charges of espionage.

Even had file searching been feasible, it would probably have been fruitless. Few sections kept efficient files, and no file was cross-indexed; aides in charge of records were so inexpert and changed so rapidly that almost no section had a librarian fully familiar with its resources. Most sections kept chronological files only, and, because of storage problems, bundled up their papers after a year or so and dumped them helter-skelter into basement storerooms where they were thereafter undisturbed. Some officials, withholding important documents, carried them off when they returned to the United States. At least one section solved its storage problem by burning records.

Trained librarians were never numerous, and the few who, like Muriel Weins of CHS, served in Occupation offices had little success in establishing a central repository or even a general catalogue of reports, documents, and papers. Much of the opposition came from CHS section chiefs who, as nominal custodians of published matter (but not of correspondence or of intra-office memoranda) feared that such a depository would weaken their importance. Late in 1950 agreement was reached that outdated materials would be stored, and some effort would be made to systematize holdings; but the storage was to be made in wooden chests piled in tiers four-high so that access would be difficult, and librarians expected few good results. When the Occupation neared its close, all SCAP records that had not been destroyed were hurriedly packed and shipped to the United States, where they were to be safeguarded but without calendaring or careful identification of the contents of the boxes wherein they were shipped.

In lieu of documents CHS historians interviewed personnel; but because of rapid turnover in key Occupation sections (five different men in succession, for instance, having had charge of the purge within four years) interviews yielded little information of historical value.

Each section stressed its own accomplishments and minimized the work of others. Each section, moreover, wished to credit its personnel by name, and when CHS refused to do so each section wrote its own history; but CHS ordered its middle-grade historians to complain to colonels and generals that individual section histories were biased and unacceptable. Staff sections then retorted that CHS was uninformed and hostile.

No one was satisfied. Some chiefs, notably Whitney and Sams, protested that the CHS work was botched; and others, such as Willoughby, Marquat, Schenck, Back of Civil Communications, and Nugent, sent their own men to CHS to do the job over again. In September, 1948, CHS scrapped everything that had been done during the preceding three years and started anew.

This did not relieve the basic difficulties. The foreman from the assembly-line required all research, evaluation of material, and writing of the presurrender background on any topic, regardless of complexity, to be finished within two weeks. He believed himself generous in allowing one additional week for each postwar year's activity. This forced inexperienced historians, without training, reference data, or secretarial assistance, to ferret out, analyze, absorb, and write a complete history on any topic whatever, of any magnitude or of any complexity, within five weeks of the initial assignment. To produce a scholarly work was of course impossible; but the foreman made matters worse by insisting that the writers, whom he called "journeymen historians," stay at their desks unless he gave special permission to leave the office for conferences. Having no conception of the scope of its assignments, no knowledge of the complexities involved, and no over-all plan of action, CHS administration shifted policy irresponsibly and unpredictably. Uncontrolled whim caused one monograph to be rejected because the writer did not believe that Japan's great knit-goods industry had begun in the eighteenth century when a prostitute taught a Dutch trader how to knit. The monograph on Freedom of the Press was thrown back for rewriting because it did not list the names of ten "newspapers" allegedly issued prior to 1868 nor mention the prewar accomplishments of the Chief Historian's friends. The monograph on Police Reform was condemned, first because it was not based on the police bureau's unreliable reports, and secondly because it quoted "weird statements" drawn from those same reports. CHS authorities rejected manuscripts that did not wholly agree with the contents or the viewpoint of whatever they had read, or with whatever they thought they remembered.

Generally speaking, CHS regarded a monograph as satisfactory if it did not criticize the Supreme Commander, if it stated that all actions had been successful, if it avoided controversial material, and if it were copiously documented according to an elaborate and confusing footnote system.

The sourcing while impressive, was highly questionable. Not even MacArthur was acceptable authority, because he had contradicted himself upon occasion and, according to CHS, made extravagant claims for propaganda purposes. Anything, however, published by any other SCAP agency was acceptable, no matter how unreliable it might be. CHS historians were forbidden to cite newspaper accounts, unless an Occupation section assumed responsibility for accuracy. Interviews with Japanese were disapproved and first-hand investigation was forbidden.

While careless or amateurish SCAP papers became gospel, such established sources as Jerome B. Cohen's *Japan's Economy in War and Reconstruction,* the Mitsubishi Economic Research Bureau's *Japanese Trade and Industry,* Yosaburo Takekoshi's *The Economic Aspects of the History of the Civilization of Japan,* and the at least semiofficial *Oriental Economist* were rejected as unsatisfactory.

Monographs, therefore, failed to fulfill the requirement of "a comprehensive factual, fully documented exposition of SCAP activities and of such Japanese governmental, political, economic and social activities as relate to SCAP policy and action." The adjutant general's call for explanatory comment was ignored, even when MacArthur himself had made such remarks.

A code of rules, never issued formally but clearly understood by all CHS personnel, controlled CHS output:

1. No criticism was permitted of the Supreme Commander, or of Occupation policies, methods, or members.

2. All policies and actions were to be described as though originated by the Supreme Commander.

3. Monographs were to prove that the Supreme Commander quickly and completely fulfilled all duties entrusted to him.

4. No Occupation individual was to be mentioned by name, and no staff section to be identified. MacArthur was to be referred to as Supreme Commander, but no other official was to be identified even by title.

5. No mention was to be made of the Far Eastern Commission or the Allied Council for Japan. The Joint Chiefs of Staff were to be mentioned in footnote citation, but sparingly; nor was there to be direct quotation of their directives.

6. No postwar writings other than those issued by the Occupation were to be cited unless unavoidable, nor was any book to be cited if published after 1937 unless specifically approved by the CHS Chief.

Even with all these handicaps, speedier and more efficient writing might have been attained had CHS not been obsessed with minor details of paragraph numbering, punctuation, and insistence upon form. Manuscripts were rewritten over and over again to avoid even one word's interlineation, an erasure, or a correction in spelling. Any departure from a legalistic, dull style invited rejection; all monographs were stripped of human interest and of concern with human problems.

Not until January 28, 1950, more than four years after CHS was organized, was even a general idea formed concerning the philosophic history which the monographs were designed to support; and even then the idea was kept secret from the staff. New section chiefs, succeeding one another in rapid succession subsequent to the assembly-belt foreman's transfer to a mental hospital, vaguely hoped that some "high level historian, internationally recognized" might undertake responsibility. One colonel who had heard of Arnold Toynbee's philosophy of history considered him for the purpose until he learned that Toynbee was British; the award of Pulitzer prizes led to mention of Arthur M. Schlesinger, Jr., and Bernard De Voto. The publication of the *Literary History of the United States* brought Robert E. Spiller's name into consideration since he, too, had supervised a committee of writers.

Such Far Eastern specialists as Harold M. Vinacke of Cincinnati, Kenneth Colegrove of Northwestern, Harold S. Quigley of Minnesota, Hugh Borton of Columbia, Edwin Reischauer of Harvard, and Kent Greenfield, the top army historian, were then approached. Each, however, insisted upon access to MacArthur, freedom from military censorship, and independence of position; and, since these could not be granted, the editorship of the official history, to contain philosophy, causes, effects, and appraisal of ultimate consequences fell to the gentleman whose educational training had ended in his freshman college year.

Under such conditions CHS failed utterly to finish its work. After six years only a fraction of the commitment had been accomplished, and the great over-all philosophic history was virtually untouched. At that time the Occupation cut down personnel, CHS disbanding its high-priced staff.

None of the fifty-three monographs had been completed—much less the final history; nor had any Supreme Commander expressed even the most cursory curiosity concerning them. No specific guidance had ever arrived on philosophy, purpose, or content. Although portions of each monograph had gone to the chief of staff, his only comment—relayed to the CHS staff—concerned misspellings, poor grammar, or typing. One monograph had been enthusiastically approved by Dr. E. Herbert Norman, the Canadian Ambassador, to whom, for some strange reason, it had been sent; but CHS itself rejected it.

This indifference contrasted strangely with MacArthur's meticulous scrutiny of his military report, which he three times personally edited. The impression inevitably grew that "topside" cared little what was offered on nonmilitary affairs, nor how repetitious, how clumsily written, how elementary, how incomplete it might be.

Perhaps the inattention after all benefited bewildered CHS historians. Gordon Prange's military historians wrote a smooth, careful narrative which Prange described as "high-polished as fine mahogany," but which MacArthur pigeonholed. One incident, however, which spoke of failure led to the penciled notation, "This never happened." CHS suffered no such embarrassment; it merely was ignored. The Section made no errors of judgment; if events turned out contrary to MacArthur's expectations, CHS historians simply omitted mention of them. Thus, no word appeared concerning the destruction of cyclotrons, the changed Occupation policy toward big business, the political uses of the purge, the violent controversies over birth control, the unwanted Eurasian children, breaches of trust by a few Allied officers, or wholesale wastes of funds.

The caution proved to be unnecessary. None of the writings so laboriously compiled at so heavy an expense was allowed to see the light of day as an official publication for the general reader.

Antiforeignism Revives

At no time did the Occupation accurately report the true state of Japanese opinion. Save for the few Japanese-speaking military government men in the prefectures, Occupationnaires never knew what people were saying, much less thinking.

Top brass relied upon counterintelligence agents who understood their task as one of countering Communism or detecting ultranationalist revival rather than as reporting constructive trends. Section chiefs rejected pleas that they set up information gathering units. Though Herbert Passin was allowed to start a small Public Opinion unit group, he lacked the proper men to make exhaustive surveys and was obliged to draw material from well intentioned but untrained Japanese "Gallup-poll" agencies or from items published in a closely controlled press.

Such reports as were available exaggerated danger. They showed a rise in nationalism and a growing distrust of the United States. An *Asahi* poll in June, 1953, showed, for instance, that pro-Americanism had dropped from 55 per cent of the respondents in May, 1952, to 35 per cent. This was an understandable reaction from Japan's recovery of independence and from American failure to combat Communist distortion. It was noteworthy that Communism had not gained great support, the poll showing that the 0.4 per cent of Communist respondents in 1952 had risen only to 1 per cent while "neutrals" and "don't knows" had gone from 44 to 62 per cent. (The failure to balance, it should be added, is typical of Japanese statisticians.)

Lessened admiration for America meant only the recovery of pride and patriotism; but many Americans who recalled the prewar excesses suspected, like Professor Robert A. Scalapino of the University of California, that emotionalism might again be turned into what he called superracialism and superculturism.

While Westerners warned of possible return to antialienism, many Japanese, in the intoxication of newborn independence, were carried away by the Communist-inspired rumor that the United States was plotting to reduce Japan to the status of a colony. Among them were such military men as Colonel Hattori who, now that he was free from Willoughby's supervision, headed a move to build a new army, and Colonel Masanobu Tsuji who was elected to the Diet on a neo-nationalist platform. The unreality of the movement was illustrated by Tsuji's demand that the United States withdraw its forces from Japan but only after it had pledged itself to equip a 500,000-man army and navy, to present Tokyo with 700 transport planes and 2,000 fighter planes, and to look benevolently on the resumption of full trade between Red China and Japan.

Both American and Japanese alarmists were wrong. Japan, like every other nation that had weathered such ordeals, was proud and probably overexuberant but was not dangerously aggressive. Some foreign residents, particularly those tasting freedom for the first time, were cocky and unduly demanding, but none dreamed of domination.

Save for a few months during 1946 when neither the Occupation nor the Government effectively checked newly liberated Koreans and Formosans, aliens offered no threat to Japanese security, the attempted riotings by a handful of malcontents even at that unsettled time being at once repressed.

Nor, generally speaking, were foreigners numerous. Takuyo Ito, chief of the Immigration Bureau, reported that 633,699 civilian aliens resided in Japan on July 13, 1952. To them must be added some 120,000 soldiers, supporting personnel, and "dependents"; but this group, while large, actually formed less than 1 per cent of the total population. Moreover, more than 97 per cent of the aliens were Asians with traditions, standards of living, customs, and food habits not too dissimilar from those of Japanese.

Even with the inclusion of military personnel and their dependents, most of whom lived apart from the general population and came but rarely into intimate contact with it, American and European residents, the outstandingly different ethnic group, numbered 137,000, or approximately 0.16 per cent of all people in Japan. The number was rapidly declining: from a peak of 3,850 Department of the Army civilians (DAC's) the number dropped to 1,050 in May, 1951 and only 400 in January, 1952; and most of these separated from service soon after. Many of the 2,500 foreign traders whom Brigadier General William A. Beiderlinden reported as arriving between August, 1947, and May, 1949, had departed; and, while there had been an addition to the 1,800 missionaries, the slight gain was counterbalanced by the departure, during the second half of 1952, of at least 20 per cent of the nonmilitary civilians who had come to Japan. At New Year's, 1953, the census showed 6,556 Americans, 1,437 United Kingdom nationals, 1,005 Canadians, and 865 Germans remaining in Japan. No other civilian group numbered more than 500 persons.

This small handful of white residents—who as representatives, for the most part, of conquering nations claimed, and until 1952 enjoyed, extraterritorial status, thus advertising, usually unintentionally, Japan's inferior position among world powers—irritated many Japanese. Knowing this, many such residents consciously leaned backward with a refusal of special privilege; but their gestures of modesty or desire to demonstrate equality sometimes led unthinking Japanese to underestimate them as unimportant or as outcasts.

A very few thoughtless or callous aliens demanding preferred treatment as their right, misusing such privileges as were graciously accorded, or loudly complaining of what they regarded as shortcomings in the Japanese way of life, antagonized supersensitive Japanese who believed that all whites regarded Orientals as inferior. Exaggerated reports of such improper behavior spread rapidly by word of mouth and, while often balanced by other accounts of kindnesses or courtesies performed by foreigners, created a poor impression on the Japanese.

Late in the Occupation army leaders began to guide service personnel toward more considerate behavior; but at no time did any high authority endeavor to improve the standards of delinquent civilians or dependents.

Unlike most alien colonies elsewhere, Westerners in Japan generally had a higher standard of living than the people around them. Their special foods and their access to luxuries unavailable to most Japanese often made them objects of envy, while language barriers and cultural differences hampered mingling on equal terms.

Whether isolation was due, as foreigners believed, to Japanese exclusiveness, or, as Japanese were sure, to Western race prejudice, neither group understood the other. The foreigner, all too often, made no pre-

tense of trying to understand. Beyond a few elementary language lessons, which virtually never went so far as reading and writing, a dilettante interest in flower arrangement or tea ceremony, and perhaps two
or three visits to kabuki, the ordinary foreigner took but slight interest
in Japan's culture.

The four daily newspapers, in addition to the army's edition of *Stars
and Stripes,* and the half-dozen English-language magazines that served
the 17,000 foreigners paid relatively little attention to local Japanese
news and almost wholly ignored Japanese literature, art, drama, science,
religion, social welfare, education, or native music.

In this respect the postwar English-language press fell short of prewar models, certain earlier journals having devoted space generously to
such matters. Newsprint shortages during the Occupation limited feature articles, except in *Stars and Stripes,* whose interests lay in "stateside" rather than Japanese affairs.

The indifference of Occupation to cultural or sociologic affairs, its
pointed ignoring of human values and of other matters not directly
concerned with decentralization, demilitarization, or security, offered no
encouragement to persons interested in understanding psychologies or
philosophies. Soldiers were but lightly briefed on such topics; "dependents," not at all. No Occupation agency offered consistent, effective aid
to those few groups, chiefly women's clubs, which tried to glean accurate
information concerning the country to which they were assigned.

Prior to the war the cultural gap between foreigners and Japanese had
attracted comparatively little attention; but postwar insistence that
Japan end her cultural feudalism turned a microscope upon the foreign
communities. Japanese closely studied the social and cultural life of
the "Little Americas" of Washington Heights and Grant Heights in
Tokyo, the 1,700 American families living in commandeered Japanese
mansions, and the occupants of army hotels and other billets.

From the very opening of the Occupation, but more particularly after
the spring of 1946 when American "dependents" began arriving, Japanese Cabinet members seriously proposed that domestic help be considered as government spies. Although the suggestion was not accepted,
house boys, maids, and other employees in position to observe private
lives and cultural interests regularly relayed reports to the general
population of Japan.

These comments, gathered haphazardly by untrained observers and
repeated uncritically, must have been astonishingly confusing; but a gen-

eral impression evolved that foreign standards might be different from Japanese but were not necessarily higher. Wide differences between the urgings of CIE spokesmen and the daily life of Americans attracted particular notice. For many Japanese the home life of Occupationnaires failed to corroborate official statements that Americans revered democracy, equality, and culture.

Shortcomings seemed to the Japanese to be particularly apparent in the spiritual interests. These were not construed as religious but as intellectual concerns. Expecting a higher standard than their own, Japanese expressed disappointment that relatively few Occupation families displayed proficiency in music or art, or other accomplishments which traditional Japanese education considered as social graces essential for an aristocracy.

Americans read less than Japanese, and most of their reading was trivial—the GI's, in particular, being devoted to comic books, detective stories, and westerns. Armed Forces Radio Service broadcasts offered less classical music than did Japanese station recordings. Relatively few white foreigners attended Japanese recitals, concerts, art exhibitions, or English-language lectures; for months, indeed, these functions had been off limits.

Foreigners entertained frequently, but at cocktail hours, dinners, or bridge parties rather than at intellectual gatherings. Invariably the Union Club's bingo evenings attracted ten times as many people as did sessions of the Asiatic Society of Japan or the Society for International Cultural Relations. The Tokyo American Cultural Center long discouraged use of its 18,000 books by non-Asian aliens and, in addition, was closed to Japanese and foreigners alike for eleven months during 1953.

The picture was unbalanced and unfair, the same situation being found among most Japanese. Foreign residents, drawn from a cross-section of the younger American group, were certainly not chosen primarily as ambassadors of culture; but the reports contained sufficient truth to cause Japan to look skeptically and suspiciously at propagandists who incautiously proposed that Japan follow the American model.

Japanese, whose living standards had never been high, and who had lived under rationing or other straitened circumstances for more than a dozen years, frowned upon American waste and extravagance. Taught prior to the war to regard imported goods as "luxuries," to eat frugally, to endure cold, mud, and broken roads, to travel in crowded trams, and to endure privation, they were shocked when Americans demanded the identical foods to which they had been accustomed at home, overheated houses, smoothly paved streets, big motorcars, restricted special trains, and all the creature comforts.

As long as Japan remained subject to the conquerors, these indulgences could not be denied the Occupation forces; but, immediately upon recovery of sovereignty, the Government set itself to limit luxuries used chiefly by the aliens and to tax foreign goods which Japanese regarded as unnecessary. A third device, not officially adopted but generally condoned, was to exact higher prices from foreigners than from Japanese.

Since foreigners, particularly civilians attached to the Occupation, received salaries far in excess of those Japanese received for comparable work, many Japanese explained engagingly that to foreigners the added costs meant nothing.

The Government encouraged this discrimination. Rent ceilings held down the cost of Japanese housing but did not apply to buildings rented to foreigners; a house which a Japanese might rent for 5,000 yen cost the foreigner several times as much. Foreigners rented the cream of the residences; but heavy taxes sliced off great shares of the added income, so that landlords failed to profit as heavily as they hoped.

Occupation personnel with access to the post exchange or the army-operated commissary escaped the worst price inflations; but missionaries, businessmen, and teachers paid exorbitant prices for necessities. Foreigners with inelastic standards of living suffered heavily. Tariff duties of more than 350 per cent on American cigarettes, of 65 per cent on coffee and motorcars, of 35 per cent on butter, cheese, margarine, milk, and soap raised living costs. Additional controls, through restrictions on the use of foreign currency for such "luxuries," gave them an additional scarcity value that drove prices to high levels. Coffee sold at $2 a pound; butter and cheese, at $1; canned soups cost 30 cents; margarine, 60 cents; sugar, after returning to the free market, 20 cents.

Kiyohide Okano, formerly in charge of local government but in 1953 Minister of International Trade and Industry, led the war on extravagance, especially in such luxuries as suitings, fine cars, and television sets. He instructed Tetsuo Nakano, chief of his Enterprise Bureau, to slash currency allotments from $8,200,000 in April–September, 1952, to $5,600,000 in the succeeding six months. In actual operation, while total amounts fell, some categories showed heavy increases, the allotments for liquor almost quadrupling, and cosmetics tripling while machinery allotments rose but 50 per cent. He saved heavily in medicine and chemical imports, down two-thirds; in textiles, cut by half; and in foodstuffs, reduced by 12 per cent.

He further lessened allotments to $4,000,000 for April–September, 1953, and abolished them entirely thereafter. "The amounts," he said, "are small, but the mental attitude is important. Foreigners should eat food produced in Japan and should dress in Japanese materials."

The restrictions encouraged, if they did not cause, the closing of specialty shops which had mushroomed to serve foreigners following surrender, Japanese nationals being at first forbidden to enter. At least 900 of these stores existed in July, 1950, to supply foreigners ineligible to purchase in the army post exchange, but much of their $10,000,000 total yearly business was believed to cloak black-market operations, the 5,000 American Nisei and the large Chinese trading group being particularly singled out—though without adequate proof of any illegality. The number was therefore reduced in March, 1951, to 400 stores and in January, 1952—when for the first time Japanese were given access— to 330 stores. They were ended in October, 1953, when their currency allotments were shut off.

Treatment of specialty shops reflected prewar prejudice against foreign banks and alien businessmen. Japan, whose foreign trade in normal years almost invariably showed unfavorable balances, resented the draining abroad of profits. Prior to the war, home industry of all sorts had been protected by monopolies and cartels, government subsidies, centralized direction, and various discriminatory laws and preferential treatments.

Explicit provisions in the Occupation-drafted Constitution prohibited such favoritism; but new tax laws, licensing procedures, and foreign currency controls provided partial substitutes for outlawed antiforeign practices.

Revived national patriotisms accompanying recovery of sovereignty furthered the campaign to discredit foreign business. Few Japanese protested when *Yomiuri* sweepingly condemned most British merchants as "dollar speculators" or as tax evaders who "diverted 100,000,000,000 yen to illegal channels at usurious rates"—a charge that led the Finance Minister in 1953 to audit the books of 450 foreign firms and 300 private traders. Tokyo police in the same year raided night clubs patronized by foreigners but did not molest those whose clientele was usually Japanese. Only the newly founded Tokyo *Evening News* objected when the National Rural Police proposed in 1952 to revive the prewar special Guard Section that had spied upon and interfered with private lives of unoffending foreigners; by 1953 the conviction had again become deeply rooted that foreign businessmen were unruly, immoral, and often drunken.

Revival of prewar antialienism explained much of the burst of opposition to foreigners; but more was sheer reaction against excessive proforeignism during the Occupation. Precisely as aliens received, even when they did not claim, credit for the democratization and improvement of Japan, so they were held responsible for postwar lapses in public and private morals, undesired social innovations, and vulgarities in music, art, and literature. Admiration for American ways became less fashionable. French and other Continental influences won wider vogue, the smart set professing to see shortcomings in ways that previously had been popular. One shrewd observer, Toshiko Imagawa, explained pro-Gallicism by the remark, "There are no Frenchmen in Japan."

The trend away from America and Britain grew more pronounced when, following the peace treaty, the United States retained land-force and naval bases upon Japanese soil. However necessary these may have been for Japanese as well as American protection, and however profitable may have been the business thus provided—it was a commonplace that only Korean War procurement orders kept Japan solvent during 1951–1953—superpatriots disliked the continued presence of foreign troops. They condemned the Western insistence that foreign soldiers continue to be exempt from Japanese control.

By various postsurrender agreements the United Nations, in this instance a polite synonym for Americans, rented air, land-force, and naval bases, together with areas required for barracks, training, weapons testing, and recreation. To soften Japanese sensitivities, as well as to assure military security, actual leaseholds were seldom clearly publicized. Yukiro Iseki, chief of the Foreign Ministry's International Cooperation Bureau, disclosed that in January, 1953, the United Nations had 733 "facilities"; but as this compilation sometimes counted individual buildings as units equal statistically to each of the 44 airfields, he afforded little clarification. The total area throughout Japan held by alien forces covered at least 400 square miles.

Patriotic Japanese resented this diversion of territory to foreign control, particularly when soldiers stationed thereon were exempt from Japanese jurisdiction; independent Japan, they said, should not permit infringements on her sovereignty. Others protested when profit seekers ran up jerry-built saloons, dubious "entertainment parlors," and bawdy-houses to cater to GI trade. Such resorts, while certainly not unknown in prewar Japan, had been limited to the cities, for the most part; to introduce them into rural regions threatened the supposedly pure morality of the countryside. Antagonism was more intense against the rural resorts than against the 500 Western-style hotels which *Yomiuri* listed in 1954 as catering to foreign troops in Tokyo. At least $100,-000,000, *Yomiuri* said, had been invested in this shady hotel industry.

Logic and facts played no restraining role. Though the clip joints, strip teases, bordellos masquerading as "hot springs hotels," and unsavory night clubs were built by Japanese, paid for by Japanese money, staffed by Japanese, and served by Japanese pimps to lead customers to the 50,000 Japanese "waitresses," barmaids, and "pillow geisha," blame for their existence fell upon the foreigners. Critics of the aliens ignored the fact that even worse examples of the same evils occurred in every city of Japan and in hundreds of spa hotels where Japanese men formed the overwhelming majority of patrons.

THIRTY

Hotbed of Vice

Difficulties might have been avoided had the counsels of the Joint Chiefs of Staff been scrupulously followed instead of being by-passed and evaded.

Before the Occupation opened, the Joint Chiefs had told MacArthur that neither they nor President Truman desired Occupationnaires to live in isolation. "Association of the Occupation forces with the Japanese population should be controlled," they reiterated in JSC 10, "only to the extent necessary to further the plans and objectives of the Occupation."

MacArthur agreed that this was wise. Any order to bar social contact, he said, would be useless and unenforceable; moreover, it would be "violative of the inherent self-respect of the American soldier."

Nevertheless, top brass, apparently uninformed of either the directive or MacArthur's opinion, issued, under his authority, restrictions which prevented social contacts. Soldiers paid no transportation charges, but they were forbidden to ride streetcars, subways, ferries, boats, or—except in special cars from which Japanese were barred—any trains. Restaurants, cafés, bars, and hotels were put off limits. No serviceman could legally drink Japanese water nor eat Japanese food; if he brought his own food he could not have it cooked in a Japanese kitchen. He could not visit a Japanese movie, theater, bathhouse, or bank, or any private house that was surrounded by a fence; if he entered other houses he must leave before eleven o'clock at night.

The rules were premature. Except in Kyoto, fraternization had developed slowly. In September, Frank Kluckhohn had noted, in some surprise, the reluctance of the GI to make friends. "There is no fraterni-
326

zation," he wrote. "The man in khaki is not unkind; he is indifferent." Within a month the situation changed. During October the GI struck up friendships, especially with Japanese girls.

The unwise rules almost effectively prevented normal social relationships. Decent, well-behaved GI's who at home would have taken their girl friends to parties, dances, movies, soda fountains, or other innocent recreation places could not do so in Japan. They could visit homes; but all Japanese houses were overcrowded, and the ban on public transportation usually prevented a soldier's going beyond walking distance from his billet, for while theoretically he could draw upon the motor pool for a jeep his chance of receiving one was slim. In most instances, the GI with a girl friend had no place to entertain her but the street—or public park.

The vast majority of American soldiers were good, clean kids; but for these the army made no provision. A small minority went wrong, and for these the army made excuses. Top brass did not admit that its rules were bad but threw the blame upon changes in personnel. The seasoned combat soldier, it said, had been replaced by green troops, and the younger boys had gone to seed. Japanese girls seduced them to get luxuries, specially the excess canned rations and the cigarettes, which were then being distributed free to personnel already sufficiently cared for in their billets. The boys were swept off their feet by the deference and obedience of servile Japanese women. But the army did nothing to protect them.

Japanese had other answers. Foreigners, they said, had always been immoral. This, they said, was admitted by Westerners themselves in many publications. Missionaries, especially, had always lamented the viciousness and immorality of businessmen and diplomats. Drunkenness, vice, rowdiness, and wickedness, they said, had always marred the foreign settlements. The GI, they said, was only following the pattern of his predecessors.

This slandered the average GI, and completely ignored the remarkable number of volunteer GI evangelists who were holding impromptu religious services in many public places; but Japanese did not understand the impassioned preaching and only too well understood the small amount of bad behavior. They violently resented the assumption that all Japanese women were immoral, and all association must necessarily be reprehensible and vulgar.

Callous imputations embodied in the Occupation rules against the wishes of the Joint Chiefs of Staff unnecessarily undermined sound, healthy social relationships. The regulations issued, with or without MacArthur's knowledge, in the interest of sanitation—another imputation which, of course, angered Japanese—restricted many forms of innocent association but opened the gates wide to lasting injury. MacArthur allowed the Eighth Army to say that geisha quarters and houses of prostitution might remain open "until they become a menace." Official tolerance continued even after the Japanese Recreation Association advertised that 1,500 comfort girls had been recruited to play billiards, golf, and *torompu* (cards) with servicemen, to dance and sing with them and to entertain in other ways. If these were not enough, 3,500 more reception girls were ready to assist.

Conditions became so bad at Yokohama and Yokosuka that a navy chaplain wrote an indignant letter which was read upon the Senate floor. By coincidence, this happened immediately prior to the visit to Japan of a number of clergymen sent to survey the possibility of reopening missions; in consequence, the red-light districts were at once put off bounds. As Japanese girls were also barred from the Red Cross and other clubs, such resorts as the unlighted public parks became notorious. In December, 1945, *Asahi* would have printed an appeal to Japanese girls not to act like prostitutes in Hibiya Park and not to walk hand in hand in public; but a zealous Occupation censor forbade the item to be published.

The same restrictions did not apply to officers. For months after the Occupation opened, girls and women were allowed free access to officers' billets. Field-grade officers with individual rooms in the Dai Ichi and Imperial hotels entertained lavishly and far into the night; the sedan motor pool grew accustomed to telephone calls for transportation to take girls home early in the morning. Other girls moved in for more or less permanent residence, at least one billet posting notices that they must not use the washrooms from six to eight o'clock in the morning, when their hosts were preparing to go to work. In billets where two, four, or six officers shared a room, blankets were hung for partial privacy.

These abuses, too, concerned only a minority of Occupationnaires and could have been corrected had the top brass cared to do so; but, apart from assigning military police to patrol the Dai Ichi Hotel corridors at night—not to restrict the girls but to control drunken Russians —nothing was done.

Harmless fraternization was difficult to arrange, especially for the

GI; illicit fraternization went unchecked in top-brass billets. By the spring of 1946, however, when American civilian girls began to arrive to work in Occupation offices and especially after April, when wives and other "dependents" were expected, Headquarters and Service officers became embarrassed at the flagrant immorality. On June 7, Brigadier General Rupert E. Starr barred Japanese women (with a few exceptions) from using Occupation motorcars and forbade them to enter billets.

Motor-pool officers reported that their night business dropped 60 per cent immediately after the order was effective.

Starr's order so angered young lieutenants and captains at St. Luke's Apartments that they threatened, only half in joke, to quit the army or, if they stayed, to ignore the regulation. At the Yuraku Hotel, 600 junior officers signed a manifesto of protest; if the order remained effective, they said, American girls should also be forbidden to visit men in their rooms. The extension was not made.

Simultaneously, General Eichelberger, conscious of deteriorating morale, ordered his men to refrain from "deliberate, arrogant, bullying attitudes." Issuance of a similar order by MacArthur against flagrant immorality would have cleaned up SCAP without insulting the great numbers of decent Japanese.

Sociologists will some day use the experience of the first Occupation year, September, 1945, to August, 1946, as material for a thoughtful study of social and family relationships. The impact of different mores, particularly sexual, on thousands of mature men without their women, and without disapproving neighbors, in an alien culture opens the way for analysis of the validity of Western tabus and conventions. Occupation records would indicate that many marriages collapsed, that many wives returned in haste to stateside homes, and that competition vitally affected the behavior of many American girls. Drink and sex irregularities were only part of the story; the lessons might well be drawn upon to understand civilization elsewhere than Japan.

Certainly the arrival of wives and the subsequent establishment of permanent American-style living corrected much, but not all, of the maladjustments. Occupation billets settled down to quieter and undoubtedly more normal life.

In September, 1949, MacArthur at last complied with JCS 10 by orders "to establish in general effect as far as practicable the same relationship between Occupation personnel and the indigenous population of Japan as exists between United States troops stationed in the United States and the indigenous population of the United States." This was precisely what JCS 10 had contemplated in much simpler words. Approved restaurants, inns, cafés, movies, theaters, and other places of resort were put on limits; the giving of gifts was authorized. Previously, it had been an Occupation crime to give a cigarette, a bar of candy, or leftover food to any Japanese—an order which was ignored by probably 90 per cent of Occupation personnel, including General MacArthur himself.

The damage had, however, been done. Army installations had come to be considered as centers of vice, where prostitution, gambling, drunkenness, and crime were mistakenly believed to run unchecked.

Late in 1953 Chitose, a small community of less than two square miles in Hokkaido, became the symbol of army-camp immorality. Brigadier General Orlando C. Troxel, newly assigned commander of the First Cavalry Artillery, was shocked to find 564 houses of prostitution, 66 beer halls, and "hundreds of lesser sucker traps and deadfalls" operating so outrageously that Japanese called Chitose "the world's most evil town" and Americans nicknamed it "the sex circus."

Putting the town off limits to the 15,000 soldiers and airmen billeted close by would have been an obvious solution. Similar action at Sasebo in Kyushu, at Yokosuka, at Tokyo, and elsewhere had so hurt the pocketbooks of Japanese merchants that they had quickly remedied conditions; but Chitose was the only sizable settlement within miles of the camp, and all ground communication passed through its muddy streets, so that posting off-limits signs would work unnecessary hardships on Troxel's men.

Mayor Tomoyoshi Yamazaki, moreover, assured the general that a local Self-Improvement Promotion Association had already brought reform. Admitting the presence of 2,400 registered prostitutes, 4,000 clandestines, and 2,000 "onlies," he declared Chitose was more moral than other towns near military bases; it was, he explained, no longer true that marijuana was easier to find and cheaper to buy than American tobacco cigarettes, and that the Self-Improvement Promotion Association had so successfully opposed drugs that heroin and morphine, while available on any corner, now cost a dollar a shot.

Similar publicity about other army camps led to the screening of numerous anti-American movies, including *Nara Base* and *Kichi no Kotachi* (Children of a Military Base), which purported to be valid documentaries of vice, rape, and crime taken by telephoto lenses.

These supposedly pacifist films, some of them inspired or made by well known Communists, preceded other frankly militarist films. Biographies of Admiral Isoroku Yamamoto and General Tomoyuki Yamashita—"the flower of military chivalry murdered by a prejudiced Allied court martial"—the story of the battleship *Yamato,* and *Reimei Hachigatsu Jugonichi* (Dawn of August 15) revived Japan's patriotic sentiments and, as in the case of the Yamashita film, which showed three hundred Japanese wounded being bombed in hospital and American tanks driving into throngs of fleeing Japanese civilians, stirred anti-American feelings.

So open was the Communist hand in some of these pictures, and so obviously did Communists aid the distribution of others that the Motion Pictures Times pointed out that all the antiforeignism was aimed against the Allies, no major studio having filmed a single picture warning against the Communist menace or telling of any ill inflicted on Japan by Soviet sympathizers. While a special movie industry committee protested in February, 1952, against showing Shu Taguchi's film with the title, rendered into English, I Was a Prisoner in Siberia, lest it offend the Reds, no objection of any sort was raised against the more flagrant anti-Allied stories. Production of this single anti-Soviet film had been interrupted by pickets who warned studio employees against helping make the picture, by a fire of arsonist origin in the studio, and by the murder of the police chief assigned to investigate the cause of the fire.

Much unfriendly gossip centered around half a dozen foreigners, mostly Americans, who played important roles in one or more of these pictures. No one alleged that any of the men (one of whom participated in at least three of the pictures) were Communists or even fellow travelers; but all were severely criticized, especially by an evening English-language paper, for stupidly aiding Communism against the interests of their own country. Most of the men thus accused explained that they had been duped into taking parts, that they knew only the roles which they had played, and that they had not seen the finished pictures until, to their anger and chagrin, the antiforeignism became apparent.

Production by the Japan Teachers Union in August, 1953, of *Hiroshima,* a film containing sequences which featured a pilot's confession that Americans had killed 200,000 people as guinea pigs in the atom-bomb experiment, and which showed the peddling to GI's of bomb victims' bones as souvenirs, brought the anti-American tendency into clear light. Five major film companies declined to distribute the picture unless the offending sequences were deleted; but this the union refused on the ground that it "would nullify the purpose of the film."

A private viewing was then attended by four American correspondents, a Swede, and an interpreter, and the union cabled to the London *Daily Sketch* that these reporters had found no anti-British or anti-American propaganda; but two of the witnesses declared that they had been misquoted. A second sneak preview, given to eight physicists attending an international convention, also brought favorable reports, though the publisher of *Rengo Film News* said that the union had again distorted comments.

W. R. Wilkerson, president of the *Hollywood Reporter,* stated in an article that 99 per cent of Japanese producers were Communist-influenced, and that two executives of CIE's Motion Picture Division had aided the Red domination. The statement undoubtedly contained exaggerations and Noshinobu Ikeda, chief secretary of the Japan Motion Picture Association, answered that, while Red actors and directors were active, only 20 of the 270 pictures recently produced had been Red-slanted.

Almost immediately thereafter, Toho produced *Akasen Kichi* (Red-Line Base) which the Tokyo *Evening News*, in a double-column front-page editorial, condemned as "Anti-Americanism at Its Worst." The film described American military bases in Japan as centers of dope addiction, prostitution, and crime, charged that the noise of gun practice and the open lechery of soldiers prevented children from studying, and, continuing to follow the Communist line, demanded that the Yankees go home before Japan became a colony. Three of the careless American actors who had appeared in other antiforeign films also played roles in *Akasen Kichi*. Members of the American Chamber of Commerce in Japan, after hearing Frank Waring of the American Embassy report that the *Evening News* editorial had not been exaggerated, voted to ask Toho to withdraw the film; and the new Toho president, Ichizo Kobayashi, saying he had not seen the film, withheld it for further study and possible deletions. After minor changes, it was released in December, 1953.

Communists and other professional agitators exploited fears that vice would run riot in the neighborhood of army camps; but well-meaning conservatives also were swept off their feet.

Wildly exaggerated reports of illegitimate GI babies spread recklessly. Mme. Miki Sawada, daughter of the wealthy Iwasaki family which once owned the Mitsubishi industries, and wife of one of Japan's Christian ambassadors, toured the United States to call attention to the sad plight of 100,000 "children of Mme. Butterfly," who, she said, had been deserted by their soldier fathers. Masami Takada, then chief of the Welfare Ministry's Children's Bureau, raised the estimate in July, 1952, to 150,000 GI babies, while Mrs. Tamaki Uyemura, president of the Japan Y.W.C.A., sent a tearful "open letter" to Mrs. Matthew B. Ridgway asking simple justice for 200,000 abandoned half-caste orphans.

Had the Occupation possessed more courage, or been more interested in matters of humanity, these widespread slanders against GI morality might have been entirely halted; but timorousness stepped in. As early as 1947 the Welfare Ministry's Population Problems Research Institute proposed a census of the *konketsuji,* or half-castes; but Colonel Sams blocked the plan; it would, he said, be unwise to probe so serious a sore. To investigate GI babies in Japan might inspire similar surveys of 30,000 illegitimate children said by the Indonesian Government to have been fathered by Japanese; there were also rumors of other thousands of fatherless babies whom Japanese had abandoned in China. In addition to vetoing the proposed census, the Ministry reported, he suggested closing the Elizabeth Saunders Orphanage at Oiso where Mrs. Sawada was supporting 247 Eurasians until they could be reclaimed by their fathers or adopted by other Americans.

With nothing but hysteria and hearsay to support the inflated estimates, unwarranted attacks upon GI morality ran high. Children of the Elizabeth Saunders Orphanage appeared in two motion pictures that blackened the reputation of the American soldier, and one of them, *Konketsuji,* utilized Occupation Force equipment and personnel. *Konketsuji,* it was later disclosed, was directed by a card-carrying Communist Party member.

Yet, when the Occupation had ceased and the Welfare Ministry was free to investigate, a questionnaire sent to registered physicians and midwives revealed only 5,013 Eurasian children in all Japan. Mrs. Sawada explained that not all physicians had been consulted, that others had kept faulty records, that many children had not been officially registered, and that many more had been borne in secret. In August, 1953, the Welfare Ministry revised its estimate, saying that only 3,490 half-castes had been born.

The Education Ministry, however, confirmed the small number of GI babies by reporting in April, 1953, when the children born in 1946 and 1947 were entering school, that only 323 half-caste children had enrolled.

The number of illegitimate children was certainly exaggerated. Nevertheless prostitution, whether of the streetwalking type or by "onlies" who catered to but one soldier, flourished near army installations. The army contented itself with warning lectures, prophylaxis, and requirement of physical inspection, adding the injunction that soldiers must not "fraternize" too flagrantly in public.

Other misconduct was alleged. In June, 1952, Mayor Jutsu Suzuki of Kure complained of terrorism by British soldiers; a Socialist Diet member charged that Japanese dared not protect a girl from rape for fear of being shot. These, too, were exaggerations; but official British replies that the charges were irresponsible, provocative, and unproved did little to relieve the tension. Antiforeignism mounted when the National Rural Police announced that foreign troops had committed 3,382 crimes in the fiscal year ending April, 1953, including 6 murders, 229 burglaries, and 43 rapings. This, however, was a decline from the previous fiscal year, when 6,257 crimes, including 8 murders, 301 burglaries, and 103 rapings, were recorded.

The press, in reporting actual or rumored crimes by Allied personnel, increased popular resentment. Any misdeed by foreign troops received huge headlines, preferred location, and reiteration of lurid details; but when Provost Marshal Colonel R. T. Chaplin and Foreign Minister Katsuo Okazaki explained that the offenses were minor and were decreasing with tightened discipline the news was less excitingly presented. A sharply worded British Embassy complaint in November, 1952, against press misrepresentation which "seems calculated to rouse antiforeignism" brought no lasting or effective reform. The arrest of foreign businessmen for tax evasion and for bribery of customs officials, whether or not justified, received far more sensational treatment than comparable arrests of Japanese. The tossing by drunken GIs of three Japanese, one of them a pimp, into a central city Tokyo canal just before Christmas 1953 was magnified into an American plot to drown defenseless and innocent Japanese.

Misdeeds, whether real or imputed, convinced many Japanese that alien service personnel endangered peacefulness, morality, and life. Thus Communists converted even conservatives to antialienism and, when new bases were proposed, to anti-American demonstrations.

For such reasons, Uchinada became a national patriotic symbol in 1953. Near this fishing village of 1,120 households, located on the Japan Sea, Americans proposed to test ammunition purchased from Japanese munition firms. The area, a long beach backed by sand dunes, was poorly suited for farming and had been used by the Japanese themselves for gun practice and for a proving ground.

To compensate for taking over the land, the Japanese Government proposed to pay Uchinada residents an amount approximately equal to the $200 annual income received by the average fishing family, the people being free to earn whatever extra income they might find. The Government built a new wide road to link the previously isolated village to the prefectural capital and also spent approximately $1,000,000 on harbor improvements and public services.

Agitators, ignoring the betterments and making no mention of the generous compensation, filled the press and the air waves with lamentations that Uchinada was being martyred; incessant gunfire, it was said, would scare away the fish, and Uchinada's people would be starved. The prefectural governor and the local Diet members, all of whom were stanch conservatives, and one of whom was Colonel Tsuji, protested to Tokyo; the railwaymen's union threatened refusal to transport materials needed by the proving ground, and local teachers warned that the twenty Americans to be assigned there would corrupt the youth of Uchinada. Even after the Government raised the compensation to be paid to four times the previous average annual income, student and labor delegations from other parts of Japan hurried to Uchinada to assist in demonstrations. When, in June, 1953, the Government, overriding protests, granted the lease, Uchinada residents started sit-down strikes from which they had to be removed forcibly.

Daily repetition of lies, insults, libels, and misrepresentations revived the xenophobia which had marred the late 1920's and the early 1930's. Occupationnaires misjudged the campaign by ascribing it entirely to Communist anxiety to discredit Western democracies; the antiforeign movement had deeper psychologic roots. Partly it had developed out of an innate inferiority complex heightened and strengthened by defeat and subjection, followed by an imposed peace, a security pact forced upon the nation, and continuance of foreign troops on sovereign Japan's soil. With Japan becoming what Communists invariably described as an American colony, struggle for freedom and self-rule assumed the guise of heroic patriotism.

Mamoru Shigemitsu, Progressive Party leader and Yoshida's rival for the premiership, explained the rapid change from obedience to Western wishes to frank suspicion of Western ways by referring to what he described as the age-old Oriental custom of fawning upon the mighty only to besmirch the great as soon as they had lost their power.

Coupled with these tendencies was a realization that Japan, no longer subject to conquerors, was being courted by both democracies and Soviet powers, from either of whom she might receive reward. Under such circumstances Japan, to heighten her bargaining ability, retired into her old secretive shell, hiding all she could from foreigners and discouraging alien ways.

Thus, inevitably, nationalism revived and patriotism flourished; but Japan in her exuberance exaggerated nationalism into a glorification of all things Nipponese—including often the discredited past—and perverted patriotism by confusing it with antiforeignism.

More tactful diplomacy would have given Japan a stronger sense of equality among free nations. Closer attention to ruffled Japanese feelings, even at the risk of violating minor points of protocol, could readily have saved the day. But diplomats in Washington and Tokyo lacked understanding, plasticity, and sensitivity.

THIRTY-ONE

In Retrospect

Viewed in retrospect, nine years after the surrender, the brightness of the Occupation faded; it had become obvious that Macmahon Ball had been shrewd in saying, back in 1947, that MacArthur erred not in accomplishing so little but in claiming too much.

Little remained of the highly lauded innovations and reforms. Launched amid fanfares of publicity and promises, most of them had been repealed or, if remaining on the books, had been distorted or ignored. The Emperor was as popular as ever in the past, perhaps more so; except in mere lip service none seriously upheld the fumbling Diet as the highest organ of the state. The purge had been abandoned and forgotten, except by victims who resented its unfairness; police and bureaucrats regained their old control if, indeed, they ever really had loosed their hold. Zaibatsu firms revived under their once proscribed names; political and gang bosses flourished; decentralization of schools and local government reversed itself and old-line thoughts and methods reappeared in editorial offices, movie studios, and courts of law. Americans who had hailed Japan's constitutional renunciation of armed force were offering as gifts large fleets of warships, munitions in huge quantities, money to rebuild an army, and skilled instructors to teach Japan to fight. Army pride had been revived, crowds thrilled to the Navy March, and Japan's Wild Eagles were returning to the skies.

If these reversals were fair criteria, as cynics said, the Occupation had failed. For those who, like many top-brass Occupationnaires, cared little for the intangibles of social attitudes, human values, and the spirituality of which MacArthur talked so often, the proofs were convincing;

337

many Occupation chiefs, despite their pride that the Occupation had survived without a single major hostility, and that they had returned postwar Japan to the economic level of 1936, must have been deeply saddened.

But those who, like Ridgway, Clark, and Hall, had broken the chains that kept the top brass imprisoned in Tokyo, who, unlike MacArthur, mingled freely with others than top officials on their best sycophantic behavior, and who saw individuals as something more than units in a table of statistics, knew that much had been accomplished.

Japan had not become Utopia. No nation could gain freedom and democracy by fiat or by proclamation. No serious student of sociology, of history, of psychology, or even of Japan itself could have supposed, as did MacArthur, that he had "almost overnight torn asunder a theory and practice of life built upon two thousand years of history and legend and tradition." To make the claim was to confess ignorance of actual conditions and to invite the equally untrue retort that Japanese remained at heart a feudalistic people.

Nor was there spiritual revolution: to assert that war, defeat, and Occupation had wrought such a miracle within a few short months, weakened faith in the Occupation's wisdom. Japan knew well that graft, crime, and corruption, malfeasance and eroticism had increased, and that Occupationnaires were very well aware of the conditions.

In some respects, the Occupation was its own worst enemy. Committed to democracy, in which it earnestly believed, but which it often did not practice, it copied prewar Japanese methods against which it thundered condemnation. Secret police, censorship and inquisitorial methods, dictation to the Diet, orders to the courts, commandeering of goods, facilities, and services, discrimination against the lower ranks— all these existed in the name of freedom, equality, and democracy. New ways were forced upon Japan in precisely the same manner as dictators had forced totalitarianism on the Empire. MacArthur and his aides insisted on the dignity of individuals, in which each sincerely believed; yet some high officials always, and many others sometimes, behaved as haughtily as any prewar Japanese.

Japan, to be sure, expected nothing else; she herself had so behaved in occupying China, the Philippines, and other conquered areas. Many Occupationnaires, moreover, knowing that Japan had brought on war, and only too painfully conscious of the cruelty inflicted on war prisoners, argued that Japanese deserved no consideration. Some recalled Mac-

Arthur's testy denial that he intended to be "soft" against Japan, and that he had assured an editor that for years Japan would be hard pressed to get enough to eat.

The evil did not lie in Occupation firmness nor in the policy of retribution nor even (where it existed) of reprisal; it lay in the continued denial that undemocratic practices were being followed. Officially there was no censorship, no dictation to the government, no punitive purge, no unnecessary denial of civil liberty, no militarism, and no reversal of policy. The pretense of noninterference in Japanese domestic affairs, though never laudable, may have been necessary during the first weeks of the Occupation; but Occupation section chiefs angrily insisted on the myth long after every informed Japanese knew that he must slavishly obey the slightest Occupation wish.

No one denied the necessity of safeguards against danger; failure to provide them would certainly merit court martial, but Occupationnaires trembled at shadows. Many of them came, at the time of MacArthur's "greatest gamble in history," expecting to be ambushed; as late as May, 1946, when this peril had been shown to be imaginary, MacArthur's press agents dreamed up a murder plot of which no more was ever heard. For months, high policy makers shuddered at a non-existent Rightist conspiracy to bring back Tojoism; and they hid, or scattered, the ashes of executed war criminals lest Japanese, who heartily hated the memory of the leaders who had brought them to destruction, make shrines above the martyrs' graves. Though Japan had been disarmed so completely that, as the Occupation said, she could not make war for a century, a scared SCAP filled a reporter's ears with tales of a horrible plot whereby Japan would retake Korea and Manchuria.

These exaggerated fears of reactionary ghosts, the continued (and certainly understandable) suspicion of treachery and insincerity by Japanese, the practice of saying one thing and doing the opposite, the unreality of official statements, and the silencing of criticism—all hurt the Occupation's reputation. Rightly or wrongly, justly or unfairly, many Japanese considered that Americans were hypocritical and unreliable. By shutting its eyes to reality and by rebuking even the mildest opposition as Communist-inspired, the Occupation jeopardized its cause.

Yet, despite the Occupation and despite the cancellation of its edicts, important changes had occurred. The Bourbons had been discredited; war leaders, deflated; and bureaucrats had been jolted out of their insufferable arrogance. Japanese, who once had prided themselves on their uniqueness, cast off their insularity. The cake of custom had been broken, and initiative, released from its imprisonment, had opportunity for growth. Conservatism had been branded as unfashionable, and Japanese had regained their old-time love of novelty. The people were holding up their heads; laborers and farmers, especially, were displaying self-respect.

These were intangibles which could not be expressed statistically, but which were more impressive in the long run than the rise in iron and steel production, the number of visitors at record recitals, the intrigues of party politics, or the numerous other matters which Occupationnaires so fully reported. They were also matters for which no Occupation staff section was responsible, and for which none of the more than two thousand major and three thousand minor directives had been issued.

Probably the shock of defeat, possibly by a stretch of the imagination the Imperial proclamation ending the war, had shaken Japan from its complacency—as MacArthur seemed to imply in his premature claim that a spiritual revolution had been accomplished before the Occupation had more than begun. Undoubtedly the GI's helped. While never the angelic missionaries portrayed by Douglas MacArthur in September, 1945, foreign troops were far from being the beasts and devils against whom Tojo warned. The joking boys who gave candy bars to children —against strict army orders—who were polite to pan-pans, who did not dive headfirst into crowded trams as did teen-aged Japanese, and who danced at local festivals, committed grievous errors against Japan's etiquette; but they smashed the myth that Westerners were crass materialists.

They did this, too, in the face of Occupation warnings that they must not mix too freely. The American radio almost hourly warned against health dangers, especially against local foods, though Director Miller of the Yokohama Bluff Hospital declared that native food was more nutritious, of higher quality and with more vitamins than that on sale in army commissaries. So terrifying had been warnings against unsanitary practices that one colonel imported to Japan several lockers full of "good old Mississippi soil" in which to grow his own supply of vegetables.

GI's were excellent ambassadors even though a few reflected little credit on their uniform, and thousands of Occupationnaires will always be remembered for their helpfulness to Japanese; but ignorance, suspicion, and intolerance of many top policy makers stunted the growth of Japanese democracy. Whatever may have been the reason, even though it were the sordid argument that democracy paid bigger dividends, Japan honestly desired reform. Naturally, she preferred an Oriental system; but this, to most section chiefs, seemed merely to be a device to guarantee reaction. Top policy makers almost unanimously took an adamant stand that, regardless of background, Japan must accept American ideas developed for people of Anglo-Saxon heritage.

Too large and too sudden doses of Westernism brought reaction. Japanese psychologies had not changed; it would be foolish to suppose that eight years of revolutionary impact could change psychic channels cut by two thousand years of history. Though Japanese were far more eager to learn of liberalism, freedom, and democracy than the Occupation was to explain what these virtue words implied, they rallied to defend their folkways and traditions. But, save for planned outbursts by Communist fanatics, the reaction was peaceful, selective, and, in the main, intelligent. Rejecting extremist ideas, Japan wisely retained the best of its past culture and adopted, as in so many past instances, the more desirable of foreign institutions.

From the standpoint of statistically minded Occupationnaires, the process was unfortunate. To casual observers the junking of Occupation-sponsored reforms spelled only reaction; many superficial reporters were tempted to think that Japan was hurrying back to prewar reaction and, quite possibly, to another Tojo. Such men missed the essential spirit of a new, reborn Japan.

New Japan, Shin Nippon, bore but slight resemblance to the plans drafted in Washington and claimed by MacArthur as having been successfully applied. No revolution had been accomplished, but a highly successful Renaissance had been experienced. Students versed in history and apt at recognizing parallels would have been struck by similarities between the postwar period and the Meiji Restoration; but, though Japanese repeatedly called attention to the precedent, Occupationnaires, intent upon the present, rejected their suggestions.

This was unfortunate. Study of the past would have shown the futility of imposing reform from above, especially by alien masters, would have prevented the folly of appliquéing Western forms on Oriental foundations, and would have kept the Occupation from ignoring native leadership. It would have made it clear that the mere issuing of a directive was not enough, and that supervision and constant vigilance by skilled administrators were at least as necessary as Olympian detachment; it would have prevented MacArthur from believing that his orders were being carried out when, all too often, they were ceremoniously received and carefully ignored. Ridgway and Clark, who moved out among the people, knew the truth as Douglas MacArthur never did.

Credit for the success of the Occupation, in short, belongs to two groups whose praise the leaders seldom sang. The first group was the devoted middle brass, working without adequate direction, often under the implied disapproval of their superiors and—as far as much direct help was concerned—in direct violation of Occupation orders. The second group was an amazingly cooperative Japanese populace. Together they achieved a Renaissance which, while not unique in history, ranks with the major American accomplishments.

No stronger evidence can be found that honest people of good will, working harmoniously, can build a world of peace and fellowship.

Sources

The greater portion of this book has grown out of personal experience.

The writer, well acquainted by residence, work, and study with prewar Japan, enjoyed special advantages. As research specialist for Japan in the Office of War Information, he studied, conferred, and wrote widely on policies to be followed after the war should end; he supplemented this experience by lectures and conferences with service officers being trained at Civil Affairs Training Schools.

Following surrender, he entered Government Section in Tokyo where, during 1946 and 1947, he helped draft the new Japanese Constitution, participated in numerous staff discussions on administrative, political, and purge problems, and, in addition to sheaves of special staff studies, produced daily, weekly, and monthly news reports for General MacArthur's private information.

In this capacity, he interviewed Premiers, Cabinet Ministers, Diet members, and Government officials.

As an editor of publications in Gen. Willoughby's Historical Division during 1947–1948, he prepared papers on surrender negotiations, on the initial arrival of Allied troops in Japan, on repatriation, and on Army activities in the Occupied Areas. He also indoctrinated Counter Intelligence officers on political developments.

As chief editor of the Monthly Summation of Non-Military Activities and as chief of the Political and Social Affairs Division of Civil Historical Section (formerly Statistics and Reports Section), during 1948–1951, he directed preparation of elaborate monographs covering wide ranges of interest and acted as adviser on papers dealing with economic affairs.

Basic official material includes directives from the Joint Chiefs of

Staff (originally highly classified, later cleared for general use), instructions from the Supreme Commander for the Allied Powers to the Japanese Government (SCAPINS), as well as laws, ordinances, and regulations resulting therefrom, the Official Gazette, and various explanatory and statistical documents issued by the Japanese and American Governments. Publications of SCAP staff sections have been particularly helpful, especially those of Government, Natural Resources, Economic and Scientific, Health and Welfare, and Civil Information and Education Sections.

In addition, staff studies, memoranda, and other papers filed in SCAP offices were utilized, wherever security permitted, and SCAP attachés, ranging from generals to low-rank civilians, were interviewed. Newspaper and magazine articles, both in Japanese and in English, provided helpful clues for research.

The writer was a regularly assigned observer at the biweekly meetings of the Allied Council for Japan. He has talked to hundreds of Occupationnaires and Japanese citizens whom he thanks for their cooperation and especially for their patience in enduring his broken Japanese and his insatiable and often, no doubt, childish curiosity. He has ransacked the libraries of Tokyo University and Kokusai Bunka Shinkokai (Society for International Cultural Relations), searched Occupation files for all material that may be generally published, and enjoyed special privileges in seeing Japanese official records. To the persons who made this possible the author is extremely grateful.

He wishes, especially, to thank Professor Harold M. Vinacke of the University of Cincinnati, Kenneth W. Colegrove of Northwestern University, and Gordon T. Bowles and Mrs. Bowles of the University of Tokyo for their encouragement and Colonels Charles L. Kades, Ronald Ring, and Daniel B. Hundley, who knew what a history should include. Particularly to be thanked are Mother Elizabeth Britt of the International College of the Sacred Heart and Dr. Donald R. Renard and Dr. Lyne S. Few of the United States Education Commission in Japan for the opportunity they gave to the author to live in Japan during 1952–1953 as a Fulbright exchange professor; and Tokugen Yamamoto of the Commission's staff for his tireless contributions. Miss Helen M. Uno, editor of *Contemporary Japan* and of the invaluable *Japan Year Book* 1946–1948 and 1949–1952, is also to be warmly thanked. So is Howard Gibson who spotted grievous errors; he is not responsible for any that may remain.

Chapters 1 and 2, "Occupation Atmosphere" and "Suspicion and Uncertainty," reflect the writer's personal experiences. Official statements are taken from State Department publications, from press releases by Gen. MacArthur and Gen. Robert L. Eichelberger, from statements before the Allied Council by Gen. MacArthur and Gen. Whitney and by George Atcheson, Jr., the presiding officer.

Chapter 3, "Rule by Interpreter," also rises from personal experience, supplemented by interviews with nearly all the persons named (except Prince Konoye), as well as with former Prime Ministers Higashikuni, Shidehara, Ashida, and Katayama and with Wataru Narahashi, then chief Cabinet Secretary. Corroborative and additional detail may be found in William Costello, *Democracy vs. Feudalism in Post-War Japan* (Tokyo: Itagaki Shoten, 1948); John La Cerda, *The Conqueror Comes to Tea* (New Brunswick: Rutgers University Press, 1946); W. Macmahon Ball, *Japan, Enemy or Ally?* (New York: John Day Co., 1949); Mark Gayn, *Japan Diary* (New York: William Sloane Associates, 1948).

Chapter 4, "Revolution from Above," is wholly based on personal experience, supported by numerous conversations with the writer's friends of twenty-five years, former Prime Minister Baron Kijuro Shidehara, former Prime Ministers Hitoshi Ashida and Tetsu Katayama, Dr. Tokujiro Kanamori, who guided the Constitution through the Diet, Dr. Tatsukichi Minobe, Foreign Minister Katsuo Okazaki, President Tatsuo Morito of Hiroshima University, and many others.

Chapter 5, "The Purifying Purge," is the product of many talks with Col. Charles L. Kades, Frank Rizzo, Col. Jack Napier, Carlos Marcom, and others who administered the purge from Government Section, together with the Japanese point of view as expressed by Ichiro Hatoyama, Rikizo Hirano, Heima Hayashi, Gen. Kazushige Ugaki, Admiral Kichisaburo Nomura, and others.

Chapter 6, "Who Ruled Japan?" rests heavily upon George Etsujiro Uyehara's *The Political Development of Japan, 1867–1909* (New York: E. P. Dutton & Co., 1910)—supplemented by many conversations with former Home Minister Uyehara and on Kenneth Wallace Colegrove's "The Japanese Emperor," *American Political Science Review*, XXVI, 642–659, 828–845 (Aug. and Oct., 1932). Postwar developments are largely drawn from former Prime Minister Naruhiko Higashikuni and Foreign Minister Katsuo Okazaki.

Chapter 7, "That Sacred Emperor," in addition to the sources noted for

Chapter 6, postwar period, is based on the authority of the late Prince Chichibu, and Baron Shidehara.

Chapter 8, "Battling the Bureaucrats," follows lines laid down by Milton J. Esman in "Japanese Administration," *Public Administration Review*, VII, 100–112 (Spring, 1947), and a series of staff studies written for Government Section in 1946 by John M. Maki, now of the University of Washington. Many additional details were supplied by Blaine Hoover, W. Logan McCoy, and others named in the text. The statistics, as elsewhere, are drawn from *Statistical Year Book*, compiled annually by the Prime Minister's Office Statistical Bureau and from *The Japan Annual, 1954*.

Chapter 9, "Political Machinery," is the product of the writer's personal research among leading members of every major party, including the Communists, supplemented by corroborative evidence from such financial backers as Karoku Tsuji, Michinari Sugawara, and Usaburo Chizaki and by testimony from Yukio Ozaki and Marquis Tsuneo Matsudaira.

Chapters 10 and 11, "Puppet Diet" and "Highest Organ," in addition to personal observation, rest upon the authority of Dr. Justin Williams and Commander Guy J. Swope, together with data from former Speakers Bamboku Ono, Baron Shidehara, and Takeshi Yamazaki.

Chapters 12 and 13, "Yoshida, the Paradox" and "How to Play Politics," are composite pictures compiled from scattered data supplied by Count Nobuaki Makino, Baron Seihin Ikeda, Jiro Shirasu, Kazuo Kojima, Ichiro Hatoyama, Tanzan Ishibashi, Karoku Tsuji, and numerous other friends, past or present. The writings of Shinnosuke Abe in *Mainichi* were also helpful.

Chapter 14, "Grass-Roots Reform," is a product of talks with Lieut. Col. Cecil G. Tilton, Prof. John W. Masland, Jr., of Dartmouth College, and Andrew J. Grajdanzev (Grad), checked by inspection visits to every Japanese prefecture and to all major- and middle-sized cities and many towns.

Chapter 15, "Spiritual Revolution," stems chiefly from files of Official Gazette reporting Diet discussions, from reports of the Showa Denko corruption trial and other court records, from Welfare Ministry White Papers and from newspaper files.

Chapter 16, "Underground Empire," in addition to various SCAP staff studies, reflects results of G-2 investigations as reported fortnightly. Crime statistics come from *Annual Statistics of Criminal Justice*, published annually by the General Secretariat, Supreme Court of Japan.

Chapter 17, "Democratic Police," is based primarily upon G-2 and Government Section sources, but only such data as have been reprinted in newspaper and magazine stories are used. Frank E. Hays and Noboru Saito discuss the topic briefly—respectively in *Military Government Journal,* Vol. I, No. 7 (May, 1948), pp. 15–16, and No. 8, p. 18. The chapter is based upon an article published by the author in the *Journal of Criminal Law, Criminology and Police Science,* Vol. 43, No. 5 (January–February 1953), and reprinted by its permission.

Chapter 18, "Painless Punishment," depends for its statistics upon *Annual Statistics of Criminal Justice,* already mentioned. Alfred C. Oppler's excellent "Reform of Japan's Legal and Judicial System," in *Washington Law Review,* XXXIV, 290–324 (Aug., 1949), and his comprehensive "Courts and Law in Transition," *Contemporary Japan,* Vol. XXI, Nos. 1–3 (May 30, 1952), pp. 19–55, are invaluable. So is Thomas L. Blakemore's "Postwar Developments in Japanese Law," *Wisconsin Law Review,* July, 1947, pp. 632–653.

Chapter 19, "They Live Longer," is drawn from weekly and monthly reports of Public Health and Welfare Section. The chapter is based upon the author's article in *Contemporary Japan,* Vol. XXI, Nos. 10–12 (1953), and reprinted by its permission.

Chapters 20, 21, and 22, "Great Land Reform," "Tightening the Belt," and "What Japan Eats," rest heavily upon Andrew J. Grad (Grajdanzev), "Land Reform in Japan," *Pacific Affairs,* XXI, 115–135 (June, 1948), and *Land and Peasant in Japan* (New York: Institute of Pacific Affairs, 1952). Seiyei Wakukawa has two articles on tenancy in *Far Eastern Survey,* XV, 5–8, 40–44 (Jan. 16 and Feb. 13, 1946). Wolf I. Ladejinsky wrote "Trial Balance in Japan" for *Foreign Affairs,* XXVII, 104–116 (Oct., 1948).

Chapter 23, "Flowers of Yedo," uses statistics from the National Fire Board and the Tokyo Fire Defense Board. George W. Angell's "Report on Fire Defense" of Dec. 30, 1946, is supplemented by Takeo Shioya's article in *Contemporary Japan,* Vol. XIX, Nos. 1–3, pp. 56–68.

Chapter 24, "Cities Beautiful," draws its prewar material from official publications of the City of Tokyo, notably *Tokyo, the Capital of Japan: Reconstruction Work, 1930, Twentieth Annual Statistics,* 1923, and *The Reconstruction of Tokyo,* 1933. Charles A. Beard's

Administration and Politics of Tokyo (New York: The Macmillan Company, 1923) gives the problems and the plans as drafted before the Earthquake. Postwar material rests upon White Papers issued yearly by the Construction Ministry and on the Tokyo Metropolitan Statistics Bureau reports as well as upon official Occupation releases and reports; the situation was then checked by many conferences with Governor Yasui.

Chapters 25, 26, and 27, on Communism, when not based on personal interviews with Nosaka, Shiga, Tokuda, and other Communists, or upon classified data which must not be identified, are supported by Rodger Swearingen and Paul Langer, *Red Flag in Japan; International Communism in Action, 1919–1951* (Cambridge: Harvard University Press, 1952). See also the same authors' bibliography, *Japanese Communism* (New York: Institute of Pacific Relations, 1953), and Evelyn S. Colbert's *The Left Wing in Japanese Politics* (New York: Institute of Pacific Relations, 1952). Richard L.-G. Deverall's *Red Star over Japan* (Calcutta: Temple Press, 1952) is also extremely helpful.

Chapter 28, "Trumpets Bray," is largely also based on personal experience. Two 1952 articles in *Reporter*—Frank Kluckhohn's "Heidelberg to Madrid: The Story of General Willoughby," Aug. 19, pp. 25–30, and Jerome Forrest and Clarke H. Kawakami's "General MacArthur and His Vanishing War History," Oct. 14, pp. 20–25—are extraordinarily important in this connection.

Chapters 29 and 30, "Antiforeignism Revives," and "Hotbed of Vice," come largely from personal observation, reinforced by news articles and by interviews with the sources mentioned in the text. Richard L.-G. Deverall's *The Great Seduction* (Tokyo: The Author, 1953) while possibly too angry and over-excited, should also be read.

Special Terms and Abbreviations

ACJ, Allied Council for Japan (40)
AFPAC, Armed Forces, Pacific (7)
CASA, Civil Affairs Staging Area (5, 13)
CHS, Civil Historical Section (309)
CIE, Civil Information and Education Section (27, 28)
DAC's, Department of the (U. S.) Army civilians (319)
ESS, Economic and Scientific Section (28)
FEC, Far Eastern Commission (39)
GHQ, General Headquarters
G-Sections, General-staff sections (8)
IRAA, Imperial Rule Assistance Association (54)
IRAPS, Imperial Rule Assistance Political Society (54)
JCS, Joint Chiefs of Staff (6, 7)
NPA, National Personnel Authority (96)
NPR, National Police Reserve (49, 190)
NRP, National Rural Police (186)
NRS, Natural Resources Section (224)
PHW, Public Health and Welfare Section (214)
SCAP, Supreme Commander for the Allied Powers, either as a person
    or as his organization (6)
SCAPIN(S), instruction(s) from SCAP to the Japanese Government
    (1, 47, 344)
SRS, Statistics and Reports Section (20)
SWNCC, State, War and Navy Coordinating Committee (3)

Index